Computers in Education

Twelfth Edition

SCHOOL OF EDUCATION
CURRICULUM LABORATORY
UM-DEARBORN

EDITORS

John J. Hirschbuhl
University of Akron

John J. Hirschbuhl is the founder of the Center for Computer-Based Education and Testing, a Director of Learning Technologies, and Professor of Education at The University of Akron. He is a former consulting scholar for the IBM Corporation and served as the Senior Vice President of Development and Operations at Computer Knowledge International, Inc.

Dr. Hirschbuhl received his Ph.D. from Pennsylvania State University and his B.S. and M.A. from Temple University. He has published over 100 articles in professional journals on computer-based education and training, and he has consulted with many of the *Fortune 500* companies and academic institutions.

John Kelley
University of Akron

John Kelley graduated from the University of Akron with a B.S. in Computer Science. He has overseen the development and national rollout of multiple software applications for various Fortune 1,000 companies. John has also supervised and trained help desk personnel and has designed and developed multiple IT training courses and websites.

Mc Graw Hill **Contemporary Learning Series**

2460 Kerper Blvd., Dubuque, IA 52001

Visit us on the Internet
http://www.mhcls.com

Credits

1. **Introduction**
   Unit photo—Ryan McVay/Getty Images
2. **Curriculum and Instructional Design**
   Unit photo—image 100 Ltd.
3. **Classroom Application and Software Evaluations**
   Unit photo—image 100 Ltd.
4. **Teacher Training**
   Unit photo—image 100 Ltd.
5. **Multimedia and Technology**
   Unit photo—Brand X Pictures/PunchStock
6. **Learning Management Systems and Learning Objects**
   Unit photo—image 100 Ltd.
7. **The Internet and Computer Networks**
   Unit photo—Banana Stock/PictureQuest
8. **Distributed Learning**
   Unit photo—Digital Vision/PunchStock

Copyright

Cataloging in Publication Data
Main entry under title: Annual Editions: Computers in Education. 12th Edition.
1. Computers in Education—Periodicals. I. Hirschbuhl, John J., and Kelley, John, comp. II. Title: Computers in Education.
ISBN-13: 978–0–07–339727–6   ISBN-10: 0–07–339727–X   658'.05   ISSN 1094–2602

Twelfth Edition

Cover image © Creatas/PunchStock and BananaStock/PunchStock
Printed in the United States of America   1234567890QPDQPD987   Printed on Recycled Paper.

Editors/Advisory Board

Members of the Advisory Board are instrumental in the final selection of articles for each edition of ANNUAL EDITIONS. Their review of articles for content, level, currentness, and appropriateness provides critical direction to the editor and staff. We think that you will find their careful consideration well reflected in this volume.

Preface

In publishing ANNUAL EDITIONS we recognize the enormous role played by the magazines, newspapers, and journals of the public press in providing current, first-rate educational information in a broad spectrum of interest areas. Many of these articles are appropriate for students, researchers, and professionals seeking accurate, current material to help bridge the gap between principles and theories and the real world. These articles, however, become more useful for study when those of lasting value are carefully collected, organized, indexed, and reproduced in a low-cost format, which provides easy and permanent access when the material is needed. That is the role played by ANNUAL EDITIONS.

The twelfth edition of *Annual Editions: Computers in Education* is designed to provide you with the latest information and trends regarding computers and the role they play in people's lives. Today's learning technologies are used by a fast moving society that has focused on a media-laced Internet to teach the NeXt generation. This generation is the product of a different social reality than the current teaching generation. This can be achieved because the students and teachers have access to almost limitless amounts of information via broadband networking. These technologies provide an electronic pipeline that can reach anyone, anywhere, at any time.

Streamed media and interaction have become portals to the universe. They are providing an interconnectedness that is inherent to learning. There has been a mushrooming of learning management systems and many educators have enthusiastically embraced these developments. The combination of these technologies is providing a global education wideband network for the twenty-first century. We are now zipping our way along the worldwide digital highway toward educational and training materials that stimulate us to interact with realistic simulations and key information that enables us to conceive new and more powerful ways of thinking about solving sophisticated problems. As a result of these advances, the method of delivery and assessment shifted from cognitivist-oriented to social-constructivist orientation. In addition, there has been a shift in the mode of assessment from cumulative to more formative measures. Online managed delivery and assessment provides students with opportunities to become intelligent agents within a team of learners working within their disciplines.

Multimedia has become a common application on today's Internet. Through it we can influence the lives of people all over the globe through collaborative teaching and learning in an authentic setting. It can pull together text, pictures, voice and video to provide a richer environment that will engage the learner to become actively involved in the learning process. We have now realized the long-sought benefits of technology within all levels of education.

This volume addresses the question, "How have the U.S. education and training communities ridden the back of broadband communication in order to make us a better educated, more productive and competitive nation?" There is an abundance of articles dealing with distance learning, learning management systems, networking, the Internet, and interactive multimedia applications for the classroom, the workplace, and the home.

There is an ongoing need for a publication that brings together this wealth of pertinent information on the successful implementation of current technology into schools, homes, and businesses as well as the new hardware/ software applications that have made this possible. The Annual Editions format uniquely meets this need.

This anthology addresses the current issues and rising expectations of digital natives and digital immigrants as well as educators, administrators, and trainers. It also provides a close-up look at integrating technology into the curriculum, teacher training, interactive multimedia, the Internet, learning management systems, and distance learning applications.

This volume is designed for use by individuals involved in preservice and inservice education of educators, trainers, and administrators. It is also intended for parents, students, school board members, and others concerned with the use and impact of technology on today's education and training activities.

As always, it is expected that you will have suggestions for improving future editions of *Annual Editions: Computers in Education*. You can help shape the next volume by completing and returning the postage-paid article rating form located on the last page of this book.

John J. Hirschbuhl
Editor

John Kelley
Editor

Contents

UNIT 1
Introduction

The concepts in bold italics are developed in the article. For further expansion, please refer to the Topic Guide and the Index.

UNIT 2
Curriculum and Instructional Design

The concepts in bold italics are developed in the article. For further expansion, please refer to the Topic Guide and the Index.

UNIT 3
Classroom Application and Software Evaluations

The concepts in bold italics are developed in the article. For further expansion, please refer to the Topic Guide and the Index.

UNIT 4
Teacher Training

The concepts in bold italics are developed in the article. For further expansion, please refer to the Topic Guide and the Index.

UNIT 5
Multimedia and Technology

The concepts in bold italics are developed in the article. For further expansion, please refer to the Topic Guide and the Index.

UNIT 6
Learning Management Systems and Learning Objects

UNIT 7
The Internet and Computer Networks

The concepts in bold italics are developed in the article. For further expansion, please refer to the Topic Guide and the Index.

UNIT 8
Distributed Learning

The concepts in bold italics are developed in the article. For further expansion, please refer to the Topic Guide and the Index.

Topic Guide

This topic guide suggests how the selections in this book relate to the subjects covered in your course. You may want to use the topics listed on these pages to search the Web more easily.

On the following pages a number of Web sites have been gathered specifically for this book. They are arranged to reflect the units of this *Annual Edition*. You can link to these sites by going to the student online support site at *http://www.mhcls.com/online/*.

ALL THE ARTICLES THAT RELATE TO EACH TOPIC ARE LISTED BELOW THE BOLD-FACED TERM.

Internet References

The following Internet sites have been carefully researched and selected to support the articles found in this reader. The easiest way to access these selected sites is to go to our student online support site at *http://www.mhcls.com/online/*.

AE: Computers in Education, 12/e

The following sites were available at the time of publication. Visit our Web site—we update our student online support site regularly to reflect any changes.

General Sources

Short History of the Internet

http://w3.ag.uiuc.edu/AIM/scale/nethistory.html

Bruce Sterling begins with the development of the idea for the Internet by the cold war think tank, the Rand Corporation, and goes on to explain how computer networking works. There are links to other sites and to further reading.

UNIT 1: Introduction

Agency for Instructional Technology

http://www.ait.net

AIT is a nonprofit education organization established in 1962 to develop, acquire, and distribute quality technology-based resources. It provides leadership to the educational technology policy community as well as instructional television programs.

Goals 2000

http://www.ed.gov/pubs/goals/progrpt

The reform initiative started by the U.S. Department of Education has a progress report to share.

History of Computers in Education

http://www.csulb.edu/~murdock/histofcs.html

This site explores the history of computers and the history of computers in education. A timeline lists the dates in which important events took place and gives a brief explanation of the impact of technology on education.

UNIT 2: Curriculum and Instructional Design

Education Place

http://www.eduplace.com

Houghton Mifflin's home page contains activities for students, parents, and teachers, which include weekly author interviews and child-written book reviews. It has links to excellent education topics and organizations with synopses of research (for instance, phonics instruction).

Portfolio Assessment

http://www.indiana.edu/~reading/ieo/bibs/portfoli.html

Additional information on portfolio assessment can be found in teacher resources online, including Guidelines for Portfolio Assessment in Teaching English may be viewed at this site.

Sesame Workshop

http://www.ctw.org

The Sesame Workshop enjoys a visionary role in innovative family programming. Its new media property is custom-made for today's families. The Workshop delivers a unique approach to the Internet, melding technology and edutainment to bring families together.

Teaching with Electronic Technology

http://www.wam.umd.edu/~mlhall/teaching.html

This collection of World Wide Web sites addresses the use of electronic technologies in the classroom, which range from general and theoretical resources to instructive examples of specific applications to teaching and learning.

UNIT 3: Classroom Application and Software Evaluations

Beginner's Guide to HTML

http://www.itc.univie.ac.at/docs/html-primer.html

This is a primer for producing documents in HTML, the markup language used by the World Wide Web.

Classics for Young People

http://www.ucalgary.ca/~dkbrown/storclas.html

A growing number of children's literature classics are out of copyright and are among the books available in full text here.

ENC Online

http://www.goENC.com

The Eisenhower National Clearinghouse includes science and math resources, lesson plans, a search engine, and more.

Scholastic Network

http://www.scholastic.com

Here is a selection of Scholastic products, including Global Community, contests, Scholastic publications, and home schooling resources for Grades PreK-8.

Teachers Helping Teachers

http://www.pacificnet.net/~mandel

Provides basic teaching tips, new teaching methodology ideas, and forums for teachers to share. Download software and participate in chat sessions. Features educational resources on the Web, with new ones added each week.

The Nine Planets

http://seds.lpl.arizona.edu/billa/tnp

This planetary tour through the solar system has sound and video clips and links to related sites.

The TeleGarden

http://www.usc.edu/dept/garden

View a remote garden filled with living plants. Members care for the garden through a robot arm.

Writing HTML

http://www.mcli.dist.maricopa.edu/tut

Here is a tutorial for creating World Wide Web pages, which will allow an educator to create classroom home pages.

UNIT 4: Teacher Training

Boulder Valley School District Home Page

http://www.bvsd.k12.co.us

This is the site of a district-developed home page containing planning ideas and links to educational resources for teachers and students.

Canada's Schoolnet Staff Room

http://www.schoolnet.ca/home/e/resources

Here is a resource and link site for anyone involved in education, including special-need educators, teachers, parents, volunteers, and administrators.

Teacher Support

http://quest.nasa.gov/services/teacher.html

This NASA resource provides lesson plans, standards lists, and links to video webcasts.

Teachers Guide to the Department of Education

http://www.ed.gov/pubs/TeachersGuide

Government goals, projects, grants, and other educational programs are listed here as well as links to services and resources.

The History Channel

http://www.historychannel.com

The History Channel offers a section on classroom study guides and ideas for and from educators, along wi th many other helpful features and related links.

UNIT 5: Multimedia and Technology

CNN Interactive

http://www.cnn.com/

The latest news, including pictures and archival links, is available here, along with the Infoseek search engine.

Mighty Media

http://www.mightymedia.com

The mission of this privately funded consortium is to empower youth, teachers, and organizations through the use of interactive communications technology.

MSNBC Cover Page

http://www.msnbc.com

As the only news organization to embrace three media technologies—broadcast, cable, and the Internet— MSNBC brings you up-to-the-minute news from around the globe.

NASA Aerospace Education Services Program

http://www.okstate.edu/aesp/AESP.html

This site leads to cross-curricular projects, science, technology, space, literature, math, language, astronomy, writing projects, museum links, and space image libraries.

The Science Learning Network

http://www.sln.org

This collection of museum sites includes movies, teachers' projects, news, and links to other science education material.

UNIT 6: Learning Management Systems and Learning Objects

Consortium for School Networking

http://www.cosn.org

This site provides information and discussion on how to implement networks in schools. It offers online resources and forums.

Educators Net

http://www.educatorsnet.com

Billed as the "World's No. 1 Education Search Engine," this site has over 7,200 reviewed listings and acts as a guide to education-related resources and businesses on the Internet.

ERIC Clearinghouse on Teaching and Teacher Education

http://www.ericsp.org

This ERIC site has links to lesson plans and sites on applying technology, as well as essays on teaching with technology.

UNIT 7: The Internet and Computer Networks

ADA Compliance Center

http://www.cast.org/bobby/

Bobby is a free service provided by CAST to help Web page authors identify and repair significant barriers to access by individuals with disabilities.

CAST

http://www.cast.org

CAST is a nonprofit organization that works to expand learning opportunities for all individuals, especially those with disabilities, through the research and development of innovative, technology-based educational resources and strategies.

Google

http://www.google.com

This is a fast and weighty search engine that analyzes the full text of documents, allowing the searcher to locate keywords that may have been buried deep within a document's text. Google's ever-increasing toolset includes focused search engines for images and scholarly works.

Online Internet Institute

http://oii.org

A collaborative project between Internet-using educators, proponents of systemic reform, content area experts, and teachers who desire professional growth, this site provides a learning environment for integrating the Internet into educators' individual teaching styles.

The Teachers' Network

http://www.teachers.net

Bulletin boards, classroom projects, online forums, and Web mentors are featured, as well as the book *Teachers' Guide to Cyberspace* and a course on how to use the Internet.

WebCrawler

http://webcrawler.com

This is a fast and weighty search engine that analyzes the full text of documents, allowing the searcher to locate keywords that may have been buried deep within a document's text.

Yahooligans! The Web Guide for Kids

http://www.yahooligans.com

An excellent site for children, this resource can be used if you wish to limit access by your students but still allow independent searching.

UNIT 8: Distributed Learning

The Chronicle of Higher Education: Distance Education Page

http://www.chronicle.com/distance

This site, maintained by The Chronicle of Higher Education, provides daily updates, articles, and resources concerning distance education.

Distance Learning on the Net

http://www.hoyle.com

Distance learning and education is the subject of this home page. Included are descriptions of distance education Web sites along with links that lead to further distance learning and education resources on the Net.

www.mhcls.com/online/

Weblearning Resources

http://www.knowledgeability.biz/weblearning

A bibliography of Web-based educational tools, theory, and practices.

We highly recommend that you review our Web site for expanded information and our other product lines. We are continually updating and adding links to our Web site in order to offer you the most usable and useful information that will support and expand the value of your Annual Editions. You can reach us at: *http://www.mhcls.com/annualeditions/.*

UNIT 1

Introduction

Unit Selections

1. **Digital Natives, Digital Immigrants,** Marc Prensky
2. **The Myth about Online Course Development,** Diana G. Oblinger and Brian L. Hawkins
3. **Creating Flexible E-Learning Through the Use of Learning Objects,** Marie Lasseter and Michael Rogers
4. **Meeting Generation NeXt: Today's Postmodern College Student,** Mark L. Taylor
5. **General Education Issues, Distance Education Practices,** Jeri L. Childers and R. Thomas Berner

Key Points to Consider

- How will instructional technology change the way teachers and today's students teach and learn? Why?

- What is the greatest obstacle to the use of technology in the classroom today? Discuss.

- How will distance learning practices actually enhance the delivery of content and interaction between students, teachers, and the community?

- How would you use technology to provide student centered instruction in an online environment?

Student Web Site

www.mhcls.com/online

Internet References

Further information regarding these Web sites may be found in this book's preface or online.

Agency for Instructional Technology
http://www.ait.net

Goals 2000
http://www.ed.gov/pubs/goals/progrpt

History of Computers in Education
http://www.csulb.edu/~murdock/histofcs.html

Today, learning technology is ubiquitous in the home, workplace, and schools. We are teaching the NeXt generation which is the product of a different social reality than the current teaching generation. Today's students are the first generation who were "born with a mouse in their hand and a gaming paradigm as their model for problem solving." Students and teachers have increasing access to almost limitless amounts of information via broad band networking. The onrush of new telecommunication applications is forcing educators to adapt and utilize these new technologies and to measure their impact on learning in both classroom and e-learning environments. The Internet, PowerPoint, and Learning Management Systems such as WebCT, Blackboard, and Desire2Learn are at the center of the e-learning/telecommunications explosion. These mainstream technologies combined with student demands for new technology-based instructional delivery are transforming schools and colleges and the way students of all ages learn. Teachers are improving their proficiency in utilizing alternate delivery systems that are designed to meet the needs of students in the classroom or those who wish to learn in either a synchronous or asynchronous mode. The rising tide of technology is lifting all of education to higher levels of excellence.

The articles for this unit track the concerns and dreams of educators who have come face-to-face with the promises and problems connected with the current and future implementation of instructional technology into the mainstream curriculum.

In the first article, Marc Prensky states that our students have changed radically. They are no longer the people for which our educational system was designed. They are the product of a different social reality than their teachers. Post modern influences and sensibilities permeate their expectations and may be at odds with what the schools intend to offer.

In the following article, "The Myth about Online Course Development," Oblinger and Hawkins claim that online instruction is more than a series of readings posted to a Web site; it requires deliberate instructional design that hinges on linking learning objectives to specific learning activities and measurable outcomes. Institutions are finding that teams, not individuals, develop and deliver the most effective online courses.

In the next article, Lasseter and Rogers state that their university deconstructed their existing online courses to create separate files of reusable content. They rearranged the individual pieces of content and placed them into a hierarchy consisting of learning objects that fall under objectives named by topic. The result was a course that is SCORM compliant.

Then, Mark Taylor describes current students as Generation NeXt, the product of a very different social reality than the members of the Baby Boom that predominate college faculty and staff. This paper provides an overview of some characteristics of Generation NeXt, their social genesis, these Postmodern times, with suggestions for assisting Generation NeXt to be successful in higher education.

Finally, Childers and Berner describe an approach to designing a distance education course in a learn-by-doing experience. They discuss what worked and what didn't work within the context of general principles outlined by researchers in the area of general education and distance learning. They found that distance learning practices actually enhanced delivery of the content and increased interaction between the students to maximize the goals of general education.

Digital Natives, Digital Immigrants

MARC PRENSKY

It is amazing to me how in all the hoopla and debate these days about the decline of education in the US we ignore the most fundamental of its causes. *Our students have changed radically. Today's students are no longer the people our educational system was designed to teach.*

Today's students have not just changed *incrementally* from those of the past, nor simply changed their slang, clothes, body adornments, or styles, as has happened between generations previously. A really big *discontinuity* has taken place. One might even call it a "singularity"—an event which changes things so fundamentally that there is absolutely no going back. This so-called "singularity" is the arrival and rapid dissemination of digital technology in the last decades of the 20th century.

Today's students—K through college—represent the first generations to grow up with this new technology. They have spent their entire lives surrounded by and using computers, videogames, digital music players, video cams, cell phones, and all the other toys and tools of the digital age. Today's average college grads have spent less than 5,000 hours of their lives reading, but over 10,000 hours playing video games (not to mention 20,000 hours watching TV). Computer games, email, the Internet, cell phones and instant messaging are integral parts of their lives.

It is now clear that as a result of this ubiquitous environment and the sheer volume of their interaction with it, today's students *think and process information fundamentally differently* from their predecessors. These differences go far further and deeper than most educators suspect or realize. "Different kinds of experiences lead to different brain structures," says Dr. Bruce D. Berry of Baylor College of Medicine. As we shall see in the next installment, it is very likely that *our students' brains have physically changed*—and are different from ours—as a result of how they grew up. But whether or not this is *literally* true, we can say with certainty that their *thinking patterns* have changed. I will get to *how* they have changed in a minute.

What should we call these "new" students of today? Some refer to them as the N-[for Net]-gen or D-[for digital]-gen. But the most useful designation I have found for them is *Digital Natives*. Our students today are all "native speakers" of the digital language of computers, video games and the Internet.

So what does that make the rest of us? Those of us who were not born into the digital world but have, at some later point in our lives, become fascinated by and adopted many or most aspects of the new technology are, and always will be compared to them, *Digital Immigrants*.

The importance of the distinction is this: As Digital Immigrants learn—like all immigrants, some better than others—to adapt to their environment, they always retain, to some degree, their "accent," that is, their foot in the past. The "digital immigrant accent" can be seen in such things as turning to the Internet for information second rather than first, or in reading the manual for a program rather than assuming that the program itself will teach us to use it. Today's older folk were "socialized" differently from their kids, and are now in the process of learning a new language. And a language learned later in life, scientists tell us, goes into a different part of the brain.

There are hundreds of examples of the digital immigrant accent. They include printing out your email (or having your secretary print it out for you—an even "thicker" accent); needing to print out a document written on the computer in order to edit it (rather than just editing on the screen); and bringing people physically into your office to see an interesting web site (rather than just sending them the URL). I'm sure you can think of one or two examples of your own without much effort. My own favorite example is the "Did you get my email?" phone call. Those of us who are Digital Immigrants can, and should, laugh at ourselves and our "accent."

But this is not just a joke. It's very serious, because the single biggest problem facing education today is that *our Digital Immigrant instructors, who speak an outdated language (that of the pre-digital age), are struggling to teach a population that speaks an entirely new language.*

This is obvious to the Digital Natives—school often feels pretty much as if we've brought in a population of heavily accented, unintelligible foreigners to lecture them. They often can't understand what the Immigrants are saying. What does "dial" a number mean, anyway?

Lest this perspective appear radical, rather than just descriptive, let me highlight some of the issues. Digital Natives are used to receiving information really fast. They like to parallel process and multi-task. They prefer their graphics *before* their text rather than the opposite. They prefer random access (like hypertext). They function best when networked. They thrive on instant gratification and frequent rewards. They prefer games to "serious" work. (Does any of this sound familiar?)

But Digital Immigrants typically have very little appreciation for these new skills that the Natives have acquired and perfected through years of interaction and practice. These skills are almost totally foreign to the Immigrants, who themselves learned—and so choose to teach—slowly, step-by-step, one thing at a time, individually, and above all, seriously. "My students just don't _____ like they used to," Digital Immigrant educators grouse. I can't get them to ____ or to ____. They have no appreciation for _____ or _____ . (Fill in the blanks, there are a wide variety of choices.)

Digital Immigrants don't believe their students can learn successfully while watching TV or listening to music, because they (the Immigrants) can't. Of course not—they didn't practice this skill constantly for all of their formative years. Digital Immigrants think learning can't (or shouldn't) be fun. Why should they—they didn't spend their formative years learning with Sesame Street.

Unfortunately for our Digital Immigrant teachers, the people sitting in their classes grew up on the "twitch speed" of video games and MTV. They are used to the instantaneity of hypertext, downloaded music, phones in their pockets, a library on their laptops, beamed messages and instant messaging. They've been networked most or all of their lives. They have little patience for lectures, step-by-step logic, and "tell-test" instruction.

Digital Immigrant teachers assume that learners are the same as they have always been, and that the same methods that worked for the teachers when they were students will work for their students now. **But that assumption is no longer valid.** Today's learners are _different_. "Www.hungry.com" said a kindergarten student recently at lunchtime. "Every time I go to school I have to power down," complains a high-school student. Is it that Digital Natives _can't_ pay attention, or that they _choose not to_? Often from the Natives' point of view their Digital Immigrant instructors make their education _not worth_ paying attention to compared to everything else they experience—and then they blame them for not paying attention!

And, more and more, they won't take it. "I went to a highly ranked college where all the professors came from MIT," says a former student. "But all they did was read from their textbooks. I quit." In the giddy internet bubble of a only a short while ago—when jobs were plentiful, especially in the areas where school offered little help—this was a real possibility. But the dot-com dropouts are now returning to school. They will have to confront once again the Immigrant/Native divide, and have even more trouble given their recent experiences. And that will make it even harder to teach them—and all the Digital Natives already in the system—in the traditional fashion.

So what should happen? Should the Digital Native students learn the old ways, or should their Digital Immigrant educators learn the new? Unfortunately, no matter how much the Immigrants may wish it, it is highly unlikely the Digital Natives will go backwards. In the first place, it may be impossible—their brains may already be different. It also flies in the face of everything we know about cultural migration. Kids born into any new culture learn the new language easily, and forcefully resist using the old. Smart adult immigrants _accept_ that they don't know about their new world and take advantage of their kids to help them learn and integrate. Not-so-smart (or not-so-flexible) immigrants spend most of their time grousing about how good things were in the "old country."

So unless we want to just forget about educating Digital Natives until they grow up and do it themselves, we had better confront this issue. And in so doing we need to reconsider both our methodology and our content.

First, our methodology. Today's teachers have to learn to communicate in the language and style of their students. This _doesn't_ mean changing the meaning of what is important, or of good thinking skills. But it _does_ mean going faster, less step-by step, more in parallel, with more random access, among other things. Educators might ask "But how do we teach logic in this fashion?" While it's not immediately clear, we do need to figure it out.

Second, our content. It seems to me that after the digital "singularity" there are now _two kinds_ of content: "Legacy" content (to borrow the computer term for old systems) and "Future" content.

"Legacy" content includes reading, writing, arithmetic, logical thinking, understanding the writings and ideas of the past, etc—all of our "traditional" curriculum. It is of course still important, but it is from a different era. Some of it (such as logical thinking) will continue to be important, but some (perhaps like Euclidean geometry) will become less so, as did Latin and Greek.

"Future" content is to a large extent, not surprisingly, digital and technological. But while it includes software, hardware, robotics, nanotechnology, genomics, etc. _it also includes the ethics, politics, sociology, languages and other things that go with them_. This "Future" content is extremely interesting to today's students. But how many Digital Immigrants are prepared to teach it? Someone once suggested to me that kids should only be allowed to use computers in school that they have built themselves. It's a brilliant idea that is very doable from the point of view of the students' capabilities. But who could teach it?

As educators, we need to be thinking about how to teach _both_ Legacy and Future content in the language of the Digital Natives. The first involves a major translation and change of methodology; the second involves all that PLUS new content and thinking. It's not actually clear to me which is harder— "learning new stuff" or "learning new ways to do old stuff." I suspect it's the latter.

So we have to invent, but not necessarily from scratch. Adapting materials to the language of Digital Natives has already been done successfully. My own preference for teaching Digital Natives is to invent computer games to do the job, even for the most serious content. After all, it's an idiom with which most of them are totally familiar.

Not long ago a group of professors showed up at my company with new computer-aided design (CAD) software they had developed for mechanical engineers. Their creation was so much better than what people were currently using that they had assumed the entire engineering world would quickly adopt it. But instead they encountered a lot of resistance, due in large part to the product's extremely steep learning curve—the software contained hundreds of new buttons, options and approaches to master.

Their marketers, however, had a brilliant idea. Observing that the users of CAD software were almost exclusively male engineers between 20 and 30, they said "Why not make the learning into a video game!" So we invented and created for them a computer game in the "first person shooter" style of the consumer games *Doom* and *Quake*, called *The Monkey Wrench Conspiracy*. Its player becomes an intergalactic secret agent who has to save a space station from an attack by the evil Dr. Monkey Wrench. The only way to defeat him is to use the CAD software, which the learner must employ to build tools, fix weapons, and defeat booby traps. There is one hour of game time, plus 30 "tasks," which can take from 15 minutes to several hours depending on one's experience level.

Monkey Wrench has been phenomenally successful in getting young people interested in learning the software. It is widely used by engineering students around the world, with over 1 million copies of the game in print in several languages. But while the game was easy for my Digital Native staff to invent, creating the content turned out to be more difficult for the professors, who were used to teaching courses that started with "Lesson 1—the Interface." We asked them instead to create a series of graded tasks into which the skills to be learned were embedded. The professors had made 5–10 minute movies to illustrate key concepts; we asked them to cut them to under 30 seconds. The professors insisted that the learners to do all the tasks in order; we asked them to allow random access. They wanted a slow academic pace, we wanted speed and urgency (we hired a Hollywood script writer to provide this.) They wanted written instructions; we wanted computer movies. They wanted the traditional pedagogical language of "learning objectives," "mastery", etc. (e.g. "in this exercise you will learn …"); our goal was to completely eliminate any language that even *smacked* of education.

In the end the professors and their staff came through brilliantly, but because of the large mind-shift required it took them twice as long as we had expected. As they saw the approach working, though, the new "Digital Native" methodology became their model for more and more teaching—both in and out of games—and their development speed increased dramatically.

Similar rethinking needs to be applied to all subjects at all levels. Although most attempts at "edutainment" to date have essentially failed from both the education and entertainment perspective, we can—and will, I predict—do much better.

In math, for example, the debate must no longer be about *whether* to use calculators and computers—they are a part of the Digital Natives' world—but rather *how* to use them to instill the things that are useful to have internalized, from key skills and concepts to the multiplication tables. We should be focusing on "future math"—approximation, statistics, binary thinking.

In geography—which is all but ignored these days—there is no reason that a generation that can memorize over 100

Pokémon characters with all their characteristics, history and evolution can't learn the names, populations, capitals and relationships of all the 181 nations in the world. It just depends on how it is presented.

We need to invent Digital Native methodologies for *all* subjects, at *all* levels, using our students to guide us. The process has already begun—I know college professors inventing games for teaching subjects ranging from math to engineering to the Spanish Inquisition. We need to find ways of publicizing and spreading their successes.

A frequent objection I hear from Digital Immigrant educators is "this approach is great for *facts*, but it wouldn't work for 'my subject.'" Nonsense. This is just rationalization and lack of imagination. In my talks I now include "thought experiments" where I invite professors and teachers to suggest a subject or topic, and I attempt—on the spot—to invent a game or other Digital Native method for learning it. *Classical philosophy?* Create a game in which the philosophers debate and the learners have to pick out what each would say. *The Holocaust?* Create a simulation where students role-play the meeting at Wannsee, or one where they can experience the *true* horror of the camps, as opposed to the films like *Schindler's List*. It's just dumb (and lazy) of educators—not to mention ineffective—to presume that (despite their traditions) the Digital Immigrant way is the *only* way to teach, and that the Digital Natives' "language" is not as capable as their own of encompassing any and every idea.

So if Digital Immigrant educators *really* want to reach Digital Natives—i.e. all their students—they will have to change. It's high time for them to stop their grousing, and as the Nike motto of the Digital Native generation says, "Just do it!" They *will* succeed in the long run—and their successes will come that much sooner if their administrators support them.

See also: Digital Natives, Digital Immigrants Part 2: The scientific evidence behind the Digital Native's thinking changes, and the evidence that Digital Native-style learning works!

MARC PRENSKY is an internationally acclaimed thought leader, speaker, writer, consultant, and game designer in the critical areas of education and learning. He is the author of Digital Game-Based Learning (McGraw-Hill, 2001), founder and CEO of Games2train, a game-based learning company, and founder of The Digital Multiplier, an organization dedicated to eliminating the digital divide in learning worldwide. He is also the creator of the sites www.SocialImpactGames.com, www.DoDGameCommunity.com and www.GamesParentsTeachers.com. Marc holds an MBA from Harvard and a Masters in Teaching from Yale. More of his writings can be found at www.marcprensky.com/writing/default.asp. Contact Marc at marc@games2train.com.

The Myth about Online Course Development

"A Faculty Member Can Individually Develop and Deliver an Effective Online Course."

DIANA G. OBLINGER AND BRIAN L. HAWKINS

In the early days of online course, a widespread production model was to provide faculty members with release time and/or stipends in return for developing and delivering their own courses. These early online courses were developed by a cadre of faculty "zealots" who believed that information technology could transform learning. Such faculty were willing—and able—to master the required skills, whether that meant learning Java, HTML, or a graphics package. Often re-creating the lecture, the resulting courses frequently had an idiosyncratic structure and might—or might not—use good instructional design. Being a "Lone Ranger"[1] often meant figuring things out alone, so solutions were stitched together with whatever resources were available to the faculty member. Today, the legacy of these early courses is a boutique of different applications, approaches, and instructional designs scattered across a campus.

Developing and delivering effective online courses requires pedagogy and technology expertise possessed by few faculty. Consider pedagogy, for example. Good pedagogy implies that the instructor can develop targeted learning objectives. Online instruction is more than a series of readings posted to a Web site; it requires deliberate instructional design that hinges on linking learning objectives to specific learning activities and measurable outcomes. Few faculty have had formal education or training in instructional design or learning theory. To expect them to master the instructional design needed to put a well-designed course online is probably unrealistic. A more effective model is to pair a faculty member with an instructional designer so that each brings unique skills to the course-creation process.

But what is a course? And how should a course be put online? Instructors are being challenged to move beyond the notion of a course as covering content to the idea of a course as constructing a series of learning environments and activities. Effective learning motivates learners, develops their skills, and enables learners to transfer their new skills to other settings. Interaction is a critical part of the learning experience. How will that be facilitated online?

A first step is to rethink the roles of both the faculty member and the learner. Beyond lecturing, the faculty member might serve as architect, consultant, resource, reviewer, or role model.

Students may assume multiple roles as well. Besides being a listener, the student might be an apprentice, builder, mentor, peer teacher, team member, or writer. With these alternative roles for faculty and students, the range of possible learning activities expands to include options such as authentic projects, peer exchange, case studies, debate, brainstorming, coaching, journaling, and so on. Can—and should—a faculty member who is a subject-matter expert be expected to think through these nuances of instructional design on his or her own?

Technology is another significant responsibility when developing and delivering an online course. One of the first issues to address is the application that should undergird the course. Should the course be built using a course management system? What other tools should be used to enhance the course? Is a chat room appropriate, or is using blogs or wikis better? Once the platform is chosen, who is the developer? Is learning HTML a good use of the faculty member's time?

The technology questions don't end when the course is developed. The support implications of any online course are significant. If the course includes links to readings or other Web sites, who is responsible for keeping those links updated? If a new version of software is released, who updates the course? And who worries about the security of the system, ensuring that students' assignments and grades are not tampered with? Who provides help-desk support for the course? If a student has trouble with the Web browser, should the student go to the faculty member, or is there an IT support desk that can handle technical questions? Is there a different place where students can get academic assistance?

Beyond the technical mechanics are IT policy issues such as copyright and intellectual property. Initial questions deal with ownership. If a course is developed as a part of a faculty member's regular responsibilities, does it belong to the faculty member (analogous to how textbooks are often handled), or does the institution own the work? If the author receives compensation for the course, such as a special stipend, is the course considered a work for hire? Who has the right to modify the content? If the work is commercialized and revenue is generated, is a royalty due to the developer? The level of complexity increases when the "developer" is not just the individual faculty member. What ownership rights are vested in the technical staff, graphics designers, and instructional designers who supported the faculty member? And what about the use of material provided by others? Although it is tempting to assume that fair use will allow faculty to use any material for educational purposes, few institutions can take the risk of such an assumption. If students' material becomes part of the course (e.g., discussion boards), does the institution have the necessary approval to keep the student's intellectual property for future classes?

Online instruction is more than a series of readings posted to a Web site; it requires deliberate instructional design that hinges on linking learning objectives to specific learning activities and measurable outcomes.

Developing and delivering an online course requires numerous and varied skills—skills that are unlikely to be found in a single individual. Teams will probably be more effective. For many faculty, working as a member of a course-development team is a unique experience, one in which autonomy yields to collaboration.

For any institution that wants to develop and deliver online courses, the members of the executive team should ask themselves the following strategic questions:

1. *What is the best use of the faculty member, an expensive institutional resource?* Online courses involve many components: technical architecture, instructional design, graphic design, intellectual property and copyright clearance, and subject-matter expertise. Faculty make up an institution's most highly trained, valuable resource. Is making them responsible for activities for which they are not trained (e.g., instructional design) and in which they may not be interested (e.g., technical architecture) the best use of their time? Or would a team approach work better?

2. *Do we have a process for strategically investing in course development?* What brings more value to an institution from online courses: having random courses available online, or having an entire program available online? In the early phase of online course development, faculty pioneers proved that putting courses online was possible. But to sustain the required investment—in faculty time and in support—online learning must be visible and viable. Are the advantages of online learning undercut because only one course per department is offered? Visibility becomes important once the pioneering phase has passed, as does also critical mass: programs must have enough online courses available to attract students to the offerings. In addition, the more courses that are developed within an individual unit, the deeper will be that unit's expertise,

making success increasingly likely. Pursuing the "let a thousand flowers bloom" approach to online course development may not result in maximum impact for the investment.

3. *Do we confuse providing content with creating a learning environment or delivering a course?* When putting a course online, an institution may be tempted to focus on the content. But institutions should be clear about what defines a course. If a course is simply the equivalent of its content, why are courses not defined by books rather than classrooms and faculty? A course involves content, to be sure, but it also involves interaction, dialogue, mentoring, and coaching. Clearly, content can be hosted on the Web, but how will interaction be handled? What technical infrastructure will facilitate communication and collaboration? And what pedagogical approaches will draw students in, motivating them to learn more? How an institution defines a course may well determine its success with online learning.

4. *What is the return we hope to see from our investment in course development?* In the early days of online learning, many institutions believed they would "strike it rich" by enrolling tens of thousands of students. Today's expectations are more realistic. Online learning offers needed flexibility to time-constrained students. Investing in online course development may help the institution graduate students on time while avoiding opportunity costs for the student and capacity constraints for the institution. But online course development typically catalyzes a fundamental rethinking of the course, the content, the learning activities, and the desired learning outcomes. This reexamination exists at the program level as well. With information changing rapidly, with new disciplines arising constantly, and with the understanding of how people learn growing progressively more sophisticated, the reexamination catalyzed by online learning may be one of the best investments an institution can make.

Although the "Lone Ranger" approach to online learning has worked in the past, it does not scale well. Institutions that are sincere about providing high-quality, flexible educational experiences are finding that teams—not individuals—develop and deliver the most effective online courses.

Note

1. Tony Bates, of the University of British Columbia, first used the term "Lone Ranger" to describe this approach to online course development. See A.W. Bates, "Restructuring the University for Technological Change," June 1997, <http://bates.cstudies.ubc.ca/carnegie/carnegie.html>.

DIANA G. OBLINGER is Vice President of EDUCAUSE, where she is responsible for the association's teaching and learning activities and for the EDUCAUSE Learning Initiative (ELI). **BRIAN L. HAWKINS** is President of EDUCAUSE.

Creating Flexible E-Learning Through the Use of Learning Objects

The University System of Georgia deconstructs existing online courses to create separate files of reusable content

MARIE LASSETER AND MICHAEL ROGERS

For five years, Advanced Learning Technologies (ALT), a unit within the Board of Regents of the University System of Georgia (USG), has worked with faculty and staff to develop the eCore, an electronically delivered core curriculum for the University System of Georgia. The eCore contains courses leading to the completion of the first two years of an undergraduate degree.

The ALT unit is also charged with assisting faculty and staff in using technology successfully, creating meaningful learning experiences, and expanding access to educational opportunities and resources. ALT leveraged eCore to meet these challenges by making the eCore courses available for faculty to reuse in developing their own face-to-face and online courses. In 2000, we began making these courses available on a Web site called SCOUT—Sharing Content Online for University Teaching. Stored in the WebCT Campus Edition course management system, courses were available only in their entirety. While this proved a good first step for content sharing, faculty members had to take an entire course even if they wanted just a single element, making the content somewhat cumbersome to use. They had to navigate through the course in linear fashion to find the text, images, graphs, charts, or clips they wanted for their own courses, as there was no efficient way to search a course or collection of courses for specific resources.

While faculty response to SCOUT was encouraging, feedback indicated that what they really needed was a quick way to find specific pieces of learning content so that courses could be custom designed. In addition, faculty wanted to use course content across disciplines (for example, using a history lesson on Romanticism in an American literature course). To meet these needs, ALT had to find a way to make the different course elements easily available to faculty. In simple terms, ALT wanted to provide a level of search efficiency analogous to when the telephone company Yellow Pages started listing physicians by specialty rather than just alphabetically.

Transition to Learning Objects

In February 2003, ALT began a pilot project with the specific goal of deconstructing the eCore courses and reassembling them into smaller, more modular components of instruction (specifically, learning objects). For our purposes, we use the definition of learning objects offered by David Wiley as "any digital resource that can be used to support learning."[1] We chose to store the learning objects in WebCT Vista, since it was the course management software already in use throughout the USG. Through these two actions, we believed we could decrease the cost and time of course development by making hundreds of learning objects available to faculty throughout the USG.

One of the first decisions we made concerned the level of granularity for the learning objects, since faculty would find and retrieve them by browsing sections of course content in specific topic areas. Labeling and organizing the learning objects so that faculty could easily search, retrieve, mix, match, reuse, and assemble these components into entirely new online or offline courses was crucial for success. Based on the WebCT Vista functionality and the type of content available in the original courses, we organized learning objects as groups of content pages concentrated around specific learning objectives and stored in topic areas. We organized the content related to topic areas in Vista learning modules. A table of contents on the left of the learning module screen lists all the content pages addressing a particular learning objective. The last item in the table of contents is a link to download the contents for that particular learning objective.

Deconstructing courses and reorganizing them as learning objects was technically straightforward and did not require buying a special digital content repository or any other new software. To deconstruct a course, we copied an existing course template in Vista. We then rearranged the individual pieces of content from the original course into a hierarchy consisting of learning objects that fall under learning objectives organized by topic. The key to accomplishing this process simply, efficiently, and affordably was to build this scheme not as a separate hierarchy in separate software but from the software's perspective, as a new content template in WebCT Vista course spaces.

Instead of navigating to a course, faculty members navigate to a course section in Vista, such as Precalculus Learning Objects. Instead of the first page welcoming visitors to Jane Smith's precalculus course, the welcome page is an introductory screen to topics rather than lessons, for example, "Equations" instead of "Lesson 1: Equations."

Clicking deeper into "the course" brings up learning objectives from the original equations lesson. Clicking on an objective brings up learning objects, which are groups of content pages that map to the objective. This approach means that any institution with a course management system can do what we've done and make learning objects available to faculty without additional software investment. And since WebCT Vista is SCORM compliant, we can share our courses with any SCORM-compliant system.[2]

Now, faculty looking for learning objects related to equations, for example, no longer have to navigate to the precalculus course and wade through it from start to finish. Faculty come to the faculty portal, click on a topic, and find a set of learning objectives as well as learning objects that fulfill them. For example, they can navigate to a subject (such as Precalculus), choose a topic (Polynomials), select a learning objective (Recognize a function as a Polynomial Function), and view all content, including text and media, that addresses that learning objective.

To download a learning object, faculty use the course management software's assignment tool and point and click as if they were students downloading an assignment. Prompted by Windows, they save the object to their hard drives or a new course area.

We label every learning object with a metatag to make it even more searchable. If a history professor wants images of presidents for a handout, she can query courses for images of presidents. Using the Media Library in Vista, we've also set up areas that organize learning objects by media type. All animations and simulations (images and graphics) are available for browsing individually rather than only in context in the course content.

After work on the prototype was completed in late July 2003 and faculty provided positive feedback, we outsourced technical work on 20 courses to a private consultant. Although the deconstruction work isn't complex, it is time-consuming. By the end of August 2004, 16 of the original eCore courses will be deconstructed and reconfigured as learning objects.

A Repository for Version Control

In addition to downloading the materials for reuse, the learning objects—which are stored in a centralized content database—can be made available to departments and users across the system or institution based on predefined rules or permissions, including user roles. This eliminates the need for duplicate copies of the materials and ensures that the most accurate version of the content can be automatically distributed across courses.

Faculty now have a variety of options for developing new online courses or supplementing face-to-face courses. When they attempt to reuse content, they're not locked into a course/unit/lesson format. They have the freedom to develop their courses as they like without starting from scratch.

Surprisingly, what began as a plan to provide courses as learning objects—a big undertaking—has become something even bigger. A faculty portal called FacultyVIEW[3] has emerged to provide storage and sharing of reusable learning objects and instructional design resources, an active community of scholars, and an avenue for announcements and upcoming events of interest to USG faculty and staff.

One of our goals moving forward is to perform a return on investment analysis on the project so that we understand how much time and money we are saving in course development. We will document the comparative effectiveness of courses that incorporate learning objects. Although we lack a current analysis, we believe the project will produce better courses more quickly and efficiently, especially as the learning object exchange model scales to encompass higher education on a national and global scale.

Lessons Learned

We're pleased with the project and have learned lessons along the way that may help other institutions pondering the same move.

- *Plan:* Identify teams, processes, timetables, and milestones and review procedures in advance. Anticipate that the project will take longer than you think.
- *Distill:* Consider granularity up front. We chose two levels of granularity based on our materials and the advantages offered to us by the program already in use—learning objectives and media components—on which to anchor our course transformation. Organizing learning objects around the learning objectives they map to works for us; it is straightforward in empirical courses such as math and science, but can be complex with more abstract subjects such as history and communications.
- *Design:* The quality of a course's instructional design will dictate the success of object-to-objective linking. Ideally, you will find at least one learning object and assessment per objective. Unfortunately, it doesn't always work out that way. Even in well-designed courses, you may find learning objectives with no content to back them up. We're also applying what we've learned in deconstructing courses to support effective online instructional design for new courses.
- *Describe:* Every learning object needs a name of its own. Files in WebCT Vista can't have duplicate names or title tags. When you start your project, you'll likely find a host of files named "introduction" and "chapter 1." One of the most important things to do is to enforce a naming scheme that conveys the course, the topic, and the learning objective and that provides a name referring to the lesson (for example, precalc_equations_01_polynomials).

- *Research:* Make sure your faculty are ready, willing, and able to take advantage of learning objects. We tested the precalculus pilot prototype with a small group of faculty who responded enthusiastically. With that faculty feedback, we confirmed we were on the right track and could proceed with the rest of our courses.

- *Market:* Faculty need consistent reminders that learning objects are available and that the benefits of using them can be significant. It is important to market the merits of learning objects to faculty regularly.

Taking these steps will dramatically increase your chances of success with learning objects. Best of all, successful use of learning objects translates into increased faculty productivity and new, higher-quality educational opportunities for your students.

Endnotes

1. D. Wiley, *The Instructional Use of Learning Objects*, D. Wiley, ed. (Bloomington, Ind.: Agency for Instructional Technology and Association for Educational Communications and Technology, 2002), <http://www.reusability.org/read/> (accessed September 8, 2004).
2. SCORM stands for "Shareable Content (previously Courseware) Object Reference Model," a set of technical standards that permit Web-based learning systems to find, import, share, reuse, and export learning content.
3. To view public portions of FacultyVIEW, please visit <http://www.alt.usg.edu/projects/facultyview/index.html.> (accessed September 8, 2004).

MARIE LASSETER (marie.lasseter@usg.edu) is Project Coordinator and **MICHAEL ROGERS** (michael.rogers@usg.edu) is Project Manager for Instructional Development for the Advanced Learning Technologies department of the Board of Regents of the University System of Georgia.

Meeting Generation NeXt

Today's Postmodern College Student

Mark L. Taylor

Introduction

The traditional age college student; Generation NeXt; is the product of a very different social reality than the members of the Baby Boom that predominate college faculty and staff. Postmodern influences and sensibilities permeate the expectations of students, and may be at odds with what the schools intend to offer. This presentation will overview some characteristics of Generation NeXt, their social genesis, and these Postmodern times, with suggestions for helping Generation NeXt be successful in postsecondary education.

Generations

Making generalizations about generations is a slippery prospect at best, especially about a group as diverse as Generation NeXt. The concept of "modal personality" from sociology and anthropology has long been used to describe the central tendencies of the personality characteristics found in a given group or population (Howard 1996). As long at it can be remembered that there is great variation within any group, and if the modal tendencies are not held to rigidly as stereotypes, some generalizations can help in understanding groups. This is especially true when the social impacts on characteristics are considered, and in comparing generational cohorts.

The description of generations has been popular in the academic and popular press, especially of the post-Baby Boom generations (Howe and Strauss 1993, 2000; Levine and Cureton 1998; Losyk 1997; Lyotard 1988; Raines 1997; Sacks 1996; Smith and Clurman 1997; Strauss and Howe 1991; Young 2003). While the traits of earlier generational cohorts are described more or less consistently, there is much disagreement about the status of and prospects for today's traditional age students, even about a naming term for the group.

A brief review of the generations might help place today's students in context (Strauss and Howe 1991). The earliest generation still represented in significant numbers on campuses would be those from the Silent Generation. Born 1925 to 1944 and currently ages 77 to 59, these Americans were very influenced by the Great Depression and World War II. Also called "Matures" they were socialized to and still tend to value

duty, discipline, delay of gratification, sacrifice and conformity (Smith and Clurman 1997). They tend to be comfortable in hierarchical authority structures and have a strong work e thic. Popularized as "The Greatest Generation" when combined with the G.I. Generation before them, born 1901 to 1924 (Brokow, 1998) these citizens expected to work hard for what they had, and not to squander resources. Many of their social conventions and values were more typical of Premodern than Modern times, especially the permeation of religion into social institutions and the emphasis on religious values and traditions over science in decision making. Though Modernism with its belief in reason dates back two centuries (Sacks 1996) the truly Modern shift toward science, and a belief in the promise of science and progress did not take significant cultural hold until World War II. Higher education was certainly less available for members of the Silent generation than it is today, but opened significantly after World War II.

After World War II, the Silents and the G.I. Generation created the greatest economic expansion in the twenty century, and produced the Baby Boom; the Boomers. This post-war generation is generally demarcated from 1945 until 1965 (now ages 57 to 37), and make up the majority of college faculty and staff. Boomers were, and still are, the "pig in the python" moving through social institutions as each grew to accommodate them then faced contraction when birth rates dropped in 1965. From maternity wards, to public schools to colleges, through the workforce, healthcare and soon into the retirement industry everyone makes way for Boomers.

Truly children of a Modern age, social and civil ideals were articulated and acted upon in civil and women's rights and anti-poverty initiatives. Scientific advancements in medicine, space travel, agriculture, electronics and consumer "labor saving" devises supported the Modern belief in science as a positive tool for social progress that would eventually liberate all mankind from the bondage of toil, and continued to usurp religion and traditional beliefs in decision making. Religion was certainly not abandoned nor churches closed, but the separation of church and state became more of a reality and ideas like evolution took greater social hold. Modernism tends to place religion as one of the pieces of the social structure, but not necessarily the central hub. The school with its focus on secular learning and science (as well as sports and child development) did replace the church as the center of social activity for many communities.

Baby boom children had all the advantages of a traditional family structure, with the "Leave it to Beaver/Father Knows Best" family of working father, stay-at-home mother, and at least one child the most common, representing 75 of 100 families (Raines 1997). The post-war economic expansion helped make this possible, as well did the relative affluence for a growing middle class. Dr. Benjamin Spock encouraged parents to spare the rod and nurture their children's creativity. Many children were raised in an atmosphere of optimism and economic and social growth by parents who did not know how to spend money on themselves. It is little wonder that Boomers developed values different from earlier generations. Individuality, the importance of self-development, entitlement (though tempered by some willingness to work for grades and rewards), became core values, while delay gratification became less popular. This represented a basic turning away from the values their parents held dear; the same parents who were funding their quest for personal improvement.

This Baby Boom generation might be viewed as a transitional generation between the traditionalist Premodern and Modern values of earlier times and the Postmodernists values of today. For good or ill, major social changes were wrought for and by the Boomers. It should be noted that many of the social changes conventionally attributed to Boomers were actually the result of the efforts of members of earlier generational cohorts. Society became much more inclusive for minorities and women. Education, including higher education, came to be viewed as birthright. Many negative, putative and borderline abusive parenting and school discipline methods lost favor. Rigid, patriarchal social and family structures were questioned and abandoned by many, along with the hegemony of religion. The well publicized excesses in drugs, sex and rock and roll of the 1960s and 1970s did take a toll, and society snapped back to Republicanism in the 1980s.

When the leading edge of the Baby Boom came of age to start families of their own, many chose not to. The "baby bust" of 1965 to 1979 saw the birth rate fall from the Baby Boom high of 25.3 per 1000 to 14.6 per 1000 (Strauss and Howe 1991) and produced Generation X. The freedoms of the 1960s and 1970s and Boomers' motivation for personal improvement left less room for children in the lives of Boomers, as well as for Silent generation people who were taking advantage of the new social freedoms. Increases in the availability and reliability of birth control and abortion made parenting a true choice for sexually active adults for the first time in history. Members of Generation X, now 38 to 23, were low priority children with adults believing it was more important to have a nice car than children (Raines 1977). The revolutionary 1960s that were followed by the disillusioned 1970s and the traumatic 1980s so many of these young people came of age in difficult times for children, many of whom felt like they were "late to the (Boomers') party" (Strauss and Howe 1991). They have been famously defined in both the academic and mainstream media as cynical, distrustful of authority, arrogant, naive and materialistic (Levine and Cureton 1998; Sacks 1996; Tulgan 1997). As Generation X entered the workforce they were described by Boomer managers as disloyal, not appropriately differential to authority, inattentive, uncommitted, and arrogant (Tulgan 1997). While these characteristics certainly would not apply to everyone in the Generation X cohort, they have taken hold as a stereotype many Xers are having to disprove and/or outgrow.

The "Baby Boom Echo" or the "Baby Boomlet" started in 1979 when the Boomers finally decided to follow the biological imperative and produced Generation NeXt. Continuing until 1994 these young people, now 23 to 8, number 60 million strong, and are the single largest demographic in America (Howe and Strauss 1993). These are our entering, traditional college age students. There is not a clear consensus on their character. Some describe them as "the next Great Generation" (Howe and Strauss 1993). Others believe that due to the continuing impact of Postmodern influences they are more likely to look like a continuation of Generation X than a cycling back to tradition, duty, discipline, and delay of gratification that characterized the Greatest Generation (Sacks 1996).

Postmodern Theory

Postmodernism was most famously defined by Jean-Francois Lyotard in 1979 (in French) as "incredulity towards metanarratives". Meranarratives are totalizing, all encompassing (meta) stories (narratives) about the history, purpose and goals of mankind that provide the foundation for the interpretation of information, the organization of knowledge, and the establishment of cultural practices. While Premodern times relied on religion to provide these narratives, the Modern era turned to science. Both viewed history as moving toward social enlightenment and emancipation with knowledge eventually becoming complete. All would be known, either theologically or scientifically. While the Modern era saw the scientific model becoming legitimized, Postmodernism, according to Lyotard, is an age of fragmentation and pluralism with no one model offering any predominate shared metanarrative. There has been a widespread delegitimation of previous models and authorities; religion, science, political and economic power and sources of "knowledge" (Anderson1990; Lyotard 1988; Sacks 1996).

Postmodernism arose as a reaction to the perceived limitations and failings of modernism and a questioning of its truths (Sacks 1996). In his 1992 address on "The End of the Modern Era" to the World Economic Forum, Czechoslovakian President Vaclav Havel said that modernism was an era in which there was a "cult of depersonalized objectivity" when "objective knowledge was amassed and technologically exploited" with "belief in automatic progress brokered by the scientific method" (Havel 1992). The obvious economic exploitation of scientific knowledge, as opposed to its being used for the general good, combined with the inability of science to fulfill its promise. Space shuttles exploded, antibiotics quit working, pollution and abuse of natural resources follow most civilization, and labor saving devises did not give anyone more time. Reports of scientific advancements came to be view skeptically with the assumption that the information promoted someone's agenda, as opposed to objectively presenting facts (Sacks 1996). Socially, the impact of multiculturalism (including immigration) and efforts to increase pluralism, mutual understanding and respect increased awareness that there are other people following different models and doing perfectly well. Notions of the equal value and applicability of various models of viewing the world proved especially devastating to religions whose bread and butter is their being the only path to some spiritual or everlasting goal. As Postmodernism usurped Modernism, Premodern beliefs became anachronistic.

Postmodernism lacks a prevailing model, though some would say that consumerism is most prevalent (Anderson 1990, Sacks 1996). We understand ourselves as producers and consumers. Information is a tool for people to promote their products, and may actually be the product. Self-interest, as initially developed by Boomers, may have come to maturity and replaced a larger spiritual or community good as a legitimate value model for personal choices (Sacks 1996). One implication for education has been to come to view education as a "product" and students as "customers" (Tschohl 1993).

Postmodern Generations

Generations X and NeXt are the product of these Postmodern influences and the accompanying social changes. If Boomers were defined by Jefferson Airplane's "feed your head", Nirvana's "here we are now, entertain us" might better describe later generations (Sacks 1996). The most profound shift may have been in the structure of the family. As the family changed, so changed socialization patterns, agents of socialization, and interpersonal bonding dynamics. Where in the 1960s the "Leave it to Beaver/ Father Knows Best" family of working father, stay-at-home mom, and at least one child represented 75 of 100 families, by 1997 only three in 100 families fit that picture (Raines, 1997). That is the greatest change in the family since the Industrial Revolution when fathers left the farm to work in industry. The great outmigration of mothers into the workforce, and escalation in divorce rates increased the prevalence of single parent families, led these children to have historically unique formative experiences, at least for America. The rise of day care made children consumers at a very early age, as well as subjecting them to as many parenting or supervision models as there were workers. With day care workers among the least trained and lowest paid workers in our society, socialization for these children when supervised at all was uneven at best. Many were latchkey children expected to fend for themselves after school from an early age, turning to television (which had become increasingly violent and sexual) for companionship and guidance. If Boomer children were told "you can be whatever you want to be" these young people were told "be careful" (Raines 1997).

Postmodern Education for Generation NeXt

The rise of postmodernism coincided with changes in higher education. Students changed academically as evidenced by declining test scores, reduced willingness to work for grades, increased expectations for entertainment in the classroom and

an almost knee-jerk distrust of authority. Educators, grounded in the scientific method of the Modern era were increasingly at a loss to engage Postmodern students effectively and complained of expectations for good grades with little effort, expectations by students and administrators for grade inflation, lower academic standards and lack of self-direction in learning. (Levine and Cureton 1998; Sacks 1996).

Generation NeXt is a diverse, even fragmented, age cohort who are following Generation X into college. Whether or not they follow Generation X's famous tendencies they certainly might be expected to continue to have a consumer mentality, be adaptable, pragmatic, self-reliant, and technoliterate; characteristics also applied to Generation X (Raines 1997, Sacks 1996). Today's incoming students are seen as substantially different than Generation X by the influential Howe and Strauss, who describe them as close to parents, focused on grades, active in extracurricular and community activities, demanding of a secure and regulated environment, and respectful of social conventions and institutions (Young 2003). Academic trends suggest that these traits are not being evidenced at many campuses across the country, especially less elite institutions, and they are certainly the least studious of modern cohorts (Higher education research institute 2002).

For educational delivery systems to be effective, especially with Generation NeXt, they will need to recognize and operationalize a variety of influences. Much has been written about maximizing undergraduate learning (Austin 1993; Chickering and Reiser 1993; Pascarella and Terenzini 1991). Academics to rooted in the modern and based on science; science as a method for uncovering and demonstrating "truth" and science as a body of knowledge in many fields as developed through its methods. The relationship between instructors and students tends to follow traditional lines of authority and diminished consent as instructors establish agendas for both the content and process of student learning, whether they tell students what they need to know or attempt to follow Galileo's famous maxim to help students discover for themselves. The Postmodern tendencies of students to reject both facts and authority might be in conflict with these basic premises of higher education. Few graduate programs in fields outside education address pedagogy in meaningful ways, and certainly do not prepare instructors to hold students' interest or provide the entertainment they expect (Sacks 1996).

Suggestions

Basic guidelines for educating Generation NeXt might include:

1. Establishing clear expectations, and communicating these expectations early and often. Since Generation NeXt has been required to adapt to a variety of circumstances and environments, many without clear expectations, the goal might be to exploit their adaptability by giving them clear expectations to adapt to. Whether the expectations are for class attendance and timeliness or the quality of written work, good instructors, like good parents, will communicate and hold students to consistent behavioral expectations. Increasing consistency across the campus will also

increase effectiveness, as will engaging students in the establishment of community standards and expectations.

2. Articulating all desired outcomes. If colleges are interested in developing personal, community and citizenship competencies, as well as academic competencies, these should be spelled out and quantified with codes of conduct and transcripting of community service activities.

3. Stressing the role of the scientific method in understanding, as well as the potential abuses of science and data. If science is to be viewed realistically as a set of tools for understanding, the limitations and need to critically examine data must be stressed, along with traditional education about the scientific method.

4. Avoiding pomposity and unnecessary displays of power or authority. The "whys" for everything from parking regulations to class assignments must be articulated nondefensively or risk knee-jerk rejection.

5. Expanding the parameters for class projects from the traditional "paper" to other types of demonstrations of research and learning. Expanded choices might increase student ownership of the process and outcome.

6. Maintaining technological sophistication. Hard wired youth have little patience for educational methods they see as outdated; i.e.: unidirectional lecture to rows of passive listeners. It might be easy for these students to assume that an instructor who is not aware of modern technological trends might be equally unaware of current issues in their own field.

7. Teaching "up" Bloom's taxonomy (Bloom et al. 1956). Generation NeXt is probably even less inspired by the expectation that they memorize and regurgitate unapplied knowledge level factoids than earlier cohorts, and may active rebel against them.

8. Providing real life application. Any topic, class or field that cannot demonstrate its immediate application to each student will be suspect. "You have to know this because it will be on the test" is guaranteed to discredit both the information and the instructor as it tends to show there is no other use for the information.

9. Offering opportunities for out of class interpersonal involvement from informal interaction with instructors during regular office hours to clubs and organizations might help increase students' connections to the campus, and so their learning and development.

10. Appreciating diverse viewpoints. Multicultural, paranormal/religious and traditional (even racist and sexist) perspectives must be allowed air space in classrooms to allow for each to be dispassionately examined for accuracy, veracity and utility. The knee jerk "that's just wrong" by some Boomer instructors of discredited or politically incorrect opinions does not promote this necessary analysis which offers students tools to make their own evaluations in the future.

11. Increasing flexibility in course schedules, semesters, and flexibility in entry and exit. The old "two sixteen week semesters" model has the power of decades of tradition and offers administrative convenience, but might not best meet the needs of all students who are juggling other responsibilities.

12. Moderating a customer based service model. Some of the "quality service" initiatives have helped shift the perspective from faculty staff convenience to student service (Tschohl 1993), as the "learning-centered college" movement has help shift the focus from teaching to learning (O'Banion 1999). If a student customer model is adopted it should be stressed that no rational customer expects to "get something for nothing" and that the customer is not always right.

Conclusion

Generation NeXt is coming to campus with special expectations and needs, having been raised under unique conditions in these Postmodern times. If they are to successfully matriculate and enter the workforce with sufficient intellectual and social skills, we of the Boomer and other generational cohorts must appreciate these special influences and needs and reexamine the climate, processes, and content of higher education to maximize their chances for success.

References

Anderson, W.T. 1990. *Reality isn't what it used to be.* San Francisco: HarperCollins.

Austin, A. 1993. *What matters in college? Four critical years revisited.* San Francisco: Jossey-Bass.

Bloom, B.S., M.D. Englehart, E.J. Furst, W.H. Hill, and D.R. Krathwohl. 1956. *Taxonomy of educational objectives: The classification of educational goals, Handbook I: Cognitive domain.* New York: David McKay Company.

Brokow, T. 1998. *The greatest generation.* New York: Random House.

Chickering, A.W., and L. Reiser, 1993. *Education and identify.* San Francisco: Jossey-Bass.

Havel, V. 1992. The end of the modern era. *New York Times,* March 1, 1992, 4(1).

Higher education research institute. 2002. The American freshman: National Norms of fall 2002. *UCLA graduate school of education and information studies.* Los Angeles, CA.

Howard, M.C. 1996. *Contemporary cultural anthropology.* New York: Longman.

Howe, N., and B. Strauss. 1993. *13th gen.* New York: Vintage.

Howe, N., and W. Strauss. 2000. *Millennials rising.* New York: Vintage.

Howe, N. and W. Strauss. 2003. *Millennials go to college.* New York: Vintage (not yet published, quoted from the *Chronicle of Higher Education* 49(21) page A37)

Levine, A., and J.S. Cureton. 1998. *When hope and fear collide.* San Francisco: Jossey-Bass.

Losyk, B. 1997. *Generation X.* The Futurist. 31(1): 39–44.

Lyotard, J.F. 1988. *The postmodern condition.* Minneapolis: University of Minnesota Press. (Originally published in French in 1979).

O'Banion, T. 1999. *Launching a learning-centered college.* League for innovation in the community college: Mission Viejo, CA.

Pascarella, E.T., and P.T. Terenzini. 1991. *How college effects students: findings and insights from twenty years of research.* San Francisco: Jossey-Bass.

Raines, C. 1997. *Beyond generation X.* Menlo Park, CA: Crisp.

Sacks, P. 1996. *Generation X goes to college.* Chicago: Open Court.

Smith, J. W., and A. Clurman. 1997. *Rocking the ages.* New York: HarperCollins.

Strauss, W. and N. Howe. 1991. *Generations.* New York: Quill.

Tschohl, J. 1993. *Connections.* Bloomington, MN: Noel Levitz.

Tulgan, B. 1997. *The manager's pocket guide to generation X.* Amherst, MA: HRD.

Young, J. 2003. A new take on what today's students want from college. *The Chronicle of Higher Education.* January 31, 2003.

DR. MARK TAYLOR is an educator, speaker and workshop leader based in Little Rock, Arkansas. For updates on today's postmodern college student and more information about his programs contact him at info@taylorprograms.org or visit www.taylorprograms.org.

General Education Issues, Distance Education Practices

Building Community and Classroom Interaction Through the Integration of Curriculum, Instructional Design, and Technology

JERI L. CHILDERS AND R. THOMAS BERNER

Introduction

The review of a case study of the design and development of a single undergraduate course would be a small step toward determining the role of distance learning in the implementation of the best practices in general education. For the purposes of this postmortem, key instructional design decisions, including the choices of distance learning methodologies, will be discussed in relationship to general education objectives. The role of distance learning in general education can best be determined with further critical analysis of the role of distance learning in the broader context, with a review of a variety of cases using each of Jones's and Ewell's (1993) areas of best practice as one template for evaluation.

Our approach to designing a distance education course was to learn by doing. What follows is a discussion of what worked and what didn't work within the context of general principles outlined by researchers in the area of general education and distance learning. As members of the Innovations in Distance Education (IDE) project at The Pennsylvania State University, our team members were action researchers; they started with a real teaching-learning problem, proposed solutions, and tested our assumptions along the way. We suggest that *An Emerging Set of Guiding Principles and Practices for the Design and Development of Distance Education* (Innovations in Distance Education, 1998), established as part of the IDE project, might serve as yet another important template for evaluation of the role of distance learning in effective general education.

The Case: Problems and Solutions

This case study examines the issues surrounding the integration of videoconferencing and Web-based instruction to bring the literature of journalism to life for undergraduate students. Getting students to interact with each other in a course in which the instructor is present is difficult sometimes, so taking what had been an undergraduate seminar on the literature of journalism and offering it at a distance raised the bar even higher.

This case study involves the redesign of a resident course called *The Literature of Journalism,* which is aimed at sophomore students. It has no prerequisites and, during the time of this writing, nonjournalism students and even non-College of Communications students enrolled in the course. In the past, the course had enrolled mostly senior journalism majors. In this case, of the 12 students enrolled, only two were graduating journalism students; the level of classroom interactivity and sophistication was not as high as in previous course offerings.

Adjustments were made in the course design to accommodate the student skill levels and maturity of the students, as well as to support their students' transition to the new curriculum. Before the course was redesigned for distance learning, the instructor distributed weekly five or six questions about the next reading, which provided a framework to help the students complete their essays for the next week. The instructor would then open each class by giving a brief background lecture on how the book being read came to be written. Discussion followed. The instructor had an informal evaluation, a midsemester evaluation, and an open-ended focus-group-type evaluation at the conclusion of the course.

In redesigning the course, the first problem the four-person team tackled was an analysis of the learners. This was a relatively simple task because the instructor had taught the class before.

The second problem the team needed to solve was the selection of instructional media and tools that would help them to achieve course objectives and to create the level of interactivity required. These media and tools would need to build a learning community that supported the weekly videoconference seminar, where the instructor is alone at a video desktop unit and the students are at another location on campus. The support tools the team selected were (a) the Internet and a course Web page, (b) E-mail between the students and instructor, (c) guest subject matter experts (either resident or distant), (d) the books the students read weekly, (e) library resources, and (f) in-person class visits by the instructor.

The third problem for the team was the further design and integration of the components mentioned above into a meaningful learning experience. Throughout the design process, the team dealt with problems related to the construction of the Web page, faculty development, password protection, copyright issues, privacy issues related to student information posted to the Web page, use of on-line library resources, and planning issues related to scheduling guest speakers in person and via video teleconferencing.

Class-day interaction became the next design problem for the team. Inherent in the use of interactive compressed video teleconferencing technology is the required skill to operate the system and the slight delays in audio and video transmission that require the participants to be sensitive to the subtle "delays in the conversation." This required the team to be more prepared in designing and facilitating class discussions. To solve part of this problem, the team provided an orientation to the technology the first day of class. In addition, a graduate student was stationed at the remote site with the students to manipulate the technology and to provide a warm welcome each class. The instructor also contacted all of the students before the first day of class to inform them about the course, its content, and its delivery methods. He learned about their computer capabilities (hardware and software) and their capabilities to use the Internet.

To solve the second part of the problem of the class-day interaction—choosing discussion leaders and managing the classroom interaction—the instructor had decided even before the course was redesigned for distance learning that he or she was going to require the students to submit their essays via E-mail early on the day of the class. The instructor felt that by knowing in advance what the students had written he could call on them appropriately and generate discussion. Each week after reading the students' work, the instructor would make discussion assignments based upon topics. The instructor created a list of those topics and assigned students to lead the discussions by posting the discussion list to the classroom monitor via a document camera next to the desktop unit. As the students became more comfortable talking to each other, the instructor moved more responsibility to the discussion leaders. The instructor's role became that of a facilitator and resource person. This design shifted the responsibility for learning to the student and added to the environment of community and interaction.

The team concluded that continuous evaluation of the design, technology, and curriculum was required in order to achieve the goals and objectives of the course and to determine if the use of distance learning technologies had an impact on the teaching-learning relationship. The next problem was to design the formative and summative evaluations. The team designed and distributed three E-mail surveys during the course.

Integrating Principles and Practices

In the remainder of this article, we set forth examples of principles and practices for successful integration of distance education and general education. These principles and practices have been extracted from our own experiences, and we find that it was most helpful to understand and appreciate them. There is, of course, more that can be said about these principles (Ratcliff, 1997; Innovations in Distance Education, 1998) and other examples of practices that exemplify the effective integration of curriculum, instructional design, and technology.

The staff and faculty participating in the IDE project, funded by a grant from the AT&T Foundation, summarized an emerging set of principles and practices for the design and development of distance education (Innovations in Distance Education, 1998) based on the experiences of the university teams developing distance education courses for the general education curriculum. The principles were grouped in the following categories: (a) learning goals and content presentation, (b) interactions, (c) assessment and measurement, (d) instructional media and tools, and (e) learner support systems and services. In addition, Jones and Ewell (1993) summarized the literature on what constitutes "good practice" in undergraduate education. For each of the 12 practices they articulate, we provide a description of how we implemented the practice in our context:

1. *Create high expectations for student learning and create a link between general education goals and individual course goals in ways that are motivating and appreciated by students.* In this case, the course objectives and design intended to promote an appreciation of the (a) values of freedom, power of individuals' choice, and free thought and speech; (b) one's heritage and other cultures; (c) examination of values and controversial issues; and (d) the mastery of linguistic and analytical skills, which are many of the goals of general education (Gaff, 1983; Ratcliff, 1997). In the further description of the course you will note how the distance learning design elements worked together to set student expectations and to aid in the mastery of key skills. In this course, *The Literature of Journalism,* students are advised in class and on the Web page that when they have completed the course they should have a greater appreciation for journalistic enterprise and different styles of writing. They should also gain insight on reporting and research. They should see how different writers influenced other writers. And they should get a feel for history and culture of the 20th-century writer. These objectives were accomplished in various ways beyond normal classroom discussion using distance learning technology. Content materials were placed on the Web page (described earlier) in order to provide students with a larger context: background on the author, critical reviews, and how books were originally received by the public.

2. *Provide coherent, progressive learning and set reasonable and clear course goals and assignments that progressively*

build on each other to maximize student learning. Of particular interest in this design is the integration of the Web page, E-mail, and teleconferencing to post student papers to the Web page with the expectation of their use as resource material in subsequent assignments. Students could see their individual and group progress in building analytical skills. Students were required as the course progressed to write essays that compared the books they were currently reading to the books previously reviewed in class. Because students' essays were posted on the Web page, class members could read what their classmates had written and use them as additional resources in future essays. The weekly writing assignments were intended to build writing and analytical skills.

3. *Create synthesizing experiences.* Requiring synthesis in the learning experience provides benefits to students and can be accomplished through essays, journals, capstone courses, and service learning. The instructor created synthesizing experiences through the assignment of weekly essays. The design team used distance learning strategies to enhance the experience by providing the essays in a "virtual gallery" so that all students could benefit from each student's individual synthesis.

4. *Integrate education and experience.* Education should support the students' aspirations and experiences by being relevant and easily applied. Students were encouraged to write their essays from a number of points of view and to bring in outside resources, including their own background and experiences. Students were afforded the opportunity to explore different aspects of the journalism and writing professions. To ensure that the resources provided were current and relevant, the team wanted to integrate multiple media and provide the materials at the students' computer desktops thereby creating a "virtual toolbox."

5. *Create active learning experiences.* Fully engaged students learn more and quicker. The design of this course allowed for no passive learning. At times, this design stretched the students. In fact, this learner-centered approach was sometimes a new experience or uncomfortable experience for some students. Prior to each class, students' essays were submitted and students were to be prepared to participate and lead class discussions. Each student took the lead on one class discussion topic weekly.

6. *Require ongoing practice skills.* Practice, practice, practice strengthens new skills. Nothing can demonstrate the application of skills more than the requirement of weekly essays. Grades for the redesigned course were based upon writing skills and discussion skills. The E-mail allowed for the submission of assignments and querying of peers and instructors related to the competencies being developed. The virtual gallery demonstrated that practice had its rewards. Students could easily see their skills increasing. The students began to enjoy the discourse pre- and post-class and requested a variety of on-line resources such as listservs and chat rooms to be used in the future to continue their practice and learning.

7. *Assess learning and give prompt feedback.* Confidence and skills improvement comes hand in hand with constructive feedback. For this course, students received immediate feedback in a number of ways from a number of sources. First, the instructor's immediate receipt of the essay assignment (a) provided feedback via E-mail directly to the student, (b) acknowledged the student's work that day through in-class discussion, and (c) provided comments on the essays themselves, which were returned to the students and posted to the Web page. Secondly, students received continuous feedback from the instructor and their peers: papers were posted the day of class. Students were encouraged to visit the virtual gallery and comment on each other's written or oral analysis or both of the current class discussions or refer to each other's work in subsequent discussions or essays.

8. *Plan collaborative learning experiences.* Team skills and collaborative learning are expected after college. Students' experience and learning is enhanced and reinforced by their peers' support, criticism, and collaboration. As noted earlier, some students would read their classmates' papers on the Web and sometimes would cite them in subsequent papers or discussions. Students also requested additional distance learning resources to collaborate.

9. *Provide considerable time on task.* The assignments and the use of the distance learning materials designed required a great deal of time on task. Formative and summative evaluations indicated that distance learning allowed students to achieve the course goals, often with more interactions than in resident courses. However, some students felt the time on the task was excessive.

10. *Respect diverse talents and ways of knowing.* Key knowledge skills and abilities are instilled and strengthened by explanation, discussion, practice, and application. Just as the Web page enhanced delivering the goals and objectives, it also helped enhance interaction among the students of disparate backgrounds. The instructor urged students to submit biographies and photographs to him before the start of classes so he could post them on the Web page as a way of creating a community and facilitating interaction, as well as acknowledging the diverse talents of the class.

11. *Increase informal contact with students.* Class time is a small percentage of the time spent in the learning-teaching relationship. Students benefit from and value feedback and mentoring from their peers and faculty outside of class. Using distance learning technology to enhance the learning-teaching interaction was the primary goal of the team. The Web page was designed as a way of creating community among the students, who, though even in the same room with each other, came from diverse majors and with two exceptions were unknown to each other. Student and instructor biographies, photographs, and E-mail information were added to the page to stimulate interaction. (Originally, the course was designed to accommodate students at two or more remote sites.) Students used a

variety of means to contact each other and the instructor. The instructor did have campus office hours but was most often contacted by E-mail. The majority of the informal interaction occurred via distance means.

12. *Give special attention to the early years.* Transitions to college, between colleges, or between major curricula require substantial academic and social adjustments for students. Supporting and motivating students during this transition is important. Sophomores, for example, may require more support and different learning strategies than seniors may. As described earlier, the instructor slowly shifted the class discussion responsibility to the students at the distant site. The pace of the class and the expectations of class participation were adjusted to accommodate the students' stage of development and comfort with the technology.

Course Evaluations: What Did the Students Tell Us?

In all of the resident courses, the instructor offers students the opportunity to provide feedback about midway through the course. The instructor typically asks six open-ended questions about the pace of the course, the use of E-mail, and teaching style. At the end of the semester the instructor would conduct focus-group-type assessments.

For this distance learning course, the four-person team designed three evaluations that aimed to anticipate different problems. The evaluations were solicited via E-mail and were filtered through someone other than the instructor. Unfortunately, the return rate was about 50%, even when deadlines were extended. When the instructor conducted anonymous evaluations at the end of a class, the return rate was 100%.

The first instrument surveyed the students' affinity to the technology and their perceptions of the quality of the distance learning experience, particularly video teleconferencing. This survey included questions related to the teleconferencing experience, the Web page (both content and design), the use of E-mail, and the general impact of the technology on their ability to interact with their peers and their instructor. The team wanted to make sure everyone was comfortable with the technology. Prior to taking this course, none of the students had experienced video teleconferencing. Some of the students had experienced the use of Web pages in instruction. All of the students were proficient with the use of E-mail. The results of the survey indicated that all of students reported being comfortable with the technology. By the time the first evaluation was administered, 3 weeks into the course, all of the students had accessed the Web page and used the materials, four of the students had used it 10–14 times in a 3-week period, and no student had used it less than five times.

The second instrument surveyed the students' perceptions of the course workload, pace of the course, written assignments, the amount of feedback, timeliness of feedback, and other issues related to the Web page. This evaluation focused less on the technology itself and more on the course content and the amount of interaction with the instructor. It was at this point in the course that the team learned that the students wanted to see the instructor more often on their monitors. In his facilitator role, the instructor had been placing items on the document camera in lieu of projecting his own image on the students' monitor, but the students wanted to see his face.

The third instrument surveyed the students for their perceptions of the course and the technology. Students' comments included:

> "Enjoyed course material, but was discouraged from asking questions."

> "Learnt [sic] alot [sic] from class. Interaction format of course [was] very good. Maybe a weekly meeting place and time [e.g., at student union] to discuss ideas and concepts [would be helpful]."

> "[I] would have liked more interaction from instructor. [I] felt like he was acting as moderator."

> "Liked the structure of the course. [It] was like a book group, but for credit. [I] would have liked it better if teacher was in the classroom."

Of the five students who indicated that their view of video teleconferencing had changed, one student indicated that distance learning was more personalized than he or she originally thought. Another student felt distance learning enhanced classroom interaction more. Another student felt that, as the class progressed, she was interacting with the instructor and not a TV monitor. Yet another student indicated the technology opened up possibilities for increased interaction not available in a traditional classroom.

In addition to what we reported earlier, students also reported that they would have liked:

1. more students profiles on the Web page;
2. E-mail links to students;
3. Web links from the current Web page essays written by the instructor to additional Web pages (The instructor started adding links as he became more comfortable with the Web and with formatting.);
4. more comments on their papers (This comment is something with which the instructor agrees. Since papers arrived in different electronic formats, the instructor found it difficult to return to the students heavily annotated papers. This problem can be overcome if all papers are written in and then evaluated in the same software.);
5. peer tutoring (The instructor intends to incorporate peer tutoring into the course when he teaches in residence. Students would be expected to share their view of the current reading during the week on E-mail.);
6. more guest speakers brought in via videoconference (This is something the instructor will explore the next time the course is taught.); and
7. more student interaction (although a majority of respondents felt the interaction format worked well).

The team's assessment is that distance learning enhanced the attainment of the course goals. The team recommendations and those of the students will be used to further refine the course for its next offering.

Conclusion

We found that distance learning practices in our case complemented general education principles. Distance learning practices actually enhanced delivery of the content and increased interaction between the students to maximize the goals of general education, which were met in this case, and actually facilitate the use of general education principles. Distance learning practices did not significantly impact on the students' ability to learn or to experience the intended general education or course goals.

Compared to the preparation required for resident education, a distance learning course required more time during the design stage, equal time during delivery (a Web page is labor intensive, but the instructor weighed that against lower-technology alternatives, distributing photocopies of papers, for example, and decided that the higher technology approach was ultimately more efficient). Evaluation data indicate that students and the instructor expressed the benefits of the extra investment in support resources.

Distance learning and its design and development requires support resources for instructors and time for faculty development. The team approach had several advantages: (a) the team allowed the instructor to focus on the content and resource development, (b) the use of the team significantly reduced the total development time by utilizing team expertise quickly, and (c) the team environment was an efficient form of faculty development (the team provided "virtual scaffolding" and coaching when needed). Instructors vary in their expertise and affinity for distance learning practices. This team benefited from the fact that the instructor was a self-directed learner and an early adopter of technology and classroom innovation. In other cases, more faculty development would be required and would add to the lead time required. The team approach is resource intensive. Depending upon the nature of the course, the needs of the audience, and other factors, development time and team resource needs will vary.

Distance learning practices, that is, the use of Web pages and video teleconferencing, allows for continual addition of resources that add a richness and relevance to the student experience. It also allows for customization for students' needs.

Some student-instructor interaction and exchanges of data will be enhanced with the improvement in software; currently the inability to work across platforms limits the ease of giving feedback on student assignments (i.e., detailed comments in the body of essays).

Design teams and instructors must anticipate isolation that can be felt by instructors who are separated from their students. This isolation may affect instructor satisfaction, motivation, and potential long-term involvement in distance learning. These feelings of isolation may be offset by the instructor's ability to work with peers in other institutions or with students across the globe.

By nature, a distance education course forces an instructor to face pedagogical and technological issues and problems he might not face in a typical course. What we learned is that the solutions we developed can be used just as effectively in any classroom and will enhance any instruction.

References

Gaff, J. G. (1983). *General education today: A critical analysis of controversies, practices, and reforms.* San Francisco: Jossey-Bass.

Innovations in Distance Education. (1998). *An emerging set of guiding principles and practices for the design and development of distance education.* University Park, PA: The Pennsylvania State University.

Jones, D. P., & Ewell, P. T. (1993). *The effect of state policy on undergraduate education: State policy and collegiate learning.* Denver, CO: Education Commission of the States.

Ratcliff, J. (1997). Quality and coherence in general education. In J. G. Gaff, J. L. Ratcliff, & Associates (Eds.), *Handbook of the undergraduate curriculum: A comprehensive guide to purposes, structures, practices, and change* (pp. 141–167). San Francisco: Jossey-Bass.

JERI L. CHILDERS, Ph.D., is Assistant Director in the Office of Program Development, Outreach and Cooperative Extension at The Pennsylvania State University. In addition to her administrative role, she is an instructional designer and program planner. Dr. Childers is working on ways to bring innovations to the teaching-learning environment for undergraduates, postbaccalaureate students, and professionals using a variety of designs, media, and modes of delivery.

R. THOMAS BERNER, Ph.D., is Professor of Journalism and American Studies in the College of Communications at The Pennsylvania State University. He is the author of five textbooks on professional journalism practices and has just completed *The Literature of Journalism: Text and Context.* In the spring of 1994 he taught in the China School of Journalism in Beijing.

UNIT 2

Curriculum and Instructional Design

Unit Selections

Key Points to Consider

- Imagine that you are assigned to design an Internet enhanced writing course for high school students. How would you use the Internet and the World Wide Web to aid students in the writing process?

- Describe how you would revise and convert a set of paper-based tutorials so they could be distributed on the World Wide Web.

Student Web Site

www.mhcls.com/online

Internet References

Further information regarding these Web sites may be found in this book's preface or online.

Education Place
http://www.eduplace.com

Portfolio Assessment
http://www.indiana.edu/~reading/ieo/bibs/portfoli.html

Sesame Workshop
http://www.ctw.org

Teaching with Electronic Technology
http://www.wam.umd.edu/~mlhall/teaching.html

A curriculum is an educational plan for action that includes strategies for achieving desired goals. Curriculum design is the organizational pattern or structure of a curriculum. There is a broad level that involves basic value choices. There is a specific level that involves the technical planning and implementation of curricular elements. The curricular elements include needs, student characteristics, problems, goals, objectives, content, learning activities, and evaluation procedures. These elements can be used as a blueprint for developing instructional strategies and human interfaces in different learning situations. For example, interactivity is a learning activity that can be used in various learning environments. Interface design and usability assessment provide learners with a comfortable way to manipulate data and other learning objects and in so doing increase learner interaction and performance.

In addition, it is necessary to provide adaptive learning facilities that use graphical user interfaces to provide learning opportunities that meet the learner on the appropriate learning plane. In order to provide such a curriculum, teachers and designers must infuse technology-based learning tools into teacher-designed lesson plans. If this can be done, each school could contribute to the creation of a technology-based interactive instructional curriculum library.

It begins with Judith Boettcher taking a look at the characteristics of "well structured content" as it relates to the design of instructional technology resources. She describes the meaning of well-structured and focuses on the principles of designing for learning. In addition, she describes each of the three levels that formulate the characteristics of digital learning resources.

In "Integrating Technology into the Instructional Process: Good Practice Guides the Way" Marianne Handlers states that the computer is a tool for students and teachers and they need to put away their concerns of dealing with a variety of technology-based learning and teaching experiences. She describes in detail the ways computers can be integrated into the curriculum by thinking of using this resource as another tool available to students rather than thinking of "teaching computers" as a subject itself.

Then, Smith and Smith describe an online resource that helps teachers and students organize and annotate Web sites into lessons, presentations, assignments, or instructional resources. They also describe TrackStar which provides a set of tools that can help teachers locate, organize, and structure Web-based materials into a set of curriculum based learning tools.

Douglas Leigh describes the discipline of Instructional Systems design from Aristotle through Seymour Papert. Throughout the article the events of cognition are described from the cognitive basis of learning and memory to the current trends of constructivism. This decade by decade description to the development of Instructional Design's taxonomy is very informative.

The next article capitalizes on the notion of distribution as a key concept in statistics and makes generalization and justification as well as explicit focus of instruction. If you are interested in improving student learning and achievement in mathematics and science read this article.

In the final article, Elise Temple discusses the remediation program, Fast Forward Language, and the result this program had on improving the reading ability of dyslexic children.

Designing for Learning: The Pursuit of Well-Structured Content

How do you make course content really accessible to your students? Just as being an expert in your discipline is not by itself a guarantee of good pedagogy, your best-laid technology plans might miss the mark if they are not fine-tuned to the content you wish to present. And the best technology strategies benefit from semantically clear, structured content. Here, Judith Boettcher takes a look at the characteristics of "well-structured content" as it relates to the design of instructional technology resources.

JUDITH V. BOETTCHER

With the emergence of the Web as a new space for instruction, the focus of most analyses of teaching and learning has been on process—overhauling what faculty and students are doing within the learning experience. The organization of what is being taught and its availability in various formats—the structure of the course content—has received much less attention.

Meanwhile, content development has certainly not been neglected. Digital libraries, national content projects such as MERLOT (www.merlot.org/), and the work by the W3C on Web accessibility (www.w3.org/WAI/Resources/) are all efforts that foster the evolution of standards and tools for interoperability and easy access to content resources. There is clearly a trend toward further development of knowledge repositories within the disciplines.

But I think it is time now for a renewed emphasis on content resources for learning, along with increased efforts to make course content efficient and effective for students—in other words, well-structured content.

The Meaning of Well-Structured Content

The dictionary definition of the word "structure" is useful. The basic definition of structure is "the result of the action of building or constructing." This definition links well to the currently favored learning theory of constructivism.

A more elaborate definition of structure is "something arranged in a definite pattern of organization." This definition suggests one of the desirable characteristics of well-structured learning content. That is, content for which an organization is clearly visible and in which concepts are presented clearly and precisely.

Course content—the material to be learned or studied—is one of the four core components of the learning experience. The other three are the *teaching*, the *learner*, and the *environmental* components.

Consider the relationship of well-structured content to the design of an online course. Online learning based on well-structured content impacts the identification, selection, and development of course content in three ways:

- Content must be semantically well-structured for instruction; this corresponds to the *teaching* component of the learning experience
- Content must be a good fit or well-structured for a particular student; this corresponds to the *learner* component of the learning experience
- Content must be technologically well-structured; this corresponds to the *environmental* component of the learning experience

Note that the meaning of well-structured content goes well beyond the dictionary definitions of structure. It includes the nuances of interaction with the other three components of the learning experience—teaching, learner, and environmental.

Principles of Designing for Learning

Before delving more deeply into the characteristics of well-structured content for digital learning resources, let's review a few basic principles. A core principle of designing for learning is that existing knowledge structures in the brains of faculty and students are different. A student approaching a discipline such as physics, psychology, or biology for the first time will likely have few core concepts, principles, or facts to build on. At this first approach to a subject, students' thought processes might be compared to the tundra, a bare and cold landscape. The students' brains might have other areas with rich growths, but in the area of physics, their brain space might be called Tundra Territory.

But the discipline knowledge of the physics faculty, at least in the area of physics, might be comparable to jungles—rich, dense growths representing complex structures of knowledge, concepts, principles, applications, and problems. The lectures by physics faculty to the students in large undergraduate courses might be described as "Where the Tundra Brains meet the Jungle Brain."

Research into the differences in the knowledge structures in the minds of students and faculty has a long tradition in cognitive research, studying the distinctions between the knowledge structures and behaviors of novices and the knowledge structures and behaviors of experts. Well-structured content can figuratively warm the landscape of the mind and support the building of foundations for complex knowledge structures.

Multi-Modal Learning Resources

A recognized principle in educational research that works well with the notion of well-structured content and technology use is that efficient learning can be facilitated with sensory input. This includes multi-modal experiences, incorporating multiple senses. Fortunately, the current ready availability of multimedia resources makes designing for learning easier than ever.

Well-structured content can make the "jungle" of concepts, rules, and principles more readily learned by students. Multimedia resources, such as animations, simulations, and microworlds encourage student involvement and increase sensory input. Dialoguing online—with other students, with faculty, and with other online resources—also increases sensory inputs.

In addition to being well-structured semantically, content resources ideally fit student goals, readiness, and the individual's current preferred learning environment.

Some students will come to a particular discipline with rich knowledge structures of their own, but still sparse in comparison to the faculty. For faculty, this means identifying and selecting a rich set of resources that may meet the needs of many students. Nishikant Sonwalker (Syllabus, November 2001) suggests the selection and identification of many sets of resources, providing multiple paths through a course.

Studying a Subject versus Taking a Course

I was reminded of the importance of content recently when I was chatting with a new college graduate. Her new position involved work with physics materials, so I asked her if she had studied physics in college. She replied quickly and emphatically, "Oh, no, I didn't study physics. I did take a couple of physics courses, but I didn't study physics!"

A curious response! Why would this graduate make a distinction between studying a subject and taking a course? In taking a course, was she describing a learning experience that might have covered content but resulted in few knowledge structures in her memory. And she was well aware of that lack of structure. Might better-structured content have helped to ensure the development of a lasting knowledge of physics?

A student who has successfully earned a grade by "taking the course" might have knowledge structures that were created and linked to each other, but not grounded. These knowledge structures might have been suspended in mid-air, inaccessible after being temporarily constructed for testing purposes. Continuing our climate metaphor, the student essentially created a climate that was temporarily nurturing of isolated knowledge facts, but without integration into other knowledge structures, the learning was lost.

Characteristics of Digital Learning Resources

In designing an online course, a course with online components, or a course that includes digital resources, an instructor makes a host of decisions about the goals and framework, as well as identifying and selecting content. In selecting content, the instructor defines the parameters for the breadth and depth of the course and the expectations of students.

Developing knowledge structures that survive a course and provide transferable knowledge and skills generally requires different types of content. While there are many hierarchies of content types, the simplest paradigm of content has three levels: (1) core concepts and principles, (2) well-structured problems with known solutions and (3) less-structured, complex problems without known solutions. Below are some guidelines for selecting well-structured content and incorporating new digital media resources within these three levels.

Level One: Core Concepts and Principles

At this content level, a faculty designer identifies content that:

- Provides descriptions of core concepts dynamically using visual, audio, and graphic illustrations
- Provides animations that involve the students interacting with the resource and rehearsing processes
- Demonstrates relationships among core concepts, such as concept maps
- Provides clustering and chunking of information
- Reveals relationships and patterns
- Reveals differentiations and distinctions among concepts
- Links core concept knowledge with current happenings

Level Two: Well-Structured Problems with Known Solutions

At this content level, a faculty designer identifies content that:

- Presents consistent elements of the problem sets to the students
- Reveals patterns inherent to the problems
- Reveals sources and types of knowledge that contribute to problem solutions
- Engages the learner in the solutions, gradually increasing the complexity of the applied rules and principles
- Uses simulations that chunk and cluster the elements of the solutions

Well-Structured Content: Coming to You Soon via XML

One of the emerging content standards is that of XML, eXtensible Markup Language. Well-structured content is what designers have when they use XML to mark up content.

XML is complementary to the HTML standard. Jeff Jones (www.swynk.com/friends/jones/articles/xml_101.asp) used the following analogy to describe the difference between XML and HTML: XML is to defining information as HTML is to displaying information. He goes on to note that while XML and HTML both are text-based and both use tags, elements, and attributes, XML allows users to structure and define the information in their documents. Additionally, XML is a metalanguage that allows users to create their own tags, elements, and attributes as necessary.

What's powerful for designers of today's online learning environments is that the same XML document can be displayed in a variety of formats, such as HTML, MS Word, Adobe PDF, or text. Easy portability to handheld devices is also on the horizon. XML is the future for describing, manipulating, and transmitting data. The W3C (www.w3c.org/XML/) is the place to start learning about XML and its design roles for content.

Level Three: Less-Structured, Complex Problems Without Known Solutions

At this content level, a faculty designer identifies content that:

- Provides complex scenarios, such as Harvard case studies
- Engages the learners in solving problems where neither the elements or the solutions are known
- Provides simulations of complex interactions
- Provides real-world problems such as those worked on in engineering and applied disciplines
- Provides opportunities for dialogues with experts on real-life problems
- Uses case studies and problem-based learning

Level three, "less-structured" problems without known solutions maps well to more advanced students, who can build on knowledge structures already in place and apply their creativity to problem-based learning sets. Ideally, students involved in level-three problems will already have well-constructed knowledge, resulting from previously effective engagement with highly structured learning modules.

Digital content resources in support of learning need to map to students' needs and to students' readiness. Supporting the development of lasting knowledge structures continues to be art as well as science.

What Is Different about Digital Content?

Given the richness of the digital resources available, we now think about content differently. Because content is digital, it is no longer bounded by space and less and less bound by format. Because content is digital, it may be combined and recombined. Because content is digital, it can draw on the combined power of graphics, animations, audio, and video. And because content is digital, it is easier for students to become creators of content that is custom made for the growing and nurturing of the knowledge structures in their own minds—to help them move from the Tundra Territory to the Garden State.

The development of course content is increasingly the work of artists, in particular those faculty who think visually. Edward Tufte, the author of seminal books on the display of graphic information, said it this way, "To envision information—and what bright and splendid visions can result—is to work at the intersection of image, word, number, art."

JUDITH V. BOETTCHER, Ph.D. is an instructional designer and consultant with expertise in distance education and online learning programs. Send her questions and comments at judith@designingforlearning.info.

Integrating Technology into the Instructional Process:

Good Practice Guides the Way

Marianne Handler
National-Louis University

The computer as a tool for students and teachers is not going to disappear from our world; not from business, not from home use and not from the school. Yet, even with that knowledge many teachers are still concerned and uncomfortable with finding ways in which a variety of technology-based experiences can expand and enhance what is happening in their classrooms. In order to alleviate theses concerns and discomforts, the learning community, made up of teachers and students, is finding new ways of working and learning together.

These changes are not easy. Helping teachers develop their skills during a transition period takes time and effort. Teachers are aware that change is never comfortable and that time and effort will be required. It is important for the school administration to provide the time and support necessary for teachers to explore and experiment with the range of ways the technologies can be woven into the school environment and curriculum.

When describing the ways computers can be integrated into the curriculum it is important to think of using this resource as

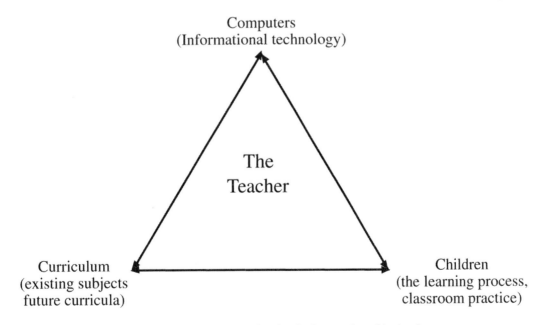

Figure 1 The teacher is a key factor in planning for the integration of technology

another tool available to students, rather than to think of 'teaching computers" as a subject onto itself.

Preparing to Use Technology

When thinking about best practice in the use of technology, one must carefully consider the possible uses of the computer within the classroom. These possible uses include using the computer:

- to teach the student.
- as a tool with which students can learn.
- as a tool to assist in the learning process.
- to develop open-ended exploratory experiences for the students.

Blending appropriate technology tools into the curriculum supports many of the dimensions of learning described by Marzano (1992) in his book, *Dimensions in Learning*. His model establishes a learning environment in which students develop positive attitudes and perceptions about learning, in which they have experiences where they can acquire and integrate knowledge, where they have opportunities for extending and refining knowledge, where they can use knowledge in a meaningful way and where they can develop what he refers to as productive habits of mind.

Planning for Technology Use

Keeping all of these factors in mind the teacher chooses ways in which the computer can best fit into a particular instructional environment. S/he identifies the instructional goals for the assignment. The next step is to match the teaching/learning task to a particular computer-based tool and finally to use these tools to complete the task. It is critical for the student to understand that the teacher values the technology-based activity and that it is seen as a part of the curriculum and the learning process.

One method might be to list a particular goal, such as having students practice using their knowledge in a meaningful way. The next step would be to think about how to achieve the particular goal. For the goal listed above the teacher would seek out software that provides a meaningful task for the student, tasks such as having to investigate a problem, determine the appropriate problem solving strategy, or, invent a solution to the problem. The tool might be a simulation, a data base, a spreadsheet or another appropriate tool (Marzano, Pickering and Tighe, 1994). Examples of this kind of planning will be discussed in more detail later.

In reflecting about the software that will be used the teacher's first concern is with the purpose of the software ... is it appropriate for the content area goals? In recent work Marzano, Pickering and Tighe (1994) have written at length on assessing student outcomes and have identified what they consider to be five lifelong learning outcomes of importance for today's students; the ability to be a self-directed learner, a collaborative worker, a complex thinker, a quality producer and a community contributor. Technology can help achieve these outcomes.

Making Technology Work for You

It is an absolute necessity for the teacher to become familiar with the software before using it with students. It is a good idea to try the software out with a small group of students to determine if it is truly appropriate for the task. As with other instructional materials it is important to know that the directions are easy for the student to follow and the reading level is appropriate for the group with which it will be used.

Keep in mind that the goal is to make the software invisible as much as possible. In other words the focus is on the curriculum, not on the software. Software woven into the classroom experience can best meet the goals of the lesson. One way to think about this is to aim for the use of **curriculum-driven software; not software-driven curriculum.** No matter how exciting the software may appear to be it will not add to the learning environment unless it has been chosen to meet a curricular application or provide an experience that adds to the goal of the lesson such as cooperative learning or peer collaboration. It is key that the software be evaluated and considered in light of the learning experiences in each particular context.

There is a current focus on helping students to develop higher-order thinking skills.... problem solving strategies, if you will. Such generic descriptions sound very good but do not help students became aware of the particular thinking skills or problem solving strategies they are being asked to use. When working with students, and when selecting the particular piece of software to be used there are three key questions they will be helpful in the planning process:

1. What strategy is being introduced?
2. When a cognitive strategy is being introduced to be used with the particular technology, provide the student with a name for it. Demonstrate why it is a particularly good strategy and that the student is adding it to a repertoire of strategies that can be used when solving a problem.
3. Have students had prior experiences with this strategy? Provide reminders of early occasions for using the strategy. Stress the importance of using strategies in more than one setting.
4. What opportunities are planned for students to practice this skill in other settings? When discussing the strategies with students it is important they become aware of their own thought processes as they learn to use varying thinking or problem solving skills. Have they studied the question posed in the setting? Can the students discuss the various strategies they already know about? Can they select the one to be used to solve this particular task? This meta-cognitive approach can be practiced with a variety of software programs available in many schools.

Graphic organizers are one example a group of tools that can be used across content areas. Data bases, word processors and hypermedia software are examples of this group. Inspiration (1992; Fig. 2) allows the user to brainstorm ideas, develop concept maps in an open, exploratory environment. With a click of the mouse the same information can be displayed in an outline format for further exploration.

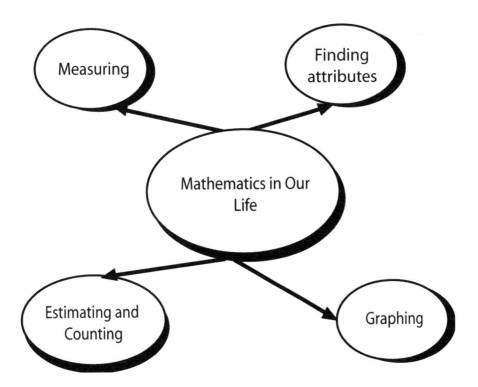

Figure 2 Using *Inspiration* for brainstorming.

Spreadsheets (Fig. 3) provide opportunity for students to work with real, authentic problems. It is possible for students to gain a variety of experiences while using this approach. They can learn to use the spreadsheet, and once learned, they can create graphs and interpret data displayed on spreadsheets. Working with the "what if?" questions that are inherent in the use of spreadsheets helps students use their knowledge of the problem and prior knowledge of similar situations and content meaningfully.

Creating and interpreting **graphs** does not always come easily to students. Many have had the opportunity to work with graphs where the form and content have been already decided for them. Developing problems with no 'one way' to answers gives groups of students opportunities to use the spread sheet to try out more than one approach. The focus can be on finding the solution, thinking about the process or focusing on the creation of graphs. These open-ended exploratory experiences give students that chance to try out problem solving strategies that have been previously practiced. It is important for students to be able

to identify the particular strategies and begin to learn in what settings the various approaches can best be to put to use.

Graphing lessons frequently give the students the numerical data for the assignment and the type of graph that should be created. Programs such as ClarisWorks or Microsoft Works are examples of the kind of software that allow children to quickly create graphs from a body of data. Time can then be spent discussing the issue of interpreting graphs.

The Graph Club (Tom Snyder Productions, 1994) includes an experience for beginning graphing that provides insight into the meaning of the data displayed. This software contains a different approach to graphing; an opportunity for demonstrating an understanding of graphs that is not always included in graphing instruction. One of the segments of the program presents a completed graph with the numerical data appropriately displayed. Students often have difficulty understanding the appropriate display for a 'data story.' In this case there is an opportunity to teach strategies for graph selection or assessing student understanding.

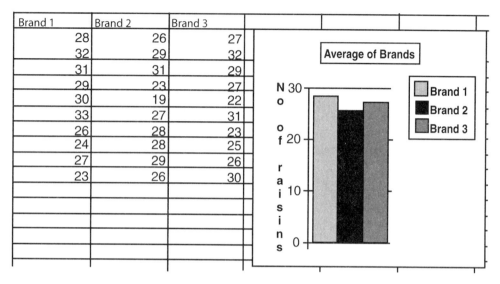

Brand 1	Brand 2	Brand 3				
28	26	27
32	29	32
31	31	29
29	23	27
30	19	22
33	27	31
26	28	23
24	28	25
27	29	26
23	26	30

Figure 3   Using a spreadsheet and creating graphs.

Kid Pix can be used to develop opportunities for students to practice new strategies or it can be used as an assessment tool. When it first was released many teachers thought of this as a 'cute program for young children'. In fact it is an example of how the use of open-ended programs can emerge in the hands of excellent teachers. As in many areas of teaching and learning we are limited only by our own imaginations and ability to think in new ways. This screen is an example from KidMath, a series of mathematics activities for Kid Pix developed by Paul Becher, a teacher from Waukesha, Wisconsin. This can be a tool to teach the student or to allow practice in new skills thus assisting in the learning process.

Simulations lend themselves to the creation of powerful learning experiences. They often fall into the category of open-ended activities and require thoughtful decision making on the part of the student. They are excellent opportunities for students to open their tool box of problem solving strategies and determine which ones can best help them. Simulations frequently allow for student interactions as they learn to collaborate on finding a solution that all can agree upon. Several excellent pieces of software fit into this category. Operation Frog is a useful simulation in the science area and the Sim City series has been used in social studies programs in middle schools and in high schools.

Telecommunications

During the past several years an explosion has occurred in the area of telecommunications. Local bulletin boards often provide a resource for teachers looking to network with others. The anonymity of telecommunications has also added an element of comfort for some students who are not comfortable in social settings. Remember that when 'your fingers do the talking' such things as stuttering, acne, being overweight, and other such elements that make life painful for some students, do not show.

Commercial on-line services such as America On-line provide resources for both students and teachers as well as a gateway to the resources of the newest telecommunication resource, the super highway, or the Internet. Students find new resources as they explore open-ended activities that require them to use many information tools to support their projects.

E-mail between students or teachers in almost every country of the world allows for the creation of a global network and access to global centers of information. America On-line and other commercial networks also provide opportunities for private chats. In other words it is possible for students in different classrooms to talk to each other in real time in a planned and private environment.

Where Does it Lead?

It is the intention of this article to encourage teachers to take the risks needed to teach in new ways, to try new tools and enjoy the challenge of learning with students. Teachers hold the key to helping these students learn to become users of knowledge, learners willing to explore different ways to attack a problem, as will as citizens with a variety of communication skills in our global community.

The challenge is there for you to take. Think about the lessons you as a teacher have designed for your classroom. Some work very well. Others may not be achieving the goals for the students in either the content itself or in the ability to work together or to clearly communicate ideas. How can that lesson be reshaped to become more successful for the students? The reshaping of the lesson might be a time to think about incorporating the use of technology. Could it be that one of the forms of available technology; computer software, laserdisc, CD-ROM or video help meet the planned goals?

This article has mentioned many examples of software, but it is important to remember that each classroom has different needs based on the students in that classroom. Suggested software, here or elsewhere, is just that. It is up to the teacher to look for reviews of software and to find ways in which to evaluate the software in light of the goals for the particular lesson and setting. As you continue to reshape your lessons and activities you and your students will discover the pleasure in practicing the skills of becoming life-long learners together.

References

Marzano, R.J. (1992). *A different kind of classroom: Teaching with dimensions of learning*. Association of Supervision and Curriculum Development.

Marzano R.J., Pickering, & Tighe (1994). *Assessing Student Outcomes*. Association of Supervision and Curriculum Development.

On the Right Track:

Technology for Organizing and Presenting Digital Information

SEAN J. SMITH AND STEVEN B. SMITH

This article describes an online resource that helps teachers and students organize and annotate Web sites (more specifically, the addresses or URLs to the Web sites) into lessons, presentations, assignments, or instructional resources. TrackStar was created to assist teachers to integrate the Web more effectively into their classroom to meet the needs of all students. Each Track provides a user with a list of Web-based resources offering easy access to the content.

The tremendous growth of the World Wide Web (Web) has created rich instructional environments for all teachers to address the learning needs of diverse learners. Easy access and immediate applications to classroom instruction allow for an instructional tool unique in access as well as use. Currently, over 46% of schools have reported that the majority (50% or more) of their teachers are intermediate-level users of technology and are able to use a variety of computer applications (i.e., word processors, CD-ROM programs; Market Data Retrieval, 2001). Further, more than 60% of schools in the United States reported that the majority of their teachers use the Internet for instructional purposes and that more schools provide Internet access in classrooms (82%) than in any other location. However, these same reports also indicated that most teachers are still not adept at integrating technology into their curriculum (Market Data Retrieval, 2001). There exists a need for educators to become proficient at integrating technology effectively and efficiently within their classroom, a need that can be addressed by providing them with skill, opportunity, time, and tools (Meyer, 2001).

Educational applications of the Web vary and continue to grow as schools, government agencies, nonprofit organizations, companies, and a variety of other organizations create resources for classroom application. Recently, it seems that not a day goes by that a Web-based resource has not been created to address the learning needs of a particular student. Unfortunately, although evidence of the educational benefits of technology abounds (Edyburn, 2001) and investment in hardware and software has increased dramatically, relatively few teachers use technology regularly in their teaching, and the effect of computers on existing curricula is still very limited (Zhao & Cziko, 2001). Today the tremendous growth of Web-based resources offers teachers and parents both instructional opportunities as well as challenges. The catch-22 for many teachers involves the process of finding resources in an efficient manner, reviewing and identifying instructionally appropriate resources to enhance current curriculum, and then constructing an effective delivery format to ensure appropriate integration and subsequent learning (Higgins, Boone, & Williams, 2000).

Finding the Right Technological Resources

Take Emily, for example. Emily is a fifth-grade teacher about to complete her 15th year teaching in an elementary classroom. For the past 2 years, Emily has tried to integrate technology, specifically the Web, into her classroom instruction. Limited in her abilities, she has witnessed its potential when her fifth graders share work they have completed at home or in the library using Web-based resources. Determined to integrate more technology into her teaching, Emily decided to supplement her traditional unit on *Charlotte's Web* with Web-based resources. She hoped the integration of the Web might expand student understanding, specifically for those with learning disabilities (LD) who had been increasingly included into her general curriculum classroom.

Emily began her Web investigation by speaking with Mrs. Hayes, the librarian, as well as the school technology coordinator and other teachers she knew who had begun to experiment with the Web. Two peers offered some basic tips but were not able to direct her to specific resources on *Charlotte's Web*. Undeterred, Emily decided to locate her own. Unfortunately, finding the time to focus on this task was a challenge. With her planning periods filled for the next several weeks, Emily was left to searching the Web before or after school. Having two young children of her own, the morning offered limited opportunities; instead, she found herself sitting down at her home computer around 8:00 pm one Tuesday evening.

Finally, after her two children were asleep, Emily dialed in and accessed the Web from home. As she patiently waited for the modem to connect, she remembered why she preferred her direct Internet connection at school, especially at this time of night. She plodded on and began to search using the only search engine she was familiar with, Yahoo® (http://www.yahoo.com). Although not adopt at the ins and outs of Yahoo, she was knowledgeable enough to type in various terms related to *Charlotte's Web*. After several hours, Emily was getting frustrated. Besides her patience being significantly tested by the limited speed of the modem and her home computer, the resources she had located were either too simplistic or too challenging for her fifth-grade classroom. Determined to use the Web to supplement instruction, Emily selected several resources from what she found and decided to use them over the next week. By the end of the week, Emily realized she had made a mistake trying to integrate these Web-based resources. Her students quickly found that the materials were either too easy or too hard. Instead of using the resources she had selected, Emily observed that students were searching for themselves or that they were surfing the Web for material unrelated to the *Charlotte's Web* assignment. Discouraged, Emily struggled with how to proceed and improve the Web-based supplement. Looking ahead, Emily wondered if the upcoming weekend would offer any time to search the Web for additional resources.

Emily learned the hard way about how not to integrate the Web into her teaching. Unfortunately, Emily is not alone. Many of her peers have experienced the same frustrations and have given up on the possibility of integrating Web resources into their teaching. For many teachers, integrating the Web often means settling on resources inappropriate for student learning, especially for those with specific learning disabilities.

Although there has been tremendous growth in the Web, teachers continue to struggle with accessing the right resources for their classroom needs and, more important, the learning needs of the student (Meyer, 2001). For students with disabilities, the need to identify an appropriate Web-based instructional tool is critical. Although many teachers have begun to recognize the unique capabilities of the multimedia and hypermedia components of the Web, teachers often struggle with identifying and, subsequently, integrating the appropriate technology tool. For instance, like many software applications, Web-based resources may have been constructed for a particular grade level. Thus, simply accessing a Web site on whales does not ensure that it is appropriate for fourth graders. Instead, teachers must be able to review the Web-based resource and identify whether it addresses the subject area, students' specific learning needs, and various student learning preferences.

As Emily will soon discover, there are solutions that address the problems of locating, organizing, evaluating, and integrating Web resources into instructional environments. The Regional Technology in Education Consortia (R•TEC; see http://www.rtec.org) program, established by the United States Department of Education (Grant No. R302A000015), has funded the development of several Web-based tools that teachers can use to locate, organize, evaluate, and integrate Web resources into their

teaching. The R•TEC program was originally established to help states, local educational agencies, teachers, school library and media personnel, administrators, and other educational entities successfully integrate technologies into K through 12 classrooms, library media centers, and other educational settings, including adult literacy centers. Today, the 10 national R•TEC programs continue to be an online resource for educators across the country.

Teachers continue to struggle with accessing the right resources for their classroom needs

One of the R•TEC's, the High Plains Regional Technology Consortium (HPR•TEC), located at the University of Kansas in the Department of Special Education (http://hprtec.org), has developed a number of tools designed specifically for educators to use. Some of the most popular tools are TrackStar, Profiler, QuizStar, RubiStar, and Web Worksheet Wizard. Each of these tools offers the educator (novice to expert), an accessible system for organizing, displaying, creating, evaluating, and managing Web resources for use in the classroom. For example, TrackStar offers teachers like Emily an online database that structures Web resources for searching, lesson integration, and general use by students and teachers. More important, TrackStar (see Note) offers a structure and easy-to-use format that allows novices to quickly learn, develop, and use the application. It is the ease of use function that has made TrackStar so attractive to us and other educators, literally across the country. Similarly, TrackStar addresses one of the primary issues for many teachers who are attempting to incorporate the Web into their teaching. That is, how does someone locate instructionally appropriate Web-based resources, organize what is found, and make these selected resources available to all students without investing a significant amount of time and effort?

At the University of Kansas in the teacher preparation program, TrackStar is an integral component within the introductory technology course for both general and special education teacher education preservice students. Required for all School of Education students, this course is taught every semester with approximately 70 participants per semester. Students use TrackStar to create technology-enhanced lessons, creative research tools, extended learning exercises, and a variety of other learning products. Many students use the TrackStar program in other education courses as well. For example, in the Characteristics of Exceptional Learners course, students are asked to expand on their initial tracks (created in the introductory technology course) to ensure the tracks are relevant to the specific learning needs of students with high incidence disabilities. The intent of the assignment is to bridge the technology application to content relevancy and instructional effectiveness.

Why have we selected this program? The benefits of the program are numerous. For instance, a student does not need to learn a sophisticated program or hypertext mark-up language (HTML) to create a Track. The program is simple to learn and easy to use, and most students can have a complete Track created in approximately 20 minutes. TrackStar not only provides students with the means to organize and annotate their selected Web sites but also makes available to them a rich library of Tracks created by other educators and students. This resource provides teachers with just-in-time and content-specific resources for use in their classroom. Similarly, as we express to our students, TrackStar represents the essence of technology integration. By providing a simple, easy way to organize and annotate educationally appropriate Web sites, teachers are able to

- control access to specific Web sites,
- provide educationally appropriate and safe Web resources for all students,
- control scope and sequence of instruction,
- address specific needs outlined in a student's Individualized Education Program,
- create a renewable educational resource,
- share their Tracks with other educators, and
- acquire just-in-time resources and lessons created for special education classrooms.

Thus, technology is not used simply as a reward system or unrelated motivational tool; instead, the Web is integrated as an instructional tool.

What Is TrackStar?

TrackStar is an online resource that helps teachers and students organize and annotate Web sites (more specifically, the addresses or URLs to the Web sites) into lessons, presentations, assignments, or instructional resources. Similar to bookmarks (Netscape®) or favorites (Internet Explorer®), TrackStar allows users to organize favorite Web sites into Tracks under a specific topic and make them accessible to anyone with Internet access.

Tracks are created by teachers or students and are stored on servers at HPR•TEC. All of the Tracks, approximately 63,000, are organized and cataloged by grade level. Users can select from Tracks created for early childhood, primary grades (K–2), intermediate grades (3–4), middle school (5–9), high school (9–12), college/adult, or all grades. Likewise, users can select Tracks organized by keyword (i.e., special education), by author, or by themes and standards. If you are interested in the most popular Tracks, users have access to the month's Track-A-Day, a list of all "Top Tracks," and Tracks by subject/category. For the user uncertain of how to begin locating a Track, TrackStar has a "How to Find a Track" tutorial.

Each Track provides a user with a list of Web-based resources offering easy access to the content. For example, in the case above, Emily was searching for resources concerning *Charlotte's Web*. A keyword search using this title brings up 64 Tracks created by other educators or students. Each Track offers a title, an annotated summary for the entire Track, and a reference (and often an e-mail address) to the author. For example, one teacher

has created a Track entitled *Charlotte's Web*. According to her summary, she located Web-based resources concerning *Charlotte's Web* that would help students who had difficulty decoding unknown words. She has included five *Charlotte's Web* Web sites and provided a summary for each one. Her second Web site, for instance, directs users to answer a set of questions in an effort to improve comprehension skills as well as word recognition skills when reading *Charlotte's Web*. When users select this site, they are linked to teachnet.com (http://www.teachnet.com) and its list of questions and possible activities for students.

TrackStar was created to assist teachers like Emily in using the Web more effectively. By creating a structured template, teachers and students can organize lists of resources to be integrated into classroom instruction. Similarly, by making these Tracks fully accessible via the Web, students and teachers can access this information at any time. Format considerations also apply the principles of Bobby (see http://www.cast.org/bobby), thus offering access to all users, including those with disabilities.

As teachers and students create their individual Tracks, they are adding to an ever-growing database of subject-specific Tracks for teachers and students across the K through 12 curriculum. More important, although these Tracks are fully accessible to anyone using the Web, the author of the Track is the only individual who has the ability to alter the content of the Track. For example, Emily and her students may use the Track on *Charlotte's Web*, but they do not have the ability to add or delete information or sites from this Track. Emily, however, can create her own Track (please see the Appendix for details), modify an existing Track thereby creating a new Track, or e-mail the Track author with possible suggestions to improve the current Track.

TrackStar Tracks are intended to be used by teachers and students and are therefore carefully reviewed for content and appropriateness by HPR•TEC staff and teacher consultants. When reviewing Tracks they make certain that each Track contains a first and last name, a usable email address, and an appropriate description. HPR•TEC staff look to see if all fields have been completed and make sure all links are working and that they are the same as described in the annotations.

Occasionally, Tracks must be placed on hold. Tracks that are held generally contain copyrighted or explicit material and/or inappropriate content. An example of inappropriate material might be linking to search engines that are inappropriate for young students or educational environments. Reviewers also look to see what type of advertising is used on the Web pages. If any site uses advertising dealing with sex, drugs, gambling, or other such material, the Track is deemed inappropriate. A Track can also be placed on hold for 30 days if it has fewer than two links, three or more broken links, or noneducational links. Once all links have been checked for appropriateness and functionality, staff submit the Track as reviewed.

If a Track is placed on hold, the author has 1 month to correct any problems. Once the problems have been corrected, HPR•TEC reviews the Track again. If the problems are not corrected within the prescribed time limit, the Track is deleted from the TrackStar database. Once a Track has been deleted, there is no way to retrieve the Track. Similarly, Tracks are deleted if there is no usable e-mail address or if the Track contains no links.

Teachers and students can save a considerable amount of time generally spent searching the Web, using popular search engines with varying degrees of success, by using TrackStar, which offers a Web-based structure that locates Tracks and organizes them specific to content and grade level. Tracks are also often accompanied by Web-based quizzes (QuizStar; http://quiz.4teachers.org/), rubrics (RubiStar; http://rubistar.4teachers.org/), and lesson plans. As a result, users like Emily can save time and frustration by avoiding numerous search engines and instead, spend only limited time exploring various Tracks created by peers.

Searching for the Right Track

Although not created to replace search engines, TrackStar has evolved into a database of Web-based resources that have been located, organized, and summarized to assist teachers, students, and parents. Thus, teachers like Emily can access educationally appropriate Web sites without having to weed through hundreds if not thousands of irrelevant sites. Teacher-created Tracks may not contain every relevant link, but these Tracks generally offer a reference point from which to begin a search. To find the right Track, teachers and other users must understand how TrackStar organizes Tracks as well as the tools available to locate them.

As the use of TrackStar has grown, the need to organize the thousands of Tracks in a searchable format has become vital. As mentioned earlier, a popular way to access Tracks is via a keyword search to identify specific topics. To begin a search, click inside the search box and type the word or phrase that best describes the topic for which you are hunting. Click **Go** to start the search. For example, if looking for Tracks about strategies, type the word *strategies* in the search field and click **Go.** After a few moments, a page with a listing of all the Tracks that have the word *strategies* in their title, description, annotation, or link titles will appear. Click on the title of a Track that appears to meet your needs, and you will be taken to the Description Page of that Track.

If you want to search for a phrase, such as *learning strategies,* enclose the phrase in quotation marks when typing it in the search box (e.g., "learning strategies"). Use lower case when typing search queries if you want the maximum number of results. Similarly, if you want to limit your search to Tracks appropriate for certain grade levels, also click on the checkbox(es) in front of the desired grades. For example, if looking for Tracks about *dinosaurs* that could be used by second graders, type the word *dinosaur* in the search field and check the Grades K–2 box and click **Go.** After a few moments, a page with a listing of all the Tracks that have the word *dinosaur* in their title, description, annotation, or link title will appear.

If you happen to know the name of the author who created a Track, click on the **by Author** search link on the TrackStar home page. You will be taken to a page that asks for the author's name or complete e-mail address.

Click inside the search box. Type the first, last, or entire name of the desired author. Click **Go** to start the search. After a few moments a page with a listing of all the Tracks made by that person will appear. Click on the title of a Track that meets your needs, and you will be taken to the Description Page of that Track. If you find a Track that is particularly well done, you might be interested in other Tracks made by that same author. You can also locate Tracks made by an author from the Description Page of a Track. Look for "Search Tracks" and simply click the **All Tracks by this Author** link to see a list of all that author's Tracks.

Finally, as national and state curriculum standards continue to direct teaching, TrackStar has organized Tracks based on a limited number of state standards as well. The states represented in this database are Texas, Oklahoma, Kansas, Missouri, and Nebraska. Additional states will be forthcoming but probably limited to the states that the High Plains Regional Technology Consortium serves (Kansas, Colorado, Nebraska, Oklahoma, North Dakota, South Dakota, and Wyoming); however, a quick review will find these state standards similar to the national curriculum standards and, thus, applicable to many states across the country. To use the standards search tool, click on the by **Themes & Standards** link on the TrackStar home page. This will take you to a page listing the searches available. Choose the Subject/Grade Level combination of interest (e.g., Social Studies, Grades 5–8). You will be taken to the Themes page for that academic subject and grade level. From the left-hand column choose a theme (e.g., American Revolution) by clicking on the link. This will return a list of all Tracks in the database that fit this topic. At the top of the page you will also see the five states listed. Click on the name of your state to see that state's Social Studies Academic Standards related to the topic of the American Revolution. You can keep this window open when reviewing Tracks to help you decide which Tracks (or sites within a Track) will help your students meet the standards.

Integrating Tracks to Improve Student Learning

Successful technology integration for teachers begins with an understanding of how a technology will affect student learning and comprehension. Many teachers too often rely on the technology itself to provide all the necessary instruction, content, and feedback (Smith, 2000). Students can easily become engaged in the wrong learning experience by focusing their attention on the hardware (the computer) and not the content or instruction being presented. Our experience with TrackStar with current and future general and special education teachers has shown us that teachers who have successfully integrated TrackStar Tracks into their teaching have blended the use of technology with traditional educational practice in a way that provides resources, activities, or extended learning opportunities. For example, our teacher Emily might develop an instructional unit on the topic of amphibians and use a Track she created that encourages students to "hunt" for different amphibians by clicking preselected links and searching the selected Web site for "clues." This exploration

Table 1   Ideas for Integrating Tracks

Presentation	Resource List	Homework Assignment	Scavenger Hunt
Worksheet	Test preparation/review	Student research project	Extra credit
Integrate state and national standards	Lesson plan development	Introducing technology	Introducing interactive learning
Provide in-depth learning opportunities	Teaching organizational skills		

activity, similar to a scavenger hunt, would serve as a single activity within the amphibian unit. Using her Track in this way, she could address more learning preferences and could engage her students in an interactive learning activity while allowing time for interaction with individual students and opportunities to give more attention to their specific learning needs.

There are many ways in which a teacher can use TrackStar to enhance the learning opportunities of students, especially those with disabilities (see Table 1). Each opportunity a teacher has to explore new ideas, be creative, and be inventive is bound to have a positive effect on their students. TrackStar makes it easy for teachers to integrate technology into their teaching and to engage their students to use higher-order thinking skills.

Conclusion

Structuring Web-based resources is important if teachers are to use these resources in an effective instructional manner. Simply creating the resource and making it accessible does not guarantee its use, especially when effective integration for students with special needs is the goal. Instead, educators need access to Web-based programs, like TrackStar, that can help teachers locate, organize, and structure Web-based information.

Developed to help teachers and parents address some of the challenges the Web offers, TrackStar features a variety of tools. These tools attempt to eliminate the hurdles and allow teachers to focus on instruction, access resources that will enhance classroom activities, and hopefully further individualize the general curriculum. More important, TrackStar saves time.

As Emily learned, finding instructionally appropriate resources can eat up a lot of a teacher's valuable time. For the novice or experienced user, TrackStar offers an environment where a learning community has already organized relevant information in a format that can be immediately shared with others.

There are limitations to TrackStar as there might be with any Web-based educational tool. Many of the limitations are by design and contribute to the "ease of use" experienced by all users. Other limitations are directly attributed to the dynamic nature of the Internet (i.e., maintaining link accuracy and currency, and inability to link to certain Web pages). Still other limitations are timeliness, relevance, and appropriateness of the

Web sites selected. As with similar programs (i.e., WebQuest, Netscape Bookmarks v. 6.0), the user is often presented with a limited array of tools options for customizing the program. For instance, the user of TrackStar has two display modes to choose from and does not have access to alter the appearance of the program for students. While TrackStar is limiting in one sense, it can be totally liberating for educators who can master and integrate this tool into their teaching repertoire.

Persons interested in submitting material to Technology Trends should contact Marshall Raskind, Frostig Center, 971 Altadena Dr., Pasadena, CA 91107.

Note

To access TrackStar, got to http://trackstar.hprtec.org

References

Edyburn, D. (2001). 2000 in review: A synthesis of the special education technology literature. *Journal of Special Education Technology, 16*(2), 5–17.

Higgins, K., Boone, R., & Williams, D. L. (2000). Evaluating educational software for special education. *Intervention in School and Clinic, 36,* 109–115.

Market Data Retrieval. (January 2001). *Report on technology in education 2000.* Washington, DC: Author.

Meyer, L. (2001). New challenges. *Education Week, 20*(35), 49–66.

Smith, S. J. (2000). Technology integration: Teacher education column. *Journal of Special Education Technology, 15*(1), 59–63.

Zhao, Y., & Cziko, G. A. (2001). Teacher adoption of technology: A perceptual control theory perspective. *Journal of Technology and Teacher Education, 9*(1), 5–30.

SEAN J. SMITH, PhD, is an assistant professor in the Department of Special Education at the University of Kansas. His research interests include learning disabilities, cognitive disabilities, instructional technology, and teacher education.

STEVEN B. SMITH, PhD, is an assistant professor in the Department of Teaching and Leadership at the University of Kansas. He conducts research in instructional technology and teacher education. Address: Sean J. Smith, Dept. of Special Education, 1122 West Campus Rd., University of Kansas, Lawrence, KS 66045.

Appendix: Creating Your Own Track

In addition to locating existing Tracks, visitors to TrackStar can also create their own Tracks. Through the guidance of the online tutorial (http://trackstar.hprtec.org/utu.html), users are instructed in a step-by-step process of how to create a personal Track for public use. Each track is protected by an individual ID number and can only be edited by the individual who created the Track. For those new to TrackStar, there is an online guide in the tutorial section that will help with preplanning your Track (http://trackstar.hprtec.org/preplan.html). Below are some helpful tips every educator should consider.

Planning Track Content

Before you begin to make your Track, it is a good idea to decide on the main idea of your Track and what questions you want to answer by visiting links on your topic.

Checking Tracks That Are Already Online

Once you have a topic in mind, you might want to see if anyone else has created a Track on the topic that you have selected. There may be Tracks that already meet your needs or a Track that you could modify to meet your needs. To identify previous Tracks, conduct a keyword search (http://trackstar.hprtec.org/cgi-bin/search.pl?mode=keyword) using your topic of interest.

Choosing a Descriptive Title

TrackStar uses key words in Track titles for its search engine. To make your Track easy to locate, use a descriptive phrase in your title. For example, use "Math Manipulatives for Students with Learning Disabilities" rather than "Learning Disabilities." Focusing on a specific topic will improve the quality of your Track and make it easier to locate.

Writing a Useful Description of Your Track

Writing a brief but thorough description will help others to understand and use your Track. Include a concise description of your lesson or activity, the age or grade for which it is intended, the subject (such as science or art), any state standards that apply, and details that might differentiate your Track from similar Tracks, Many people judge the content of a Track solely by its description; so more people are likely to use your Track if you provide a good description. You may use HTML to format the description, but it is not required.

Searching for Useful Links

To explore online resources available on your topic, enter keywords into a search engine like Google® (http://www.google.com) or AltaVista® (http://www.altavista.com). To search for words that appear together on Web sites, like Down syndrome, enter the term in quotation marks (i.e., "Down syndrome"). To learn more about search engines, use the help file in your favorite search engine or review our helpful search engine hints (http://busboy.sped.ukans.edu/~seanj/searching_the_web.html).

Organizing Your Links

As you search for links, collect them by cutting and pasting the addresses into a word processor document like Microsoft Word® or AppleWorks.® to do this, open one of these word processing programs alongside your browser. In the browser, highlight the URL (address) of the site you want, select **Edit** from the Menu Bar and drag down to **Copy.** Then click on the window of your word processor to select it, and choose **Edit** from the Menu Bar and drag down to **Paste.** Be sure to type a title for each link as well, so you will remember the names of the sites. Collecting links in this way prevents you from is typing a long Internet address (URL). Once you have collected your links, organize them in your word processor in the order you wish them to appear in your Track. Then write annotations or directions that tell students or visitors what to look for or accomplish when visiting each link in your Track. After you've organized links and written annotations in your word processor, edit your work (spell check, grammar check, etc.). Doing all of this before you start to make a Track online will really speed up the process and leave less room for error.

Creating Annotations for Your Links

Annotations are directions that tell students or visitors what to look for or accomplish when visiting each link in your Track. The best annotations include directions for where to look on the accompanying page and what to look for, as well as answers to a variety of questions ranging from basic knowledge to synthesis of information. Well-written annotations provide direction in clear, easy-to-follow steps. When HPR•TEC selects Top Tracks or Tracks to feature in their Premier Tracks listings, they look for Tracks that help students discover, identify, understand, analyze, synthesize, and evaluate different topics. They also look for creative teaching approaches and unique uses of TrackStar.

From *Intervention in School and Clinic*, Vol. 37, No. 5, May 2002, pp. 304–311. Copyright © 2002 by Pro-Ed, Inc. Reprinted by permission.

A Brief History of Instructional Design

Douglas Leigh

As a formal discipline, Instructional Systems Design has been a long time in the making. The early contributions of thinkers such as Aristotle, Socrates and Plato regarding the cognitive basis of learning and memory was later expanded by the 13th century philosopher St. Thomas Aquinas who discussed the perception of teachings in terms of free will. Four hundred years later, John Locke advanced Aristotle's notion of human's initial state of mental blankness by proposing that almost all reason and knowledge must be gained from experience. Then, at the turn of the 20th century John Dewey presented several tenets of the philosophy of education which promoted the idea that learning occurs best when married with *doing,* rather than rote regurgitation of facts.

As the 1920's approached, a behaviorist approach to educational psychology became increasingly predominant. Thorndike's theory of connectionism represents the original stimulus-response (S-R) model of behavioral psychology, and was expanded on some twenty years later by Hull in his exposition of drive reduction—a motivational model of behavior which emphasizes learner's wants, attention, and activities. With the Industrial Revolution came an increased attention to productivity, and educational behaviorists during the 1920's such as Sidney Pressey applied mechanized technology to increase the efficiency of the learning process. Though their initial incarnation did not see much use after the Depression, many of the lessons learned research into these teaching machines regarding the delivery of standardized instruction contributed to the instructional media research & development movement of World War II.

The advent of the Second World War presented a tremendous instructional dilemma: the rapid training of hundreds of thousands of military personnel. Ralph Tyler's work a decade before WWII indicated that objectives were most useful to instructional developers if written in terms of desired learner behaviors. Armed with this knowledge and the experience of creating standardize methods of instructional delivery using teaching machines, military researchers developed a bevy of training films and other mediated materials for instructional purposes. In part, the United States' heavy investment in training and R&D was credited with the country's victory in the war. With the economic boom that followed, federal dollars followed researcher's desire to better flesh out the underpinnings of learning, cognition, and instruction.

The 1950's are characterized by a shift away from the uninformed application of instructional technology to the formulation of theoretical models of learning. The publication of B. F. Skinner's *The Science of Learning and the Art of Teaching* in 1954 canonized the basic behaviorist principles of S-R, feedback, and reinforcement. As the key element of his theory of operant conditioning, the reinforcement of desired learner responses was also incorporated into Skinner's implementations of programmed instruction. Considered by many the progenitor of contemporary instructional design, programmed instruction emphasizes the formulation of behavioral objectives, breaking instructional content into small units and rewarding correct responses early and often.

Another substantial instructional theorist of the 1950's was Benjamin Bloom. His 1956 taxonomy of intellectual behaviors provided instructors a means by which to decide how to impart instructional content to learners most effectively. Advocating a mastery approach to learning, Bloom endorsed instructional techniques that varied both instruction and time according to learner requirements. While this approach provided instructional developers a means by which to match subject matter and instructional methods, Bloom's taxonomy was not in and of itself capable of satisfying the desire of large organizations to relate resources and processes to the performances of individuals. To achieve this researchers in the military's Air Research and Development Command borrowed from Ludwig von Bertalanffy's General Systems Theory of biological interactions to integrate the operations of a wide range of departments, such as training, intelligence, and staffing. Combined with the Bloom's Taxonomy, the systems approach to instructional and organizational development allowed planners and policy-makers to match the content and delivery of instruction in a fashion which considered both super- and sub-systems (the organization as a whole, as well as groups and individuals within the organization). These advances of Skinner, Bloom and von Bertalanffy were usually employed to develop instruction in what was only *assumed* to be an effective an efficient manner. The formalization of a standardized design process still had yet to be devised.

Again it was a crisis that spurred the next evolution of instructional technology—a shift away from an emphasis in the development of instructional programs to one which focused on the design of entire curriculum. Again the crisis was a war, but this time the war was a political one. In 1957 the Soviet Union launched the Sputnik satellite and began the "space race". America was taken by surprise and the government was forced to reevaluate the education system and its shortcomings.

Science and math programs were the first to be targeted, and the government employed experts in these fields to bring the content up to date.

In 1962 Robert Glaser synthesized the work of previous researchers and introduced the concept of "instructional design", submitting a model which links learner analysis to the design and development of instruction. Interestingly, Glaser's contribution to the current field of instructional systems is not so much in the advancement of his model, but in work concerning Individually Prescribed Instruction (IPI), an approach whereby the results of a learner's placement test are used to plan learner-specific instruction.

At the same time Glaser was developing his theories of instructional design and IPI, Robert Mager published his treatise on the construction of performance objectives. Mager suggested that an objective should describe in measurable terms who an objective targets, the behavior they will have exhibited, the conditions or limitations under which they must carry out this behavior, and the criteria against which their behavior will be gauged.

As early as 1962 when he published "Military Training and Principles of Learning" Robert Gagné demonstrated a concern for the different levels of learning. His differentiation of psychomotor skills, verbal information, intellectual skills, cognitive strategies, and attitudes provides a companion to Bloom's six cognitive domains of learning. Later, Gagné extended his thinking to include nine instructional events that detail the conditions necessary for learning to occur. These events have long since been used for the basis for the design of instruction and the selection of appropriate media.

The mediation of instruction entered the computer age in the 1960's when Patrick Suppes conducted his initial investigations into computer-assisted instruction (CAI) at Stanford University. Developed through a systematic analysis of curriculum, Suppes' CAI provided learner feedback, branching, and response tracking—aspects were later incorporated into the PLATO system in the 1970's and continue guide the development of today's instructional software.

By the late 1960's America was again in crisis. Not only was the country involved in another war, but the nation's schools were unable to elicit the achievement from learners it anticipated. Grant Venn argued that since only 19% of first graders complete a bachelor or arts degree, that the current educational system is only serving the advantaged minority of schoolchildren. To counter this trend Robert Morgan proposed to conduct an experiment with an "organic curriculum" which would to incorporate into the educational system the best instructional practices identified through research. Accepted in 1967 the proposal by the US Office of Education, the project was dubbed "Educational Systems for the 1970's", or ES'70. Morgan engaged an array of experts in the field of learning, cognition, and instructional design to contribute to the project and carried out multiple experiments in a variety of settings. Of these was Leslie Briggs, who had demonstrated that an instructionally designed course could yield up to 2:1 increase over conventionally designed courses in terms of achievement, reduction in variance, and reduction of time-to-completion—this effect was four times that of the control group which received no training. In 1970, Morgan partnered with the Florida Research and Development Advisory Board to conduct a nation-wide educational reform project in South Korea. Faced with the task of increasing the achievement of learners while at the same time *reducing* the cost of schooling from $41.27 per student per year Morgan applied some of the same techniques as had been piloted in the ES'70 project and achieved striking results: an increase in student achievement, a more efficient organization of instructors and course content, an increased teacher to student ratio, a reduction in salary cost, and a reduction in yearly per student cost by $9.80.

Around this time Roger Kaufman developed a problem-solving framework for educational strategic planning which provided practitioners a means by which to demonstrate value-added not only for the learner, but the school system and society as a whole. This framework provided the basis for the Organizational Elements Model (OEM), a needs assessment model which specifies results to be achieved at societal, organizational, and individual performance levels. By rigorously defining needs as gaps in results Kaufman emphasized that performance improvement interventions can not demonstrate return-on-investment unless those interventions were derived from the requirements of these three primary clients and beneficiaries of organizational action. This approach to needs assessment and strategic planning has since been used across the world as the foundation for planning, evaluation, and continuous improvement in military, business, and educational settings.

A variety of models for instructional system design proliferated the late 1970's and early 80's: Gagné and Briggs, Branson, Dick and Carey, and Atkins, to name a few. One possible reason for this phenomenon deals with the establishment of formal education and training departments within both public and private organizations. Faced with the computerized technologies of the times, these organizations require a means by which to quickly develop appropriate methods by which to educate internal employees in the new business practices ushered into existence by the Information Age. Another explanation is that businesses, especially consulting organizations, are becoming increasingly required to demonstrate value-added not only to their organization, but to the clients they serve. The evaluation and continuous improvement components of contemporary models of ISD make far strides from the early develop-and-implement models of the middle of the century in this aspect.

In the 1990's a dual focus on technology and performance improvement has developed. For example, in his 1988 essay "Why the Schools Can't Improve: The Upper Limit Hypothesis" Robert Branson offers an argument for systemic school reform, suggesting that schools are operating at near peak efficiency and must be redesigned from the top down using technological interventions. Later in that year Branson was contracted by the Florida Department of Education (DOE) to analyze its various programs and plan a system-wide technology-based educational reform initiative for Florida called Schoolyear 2000. Over the next several years Branson's team developed and piloted multiple computerized instructional technologies, as well as models of the interaction between the internal operations of the school system and the experiences and knowledge of students, parents, and teachers.

Developments in performance improvement outside ISD during the 1990's such as Quality Management (QM), Organizational Engineering, and Change Management have required that instructional designers look outside their profession to demonstrate the utility of their practice. Introduced earlier by Deming, QM has swept public and private organizations alike in the 90's. Whereas initially thought of in terms of "quality control" or "zero defects", quality practices have evolved into tools for organizational continuous improvement. Similarly, instructional designers in the 90's often work alongside authorities in the field of organizational engineering. Characterized by a concern for an organization's culture and interaction between groups, organizational engineering seeks to improve organizations through the identification of relationships between an organization's vision, mission, goals, methods and personnel. Similarly, change management has become a business in and of itself, with leaders such as Darly Conner and Joel Barker pioneering methods for and models of organizational change.

The advent of new media, such as the Internet and hypermedia, has brought about not only technological innovations, but also coupled these with new ways of approaching learning and instruction. As opposed to the behavioralist perspective that emphasizes learning objectives, the constructivist approach holds that learners construct their understanding of reality from interpretations of their experiences. Theorists such as Thomas Duffy and Seymour Papert suggest that constructivism provides a model whereby socio-cultural and cognitive issues regarding the design of learning environments can be supported by computer tools. This philosophy has been applied to such computerized technologies as online help systems and programming language LOGO.

In the future, instructional designers are likely to choose one of two paths: specialist or generalist. In the prior path, designers will focus on one aspect of learning or instruction and act as consultants or subject matter experts, whether internal or external to the organization. The other approach is one more aligned with managerial activities. Since the field is becoming too broad for most designers to work with authority in all matters, this option allows practitioners to oversee the development of instructional projects, rather than narrow their efforts exclusively on assessment, analysis, design, development, implementation, evaluation or continuous improvement.

References

Boling, E. (1996). *Instructional Technology Foundations I: Historical Timelines Project Page* [Online]. Available: http://education.indiana.edu/~istcore/r511/datelist.html [1998, June 7].

Kearsley, G. (1994). *Learning & Instruction: The TIP Database* [Online]. Available: http://www.lincoln.ac.nz/educ/tip/1.htm [1998, June 7].

Reiser, R. A. (1987). Instructional Technology: A History. In R. M. Gagné (ed.), *Instructional Technology: Foundations* (pp. 11–40). Hillsdale, NJ: Lawrence Erlbaum Associates.

Shrock, S. A. (No date). *A Brief History of Instructional Development* [Online]. Available: http://uttc-med.utb.edu/6320/chapters/summary_ch2.html [1998, June 7].

Designing Statistics Instruction for Middle School Students

A broad consensus exists that "students need to know about data analysis and related aspects of probability in order to reason statistically—skills necessary to becoming informed citizens and intelligent consumers" (NCTM, 2000). In light of these recommendations for greater emphasis on data analysis throughout the grades (AAAS, 1993; NRC, 2000), researchers at the National Center for Improving Student Learning and Achievement in Mathematics and Science (NCISLA) examined ways teachers can make statistics accessible to all students. The research studies highlighted here feature the ways that middle school students can come to understand statistics through carefully designed instruction and teacher professional development.

The approach taken by the NCISLA research team led by Paul Cobb and Kay McClain capitalized on the notion of *distribution* as a key concept in statistics and made generalization and justification[1] an explicit focus of instruction. The research suggests that in order to support students' development of more advanced statistical reasoning, traditional middle school instructional strategies need to be reconsidered. The findings suggest ways teachers can develop lessons that are better suited to students' ways of thinking and learning. Through professional development seminars in two cities,[2] Cobb, McClain, and their colleagues examined ways that alternative instructional designs can be implemented and sustained with only minimal external resources.

Research Focus

In interviews with students and in whole-class assessments, researchers Cobb, McClain, and Koeno Gravemeijer found that most middle school students thought of data analysis as "doing something with numbers" (Cobb, 1999; McClain, Cobb, & Gravemeijer, 2000). Students typically approached problems in a procedural manner, *without considering the question or issue at hand*. For example, students often calculated means to compare data sets even for cases in which the analysis of differences in range or variability of data were more appropriate.

To re-orient students' beliefs about what it means to do statistics in ways that resemble those of professional statisticians, the

research team[3] developed two instructional sequences—one for the seventh grade and one for the eighth grade—and computer tools, which they then tested in an experimental classroom and revised based on their analysis of student learning and understanding.

The researchers were particularly interested in developing instructional sequences that fostered students'—

- ability to analyze data in increasingly sophisticated ways.
- understanding of statistical inference.
- ability to design procedures for generating sound data.

The 2–year study involved 29 racially diverse students in the seventh grade and 11 of the same students as they continued into the eighth grade.[4] The research team documented students' learning over the 12 weeks of the seventh-grade experiment and the 14 weeks of the eighth-grade experiment. The students were assessed at the beginning of the eighth-grade term to determine what they had retained from the seventh-grade course. Results from this assessment indicate that the 11 students who volunteered to continue with the course in the eighth grade were representative of the seventh-grade group in terms of their ways of reasoning about data.

The long-term nature of the study allowed the team to observe progress in student reasoning about statistics and to revise the instructional sequence as needed. In follow-up trials using the seventh-grade sequence, the team was able to reduce instructional time by two-thirds.

Instructional Activities and Classroom Norms

In the beginning of the sequence, a majority of the lessons engaged students in exploratory data analysis—an important activity that lays the groundwork for statistical inference. In exploratory data analysis, students draw informal conclusions by analyzing meaningful patterns in specific sets of data. Statistical inference takes the analysis of such patterns a step further by drawing conclusions about the population. Based on a data sample, statisticians assess the likelihood that those patterns reflect trends in a larger population, relying on notions of sampling distributions, confidence intervals, and significance tests to make probabilistic statements.

To promote student reasoning in these statistical activities, the researchers proposed using the notion of distribution as the over-arching idea around which instruction would be organized. Specially designed computer tools allowed students to reorganize data in order to identify patterns in the way that the data were distributed. (See box for more on Computer Tools That Supported Students' Learning.) Students used the computer tools to represent their models and generalizations, which in turn provided a context and focus for class discussions (McClain & Cobb, 2001).

The investigations typically required students to make a recommendation based on a comparison of two sets of data, for example data on patients who received two different medical treatments or on the braking distances of samples of two different models of cars. Students' investigations of a particular problem set began with a discussion about the data-generation process. This was important because the students did not collect the data themselves and the researchers wanted to ensure that students' analyses remained grounded in the problem or issue they were investigating. In these, often quite lengthy discussions, the teacher and students together—

- identified the particular phenomenon under investigation (e.g., two alternative treatments for AIDS patients).
- clarified why it was important to address the problem (e.g., relevance of determining the most effective medical treatment).
- identified relevant aspects that should be measured (e.g., T-cell counts).
- considered how those aspects might be measured (e.g., by taking blood samples).

A majority of classroom time was devoted to exploratory data analysis. Working first in pairs and then through whole-class discussions, students used the computer tools to structure data and present their analyses. Students were also required to write individual reports about their data analysis, outlining data-based recommendations for a target audience (e.g., the head medical officer of a hospital).

The researchers found that the computer tools served an important function in supporting student learning, as did the negotiation of norms or standards for what counted as an acceptable statistical argument. The reports required students to make explicit their reasoning and statistical arguments and, thus, also supported students' learning of reasoned argumentation in statistics.

Reorienting student thinking about statistics. Cobb and McClain reasoned that just as a proficient analyst searches for trends, patterns, and anomalies in relation to a research question, students need to conduct their data analysis in the context of problems they consider realistic and legitimate. Cobb and McClain found that by talking through the data collection process, students became engaged in the problem at hand and, ultimately, in finding ways to use statistical analysis to address the problem situation.

The research team found that if students had some familiarity with the phenomenon to be investigated, had an opportunity to talk through the data collection process, and recognized a broader purpose to the investigation, the teacher could foster and support students' pragmatic interest in analyzing the data. Initially, students recounted personal stories that related to the problem scenario, rather than focusing on generating and analyzing data to come to practical decisions or judgments.

By the second week of the sequence, students were taking a more pragmatic approach to the investigation and increasingly posed questions about forms of data that would be helpful in their analysis.

As they worked, the teacher and students established norms for discussing their analysis and making statistical arguments: Students were expected to explain and justify their reasoning. In classroom discussions, students compared different analyses and clarified statistical issues, such as the most appropriate way to partition the data for comparisons. McClain and Cobb (2001) distinguished this form of *conceptual discourse,* in which students explain the rationale for their analysis, from *calculational discourse,* in which students merely explain *how* they analyze the data but do not explain *why* they choose a particular analytical method for addressing a problem.

These discussions, in which students explained the rationale for their analytical methods, gave the researchers important insights into their reasoning. The teacher was able to capitalize on this reasoning during classroom activities and discussions using the computer tools.

Using computer tools to enhance learning. In the seventh-grade sequence, students made the transition from analyzing data based on the *absolute frequency* of occurrences in particular intervals (e.g., 15 cars going faster than the speed limit and 30 going slower) to analysis based on the *relative frequency* (e.g., one-third of the cars going faster than the speed limit). Making this transition from additive to multiplicative reasoning proved important for students, especially in analyzing unequal data sets (comparing data sets with different numbers of data points), in which a focus on absolute frequencies can lead to erroneous conclusions. (See example described in Computer Tools That Supported Students' Learning) The teacher supported students' transition from additive to multiplicative reasoning by encouraging them to think about a data set as a whole, rather than as a collection of individual data points.

By the end of the seventh-grade sequence, all 29 students came to reason about *univariate* data in terms of qualitative proportions. Nineteen out of 29 also could use the graphs representing distributions of the data sets (similar to histograms and box plots) to make sound data-based arguments, even when the data sets were unequal. Importantly, an assessment of students' data analysis at the beginning of the eighth-grade sequence indicated that none of the continuing students had regressed during the 9-month gap between the experiments.

Computer Tools That Supported Students' Learning

Statistical computer tools were designed to support development of students' statistical thinking. The tools provide a basis for learning to interpret conventional representation used in statistics, such as histograms and box-and-whiskers plots. The computer tools are available on the CD-ROM included with the NCTM publication, *Navigating Through Data Analysis in Grades 6–8* (Bright, Brewer, McClain, & Mooney, 2003).[5]

Students can use the computer tools to—

- investigate trends and patterns in univariate data by ordering, partitioning, or otherwise organizing data points. **Tool 1** represents individual data points as separate bars and allows students to compare the number of data points within any intervals they choose.
- Analyze increasingly complex univariate data sets in ways that more closely resemble standard ways in which professional statisticians structure data. **Tool 2** allow students to represent data as dots on an axis and then partition that data into groups of a specific size, with a specified interval width (a precursor to histograms), or two or four equal groups (a precursor to box plots), (See Figure 1.)
- Identify trends or patterns in data distribution of bivariate data sets. **Tool 3** provides students a variety of ways to investigate relations between two measures in bivariate data sets that are represented as scatter plots. (See Figure 2.)

The following examples illustrate how the teacher used Tool 2 to support students' learning as they investigated the effectiveness of two AIDS treatments. The number of patients in the two data sets differed significantly, challenging students to compare unequal data sets.

Using Tool 2 to plot the T-cell counts for the two treatments on two different axes, a number of the students decided to compare the data sets in terms of the number of data points falling above and below a particular data point (see Figure 1a). One group of students presented their analysis using this representation, concluding that the new treatment was more effective than the old treatment and noting that "the old treatment had 56 patients above 550, and the new ones 37." However, a fellow student pointed out that this argument was confusing because the students reported the number rather than the proportion of data points above 550 (i.e., absolute rather than relative frequency).

The analysis presented by another group of students, who used Tool 2 to divide the data into four equal groups, build off students' decision to use percentages rather than absolute numbers to make the comparison (see Figure 1b). From this analysis, the students concluded that the new treatment was better than the old treatment "because the three groups for the new (treatment) group are above 525 and on the old they are below." The data points in this graph are hidden so that students can focus on the ways the data are distributed when divided into intervals, each of which represent 25% of the data for a given set. This representation is a precursor to the box-and-whisker plot.

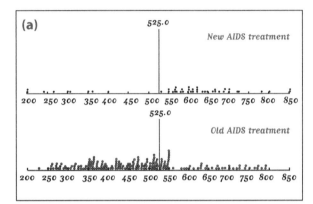

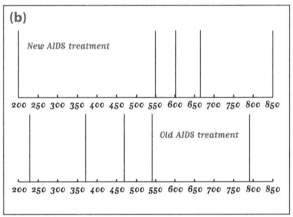

Figure 1 Univariate data organized using Tool 2 to partition data (a) at any given value and (b) into four equal groups with individual data points hidden.

In the eighth-grade experiment, distribution proved to be a crucial concept for students to understand when analyzing *bivariate* data. The research team wanted the students to be able to interpret a bivariate data set as distributed in a two-dimensional space that represented the change in one variable's distribution when other variables changed (i.e., a distribution of univariate distributions). This focus on the distribution of bivariate data encompasses and deepens a concern about direction and strength of relationships between statistical variables.

The research team structured the activities in the eighth-grade sequence so that students could learn about key concepts, such as covariation. However, their analysis of student work suggested a need to establish student understanding of a distribution of univariate distributions before students could interpret scatterplots of bivariate data in terms of the line (representing

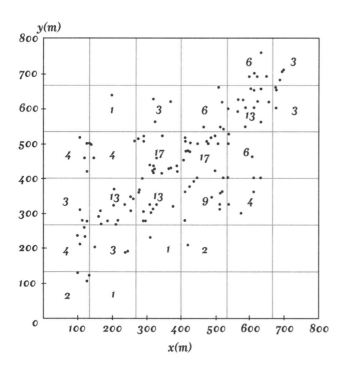

Figure 2 Bivariate data organized using the **Grids** option in computer Tool 3.

the conjectured relationship of covariation) about which the data are distributed.

The research team found that when they used the grids option on Tool 3 (see Computer Tools That Supported Students' Learning, Figure 2), students more easily interpreted bivariate data in terms of the shape of the different stacks (or slices) of univariate data. As a result of these discussions focused on shape, concepts such as "majority" and "median" took on new meanings that supported an understanding of bivariate distribution. Student understanding of bivariate data as distributed reflects a progression to a more sophisticated approach to statistical inference. Conceptually, understanding bivariate data sets as distributions is important for assessing which aspects of a data set are relatively stable. For example, if an analyst wants to repeat an experiment and collect new data, which characteristics does she examine to determine if she has a good representation of the population? Recognizing that the median of a univariate data set is relatively stable in comparison with extreme values is the first step toward statistical inference (i.e., making an inference about the population based on a given sample). Cobb and McClain proposed that this orientation to statistics can provide a starting point for understanding sampling distributions, a concept that has been problematic for most college students.

Why Focus on Students' Learning Trajectories?

A learning trajectory is the path conjectured for the development of students' thinking that leads to proposed instructional goals. By repeatedly testing and revising ways to support students' learning so that they reach learning goals, the researchers discovered more about student thinking and designing instruction that supports students in learning statistics (Cobb, McClain, & Gravemeijer, 2003). The research provides insights into the ways a proposed student learning trajectory can support instructional design (See Figure 3.)

The learning trajectories were useful in developing curricula in the NSF-funded middle school project directed by Clifford Konold (Konold & Higgins, in press) and mathematics assessment frameworks for the State of Washington. The tools and tasks are also featured in NCTM's publication, *Data Analysis in the Middle Grades* (Bright, Brewer, McClain & Mooney, 2003).

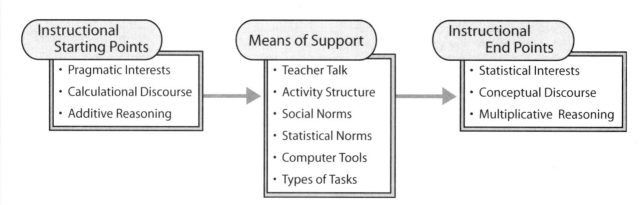

Figure 3 Students' learning trajectories.

The instructional starting points represent the understandings students bring to the course or that are established early in the course sequence; these are subsequently built on through strategies outlined under means of support to reach the instructional end points.

Teacher Practice Considerations

Based on analyses of students' reasoning and learning trajectories (Why Focus on Students' Learning Trajectories?), Cobb and McClain's research team developed computer tools and instructional sequences that support students' learning of statistics. These tools were subsequently used in research-led professional development in two urban areas with 26 teachers.

One challenge of planning a lesson based on students' learning trajectories is anticipating what students will understand and the ways students will approach the instructional activities. Through their research and professional development experience, Cobb and McClain found that teachers can design lessons responsively and effectively along three dimensions—

- instructional activities.
- tools and resources students use for analysis.
- classroom discourse.

Through these studies, the teachers and researchers identified the following issues as critical in designing effective instruction—

Fostering Student Interest in Statistics.

Cultivating student interest was considered a crucial factor in ensuring all students had the opportunity to learn statistical ideas. The extent to which students and their families see learning mathematics paying off (in terms of future educational and economic opportunities) varies as a consequence of family history, race or ethnic history, and class structure. By making the development of students' interest in mathematics an explicit goal of the instructional sequence, participating teachers were better able to provide all students with a reason to engage in statistics.

Specifically, the researchers found the types of activities selected for investigation mattered for cultivating student interest. Students were less likely to engage in analysis of the data if they had little knowledge of the phenomenon to be investigated. To develop students' pragmatic interest in the investigation and to familiarize students about a phenomenon, teachers led discussions about the data-generation process.

Allowing for Contrasting Methods of Analysis.

Fruitful statistical discussions occurred when students shared different approaches to analyzing data. The initial data sets were designed to allow for contrasting methods of analysis that resulted in different recommendations or pragmatic arguments. Later, the teachers introduced data sets that purposely had a significantly different number of data points to lead students to make comparisons in relative rather than in absolute terms. Classroom discussions were then organized, and specific tools were incorporated, in order to reach other instructional goals.

By circulating around the room during group work, the teacher was able to assess student thinking. He or she could then incorporate the students' contrasting solutions into classroom discussions in order to highlight statistically significant issues. In student interviews, one student expressed this aspect of the lesson as her favorite because "a lot of times people talked about ways that I hadn't thought of. I liked trying to figure out their way or seeing if their thing is better."

Structuring Class Discussion Around Students' Analyses of Data.

Cobb and McClain designed the computer tools as resources for teachers to use to achieve their instructional goals by capitalizing on their students' reasoning. In each investigation, which often spanned two or more class sessions, students engaged in a whole-class discussion of the data-generation process, individual or small-group activity in which the students usually analyzed the data at computers, and a whole-class discussion of their analyses, often with the use of a computer projection, system to display the computer tools. Students also learned to communicate their critical reasoning and to address the broader issues of the investigation through writing reports.

The computers tools and classroom discourse norms played important roles in all of these activities. Classroom norms helped delineate what was considered appropriate for students to contribute to a statistical discussion. Teachers and students could negotiate what Yackel and Cobb (1996) described as sociomathematical norms. Such norms included delineating what counted as a contrasting mathematical solution, what counted as a contrasting mathematical solution, what counted as a sophisticated solution, what was considered an acceptable line of reasoning and what counted as an efficient solution. Ideally, students justified their statistical reasoning by explaining how the method they used to structure the data resulted in insights into the pragmatic issues relevant to the investigation. The classroom norms evolved as students' reorganized their own thinking based on classmates' contributions and growing statistical knowledge.

Capitalizing on Student Contributions.

In order to focus discussions on statistical issues, the teacher often needed to ask students to clarify their statements or expand on comments made by other students. For example, when one student referred to the "majority of numbers," the teacher asked what he meant by "majority." Clarifying and establishing student understanding of terminology was a critical part of refining student thinking and engaging in statistical discussions.

Professional Development Implications

Teacher professional development is central to an instructional approach to statistics that builds on students' learning trajectories. (See Why Focus on Students' Learning Trajectories?) Working over the long-term in two teaching communities (12 and 14 teachers respectively),[6] Paul Cobb and Kay McClain examined ways to develop and sustain professional teaching communities. In these teaching communities, the researchers and teachers implemented a professional development program that enabled teachers to—

- identify student learning trajectories.
- establish instructional goals in light of students learning trajectories
- propose benchmarks to assess students' progress towards instructional goals.
- examine videotaped classroom sessions to investigate student learning and to evaluate the effectiveness of sequences in relation to the instructional goals.
- plan instruction by adapting sequences to fit local instructional situations and learning goals.
- engage in and facilitate statistical analysis using the computer tools.[7]
- generate evidence of students' mathematical reasoning to make the complexity of teaching and learning visible to school leaders and the educational community.
- collaborate on assessment tasks that could be used across contexts to examine student thinking.

Based on their research and professional development experience, Cobb and McClain worked to establish teaching communities that build teachers' content knowledge, pedagogical skill, and collaborative strength. Teachers commented that the professional development seminars helped them to *"become better at fine-tuning the things that really work"* and found the experience of *"being able to dialogue with teachers (and) being able to look at other work"* valuable. Working through statistical problems in the seminars proved important because it gave teachers a chance to *"find out where I struggle with, because that's the first place I know I'm going to get a question from the kids."*

The approach described here differs from one in which teachers try an innovation without necessarily understanding the underlying ideas that allow for adaption. By using an instructional sequence based on instructional learning trajectories that account for students' knowledge levels, these teachers learned that they could modify specific instructional activities and still remain faithful to a proposed instructional sequence. Through the collaborative process of testing, modifying, sharing, and critiquing, teachers formed a community of practice that contributed a significant insights about student learning in specific areas of mathematics.

When planning professional development, Cobb and McClain stress the importance of:

Evaluating Organizational Supports.

Because their professional development required significant commitment on the part of teachers, support from administrators was essential. The researchers observed that if districts become focused on a narrow range of tasks assessed through tests, teachers might likewise feel compelled to narrow their instructional focus and professional development, consequently missing opportunities to recognize and capitalize on their students' thinking and reasoning. Teachers and administrators can foster an environment that supports the development of a professional teaching community—one that builds teachers' content knowledge and pedagogical skills—by collaboratively defining a vision that recognizes students' capacities to engage in statistical reasoning and then invest in professional development to that end. (See Gamoran et al., 2003, for more detail about organizational supports for instructional change.)

Establishing "Buy-in".

Cobb and McClain found that teachers were willing to invest time and energy in changing their instructional practices when they were provided concrete evidence of students' misconceptions about statistics (often grounded in traditional instructional approaches that focused on calculating but not understanding the median, mean, mode, and range). Videos of classroom sessions, during which students' reasoning and misconceptions were evident, provided teachers a framework for analyzing their own practice.

Allocating Time and Resources.

In team meetings, middle school mathematics teachers served as resources for each other, sharing observations of students' thinking and collaboratively planning or adapting lessons. Teachers analyzed students' thinking and collaboratively planning or adapting lessons. Teachers analyzed students' reasoning and solution strategies and discussed ways they could revise problems in order to correct common misunderstandings and advance student thinking. Classroom episodes documented by Cobb and McClain during visits to teachers' classrooms were useful for analyzing instructional practices and students' reasoning in these school-supported teacher seminars.

Supporting Teachers' Work on Improving Instructional Sequences

In monthly seminars, teachers became actively involved in the process of improving and adapting the instructional sequences. A typical seminar often involved teachers in working through a lesson and then discussing the different ways that they analyzed the data. In subsequent seminars, teachers revisited the lesson and examined the ways it played out in his or her classroom, provided specific examples of students' work, discussed students' learning trajectories, and suggested ways to improve the lessons to further enhance students' engagement and learning. This iterative process not only improved lessons but also strengthened teachers' practice and content knowledge. One teacher expressed this change: *"In going through (the seminar) I had tools, for example, I've never seen a box and whiskers (plot). It's became my best friend. I can't imagine looking at data—most data—without using a box-and-whiskers."*

Additional Resources

Cobb, P., McClain, K., de Silva, Lamberg, T., & Dean, C. (2003). Situating teachers' instructional practices in the institutional setting of the school and district. *Educational Researcher*, 32(6), 13–24.

Gamoran, A., Anderson, C. W., Quiroz, P. A., Secada, W. G., Williams, T., & Ashmann, S. (2003). *Transforming teaching in math and science: How schools and districts can support change.* New York: Teachers College Press.

Implications: Supporting Students' Learning of Statistics

Cobb and McClain's research reveals ways that middle school students' learning of statistics can be better supported and suggests ways to design instruction and pursue instructional reform in middle school mathematics education.

The research shows that through the seventh- and eighth-grade sequences, students learned to—

- develop sound designs for generating data that involve both issues of sampling and of controlling extraneous variables.
- effectively develop and communicate statistical arguments.
- make recommendations that were justified in the context of the data.
- structure the data in different ways to support their arguments and to reason statistically.
- take a more active role in statistical analysis.

As a result, students' developed a more realistic perspective about what it means to do statistics.

Although NCTM's *Principles and Standards for School Mathematics* (NCTM, 2000) does not propose introduction of the topic of statistical covariation until high school, Cobb and McClain found that middle school students were capable of reasoning about data in more sophisticated ways than is generally thought possible. Cobb and McClain's findings constitute the first apparent documented instance of middle school students' reasoning about bivariate data in such a sophisticated manner.

Next Steps

The instructional sequence and computer tools developed by Cobb and McClain now serve as resources for middle school teachers, who are adapting them to achieve their instructional goals (Cobb, McClain, de Silva Lamberg, & Dean, 2003; Cobb & McClain, in press). As previous studies have shown, implementation of an innovation is less likely if teachers do not have an understanding of the underlying ideas that help them adapt the innovation to their own settings (Ball, 1989, 1993; Bransford, Brown, & Cocking, 2000; Grossman, 1990; Sowder & Schappelle, 1995). Cobb and McClain's research indicates that teacher professional development that is premised on students' learning trajectories can help teachers design goal-directed instruction that builds on and advances students' ways of thinking.

References

American Association for the Advancement of Science. (1993). *Benchmarks for science literacy.* Cary, NC: The Oxford University Press.

Ball, D. (1993). With an eye on the mathematical horizon: Dilemmas of teaching elementary school mathematics. *The Elementary School Journal, 93,* 373–397.

Ball, D. (1989). Teaching mathematics for understanding: What do teachers need to know about subject matter? *In Competing visions of teacher knowledge: Proceedings from an NCRT seminar for education policymakers. Vol. I, Academic subjects.* (pp. 79–100). East Lansing: Michigan State University, National Center for Research on Teacher Education.

Bransford, J., Brown, A., & Cocking, R. (2000). *How people learn: Brain, mind, experience, and school.* Washington, DC: National Academy Press.

Bright, G. W., Brewer, W., McClain, K., & Mooney, E. S. (2003). *Navigating through data analysis in Grades 6–8.* Reston, VA: National Council of Teachers of Mathematics.

Cobb, P. (1999). Individual and collective mathematical learning: The case of statistical data analysis. *Mathematical Thinking and Learning, 1*(1) 5–44.

Cobb, P., & McClain, K. (in press). The collective mediation of a high-stakes accountability program: Communities and networks of practice. In E. Kelly & R. Lesh (Eds.), *Design research in mathematics and science education.* Mahwah, NJ: Erlbaum.

Cobb, P., McClain, K., & Gravemeijer, K. (in press). Statistical data analysis: A tool for learning. In T. Romberg, T. Carpenter, & F. Dremock (Eds.), *Understanding mathematics and science matters.* Mahwah, NJ: Erlbaum.

Cobb, P., McClain, K., & Gravemeijer, K. (2003). Learning about statistical covariation. Cognition and Instruction, 21 (1), 1–78.

Cobb, P., McClain, K., de Silva Lamberg, T., & Dean, C. (2003). Situating teachers' instructional practices in the institutional setting of the school and district. *Educational Researcher, 32* (6), 13–24.

Grossman, P. (1990). *The making of a teacher: Teacher knowledge and teacher education.* New York: Teachers College Press.

Konold, C. & Higgins, T. (in press). Working with data: Highlights of related research. In D. Schifter, V. Bastable, & J. Russell (Eds.), *Developing mathematical ideas.* Palo Alto, CA: Dale Seymour.

McClain, K. & Cobb, P. (2001). Supporting students' ability to reason about data. *Educational Studies in Mathematics, 45,* 103–129.

McClain, K., Cobb, P., & Gravemeijer, K. (2000). Supporting students' ways of reasoning about data. In M. J. Burke & F. R. Curcio (Eds.), *Learning mathematics for a new century (2000 Year book).* Reston, VA: National Council of Teachers of Mathematics.

National Council of Teachers of Mathematics. (2000). *Principles and standards for school mathematics.* Reston, VA: Author.

National Research Council. (2000). *National science education standards.* Washington DC: National Academy Press.

Sowder, J., & Schappelle, B. (1995). *Providing a foundation for teaching mathematics in the middle grades.* Albany, NY: State University of New York Press.

For More Information

This issue of *in Brief* is based on research by Paul Cobb, Kay McClain, and Keono Gravemeijer that is reported in a forthcoming book, *Understanding Mathematics and Science Matters*, edited by T. Romberg, T. Carpenter, and F. Dremock, and in other journal articles (see References). For additional publications by Paul Cobb, Kay McClain and Keono Gravemeijer see: http://www.wcer.wisc.edu/ncisla/publications and http://www.wcer.wisc.edu/ncisla/teachers

Notes

1. Generalizations are general mathematical assertions concerning the structure, properties, or relationships that underlie key mathematical concepts. Students provide justification of their mathematical generalizations and analysis by developing mathematical arguments that are shared, discussed, and debated in class, in order to further student thinking and learning.

2. One team, located in the southern part of the United States, included 12 teachers; the other team, located in the western part of the United States, included 14 teachers.

3. The research team, led by Cobb and McClain, included Koeno Gravemeijer, Jose Cortina, Lynn Hodge, Maggie McGatha, Nora Shuart, and Carrie Tzou. Cliff Konold and Erna Yackel served as long-term consultants.

4. Although the intention was to continue with the 29 original seventh-grade students, the requirement that teachers in the cooperating school district follow a relatively prescriptive curriculum meant the researchers could not conduct the experiment during the regularly scheduled eighth-grade class. Thus, the students participating in the eighth-grade sequence volunteered to participate in an afternoon activity period. Of the 11 students, 7 were African American, three were White, and one was Asian American.

5. For more on the computer tools, also see Mclain & Cobb, Mc Clain, & Gravmeijer, 2003.

6. All the teachers had at least three years of experience in teaching mathematics in a middle school.

7. The computer tools are available on the CD-ROM included with the NCTM publication, *Navigating Through Data Analysis in Grades 6–8* (Bright, Brewer, McClain, & Mooney, 2003).
   The tools are also available online at http://peabody.vanderbilt.edu/dpts/tandl/mted/MiniTools/Minitools.html.

From *In Brief*, Vol. 4, no. 1, Winter 2004, pp. 1–5, written by Susan Smetzer-Anderson and based on research conducted by Paul Cobb, Kay McClain, and Keono Gravemeijer. In Brief was published by the National Center for Improving Student Learning & Achievement in Math & Science, at the Wisconsin Center for Education Research. Reprinted by permission.

Changes in Brain Function in Children with Dyslexia after Training

ELISE TEMPLE
Department of Human Development
Cornell University

Introduction

Developmental Dyslexia

Developmental dyslexia is defined simply as difficulty reading despite the intelligence, motivation, and education necessary for successful reading[1]. Its prevalence is still an active area of research but has been estimated at any where between 5 and 17% of the population, therefore representing a very large national and international concern[1]. Studies have shown that the reading deficits of children with developmental dyslexia have persisted into adolescence and even adulthood. The disorder cannot be explained as a simple developmental lag[1]. A number of different methods have suggested a neurobiological basis for the disorder, but the fundamental cause (or causes) remains unknown and is an active area of research on many fronts[2,3]. It is important to note that there are many risk factors for difficulties in reading that are not biological. For example, home literacy environment and socio-economic status can predict reading ability[4]. These factors can and should be addressed in educational and social policy. The biological basis for dyslexia is considered when those risk factors have been accounted for and a reading deficit remains.

Importance of Phonological Awareness

A developing consensus among many researchers is that developmental dyslexia is characterized by difficulties in phonological processing, specifically phonological awareness which is the ability to identify and manipulate the sound structure of words[1,4]. Individuals with dyslexia have impaired phonological skills, including the ability to distinguish rhyming sounds, count the syllables of words, and sound out novel or "pseudo-words" (e.g., "stroat" or "traim"). Phonological awareness skills are thought to be a required foundation for both normal-reading and dyslexic children to benefit from phonics instruction.

Auditory Processing

In addition to a deficit in phonological processing, individuals with dyslexia have been shown, by some researchers, to have a more fundamental deficit in auditory processing, specifically auditory processing of rapid auditory sounds that are entering the nervous system in the 10's of milliseconds[5,6]. This deficit in processing rapid auditory stimuli is thought to impact language and subsequently reading because some of the sounds in language, or phonemes, differ only in frequency changes that occur in the first 40–50 ms of the sound. The idea behind the rapid auditory processing hypothesis of developmental dyslexia is that without this ability to detect rapid auditory signals the child is unable to distinguish certain phonemes and develops an inadequate or "fuzzy" understanding of the phonology or sounds of his/her language. This inadequate understanding of the sounds of the words in the language is especially problematic when the child learns to read and is required to map letters onto their appropriate sounds.

Functional Brain Imaging

With the advent of new technology that allows us to visualize brain function in adults and children, researchers have begun to explore brain function and possible dysfunction in adults, and more recently children with developmental dyslexia. There are a few methods available to measure brain function in children. The type used in the current study is called functional magnetic resonance imaging or fMRI. fMRI is a variant of traditional MRI, which is used for visualization of any soft tissue inside the body (including the structure of the brain and spinal cord).

While MRI allows us to see the structure of the brain, fMRI allows us to see the *function* of the brain. The technique is based on the fact that when you think, see, or imagine there is an increase in brain function (neurons firing) in specific and localized parts of the brain. Increased brain function causes an increase in blood flow. The increase in blood flow, brings about an increase in oxygen, that can be measured by fMRI. More oxygen occurs naturally in areas of the brain that are working harder. The technique is entirely noninvasive (it requires no injections or imaging contrasts) and can be used safely in children.

Brain Function in Dyslexia

Studies of brain function in dyslexia using this and other techniques have shown people with dyslexia seem to have a neural disruption in phonological processing as well as the behavioral deficit described earlier. A number of studies, using different methods and subject groups, have found that when people with dyslexia are asked to do some tasks that require phonological processing they have less brain function (as compared to normal reading controls) in a specific brain area. This decreased activity is localized to a part of the brain on the left side called the temporo-parietal cortex, a region of the brain located a little behind and above the ear[2]. This decrease in brain function has been shown in adults with dyslexia and even non-English speaking adults with dyslexia.

More recently, children with dyslexia have also been shown to have decreased activity in this brain region, suggesting that the disruption may be fundamental to the disorder and not an effect of years of compensation. What has not been known is the extent to which this decrease in brain function could be changed with training or education.

The Current Study

The current study[7] was designed to test whether this decrease in activity could be changed in children with dyslexia. We hypothesized that we might be able to see changes in brain function in children with dyslexia after remediation and we expected two types of changes. One type of change we might see would be a normalizing of the activity in the left temporo-parietal region discussed above. We might see increases in activity in this region, bringing the dyslexic brain closer to the normal-reading brain. We also expected that we might see increased activity in other regions of the brain, perhaps reflecting a compensatory effect of the training on brain function.

Methods

Training Program

The training program used in the study was Fast ForWord Language (www.scileam.com). which focuses on auditory processing and oral language through an intensive and adaptive computer program[8,9]. One unique feature of the program is a focus on training children to discriminate rapid auditory signals. It also emphasizes other aspects of oral language, including auditory attention, memory, phonological processing, and listening comprehension. The training lasted approximately 8 weeks and included 100 minutes a day, 5 days a week.

Experimental Design

The study included children 8-12 years old with dyslexia (n=20) who underwent fMRI scans before and after training. In addition, 12 normal-reading children underwent two fMRI scans about 8 weeks apart to control for any practice effects, normal development, and scan-rescan effects. The children performed a phonological processing task while undergoing fMRI. The task was a simple rhyming task. Each child was shown two letters and asked to push a button if the names of the two letters rhymed with each other (e.g., "T" and "D" rhyme, whereas "G" and "K" do not). This was compared to a matching task where the child

simply indicated if the two letters were the same letter (e.g., "P" and "P"). The rhyming task was designed to require phonological analysis of the letters' names, but was simple enough for a poor or beginning reader to perform.

By comparing the brain function during the rhyming task with the brain function during the matching task, we could focus on the brain function specifically associated with phonological analysis rather than orthographic processing of letters or other task demands (like pushing a button, being in an MRI machine, etc.).

Results

Reading and Language Ability

We found that the children with dyslexia, as a group, demonstrated improved performance on reading measures after the training program. Their performance on the Woodcock Johnson Reading Master subtests improved significantly and, as a group, was now in the normal range. (WJR-MT scores: Word Identification: pre training = 78.2, post training = 86.0, $p < 0.0005$; Word attack: pre training = 85.5, post training = 93.7, $p < 0.0001$; Passage Comprehension: pre-training = 83.3, post training = 88.9, $p < 0.001$). Similar improvements were seen in oral language measures (CELF3: receptive: pre training = 92.5, post training = 101.3, $p < 0.001$; expressive: pre training = 95.0, post training = 102.2, $p < 0.006$).

Brain Function

In our analysis of brain function, we found a number of brain areas that showed changes in the children with dyslexia after training. In line with our expectations, we did see an increase in the left temporo-parietal cortexes in the children with dyslexia after training. This region was near the region which had been shown to be under-active in these children compared to normal reading children. This increase in brain function had a normalizing effect, in that it brought the brain function of children with dyslexia closer to that of normal reading children. This normalization was not complete however; the children with dyslexia did not reach normal levels of activity in this region.

In addition, we saw increased activity in a number of regions not normally involved in phonological processing. These regions included parts of the right side of the brain which are mirror images of the normal left-sided language processing areas. These increases may reflect more of a compensatory effect of the training, where the right side of the brain gets involved to help the damaged left side. Right-sided help for language in people who have left-sided damage has been reported in studies of stroke recovery where increased right-sided activity was associated with improved language after stroke.

In summary, we found a partial amelioration of the disrupted brain function seen in children with dyslexia after training; they showed partial normalization of activity in the left temporo-parietal cortex. In addition, we saw compensatory effects of training, especially in increased activity in the right side of the brain.

Conclusion

This study was the first to use fMRI to explore possible changes in brain function after behavioral training in children with dyslexia. The training used was Fast ForWord Language, a training program that focuses on oral language and auditory processing. After training, the children with dyslexia improved in reading and language ability. In addition, after training, the children with dyslexia showed changes in brain function. These changes in brain function were both "normalizing" and "compensating."

Normalization of brain function in children with dyslexia included increased brain function in the left temporo-parietal cortex, above and behind the left ear. After training there was increased activity in this region, which had been shown to be under-active in children and adults with dyslexia. "Compensating" effects of the training included increased activity in regions of the brain that were not normally active during such tasks. These increases were seen especially in the right side of the brain, in mirror images to the traditional left-sided language areas, perhaps reflecting a tendency by the right side of the brain to compensate for the left side's inability to function fully. This study shows that the brain dysfunction seen in dyslexia can be affected by behavioral training.

The implications of this study are numerous. First, this study shows that it is possible to study the brain effects of training in human children. Previous research on brain plasticity had been largely limited to animal research. This study opens up the possibility for further research that explores different interventions and educational strategies. Second, this study shows that a specific remediation program, Fast ForWord Language, resulted in changes in brain function in children with dyslexia while improving their reading ability. Finally, this study shows

that previously reported brain dysfunction in dyslexia can be at least partially ameliorated. These results should help give hope to the individuals struggling with dyslexia and their families and teachers. Dyslexia is not simply a matter of a child not "trying hard enough." This brain research has shows us that the biological aspects of dyslexia can be changed and at least partially normalized.

References

1. Shaywitz, S.E., *Dyslexia*. New England Journal of Medicine, 1998. **338**(5): p. 307–12.
2. Temple, E., *Brain mechanisms in normal and dyslexic readers*. Curr Opin Neurobiol, 2002. **12**(2): p. 178–83.
3. Habib, M., *The neurological basis of developmental dyslexia: an overview and working hypothesis*. Brain, 2000. 123 **Pt 12:** p. 2373–99.
4. Snow, C.E., M.S. Bums, and P. Griffin, eds. *Preventing Reading Difficulties in Young Children*. 1998, National Academy Press: Washington, D.C.
5. Tallal, P. and M. Piercy, *Defects of non-verbal auditory perception in children with developmental aphasia*. Nature, 1973. **241**(5390): p. 468–9.
6. Tallal, P. S. Miller, and R.H. Fitch, *Neurobiological basis of speech: A case for the preeminence of temporal processing*. Annals of the New York Academy of Sciences, 1993. **682** (27–47).
7. Temple, E., et al., *Neural deficits in children with dyslexia ameliorated by behavioral remediation: Evidence from fMRI*. Proc Natl Acad Sci USA, 2003. **100**(5): p. 2860–2865.
8. Tallal, P., et al., *Language comprehension in language-learning impaired children improved with acoustically modified speech*. Science (Washington DC), 1996. **271**(5245): p. 81–84.
9. Merzenich, M.M., et al., *Temporal processing deficits of language-learning impaired children ameliorated by training*. Science (Washington DC), 1996. **271**(5245): p. 77–81.

UNIT 3

Classroom Application and Software Evaluations

Unit Selections

Key Points to Consider

- Locating software that meets a particular set of objectives can be a challenge. Describe how you would search for specific application packages. Discuss what criteria you would use to determine whether you should purchase the program or develop your own.

- Develop an evaluation instrument specifically designed for your teaching area. Pilot test it with a software package in your teaching area. Does your instrument thoroughly evaluate the package? Were you able to communicate your findings in an understandable way? Refine your instrument based on these results.

Student Web Site

www.mhcls.com/online

Internet References

Further information regarding these Web sites may be found in this book's preface or online.

Beginner's Guide to HTML
http://www.itc.univie.ac.at/docs/html-primer.html

Classics for Young People
http://www.ucalgary.ca/~dkbrown/storclas.html

ENC Online
http://www.goENC.com

Scholastic Network
http://www.scholastic.com

Teachers Helping Teachers
http://www.pacificnet.net/~mandel

The Nine Planets
http://seds.lpl.arizona.edu/billa/tnp

The TeleGarden
http://www.usc.edu/dept/garden

Writing HTML
http://www.mcli.dist.maricopa.edu/tut

learner's imagination and help demonstrate ideas. However, multimedia must be chosen with certain criteria in mind, such as the purpose for using it, who will be using it, and whether it will be effective in satisfying the learner's needs. We must guard against being persuaded by combinations of immediate access, sound, graphics video, and animation that stimulate our senses but fail to meet the objectives of our curriculum or the needs of our learners. Using systematic evaluation techniques found in these articles, we can create the mind tools that are needed to meet the learner's needs.

In the first article, Doug Peterson describes how a university became one of the first to implement a full-scale Personal Digital Assistant program by giving faculty an opportunity to study how the devices can be integrated into college teaching and learning. Doug believes PDAs are likely to become an integral part of the educational landscape.

In the following article, Richard Van Eck asks the question, "Will we realize the potential that Digital Game-Based Learning has to revolutionize how students learn?" He believes that this has much less to do with attitude and learner preferences than it does with a technology that supports some of the most effective learning principles identified during the last hundred years.

In the next article, Peter Meng describes why the rapid evolution of audio-photo-video recording capabilities through phones and inexpensive hand-held devices will create a flood of multimedia content. They will be immediately adopted by the current class of students and will be looked at with disinterest or uncertainty by many of the current faculty. These technologies will quickly create demand for more bandwidth and storage for that content. In addition there will be a need for a centralized management and monetization infrastructure.

The final article discusses the use of Instant Messenger (IM) to carry out structured online class discussions. A clear distinction between casual IM use in a class setting and planned, structured implementation is provided.

Software is the fuel that brings computers to life; it is also the magic that makes Internet interactive multimedia happen. It contains the grain of creativity that causes us to wonder, "How did they do that?" Internet-based multimedia can capture the

Implementing PDAs in a College Course: One Professor's Perspective

Doug Peterson

Personal digital assistants (PDAs) have been a mainstay in the business world for several years, but their adoption in higher education is relatively recent. In the fall of 2001, the University of South Dakota became one of the first universities to implement a full-scale PDA program, giving faculty an opportunity to study how the devices can be integrated into college teaching and learning. Here, Doug Peterson shares his experience from the past year.

Underlying any attempt at integrating new technology should be a basic philosophy of the interplay between technology and education. When technology is used to support a task for which it is not well suited, failure is likely. The same is true when students are asked to use technology when it's not needed. Fortunately, both of these mistakes can be avoided by adopting the principles of "use-centered design" (Flach & Dominguez, 1995). Use-centered design replaces the traditional focus on either user or product with a concentration on the goals and tasks associated with the use of the technology.

There are two steps in applying a use-centered approach. First, learn the user's tasks; and second, consider the technology's capabilities. Ideally, the task analysis and technology reviews should remain independent of each other so as to avoid finding a need simply because the capability exists, or applying some capability just because you can. The purpose of the use-centered approach is to set objectives and then determine if they can be met by the technology. A study of PDA implementation at the University of South Dakota was done to determine how the PDA could replace traditional support materials and improve the completion of identified tasks.

Taking the PDA's Capabilities to Task

A student's primary objectives in most college courses are comprehending, retaining, and evaluating course material. Secondary supporting tasks include taking lecture notes, reading assigned materials, reviewing information to improve retention and comprehension, and completing exams and assignments properly and on time. A task analysis should identify the information necessary to complete the task, and with respect to a college course, most information comes in the form of paper or electronic text.

The PDA's strengths are flexible data handling, portability, and ease of use. Flexibility in data use is advantageous because tasks can be matched to the ideal data access format (e.g., information for the periodic table of elements can be accessed via a graphical interface instead of a text-formatted database). The portability of PDAs is an equally important attribute, because it increases the availability of the material contained within the PDA. (What instructor wouldn't want students to carry the syllabus and class notes with them at all times?) The PDA's ease of use is aided greatly by a consistent look and feel of applications.

Course Scheduling

One of the most important aspects of a course syllabus is the course schedule, indicating topics for each class period, exams scheduled, and assignment due dates. Support of this component corresponds perfectly to what PDAs were originally designed to accomplish. The problem to overcome is not how to put a course schedule in place (the calendar is the obvious solution), but instead how to make sure that the students will all have the right information on their handhelds. At USD this was done by creating a datebook archive file (in Palm Desktop) that students could download and import into their PDA. Once completed, the student's calendar contained all class meeting times, including a note identifying the topic and readings for each day. For exams and important events, alarms were pre-set to sound one or more days in advance.

Document Formats

Converting existing text-based course material (e.g., syllabi, laboratory instructions, term-paper guidelines, and the like) is the easiest of all PDA implementation problems for a course. The most difficult part is deciding which of the various available text formats to use.

The Palm doc format (unrelated to the MS Word format) is a good choice, because it is common, and PC and online document converters are freely available. The doc format can be read by many third-party readers but is not directly editable, making it desirable for materials that the student needs to read but not alter. Text editors are ideal for note-taking outlines or laboratory guides, where students may add additional information. Some are compatible with word processor formats on personal computers.

Adobe Acrobat files can also be converted for use on the PDA and offer better preservation of formatting as well as good image handling (including larger images that can be magnified and scrolled for detail). Others such as iSilo also preserve complex formatting and images and can be used to capture HTML content. An alternative to reader-based documents is a format called "Web clipping," or PQA, for the PalmOS (version 4.0 and higher). PQA files are created from HTML (with WCA-build, a free program available from Palm) and function as a stand-alone application where the user taps the icon from the main screen to launch the document. This format is ideal for documents that students need access to without additional help, such as a syllabus that explains how to use other course-related PDA applications and files.

Application Areas

The ever-growing number of applications available for the Palm is also an important consideration. However, finding the one education application you need for your course, among more than 13,000 available, can be challenging. Some courses may benefit from very specific applications such as a periodic table of the elements for chemistry classes; financial calculators for business; or even the game "Cooties" to teach the spread of disease. More general educational applications are also available.

Tracking Assignments

4.0Student (by Handmark) allows students to track assignments and due dates, and can integrate course information into the PIM function of the PDA. Instructors can set up course information in advance and beam it to the students. Students can track their performance in individual classes or overall GPA simply by recording their scores on graded work. They can also use student management applications to estimate their grade based on hypothetical scenarios (e.g., what will my overall grade be if I get 84 percent on the final paper?).

Test Preparation and Quizzing

Reviewing practice tests was identified early on in the task analysis as something students do to prepare for exams. This task can also be supported by the PDA in a number of ways, however, free applications make this very easy. After the review of several available quizzing and trivia programs, two applications emerged as the current leaders in the area of PDA-based practice tests: QuizApp and Quizzler Pro. Both products can present multiple-choice questions or flash cards in either a random or fixed order.

Each product has some unique features as well, such as a timed quiz (Quizzler Pro), or a categorical breakdown of

performance (QuizApp). Both are free to students and have minimal costs associated with the creation of quizzes (Quizzler uses a desktop application, while QuizApp uses an online converter—both options cost under $20). Quizzler allows free quiz creation using the notepad, which will appeal to students seeking practice tests for non-PDA classes. The PDA-based practice tests have been well received by students, and informal assessment suggests that this has a beneficial effect on test scores. The use of PDAs for actual in-class tests is also a possibility, through these and other products currently available.

Custom Applications

Course-specific custom applications also have potential as the ability to develop them becomes easier and more affordable. An example of this is a speech evaluation program that mimics a course rubric for grading and allows students to beam their evaluations to the speaker for review. A second emerging PDA component which will impact custom applications in the future is wireless connectivity. Stanford already has a Bluetooth-equipped classroom that allows students to ask questions and respond to in-class surveys using their Bluetooth-enabled PDAs; faculty at USD are currently working to develop a similar but portable system for the spring 2003 semester.

In the Classroom and Around the Campus

PDAs may also play a role in general campus life. Students at USD can look up campus, faculty, or community information on a NearSpace powered data system. For campus locations, students can also link to the integrated campus map and find the building or room they are looking for.

The distribution of PDA material should also be considered. Sending individual files does not take long when using a "viral beam" (each recipient passes the file on to others). Downloading and installing from a PC is probably the most common, but other approaches are also available. USD students can access data and applications for their PDAs via two other options. IR Ports connected to an XTNDConnect server allow students to sync to the server and receive data placed in course folders by instructors. A PDA Kiosk is also available to install applications selected on the kiosk screen and beamed to the PDA via an IR port.

Technology Evaluation

The overall assessment of PDA applications in a large class reveals a few simple conclusions. PDAs appear to have a much larger role outside of the classroom than inside the classroom. This is an added advantage, because it implies that the technology does not supplant classroom education, but supports it. Obviously, this may change as wireless connectivity increases. There is also variability in the multiple PDA applications students liked and used. This variability suggests that with the proper evaluation of student needs, PDA-based support for a wide variety of courses can be implemented. Like all technologies, a PDA is only a tool; if used inappropriately it can be a source of frustration, but if used correctly it can be a tremendous asset. PDAs are likely to become an integral part of the educational landscape, so course instructors can either invest in utilizing them properly or hope that their students will.

Resources

Flach, J. M. & Dominguez, C. O. (1995). Use-centered design: Integrating the user, instrument, and goal. *Ergonomics in Design,* 3, 3, 19–24.

4.0Student available from www.handmark.com (license required)

iSilo is available at www.isilo.com

NearSpace information available from www.nearspace.com

QuizApp Available at www.quizapp.com (free)

Quizzler Pro available at www.quizzlerpro.com (free)

WCABuild (to create PQA files) is available at www.palm.com

XTND Connect is a product of Extended Systems (www.extendedsystems.com)

DOUG PETERSON, Ph.D., is an assistant professor of psychology at the University of South Dakota. doupeter@usd.edu

Originally from *Syllabus*, November 2002. Copyright © 2002 by Campus Technology/1105 Media. Reprinted by permission. www.campus-technology.com

Digital Game-Based Learning

It's Not Just the Digital Natives Who Are Restless

RICHARD VAN ECK

After years of research and proselytizing, the proponents of digital game-based learning (DGBL) have been caught unaware. Like the person who is still yelling after the sudden cessation of loud music at a party, DGBL proponents have been shouting to be heard above the prejudice against games. But now, unexpectedly, we have everyone's attention. The combined weight of three factors has resulted in widespread public interest in games as learning tools.

The first factor is the ongoing research conducted by DGBL proponents. In each decade since the advent of digital games, researchers have published dozens of essays, articles, and mainstream books on the power of DGBL—including, most recently, Marc Prensky's *Digital Game-Based Learning* (2001), James Paul Gee's *What Video Games Have to Teach Us about Learning and Literacy* (2003), Clark Aldrich's *Simulations and the Future of Learning: An Innovative (and Perhaps Revolutionary) Approach to e-Learning* (2004), Steven Johnson's *Everything Bad Is Good for You: How Today's Popular Culture Is Actually Making Us Smarter* (2005), Prensky's new book *"Don't Bother Me, Mom, I'm Learning!": How Computer and Video Games Are Preparing Your Kids for 21st Century Success and How You Can Help!* (2006), and the soon-to-be-published *Games and Simulations in Online Learning: Research and Development Frameworks,* edited by David Gibson, Clark Aldrich, and Marc Prensky. The second factor involves today's "Net Generation," or "digital natives," who have become disengaged with traditional instruction. They require multiple streams of information, prefer inductive reasoning, want frequent and quick interactions with content, and have exceptional visual literacy skills[1]—characteristics that are all matched well with DGBL. The third factor is the increased popularity of games. Digital gaming is a $10 billion per year industry,[2] and in 2004, nearly as many digital games were sold as there are people in the United States (248 million games vs. 293.6 million residents.)[3]

One could argue, then, that we have largely overcome the stigma that games are "play" and thus the opposite of "work." A majority of people believe that games are engaging, that they can

be effective, and that they have a place in learning. So, now that we have everyone's attention, what are we DGBL proponents going to say? I believe that we need to change our message. If we continue to preach only that games can be effective, we run the risk of creating the impression that *all* games are good for *all* learners and for *all* learning outcomes, which is categorically *not* the case. What is needed now is (1) research explaining *why* DGBL is engaging and effective, and (2) practical guidance for *how* (when, with whom, and under what conditions) games can be integrated into the learning process to maximize their learning potential. We are ill-prepared to provide the needed guidance because so much of the past DGBL research, though good, has focused on efficacy (the message that games can be effective) rather than on explanation (why and how they are effective) and prescription (how to actually implement DGBL).

This is not to say that we have ignored this issue entirely. Many serious game proponents have been conducting research on how games can best be used for learning,[4] resulting in a small but growing body of literature on DGBL as it embodies well-established learning principles, theories, and models. On the other hand, many DGBL proponents have been vocal about the dangers of "academizing" ("sucking the fun out of," as Prensky would say) games. This is partly the result of our experiences with the edutainment software of the last decade or so, which instead of harnessing the power of games for learning, resulted in what Professor Seymour Papert calls "Shavian reversals": offspring that inherit the worst characteristics of both parents (in this case, boring games and drill-and-kill learning).[5] Many argue that this happened because educational games were designed by academicians who had little or no understanding of the art, science, and culture of game design. The products were thus (sometimes!) educationally sound as learning tools but dismally stunted as games. Yet if we use this history and these fears to argue, as some have, that games must be designed by game designers without access to the rich history of theory and practice with games in learning environments, we are also doomed to fail. We will create games that may be fun to play but are hit-or-miss when it comes to educational goals and outcomes. The answer is not to privilege one arena over the other but to find the synergy between pedagogy and engagement in DGBL.

In this article, I will outline why DGBL is effective and engaging, how we can leverage those principles to implement DGBL, how faculty can integrate commercial off-the-shelf (COTS) DGBL in the classroom, what DGBL means for institutional IT support, and the lessons we can learn from past attempts at technological innovations in learning.

The Effectiveness of DGBL

If we are to think practically and critically about DGBL, we need to separate the hype from the reality. Many who first hear about the effectiveness of games are understandably skeptical. How much of the research is the result of rigorous, controlled experimental design, and how much is wishful thinking and propaganda? A comprehensive analysis of the field is not possible here and, in any case, has already been done by others. Several reviews of the literature on gaming over the last forty years, including some studies that use rigorous statistical procedures to analyze findings from multiple studies (meta-analyses), have consistently found that games promote learning and/or reduce instructional time across multiple disciplines and ages.[6] Although many of these reviews included non-digital games (pre-1980), there is little reason to expect that the medium itself will change these results. A cursory review of the experimental research in the last five years shows well-documented positive effects of DGBL across multiple disciplines and learners.

What accounts for the generally positive effects found in all these studies about games and learning? These empirical studies are only part of the picture. Games are effective not because of what they are, but because of what they embody and what learners are doing as they play a game. Skepticism about games in learning has prompted many DGBL proponents to pursue empirical studies of how games can influence learning and skills. But because of the difficulty of measuring complex variables or constructs and the need to narrowly define variables and tightly control conditions, such research most often leads to studies that make correspondingly narrow claims about tightly controlled aspects of games (e.g., hand-eye coordination, visual processing, the learning of facts and simple concepts).

As Johnson says in *Everything Bad Is Good for You:* "When I read these ostensibly positive accounts of video games, they strike me as the equivalent of writing a story about the merits of the great novels and focusing on how reading them can improve your spelling."[7] Although it's true that games have been empirically shown to teach lower-level intellectual skills and to improve physical skills, they do much more than this. Games embody well-established principles and models of learning. For instance, games are effective partly because the learning takes place within a meaningful (to the game) context. What you must learn is directly related to the environment in which you learn and demonstrate it; thus, the learning is not only relevant but applied and practiced within that context. Learning that occurs

in meaningful and relevant contexts is more effective than learning that occurs outside of those contexts, as is the case with most formal instruction. Researchers refer to this principle as *situated cognition* and have demonstrated its effectiveness in many studies over the last fifteen years. Researchers have also pointed out that play is a primary socialization and learning mechanism common to all human cultures and many animal species. Lions do not learn to hunt through direct instruction but through modeling and play.[8] Games, clearly, make use of the principle of play as an instructional strategy.

Games are effective not because of what they are, but because of what they embody and what learners are doing as they play a game.

There are other theories that can account for the cognitive benefits of games. Jean Piaget's theories about children and learning include the concepts of assimilation and accommodation. With assimilation, we attempt to fit new information into existing slots or categories. An example of an adult assimilating information might be that when a man turns the key in the ignition of his car and the engine does not turn over, and in the past this has been due to a dead battery, he is now likely to identify the problem as a dead battery. Accommodation involves the process whereby we must modify our existing model of the world to accommodate new information that does not fit into an existing slot or category. This process is the result of holding two contradictory beliefs. In the previous example, should the man replace the battery and experience the same problem, he finds that the engine not starting both means and does not mean a dead battery. This process is often referred to as *cognitive disequilibrium*. Accordingly, our stranded motorist must adjust his mental model to include other problems like alternators and voltage regulators (although perhaps only after an expensive trip to his auto mechanic). Piaget believed that intellectual maturation over the lifespan of the individual depends on the cycle of assimilation and accommodation and that cognitive disequilibrium is the key to this process.

Games that are too easily solved will not be engaging, so good games constantly require input from the learner and provide feedback.

Games embody this process of cognitive disequilibrium and resolution. The extent to which games foil expectations (create cognitive disequilibrium) without exceeding the capacity of the player to succeed largely determines whether they are engaging.

Interacting with a game requires a constant cycle of hypothesis formulation, testing, and revision. This process happens rapidly and often while the game is played, with immediate feedback. Games that are too easily solved will not be engaging, so good games constantly require input from the learner and provide feedback. Games thrive as teaching tools when they create a continuous cycle of cognitive disequilibrium and resolution (via assimilation or accommodation) while also allowing the player to be successful. There are numerous other areas of research that account for how and why games are effective learning tools, including anchored instruction, feedback, behaviorism, constructivism, narrative psychology, and a host of other cognitive psychology and educational theories and principles. Each of these areas can help us, in turn, make the best use of DGBL.

Implementing DGBL

The positive effects of DGBL seen in experimental studies can be traced, at least partially, to well-established principles of learning as described earlier (e.g., situated cognition, play theory, assimilation and accommodation) and elsewhere by others.[9] This means that DGBL can be implemented most effectively, at least in theory, by attending to these underlying principles. How, then, can we use this knowledge to guide our implementation of DGBL in higher education?

A review of the DGBL literature shows that, in general, educators have adopted three approaches for integrating games into the learning process: have students build games from scratch; have educators and/or developers build educational games from scratch to teach students; and integrate commercial off-the-shelf (COTS) games into the classroom. In the first approach, students take on the role of game designers; in building the game, they learn the content. Traditionally, this has meant that students develop problem-solving skills while they learn programming languages. Professional game development takes one to two years and involves teams of programmers and artists. Even though this student-designed approach to DGBL need not result in commercial-quality games, it is nonetheless a time-intensive process and has traditionally been limited to computer science as a domain. It is certainly possible for modern game design to cross multiple disciplines (art, English, mathematics, psychology), but not all teachers have the skill sets needed for game design, not all teach in areas that allow for good content, not all can devote the time needed to implement this type of DGBL, and many teach within the traditional institutional structure, which does not easily allow for interdisciplinarity. For these reasons, this approach is unlikely to be used widely.

In the second case, we can design games to seamlessly integrate learning and game play. Touted by many as the "Holy Grail" approach to DGBL because of its ability to potentially address educational and entertainment equally, and to do so with virtually any domain, this professionally designed DGBL process is more resource-intensive than the first option. This is because the games must be comparable in quality and functionality to commercial off-the-shelf (COTS) games, which after all

are very effective in teaching the content, skills, and problem-solving needed to win the game. The development of such "serious games" is on the rise, and the quality of the initial offerings is promising (e.g., *Environmental Detectives,* developed by the Education Arcade; *Hazmat: Hotzone,* under development at the Entertainment Technology Center at Carnegie Mellon University; *Virtual U,* originally conceived and developed by Professor William F. Massy; and *River City,* developed by Professor Chris Dede, the Harvard Graduate School of Education, and George Mason University). However, the road to the development of serious games is also littered with Shavian reversals (poor examples of edutainment in which neither the learning nor the game is effective or engaging). Consequently, fewer companies are willing to spend the time and money needed to develop these games, for fear of revisiting their unprofitable past, and so the number of games that can be developed is limited. Although this professionally designed DGBL approach is clearly the future of DGBL,[10] we are not likely to see widespread development of these games until we demonstrate that DGBL is more than just a fad and until we can point to persuasive examples that show games are being used effectively in education and that educators and parents view them as they now view textbooks and other instructional media.

The third approach—integrating commercial off-the-shelf digital game-based learning (COTS DGBL)—involves taking existing games, not necessarily developed as learning games, and using them in the classroom. In this approach, the games support, deliver, and/or assess learning. This approach is currently the most cost-effective of the three in terms of money and time and can be used with any domain and any learner. Quality is also maximized by leaving the design of game play up to game designers and the design of learning up to teachers. I believe that this approach to DGBL is the most promising in the short term because of its practicality and efficacy and in the long term because of its potential to generate the evidence and support we need to entice game companies to begin developing serious games.

Quality is maximized by leaving the design of game play up to game designers and the design of learning up to teachers.

This approach is gaining acceptance because of its practicality, and research shows that it can be effective.[11] Entertainment Arts (EA), a game-development company, and the National Endowment for Science, Technology, and the Arts (NESTA) in the United Kingdom have entered into a joint partnership to study the use of COTS games in European schools, and similar initiatives are being proposed in the United States. If the United States is like the United Kingdom, where 60 percent of teachers support the use of games in the classroom,[12] the United States may be well-positioned to begin generating the evidence (through the use of COTS games) that the game industry needs to begin developing serious games.

Integrating COTS games is not without its drawbacks. Commercial games are not designed to teach, so topics will be limited and content may be inaccurate or incomplete. This is the biggest obstacle to implementing COTS DGBL: it requires careful analysis and a matching of the content, strengths, and weaknesses of the game to the content to be studied.[13]

There are ways to minimize these drawbacks, some of which I will discuss later, but the elephant in the room is that in our conversations about DGBL, we rarely acknowledge that the taxonomy of games is as complex as our learning taxonomies. Not all games will be equally effective at all levels of learning. For instance, card games are going to be best for promoting the ability to match concepts, manipulate numbers, and recognize patterns. *Jeopardy*-style games, a staple of games in the classroom, are likely to be best for promoting the learning of verbal information (facts, labels, and propositions) and concrete concepts. Arcade-style games (or as Prensky and others refer to them, "twitch" games) are likely to be best at promoting speed of response, automaticity, and visual processing. Adventure games, which are narrative-driven open-ended learning environments, are likely to be best for promoting hypothesis testing and problem solving. Many games also blur these taxonomic lines, blending strategy with action and role playing, for instance.

It is critical, therefore, that we understand not just how games work but how different *types* of games work and how game taxonomies align with learning taxonomies. This is not a new idea. In perhaps one of the most ambitious and rigorous examinations of the use of games to teach mathematics, a 1985 study undertaken for the National Council of Teachers of Mathematics developed eleven games for different grade levels using 1,637 participants. The study authors intended their eleven separate game studies to examine if and how games could be used to teach mathematics at varying learning levels.[14] Games, they hypothesized, might be better at promoting learning at some levels than at others. Further, they distinguished between three types of game use: pre-, co-, and post-instructional, based on when games were used in relation to the existing curriculum. The study authors found that there were indeed differences by learning level and by whether games were used prior to, during, or after other instruction and also that there were interactions between these two factors. They concluded that although drill-and-practice-type games at the time made up the vast majority of edutainment titles, instructional games could be effective for higher learning levels if designed and implemented well. Though this seems to support the development of serious games, the core principle—that games can promote learning at higher taxonomic levels—is as applicable to COTS games, which require and promote problem-solving and situated cognition *before* they are integrated with instructional activities or content.

Integrating COTS DGBL in the Classroom

It is important to understand how the theoretical issues outlined here relate to the use of games to teach. Although this section gives a practical description of the issues, it is meant more as a heuristic for understanding the issues involved than as a prescriptive tool. There are a wide range of other factors that must be considered, such as using the game outside of the classroom (as with all homework), balancing game play and other instructional activities, and rotating students' use of the computers in classrooms where there is not a one-to-one student-computer ratio. Many of these issues are not unique to DGBL, however, and are adequately treated by authors of texts that emphasize integrating computer technology into the learning process.[15]

Choosing a Suitable Game

A good number of COTS games are suitable for use in the classroom, and there are many examples of COTS games already being used in the classroom, including *Civilization, CSI, Age of Empires II, The Sims 2, Age of Mythology,* and *SimCity 4* (e.g., see <http://www.Silversprite.blogspot.com>). Prensky has put together a list of five hundred "serious" games that can be used to teach different content. Many of these can be found at <http://www.socialimpactgames.com>, and his new book and accompanying Web site (see <http://www.gamesparentsteachers.com>) provide even more guidance on using games for learning. These games can be a good match for DGBL depending on whether the explicit content is a match for the classroom content. Examples include *Civilization* to teach history, *CSI* to teach forensics and criminal justice, and *SimCity* to teach civil engineering and government. But they can also be a good match based on whether the underlying strategies and the game play match the content of the course. Games like *RollerCoaster Tycoon* and *Cruise Ship Tycoon,* for example, do not seem at first glance to be good candidates for DGBL. A closer examination of these titles, however, reveals a different story. In *RollerCoaster Tycoon,* students build roller-coasters to different specifications, which is what engineers do. And though the game does not require students to use calculus or learn physics, the principles are certainly present in the game. By asking learners to take on the role they are given in the game (the engineer), we can extend the game into the classroom by asking them to perform the tasks that an engineer in charge of the roller-coaster would do. Management might require safety reports that include maximum load capacity, force tolerances and structural integrity, speed estimates, and weight limits, for example, all of which would require the use of calculus, a demonstration of physics knowledge, and the ability to communicate (write) in ways that are authentic to real-world engineers. Both *RollerCoaster* and *Cruise Ship Tycoon* also require learners to manage a business, including monitoring expenses, revenues, and customer satisfaction. These are the same skills expected of business students, who as professionals will need to develop business plans, write reports, and manage budgets. Although the games do not cover instruction in all of these areas, we can easily augment the game with instructional activities that preserve the context (situated cognition) of the game (e.g., by extending the goals and character roles of the game into the classroom). Attending to the underlying structure of games opens up the instructional potential of nearly every game. As an extreme case in point, I could envision using *Grand Theft Auto* to teach ethics, morality, citizenship, and law enforcement. However, this is not to say that every game would be suitable; a host of other questions must be answered first.

Aligning the Game with the Curriculum

The 1985 study on using games to teach mathematics, discussed earlier, made the distinction between whether a game was used as a pre-instructional strategy (for an advance organizer), a co-instructional strategy (for examples and practice of learning in a domain), or a post-instructional strategy (for assessment and synthesis). This decision is partly determined by the curriculum and partly by the game. A balance between the needs of the curriculum and the structure of the game must be achieved to avoid either compromising the learning outcomes or forcing a game to work in a way for which it is not suited.

Aligning the Game with the Content

Educators recognize this as the biggest limitation of COTS games in DGBL. Any game designed to be engaging will tend to privilege that aspect over accuracy and completeness of content. So when we evaluate these games, we have to ask ourselves several questions. What *is* covered in the game? A game may take a breadth or a depth approach to the topic. Games like *Civilization* will cover a huge range of history across continents and cultures (breadth), whereas games like *Call of Duty* will focus on one narrow slice of history (depth). Obviously, this has implications for how the games align with the curriculum.

Any game designed to be engaging will tend to privilege that aspect over accuracy and completeness of content.

Just as important as what is covered in the game is what is *not* covered. Missing topics (for games that focus on depth) and missing content within topics (for games that focus on breadth) are key issues. What prerequisite knowledge is required to interact with the game content in a way that is appropriate for the curriculum? What does the game get wrong? One of the biggest misconceptions among educators is that if a game is missing content or has inaccurate content, it cannot be used responsibly for DGBL. However, educators can use these teachable moments to create cognitive disequilibrium (through instructional strategies

and activities) by presenting or designing activities by which *students* discover information that conflicts with the game and the student's knowledge.

In other cases, the games may present information that, though not technically incorrect, is nevertheless misleading. There may also be alternative viewpoints and perspectives that are not represented by the games. The game *Conquest of the Americas* involves several cultures over a three-hundred-year period, but as evidenced in the title, the game privileges the Western point of view. The indigenous populations of present-day Florida would tell a decidedly different story of Columbus's landing, just as those living in what is now the upper northeast of the United States would have a different account of the landing of the *Mayflower*. The curriculum may require incorporation of these viewpoints even when the game does not.

Designing and Evaluating the Game

Once we have chosen a game, and have analyzed it for content, we have to decide what to do about missing and inaccurate content. What content will have to be created to address gaps? Who will provide this content? Some believe that this is the teacher's responsibility, but current thinking in education suggests that the more students are responsible for in their learning, the more they will learn. Certainly, there is some content that will not be practical for students to address on their own, but wherever and whenever we can maximize student responsibility, we should.

We have to ask ourselves if the amount of potential learning is justified by the amount of work and time that will be needed to implement the game.

And the *way* we choose to maximize student responsibility is also important. Because we are going to have to go out of the game environment and into the classroom, we run the risk of eliminating what is fun and engaging about the game. So, rather than simply providing additional reading or handouts with the missing or accurate information, we should strive to design activities that are logical extensions of the game world. Learning is integral to the story of the game world—players are never asked to step out of the game world to do something (although they frequently do so when stuck). The constant cycle of cognitive disequilibrium and resolution—the engagement—is what leads to the experience that Professor Mihaly Csikszentmihalyi refers to as *flow*.[16] Flow occurs when we are engaged in an activity (physical, mental, or both) at a level of immersion that causes us to lose track of time and the outside world, when we are performing at an optimal level. Good games promote flow, and anything that causes us to "leave" the game world (e.g., errors, puzzles that require irrational solutions) interrupts flow. If we were to simply design "traditional" classroom activities (workbooks, textbook reading, teacher handouts, etc.) that addressed the missing, misleading, or inaccurate content in the game, we would be interrupting the flow experience. Granted, anytime we ask the players to stop the game and do something else, flow will be interrupted. But to the extent that we can keep these additional activities "situated" within the game world (i.e., connected to the problem being solved, the characters solving it, and the tools and methods those characters use or might use), we will minimize this interruption of flow. For the same reasons, we should make sure that students spend enough time in the game to promote flow and, correspondingly, significant time in the extended instructional activities. Even if these extended activities do not promote flow, the more frequently students move from the game to other activities (even those related to the game), the more frequently flow will be interrupted in each activity.

Although it is not possible to stay entirely within the game world (and therefore to keep students in flow) when implementing COTS DGBL, there is another reason we should strive to keep the activities we design situated within that game world. Malone and Lepper identify fantasy (endogenous and exogenous) as one of four main areas that make games intrinsically motivating.[17] Endogenous fantasy elements are those fantasy parts that are seamlessly integrated with the game world and story; exogenous fantasy elements are those that, though in the game, do not appear to have much relation to the story or game world. Endogenous fantasy elements not only help make games intrinsically motivating; in theory, they should also promote flow. So whenever we ask students to not be *in* the game, we should strive to keep the activities and roles they take on (the fantasy) endogenous *to* the game.

Thus, the roles we ask them to take on should be extensions of the roles they play in the game. These can be main characters, ancillary characters, or characters that could hypothetically be part of the game. The activities we ask them to perform as these characters should be authentic to the goals of the game world and the professions or characteristics of these characters. Some examples of endogenous activities might be to develop budgets, spreadsheets, reports/charts, and databases; to write diaries, scientific reports, letters, legal briefs, dictionaries, faxes; to design, duplicate, and conduct experiments; to conduct and write up feasibility studies; and to assess the veracity of game information or provide missing data. We should not be so naïve as to think that students will find these activities to be as engaging as the games, but given our need to meet curricular goals and our desire to tightly integrate the games with the learning process, this seems a good way to meet in the middle.

Making the Call

Ultimately, after this investment of time in analysis, we have to be willing to abandon a game if it is not a good fit. We have to ask ourselves if the amount of potential learning is justified by the amount of work and time that will be needed to implement the game. If it is not, we have to resist the temptation to hang on to something simply because we have invested so much effort.

DGBL and Institutional IT Support

Aside from the practical aspects of implementing DGBL, colleges and universities face significant challenges when attempting to support DGBL at the institutional level. There are several areas in which IT can help.

Documentation and Training Support

If colleges and universities leave DGBL entirely up to the faculty, some will do a good job, and some will not. Everyone will spend unnecessary time reinventing the wheel and rediscovering the principles needed to make the innovation work. Institutions should provide documentation and training for what DGBL can look like in general and within the context of the institution specifically. They should strive to provide heuristics and job aids for planning and analysis in order to address the critical issues and decisions outlined here. Faculty members need training to analyze, design, develop, implement, and evaluate DGBL. Staff members need training to support faculty during this process. Everyone involved in the design, development, or implementation of DGBL needs training on what DGBL is and how it is supported and implemented institution-wide (e.g., labs, procedures, guidelines).

Examples of best practices in DGBL should be collected and disseminated. Since DGBL requires pedagogical approaches that will be unfamiliar to many faculty members, pedagogical support should be provided to those interested in exploring DGBL. Colleges and universities should hire instructional designers who have experience with games and learning to assist with the design of DGBL and should support one-on-one development just as they have begun to do with online learning. Colleges of education can provide expertise in technology integration. They have been doing this for twenty-five years and can be invaluable resources both for establishing the models and pedagogical support mentioned above and for implementing DGBL.

Technical Support

Clearly, the technical challenges of DGBL are significant. Faculty need assistance during development and implementation of DGBL, and students need support during implementation. This means that institutions need to train help desk staff and provide documentation (e.g., common questions, current lab configurations and procedures for DGBL, course materials for ongoing DGBL classes) so that they understand the issues and can provide support when needed.

Financial Support

Although COTS DGBL is among the more inexpensive options, there are still financial issues involved. Just as it has done with productivity software, the IT unit should strive to provide assistance with licensing through volume licensing agreements with companies and negotiated discounts for students (who will, after all, have to play these games outside of class). Financial incentives for faculty to develop DGBL should be provided, as they often are for online learning, and should be tied to the established institutional models and procedures for DGBL discussed earlier.

Infrastructure Support

The existing higher education infrastructure is ill-prepared to support DGBL. Computer labs must be appropriately configured, meaning that they are not locked down to prevent adjustments to video resolution or installation of proprietary drivers and game patches and that they allow for the ability to save and retrieve games. Equipment that is not standard, such as headphones, speakers, and high-end sound and video cards, must be included in lab specifications. Given the increase in the popularity, power, and sophistication of gaming consoles like the Xbox 360, higher education institutions that are serious about supporting DGBL may even want to change the footprint of one or more labs to be consoles rather than PC boxes. Finally, labs must be accessible for game play outside of class, not just during class. This will place a heavier load on the labs, of course, and will necessitate the formulation of additional usage policies.

Research and Development Support

Finally, institutions will need to take an active role in R&D, just as they are beginning to do now with online learning. Colleges and universities should start by identifying those faculty members who are doing research in games and learning and should bring them into the planning, implementation, and evaluation process. These instructors are most commonly in the instructional design, education, and cognitive psychology fields, although faculty in virtually every area and domain are exploring DGBL.

Colleges and universities need to collect and disseminate research and examples of successful DGBL from within and without the institution. They should develop databases of examples and guidance for application and extension to additional domains. And higher education should encourage rigorous studies and game design so that we can extend DGBL as a field and we can continue to define and refine DGBL locally and abroad.

The Ghosts of Technology Past

Of the several technology "learning revolutions" during the last quarter-century, most have failed to achieve even half of their promise. Although there are many reasons for this, the primary fault lies with our inability (or unwillingness) to distinguish between the medium and the message. Two examples of such technological learning innovations from our recent past are media technology and computing technology.

Faculty members need training to analyze, design, develop, implement, and evaluate DGBL.

In the 1960s and 1970s, audio and video (and later, television) were touted as technologies that would revolutionize learning. We rapidly began implementing media wherever possible, regardless of grade, domain, or learners. Many studies were conducted during the 1970s to compare media-based classrooms to "traditional" classrooms, and some of the more sensational ones found their way into the public eye. By the 1980s, enough studies had been conducted to allow for meta-analyses and reviews of the literature. Most of these resulted in what has famously been called the "no significant difference" phenomenon—meaning that, overall, media made no significant difference to learning. This was not surprising to instructional designers, who argued that the implementation of media was not consistently of high quality and that the quality of the instruction in "media" versus "traditional" classrooms was not controlled. The key to understanding this issue lies in the difference between *use* and *integration* of media. *Using* media requires only that the media be present during instruction. Integrating media, on the other hand, requires a careful analysis of the strengths and weaknesses of the media, as well as its alignment with instructional strategies, methods, and learning outcomes. Weaknesses are then addressed through modification of the media or inclusion of additional media and/or instruction, and instruction is modified to take advantage of the strengths of the media. In cases where there is poor alignment, the media is not used.

Sadly, the history of the use of computing technology in learning parallels that of media use. The personal computer arrived in the 1970s, and predictions of revolutionized learning quickly followed. Schools spent hundreds of thousands of dollars on computers in the early 1980s, vowing to place one in every classroom. Studies comparing classrooms with computing technology and those without proceeded at the same pace as had studies comparing media-rich and media-poor classrooms. Once again, instructional designers and others pointed out that the quality of implementation varied greatly, making comparisons impossible. By the time there were enough studies to evaluate and review, the quality and diversity of the different implementations made it difficult to draw any meaningful conclusions. Once again, it seemed there was "no significant difference" between classrooms that used technology and those that did not. Once again, we had mistaken technology use for technology integration.

Eventually, though, educators learned from this and from prior experience with media. They began developing and testing better-integrated uses of computing technology. Since the early 1990s, educators have been moving toward technology integration and toward pre-service teacher training, emphasizing alignment of the curriculum with the technology. We must take what we have learned forward as we consider how, when, and with whom to implement DGBL in the future.

Many of us have been advocating for DGBL for twenty-five years—much of that time without any evidence of success. Over those same years, instructional designers and educators have been advocating for the intelligent integration of learning technologies, including DGBL, in accordance with established theory and the underlying strengths and weaknesses of the medium—much of that time watching schools mistake the medium for the message. It's not just the digital natives who are getting restless. We all want to see DGBL both accepted *and* implemented intelligently.

Will we continue to learn from the past? Will we realize the potential that DGBL has to revolutionize how students learn? This has much less to do with attitude and learner preferences than it does with a technology that supports some of the most effective learning principles identified during the last hundred years. If we learn from our past, and if we focus on the strengths of the medium and provide the support and infrastructure needed to implement DGBL, we may well be present for a true revolution.

Notes

1. See Diana Oblinger and James Oblinger, "Is It Age or IT: First Steps toward Understanding the Net Generation," in Diana G. Oblinger and James L. Oblinger, eds., *Educating the Net Generation* (Boulder, Colo.: EDUCAUSE, 2005), e-book, available at <http://www.educause.edu/educatingthenetgen>, and Marc Prensky, " 'Engage Me or Enrage Me': What Today's Learners Demand," *EDUCAUSE Review,* vol. 40, no. 5 (September/October 2005): 60–65, <http://www.educause.edu/er/erm05/erm0553.asp>.

2. "$10B Gaming Field Inspires New Curricula," *eSchool News Online,* September 30, 2005, <http://www.eschoolnews.com/news/showStory.cfm?ArticleID=5896>.

3. See Entertainment Software Association, "2005 Sales, Demographics, and Usage Data: Essential Facts about the Computer and Video Game Industry," <http://www.theesa.com/files/2005EssentialFacts.pdf>, and U.S. Census Bureau, Population Division, "Table 1: Annual Estimates of the Population for the United States and States, and for Puerto Rico: April 1, 2000, to July 1, 2005 (NST-EST2005-01)," December 22, 2005.

4. See, for example, L. P. Rieber, "Seriously Considering Play: Designing Interactive Learning Environments Based on the Blending of Microworlds, Simulations, and Games," *Educational Technology Research and Development,* vol. 44, no. 2 (1996): 43–58; R. Van Eck and J. Dempsey, "The Effect of Competition and Contextualized Advisement on the Transfer of Mathematics Skills in a Computer-Based Instructional Simulation Game," *Educational Technology Research and Development,* vol. 50, no. 3 (2002): 23–41; Alexander Lewis Aitkin, "Playing at Reality: Exploring the Potential of the Digital Games as a Medium for Science Communication" (Ph.D. diss., Centre for the Public Awareness of Science, Australia, 2004); Simon Egenfeldt-Nielsen, "Beyond Edutainment: Exploring the Educational Potential of Computer Games" (Ph.D. diss., IT-University Copenhagen, Denmark, 2005); Kurt D. Squire, "Replaying History: Learning World History through Playing Civilization III" (Ph.D. diss., Indiana University, 2005).

5. Seymour Papert, "Does Easy Do It? Children, Games, and Learning," *Game Developer,* June 1998, <http://www.papert.org/articles/Doeseasydoit.html>.

6. See M. Szczurek, "Meta-Analysis of Simulation Games Effectiveness for Cognitive Learning" (Ph.D. diss., Indiana University, 1982); R. L. VanSickle, "A Quantitative Review of Research on Instructional Simulation Gaming: A Twenty-Year Perspective," *Theory and Research in Social Education,* vol. 14, no. 3 (1986): 245–64; and J. M. Randel, B. A. Morris, C. D. Wetzel, and B. V. Whitehill, "The Effectiveness of Games for Educational Purposes: A Review of Recent Research," *Simulation and Gaming,* vol. 23 no. 3 (1992): 261–76.

7. Steven Johnson, *Everything Bad Is Good for You: How Today's Popular Culture Is Actually Making Us Smarter* (New York: Riverhead Books, 2005), 24.

8. See Chris Crawford, "The Art of Computer Game Design," <http://www.vancouver.wsu.edu/fac/peabody/game-book/Coverpage.html>.

9. See James Paul Gee, *What Video Games Have to Teach Us about Learning and Literacy* (New York: Palgrave Macmillan, 2003), for a comprehensive examination of the mechanisms by which games teach.

10. For example, see the Games-to-Teach Project (http://www.educationarcade.org/gtt).

11. See Angela McFarlane, Anne Sparrowhawk, and Ysanne Heald, "Report on the Educational Use of Games: An Exploration by TEEM of the Contribution Which Games Can Make to the Education Process" (2002), <http://www.teem.org.uk/publications/teem_gamesined_full.pdf>.

12. NESTA Futurelab, "Close to 60% of UK Teachers Want Computer Games in the Classroom," January 13, 2006, <http://www.nestafuturelab.org/about_us/press_releases/pr11.htm>.

13. See McFarlane, Sparrowhawk, and Heald, "Report on the Educational Use of Games"; and R. Van Eck and J. Gikas, "Gaming Theory as a Teaching Tool at All Levels," presentation for the annual meeting of Techsposium, Memphis, Tenn., March 31, 2004.

14. G. W. Bright, J. G. Harvey, and M. M. Wheeler, "Learning and Mathematics Games," *Journal for Research in Mathematics Education* (1985), no. 1.

15. See Gary R. Morrison and Deborah L. Lowther, *Integrating Computer Technology into the Classroom* (Upper Saddle River, N.J.: Pearson/Merrill/Prentice-Hall, 2005); and Mark Grabe and Cindy Grabe, *Integrating Technology for Meaningful Learning,* 4th ed. (New York: Houghton-Mifflin, 2004).

16. See Mihaly Csikszentmihalyi, *Flow: The Psychology of Optimum Experience* (New York: Harper & Row, 1990).

17. See T. W. Malone and M. R. Lepper, "Making Learning Fun: A Taxonomic Model of Intrinsic Motivations for Learning," in R. E. Snow and M. J. Farr, eds., *Aptitude, Learning, and Instruction,* Volume 3: *Cognitive and Affective Process Analysis* (Hillsdale, N.J.: Erlbaum, 1987): 223–53.

RICHARD VAN ECK is Associate Professor at the University of North Dakota, where he has been the graduate director of the Instructional Design & Technology graduate program since 2004. He began his study of games with his dissertation in 1999 and has taught a graduate course in games and learning every year since 2001. Comments on this article can be sent to the author at <richard.vaneck@und.edu>.

From *EDUCAUSE* Review, Vol. 41, no. 2, March/April 2006, pp. 17–18, 20, 22, 24, 26, 28, 30. Copyright © 2006 by Richard Van Eck. Reprinted by permission of the author.

Podcasting & VODcasting: A White Paper

Definitions, Discussions & Implications

PETER MENG

Defined

What is Podcasting?

The word "podcasting" is an amalgam of the word broadcasting and the name of the popular MP3 player from Apple Computer called the "iPod". It's a bit of a misnomer in that it implies that an iPod is required to podcast. In fact podcasts can be used with a variety of digital audio formats and play on almost any MP3 player or portable digital audio device—as well as any brand of desktop computer or laptop.

To define it: Podcasting is the process of capturing an audio event, song, speech, or mix of sounds and then posting that digital sound object to a Web site or "blog" in a data structure called an RSS 2.0 envelope (or "feed"). RSS stands for Real Simple Syndication and is an agreed specification of XML tags used to define objects which can be subscribed to through a "RSS news reader" (see glosssary). Using specialized news readers like iPodder or iPodderX, users can subscribe to a Web page containing RSS 2.0 tagged audio files on designated web pages and automatically download these files directly into an audio management program on their personal computer like iTunes, Windows Media Player or MusicMatch. When a user synchronizes their portable audio device with their personal computer the podcasts are automatically transferred to that device to be listened to at the time and location most convenient for the user.

Many have compared podcasting to Tivo® or a DVR (digital video recorder) because of it's "time-shifting" ability. In some aspects it is similar, but it is also different in that the recorded content is delivered in it's final format to a portable device that is independent of the recording device.

A Metaphor

Podcasts follow a simple publish and subscribe model but with a convenient twist. Imagine the following scenario: You've just heard about a great new magazine where each week a number of influential people from your profession are interviewed and share highly personal knowledge and advice–sounds interesting. You fill out the request form for your free 1 month trial and send it in. When the publisher receives your request they notify the distributor, where the latest version of the magazines are stored, and tell them send you the latest copy of their magazine each week. The distributor calls United Parcel Service (UPS) to schedule regular pickup/deliveries of your magazine. UPS picks up your magazine from the distributor for same day delivery. The UPS courier delivers the magazine to your house and puts it in your mailbox. But (... and here's the twist) instead of going out to the mailbox to pick up your magazine, Ralph, your trained Rotweiler, goes out to the mailbox grabs your magazine and places it—gently—in your briefcase. The next morning, as you ride the train to work, you open your briefcase to read the magazine you know is waiting for you there.

VODcasting (also called "vlogging")—the "VOD" stands for "video-on-demand"—is almost identical to podcasting. The difference is that the content is video versus audio, and the content is more likely to be played on a laptop than a PMA (personal media assistant) due to their newness and relative expense.

How It Works

Doing a Podcast

Podcasts are rapidly increasing in popularity because they are simple to produce and very inexpensive to deliver. At it's simplest, all that is required to create a podcast is a personal computer with a sound card, an inexpensive or built-in microphone, sound editing free ware, and an internet connection with access to a Web site. Because of the low cost of entry, anyone can be a publisher, or more accurately a broadcaster with their own "radio" show.

VODcasts are a bit more complex and require a slightly larger investment in equipment and time, but still fall well into the technical and financial realm of anyone with a digital video camera and a higher-end desktop or laptop personal computer.

The Pod/VODcasting Process

The process for podcasting and VODcasting can be broken down into five steps. The complexity of those steps is dependent on the purpose of the content to be created and the quality level at which it will be produced.

I. Create or capture and edit the content.
II. Publish content to a web site or blog.
III. Subscribe to the content using an "RSS News Reader".
IV. Download the content into content management software (CMS).
V. Play content on download device or synchronize CMS with portable media player and play.

Required Tools and Equipment
Podcasting

I. *Audio capture tools.* Nothing will affect the quality of a podcast more then the tools selected to capture it with. A quality microphone is a good start, combined with audio software and a personal computer. The microphone can be connected to a tape player, digital recorder with a memory card, or directly to the "MIC" input on the editing computer. If you use some type of recording device you will need some way to transfer the captured sound to your computer for editing and packaging for the internet. The way the recorded content is transferred to the computer depends on the type of recording tool you used, so check the instructions that came with the device or the numerous web sites that discuss digital recording.

II. *Audio editing tools.* There are numerous excellent audio editing tools available for all computer platforms. Price is not necessarily an indicator of quality or features, as there are numerous quality shareware, freeware and open source packages that will do the job admirably—www.sourceforge.net and www.shareware.com are good starting places for recording tools. Key requirements are multiple track editing and multiple audio compression formats including, AIFF, WAV, ACC and MP3.

III. *File transfer software.* Once content files are created they need to be published to a Web site or blog using any traditional file transfer method; basic FTP/SFTP, HTTP upload, virtual drive (WebDAV), or server upload will all work well. Also the software that is used for Web site or blog creation will probably transfer the content files to the desired location as well. Check the documentation of your Web or blog design tools for additional assistance.

IV. *RSS Enclosures.* Preparing the content for delivery requires it to be tagged via XML in a format known as RSS 2.0. The enclosure can be created with software designed to create RSS feeds or can be hand coded using your favorite text editor or WYSYWIG web design software. See the resource portion of this document for a list of editors and articles on creating a RSS enclosure.

V. *Specialized RSS news reader.* To automatically download the podcast requires a type of software called a RSS News Reader. It must be designed to specifically download podcasts to a specific folder on the subscriber's computer or can be modified to do so. Two packages to look at are iPodder (free—ipodder.sourceforge.net) for most popular operating systems, or iPodderX ($39.95—www.ipodderx.com) for the Apple OS X.

VI. *Content management software.* There are a number of software tools that are available for managing podcasts or any other audio content. CMS software allows the user to sort and organize their content into "playlists" which can be scheduled to automatically synchronize with a media player when you connect it to your computer or at specified times of the day.

By far the most popular CMS for podcasting is Apple iTunes which allows users to manage their audio content on both Windows XP and Macintosh OS X computers. Microsoft's Windows Media Player and Sony MusicMatch for Windows XP are excellent alternatives to iTunes and provide the added advantage that they will manage and play almost any type of media including photos and video. They also work with a wide variety of media players from a number of vendors. iTunes will natively synchronize content with both an Apple

iPod music player and other assorted MP3 players via associated plug-ins or applications.

VII. *A digital music player.* There are too many choices of MP3 players and media players to list in this document. Prices range from $15 for 32MB flash players to luxury $1500 multiple media wireless personalized players. Pricing is dependent on storage capability, features, styling and brand. The popular Apple iPods are priced from $99 to $499. Most of these players come with some type of content management software and methods for synchronizing with a desktop or laptop computer.

VODcasting

I. *Video capture tools.* Nothing will effect the quality of a VODcast more then the tools and techniques selected with which to capture it. However the quality required for a VODcast is dependent on the purpose of the VODcast. If the objective is to simply record an instructors lecture for future reference, then a simple $400 DV camcorder may be adequate, but you will need to have a strong understanding of the limitations of your camcorder to get the best results from it. However if the VODcast needs to meet broadcast standards or may be shown on a very large screen, much higher quality equipment may be required. A level of comfort and expertise will be required to get satisfactory results from the higher quality broadcast class equipment.

II. *Video editing tools.* There are variety of video editing applications that are available covering the range of capability and pricing from free for the novice, to thousands of dollars for the expert. Movie Maker from Microsoft and iMovie from Apple are both excellent products with which to create surprisingly sophisticated VODcasts. For the highest quality projects Final Cut Pro or editing products from Avid may be required.

III. *File transfer software.* Same as for podcasting.

IV. *RSS Enclosures.* Same as for podcasting.

V. *Specialized RSS news reader.* To-date we have not yet found news reader software specifically designed for VODcasting. Podcasting news readers like iPodder, iPodderX, and PlayPod will work, as well as stand alone generic news reader applications like Feedreader and Awasu.

VI. *Content management software.* iPhoto for the Mac and Adobe Album are both great products with which to organize your content. iPhoto can synchronize with the Apple iPod Photo and (currently) display stills. Rumor has it that a forthcoming software upgrade to the newest iPod Photo will also allow it to play MPEG 4 videos. Adobe Album allows organization and playback of VODcasts on a laptop computer. Although it will synchronize with some devices, none of these devices currently have video playback except for several models from Archos (www.archos.com).

VII. *A laptop computer or portable digital media player.* Although portable video devices are beginning to appear, the most popular playback environment for VODcasts is still the laptop or desktop computer. Interestingly, some of the units even have built-in personal video recorders (PVR) allowing for the creation of additional content which can then in turn be VODCast.

SCHOOL OF EDUCATION
CURRICULUM LABORATORY
UM-DEARBORN

Required Skills

Podcasting and VODcasting both require basic computer abilities and an interest in learning several new, although easy-to-use, software packages. Most students enter the university technology environment with enough basic technical skills to easily create and distribute podcasts. VODcasting takes a bit more work and planning but it is still very much within the realm of most student and staff technical abilities.

However, as the importance of the message increases, generally, so does the level of effort to create high quality content. Higher quality audio or video generally require a higher level of technical expertise. Currently many podcasts are known for their "scratchy" or homemade personalities. As the popularity of podcasting grows we will see ever more sophisticated broadcasts with increasing production values and higher level of required technical skills. The School of Journalism at The University of Missouri has already committed to producing all future podcasts and VOD casts using "best practices"—a professional quality level for their podcasts and VODcasts which they are currently defining.

The area of podcasting that currently requires the greatest skillset, is also the area that is evolving most rapidly and will soon open up podcasting to even greater numbers of individuals. The software used to manage and post the content to a Web site or blog is rapidly becoming easier to use and manipulate. At the current trend, posting audio and video content for podcasting will simply be a matter of dragging and dropping content to a virtual container where it will be automatically prepared for on-demand distribution.

Implications

Potential Uses for Podcasting and VODcasting at the University of Missouri

Even though the concept of podcasting is less than six months old, the sudden interest in podcasting and VODcasting comes from the numerous uses that the technology promises. The following table identifies different ways podcasting might be used and who would benefit from those uses.

Possible Uses of Podcasting	Prospective Users
Record and distribute news broadcasts.	The entire campus community and general public
Students can record and upload their foreign language lessons to their instructor's Web site. The instructor can then listen to the lessons on their MP3 player at their convenience.	Students, instructors
Audio/video recruiting development brochures with personalized messages.	Prospective students and parents, development and recruiting personnel
Recorded teacher's notes	Student, teachers
Recorded lectures distributed directly to student's MP3 players.	Students, teachers
Recorded meeting and conference notes.	Students, faculty, staff, admin
Student projects and project support interviews.	Students
Oral history archiving and on-demand distribution.	Students, faculty
Sport event distribution.	Students, alumni, and public

Effect on Current and Future Infrastructure

Both podcasting and VODcasting represent challenges to the current infrastructure albeit in different ways. The effects of these new technologies will be outlined for the following areas: storage needs, bandwidth, security, supporting hardware, and other requirements.

Podcasting

Bandwidth

The basic audio objects recorded at 32 kHz for speech content uses about 250 KB for every minute (15 MB per hour) of audio. In our current network environment a one hour audio segment will take about 1-2 minutes to download depending on network congestion. Because many podcasts are scheduled downloads, they can be scheduled for odd times of the day to reduce demand on the network.

Storage

At 15 MB per hour of speech based audio, the University could store approximately 65,000 hours of classroom audio on a single terabyte drive—more then the sum of all lectures at the University for a semester.

Although the storage costs of this much valuable content are dropping dramatically, the bigger cost may be in the cataloging, searching and retrieval of this information. Because of it's linear nature and data structure, it will be difficult, at best, to catalog the contents of these files without a significant effort. Most likely the files will be simply "meta-tagged" using the original editing or publishing software with generic informations such as: title, author, participants, subject, size, date, and select keywords. Actually tagging every subtopic and "time-coding" the tag for search purposes will be done on only the highest value content, or when currently nonexistent software appears that can automate the task with a certain level of reliability.

Supporting Hardware

Hardware requirements for podcasting are nominal. Any computer with an Internet connection and the ability of running Windows XP, Apple OS X, or Linux, has all the horsepower, storage, sound input/output, and memory required to create, edit, package and distribute a podcast. The only other equipment that is required is an external capture device with either an internal or external microphone. This includes both analog and digital recorders—analog recorders would require that captured content be transferred to digital format before editing and compression.

To play podcasts, the user can use the personal computer to which the media has been downloaded or can use almost any brand of MP3 or digital audio player as long as the device supports some type of synchronization software running on the users computer.

Supporting Software

The software specifically designed for podcasting is just beginning to appear. There are two types of software required—publishing and subscribing. Current publishing software needs both an audio capture application—like Win Amp, Audio Hijack Pro, or Audacity, and RSS editing package that will create an RSS 2.0 enclosure and deliver it to a web site or blog for distribution site—like FeedForAll or Feed Burner.

Subscription software retrieves the specified content feeds, on-demand or on-schedule, and can place the content directly into the specified folder of a content management application like iTunes or Windows Media Player. These same applications allow synchronization of the podcast with the MP3 player or digital audio device.

Other Requirements

A broadband Internet connection is *highly* recommended due to the relatively large file sizes and the amount of information that needs to be transmitted. Although dial-up could be used, the user would have to be selective as to the type and number of podcasts they would download.

VODcasting

Bandwidth

In our current network environment a one hour video segment will take about 10 minutes to download depending on network congestion. Because many VODcasts are scheduled downloads, they can be scheduled for odd times of the day to reduce demand on the network.

Storage

Depending on the resolution (for the purposes of this document we'll assume a frame size of 320 x 240 pixels). At 70 MB per hour of video the University could store approximately 10,000 hours of classroom video on a single terabyte drive.

The storage and searching issues for video are similar to those for audio, although it may be a bit easier to catalog the video components. Since the nature of video editing lends itself to time-coding and often uses embedded markers and comments in the video editing process, with some editing foresight, searchable tagged "bookmarks" could be embedded in the digital file, aiding the ability of the user to skip directly to a desired location or video event. An example of this is the Sports Tech system currently being used by the Athletics Department. This content would lend itself well to a database driven portable on demand video solution.

Supporting Hardware

Hardware requirements for creating VODcasts are more demanding than for audio. Required hardware would be a computer with an Internet connection and the following recommended configurations:

- Windows XP and Linux, Intel P4 3.0 Ghz +,140 GB, HO, 1 GB RAM, sound card
- Apple OSX, 1.5 Ghz + PowerPC, 140 GB, HD, 1 GB RAM

Other equipment required would include a video camera, ideally a DV cam (digital video) because converting analog video is time consuming and requires additional hardware. External microphones and lights may be required based on the location of filming and the quality of project required.

To play podcasts, the user can use the personal computer to which the media has been downloaded or can use almost any brand of MP3 or digital audio player as long as the device supports some type of synchronization software running on their computer.

Supporting Software

The software specifically designed for VODcasting is, as it is in podcasting, just beginning to appear. There are two types of software required—publishing and subscribing. Current publishing software is primarily a video capture and editing package—like iMovie or Adobe Premiere Elements. And then some type of software that will create an RSS 2.0 enclosure and deliver it to a web site or blog for distribution site—like FeedForAll, or FeedBurner.

Subscription software retrieves the specified content feeds, on demand or on schedule, and can place the content directly into the specified folder of a content management application like iPhoto, Windows Media Player and DopplerRadio. These same applications allow synchronization of the podcast with a Pocket PC and Archos personal media assistant (PMA).

Other Requirements

A broadband Internet connection is mandatory due to the large file sizes and the amount of information that needs to be transmitted. If the popularity of this technology takes-off there could be requirements for a content reservation system so that the available bandwidth and server capacity are not overwhelmed by a sudden demand for a specific piece of content. For example, if a teacher unexpectedly makes available their video lectures the day before a Psychology 101 final, we could find 500+ students all scrambling to download a 100MB file in a very short period of time.

Other Implications

Because the content types are significantly greater in storage and bandwidth requirements than text or image based files, podcasting and VODcasting will make their presence know on the existing infrastructure. In the event that a very popular class or student created "show" is released, the electronic "buzz" created by the wide variety of communication tools can quickly create tremendous demand for large amounts of content. Thus flexible and directable bandwidth may be required as well.

As the technology grows in popularity so too will the desire and demand to associate revenue with the content. Pod/VODcasting lends itself to a variety of revenue generating opportunities including subscription, sponsorship, product placement, as well as traditional blatant and indirect advertising. Revenue generation may seem antithetical to the mission of a public education institution, but with diminishing federal/state funding dollars and the rising popularity of on-line and lifelong learning, the repurposing and sale of content, All of these require supporting infrastructure as well as management tools or policies as previously discussed. By far the biggest issue generated by the evolution of these and other new technologies is aggregation of the content and then redistributing the appropriate content to the appropriate presentation device. Finding a way to search, present, and repurpose content across the greatest number of existing and upcoming mediums requires a concerted and centralized plan/effort that needs to be considered before unanticipated infrastructure consequences occur from a sudden acceptance of a particular creation/presentation technology.

Pedagogical Implications

The pedagogical implications of podcasting and VODcasting are intriguing. There are some simple and obvious uses, like recording classroom lectures and making them available for student notes. Even though this is technically easy to do, not only would a standardized recording process have to be set up, but more importantly, a permissions based distribution architecture would have to be established to limit access of the class content to approved class members. This could be done through the current WebCT and Blackboard architecture, or something completely new—again pointing to the fact that global content management and distribution in the University community is a growing issue.

Beyond simple recordings of lectures, a variety of other uses to enhance learning can be imagined for podcasting—in fact many of these are already being tested. Following is a sample list of ways that podcasting might be used:

- Audio recordings of textbook text, made available for students by the chapter, would allow students to "read" or review texts while walking or driving to class. It could also be a significant aid to auditory learners.
- Students could record and post project audio and video interviews which could be automatically downloaded to an instructors laptop or MP3 player for review. This would be an enhanced version of what is currently being done in the J-School).
- The same could be done for language lessons where students forward audio of their pronunciation dialogues. They could even swap these with peers for peer review before turning in the final form to the instructor.
- Oral reports recorded and archived.
- Musical resume's. Music critique.
- Libraries of bird sounds that the budding ornithologist could receive via seasonal subscription and take with them to the field.
- Downloadable library of high resolution heart sounds for medical students.

Beyond the technical opportunities and issues, both podcasting and VODcasting raise other significant issues. Some of the questions already being asked:

- How does podcasting or VODcasting challenge the current "talking head" model of classroom lectures ? If all lectures are available via video and audio, do students need to go to class? How often? Why? How do we keep them in class?
- Who owns the content, the school, the instructor, the user? Can this content be used outside of the university community? How is it protected or secured to the owner or subscriber?
- Who's going to edit the content? What are the guidelines for editing? What's real—what's not?
- How is copyrighted material tracked and/or verified?
- Can we make money from this?

Evolutionary Path

Both of these technologies are evolving rapidly and will become significant players in media distribution. As the tools to capture content become more prevalent and easier to use, variations on the theme will occur at a surprising pace. Already variations are occurring. Mobile blogs, called moblogs, currently allow individuals with Internet enabled camera phones to instantly submit photo images from their phone directly to the moblog, which are then in turn automatically transferred to someone else's phone through a Macromedia Flash enabled browser. Users are testing using their phones for sound recording and submitting those to specific sites that dynamically turn the file into a podcast. The new generation of videophones will naturally encourage the same thing for video.

These evolutionary steps are happening in weeks and months—not years. Defining their exact impact is impossible, but if the adoption and evolutionary trail of lifestyle digital tools in the last five years is any indication we will see highly useful, if not amazing, changes in the next five years.

Most likely pod/VODcasting will not replace traditional broadcast radio or television, but become an intelligent extension of it, offering more variety to a significantly larger audience from an ever increasing number of content providers and producers, each with their own unique, highly-targeted revenue models.

Conclusion

Podcasting and VODcasting, and their pending derivatives, are not fads. They are very real and very practical distribution technologies.

The ability to time-shift content versus traditional broadcast distribution models expands student teaching and learning opportunities significantly. The supporting technologies are relatively inexpensive and surprisingly easy to use—in fact easy enough to use that faculty and students will begin to actively produce and distribute content through this medium by summer semester 2005.

The rapid evolution of audio-photo-video recording capabilities through phones and inexpensive hand-held devices will create a flood of multimedia content. They will be immediately adopted by the current class of students and will be looked at with disinterest or uncertainty by many of the current faculty. Both distribution technologies will quickly create demand for more bandwidth and storage for that content, both for academic purposes and student-social activities. They will intensify the need for a centralized content management and monetization infrastructure, as well as an education support architecture to assist faculty in the integration of these technologies that will be demanded by the incoming class of students.

But in this challenge is also the opportunity to provide all new classes of services for on-campus, distance and life-long learners. In fact the greatest opportunities for these technologies are in the ways they will be used that have not been imagined yet. The portable and on-demand nature of podcasting and VODcasting make them technologies worth pursuing, implementing and supporting.

The Five Steps to Successful Podcasting

 start

1 Record and edit the Podcast.
Use the native record capability of your computer (use a microphone!) or simple recording software like FreeAmp, Peak Express, or ProTools. Save it as an MP3 file @ 32-64kps.

2 Put the MP3 file in an "RSS Enclosure"
You can either "hand code" them, use your blog software, or use special software like "Feedburner" or "Feed for All". There's lots of good tools and instruction on the web.

3 Changes are published to a blog or web site
Web or blog publishing software that supports RSS enclosures is required. This includes most current web creation software.

4 Set-up "news reader" software and let it run.
News reader software (try "iPodder", it's free and easy, or iPodderX - $39) will automatically download selected podcasts on the schedule set by the subscriber and put them directly into the folder of their favorite content management software (CMS).

5 Synchronize the media player with the subscribers computer
CMS software like iTunes, Windows Media Player or MusicMatch, that came with the subscribers digital media player, can be used to play, organize and synchronize podcasts.

Enjoy the Podcast
Now the subscriber can listen to *"Everything, Everytime, and Everywhere."*

end

The Five Steps to Successful VODcasting

start

1 Video tape and edit the VODcast.
Use a DV camera and good lighting to shoot video. Edit it with a simple but powerful editing program like iMovie or Adobe Premiere Elements. Then compress to MPEG4 or a streaming web format.

2 Put the MPEG file in an "RSS Enclosure"
You can either "hand code' them, use your blog software, or use special software like "Feedburner" or "Feed for All". There's lots of good tools and instruction on the web.

3 Changes are published to a vlog or web site
Web or blog publishing software that supports RSS enclosures is required. This includes most current web creation software.

4 Set-up "news reader" software and let it run.
It will automatically download your selected VODcasts on the schedule you set and put them directly into the folder of your favorite player. News readers can be found throughout the Internet.

5 Synchronize your PMA with your computer
Simply use the software that came with your Personal Media Assistant like Adobe Album or iPhoto or just watch it on your laptop!

Enjoy the VODcast
Now the subscriber can listen to *"Everything, Everytime, and Everywhere."*

 end

Resources

The following resource list will be seriously dated before this document is distributed for the first time. The number of portals, Web sites, blogs, and vlogs that are providing podcast and VODcast services is literally changing by the hour. Many of these sites will continue to change and evolve with the technology. Some of them will eventually transform into full-blown news or entertainment sites before year's end. The items found here are a starting point.

Articles

Oct 8, 2004. "*Podcasts: New Twist on Audio*". *Wired News* article by Daniel Terdiman.

Oct 23, 2004. "*Podcast: Time-shifted radio listening gets a new name*". Webtalk Radio.

Oct 28, 2004. "*New Food for iPods: Audio by Subscription*". *New York Times* article by *Cyrus Farivar*. (subscription required.)

Dec 2, 2004. "*Personal soundtracks*". *The Guardian* article by *Ben Hammersley.*

Dec 7, 2004. "*Tivo for your iPod*". A Newsweek article by Brian Braiker that describes podcasting to the layreader.

Dec 8, 2004. "*The people's radio*". An article on audiobloggers featured in *The Independent.*

Dec 10, 2004. "'*Podcast' your world*". *Christian Science Monitor* article by *Stephen Humphries* on podcasting.

Dec 30, 2004. "*Podcasts bring DIY radio to the web*". *BBC News Online* article on podcasting.

Jan 7, 2005. "*Podcasting: The Next Big Thing?*". KUOW 94.9 FM Puget Sound Public Radio (*NPR*) segment on podcasting.

Feb 7, 2005. '*Podcasting' Lets Masses Do Radio Shows. USA Today* article by Matthew Fordhal.

Feb 7, 2005. '*Podcasting' takes broadcasting to the Internet CNN.*

Feb 8, 2005. "*Wave goodbye to radio*" *Portland Tribune* article by Anna Johns.

Feb 9, 2005. "*Radio to the MP3 Degree: Podcasting*" *USA Today* article by Byron Acohido.

Feb 13, 2005. "'*Podcasters' deliver radio-on-demand*" *New Scientist* article by Celeste Biever.

Feb 16, 2005. "*Millions buy MP3 players in US*" *BBC* describes the take up of digital music players in the US.

Feb 19, 2005. "*Tired of TiVo? Beyond Blogs? Podcasts Are Here*" New York Times.

Feb 22, 2005. "*Adam Curry Wants to Make You an iPod Radio Star*" Wired.

Information

Podcast & Portable Media Expo: Trade show and conference for podcasters.

Podcast Alley: The podcast portal for everything about podcasting and a comprehensive listing of currently available podcasts (growing by more then 100 podcasts per day!).

podCast411. How to Information for Podcasting. Including How to hand code an RSS Feed and How to Explain Podcasting to the Technically Challenged (Flashing 12s).

Yahoo! Podcasters mailing list. A mailing list for podcasters and podcast listeners to communicate about podcasting for the iPodder platform.

iPodder.org: The official IPodder website.

Type II Technology Applications in Teacher Education

Using Instant Messenger to Implement Structured Online Class Discussions

LIH-CHING CHEN WANG AND WILLIAM BEASLEY

The use of the Instant Messenger (IM) environment to carry out structured online class discussions in graduate teacher education courses is described. Properties of IM are delineated, and specific procedures in using IM as a vehicle for class discussions are discussed. Attributes of Type II technology applications are addressed directly, and the characteristics of these class activities that correspond with such attributes are discussed in detail. In closing, the authors draw a clear distinction between casual IM use in a class setting and planned, structured implementation of IM as an example of a Type II technology application.

Much work in the field of computer-mediated communications (CMC) has focused on the use of tools such as computer conferencing in education. Brand (1988, p. xiii) noted significantly that "communications media are so fundamental to a society that when their structure changes, everything is affected." Eastmond (1994) proposed a systematic model for factors involved in using computer conferencing in adult distance education classes. Harasim, Hiltz, Teles, and Turoff (1995) articulated a variety of specific asynchronous online learning activities and made a strong case for these activities as fostering interaction both among students and between students and instructors.

Lauzon (1992) noted the challenge faced by distance educators to move students from being recipients of knowledge to being active participants—clearly a constructivist perspective. Bullen (1998) provided a thoughtful case study of a university-level course delivered by computer conferencing, and closely examined the effect of the technology on class participation and critical thinking. Meanwhile, Eastmond and Granger (1998) used computer conferencing, referred to as Type II technology, to enhance instructional communication.

Bullen's computer conferencing was implicitly an *asynchronous* activity, and in fact, much of Bullen's analysis was focused on that attribute of the learning experience. This article reports on a similar but significantly different technology—that of instant messaging (IM). IM is implicitly *synchronous*, but otherwise involves students gathering online in a shared text-only environment for class activities very much as does an asynchronous threaded discussion.

What is Instant Messenger (IM)?

IM software allows conversations between two or more individuals online in real time. It is much like Citizens Band radio in that it provides a "shared space" in which semi-public communication can occur, but IM takes place via keyboards rather than microphones, and on the Internet rather than the radio airwaves. Most IM programs are free to be downloaded from the Internet; two of the best known IM programs in recent times are America Online Instant Messenger (AIM) and Microsoft Network (MSN) Messenger.

The popularity (and feature set) of these programs has increased dramatically, and with these changes has come an increasing willingness on the part of educators to use IM to enhance teaching and learning activities. One of the authors has been using AIM software both for student advising and for structured class learning activities for five semesters at the time of this writing, and has found the process to be both complex and valuable.

The purpose of this paper is not to report formal data analysis, but to report the experiences observed directly by the instructor in the process of using IM for instructional purposes, and to provide more information about one potential instructional Type II technique that may be of value to other teachers and students.

Methodology

Context and Design

The activities described were conducted with graduate students from an educational technology program in teacher education at a Midwestern urban state university. They were mostly in-service K-12 educators.

The class format was Internet-based with the exception of two face-to-face class meetings. One was an initial introductory class occurring at the beginning of the semester, and the other was used for final project presentations and held at the end of the semester. All other class activities took place online. The class met once a week for four hours in the online environment, including one hour of formal online chapter discussion entirely in the IM environment; the instructor deliberately limited formal discussion to one hour at a time to avoid student fatigue and maximize efficiency. The other three hours of class time included activities such as student use of the class file server for class activities, online peer communications or collaborations on class-related activities, and use of the instructor's online office hours. See Wang and Beasley for more details on the integration of IM into online office hours.

Procedure

Skills. At the initial class session, all students were taught how to download and install the (free) AIM software. Students were taught a set of basic AIM skills, including those involved in carrying out a discussion and saving the contents of the discussion to disk. They were also taught to upload and download files using a class file server, in order to ensure their ability to post and read materials provided by any member of the class. Students learned that during the rest of the semester they would be required to participate in a series of class discussions, centering around assigned topics drawn from major chapters in the required class text. The discussions would take place entirely within the IM environment and would occur on a schedule to be provided by the instructor. Students were informed that their contributions should be chapter related and that the frequency of each student's participation in the discussion would be noted by the instructor.

To encourage students to quickly master the IM environment, the instructor actively promoted student use of IM for contacts between student and instructor as well as for contacts among classmates outside of class. During the second week, student use of IM consisted entirely of this type of contact, and students were able to consult actively with their classmates as well as with the instructor regarding any problems with using the IM software; they were also encouraged to use IM to interact with the classmate who was scheduled to lead the first discussion. After the second week, the main focus shifted to the use of IM for structured class discussions. At this time the "screen names" (aliases) employed by AIM were made available as a list to all class members, enabling any student to initiate contact with the entire class using a single mouse click within the IM environment.

Discussion leaders. The requirements for fulfilling the leader role were substantial and thoroughly documented in materials provided to the students. The instructor played an active role in choosing the leaders of the first discussions, in an effort to ensure a successful first encounter, though initial leaders were chosen with the full consent of the individual students involved.

Each leader was required to prepare a presentation Power-Point file that included preparatory materials for the topic he/she chose to lead in the discussion. Required contents included: (a) summary of the chapter, (b) feedback or critique on the chapter, (c) examples of situations drawn from the chapter that he/she could implement into a student teaching or learning setting, and (d) at least three critical inquiry questions drawn from the chapter. The file itself, along with a word-processed document addressing chapter details, was submitted by the discussion leader to the common folder in the class file server three days before the discussion.

The leader was required to log in to the discussion at least 15 minutes prior to the starting time to prepare for the discussion activities and/or to chat informally with any classmates online. At the appointed time, the leader was to invite classmates into the scheduled group chat. During the discussion, it was the student leader's role to initiate the discussion by posting discussion questions drawn from the previously distributed PowerPoint and word processor files. His/her task was then to be the teacher of the moment, to answer questions raised by the participants and to stimulate or facilitate the discussion process.

It should be noted that the instructor did not "disappear" from the discussion. Throughout the online discussion period, the instructor also participated with the students. The instructor took the online attendance, invited late-comers into the group chat, observed the discussion, answered individual inquiries, asked questions, solved problems, and facilitated the discussion as needed. In many ways, the course instructor served as a teaching assistant to the leader during these discussion periods. At the end of discussion, the leader was required to save the discussion transcript and distribute to the class.

Individual participants. After each student leader posted the chapter files in the common folder of the class file server, but before the discussion session, all other students were asked to access these files and organize their thoughts in preparation for the discussion. They were encouraged to post and share their own chapter commentary with the rest of the class, using the class file server, and awarded bonus points for doing so.

All students were required to log in to the discussion area 10 minutes prior to the scheduled discussion time. After the discussion was over (but prior to the next scheduled discussion), each participant was to electronically organize personal reflections, feedback, and notes on the chapter and then post these to his/her own personal electronic portfolio (ePortfolio) on the class file server for evaluation. Online attendance, quantity and quality of a student's online interaction, and ePortfolio constituted 10% of a student's final grade.

Outcomes. The introductory procedures worked well. All class members were able to log on at the appointed time for the first discussion, and all were able to enter the designated AIM discussion group. The assigned discussion leaders followed all guidelines provided by the instructor, showing up online 15 minutes before the discussion time, and taking care to "invite" those participants who were wandering around "outside" into the designated discussion group. The online discussions proceeded as expected, with facilitation primarily from the assigned student leader, and the instructor in the background to observe and assist.

An interesting development was the fact that less-knowledgeable students in the group continued to expand and enhance the complexity of their IM skills throughout the semester, through individual interaction with their more competent classmates as well as with the instructor. While the introductory lessons and practice in the use of AIM were sufficient to bring all students to an adequate level of competency, it quickly became evident that there was a wide range of skills in the group, and those with less mastery aspired to emulate their more sophisticated classmates.

IM-Based Learning Activities as Type II Technology Applications

Maddux, Johnson, and Willis (2001) have suggested that technology applications in education can by categorized into two types. Type I applications focus on providing more convenient or efficient ways of carrying out traditional learning or teaching activities, and tend to involve a teacher-centered focus. Type II applications are more student-centered, and focus on providing ways to teach or learn that are not possible (or practical) in the absence of technology. In explaining their categorization, they specified five characteristics of Type II applications. As implemented in the instructor's own experience, IM embodies these five characteristics in the following ways (summarized in Table 1).

Since it is abundantly clear that simply using IM in a classroom setting does not automatically create a Type II technology use scenario, we will examine in greater detail the ways in which this particular class implementation of IM embodies these five characteristics, focusing on one example through

which the appropriate use of IM may legitimately be described as "Type II."

Type II Activities Stimulate Relatively Active Intellectual Involvement

Well-orchestrated classroom discussions have long been chosen as a learning activity in order to stimulate active intellectual involvement on the part of students, and the techniques of assigning students to discussion leadership roles and requiring structured discussion preparation are time-honored procedures within traditional instruction. In our situation, IM software was used to implement these procedures in a relatively novel environment—one in which the class participants were not in physical proximity to one another.

Every student in the class was assigned to lead a formally scheduled chapter discussion within the IM environment. This role placed three major demands on an individual student: the first was a substantial level of formal preparation regarding the chapter contents; the second was to serve as the discussion leader and facilitator throughout the hour of the online session; the third was to distribute to all class members a transcript of the discussion after its conclusion. These individuals were in effect "teacher for a day." To carry out these demands required an intensively active involvement on the part of the discussion leader, and as has been noted, every student fulfilled the role of discussion leader at some point during the semester.

While individual participants were subject to fewer demands, all students were required to actively participate in all discussions. As noted, attendance was required, quality of participation was monitored, and all students were to post their reflections and thoughts about each discussion. The fact that all discussion content was automatically archived made it easy to determine quality and quantity of participation for each class member.

While the most active intellectual involvement in each discussion was that of the assigned discussion leader, the combination of the IM environment with structured participation requirements clearly stimulated relatively active intellectual involvement on the part of other individuals in the class.

Type II Activities Place the Learner Rather Than the Developer (e.g., Teacher) in Charge of the Learning Environment

In many ways the IM environment is highly egalitarian. It was originally developed not for instructional purposes, but for the use of individuals who wished to communicate synchronously with friends and colleagues. Its structure is built around an equal level of "power" to all participants. The only special capability available is the power of an individual who originates an online discussion to control the entry of others into that discussion area. In the context of this class, the teacher was the one figure who originated the class discussions, and thus retained that power. As it happens, any student could theoretically have set up another

Table 1 Summary of IM-Based Learning Activities as Type II Technology Applications

Characteristics (Type II activities)	IM Properties (as implemented)
1. Stimulate relatively active intellectual involvement	• Student was assigned the responsibility for leading and moderating chapter discussions (student as an active instructor) • All students were required to actively participate in each discussion session
2. Place the learner rather the developer (e.g., teacher) in charge of the learning environment	• Student and instructor have almost equal levels of control over IM environment, although instructor can still control access to discussions • Students retain full ability for communication among one another "on the side" without instructor's knowledge or control
3. Provide the learner with control over the interaction between the user and the machine, with extensive repertoire of acceptable user input	• Students have control over individual forms of expression within IM software (e.g., colors, styles, emoticons) • Student and instructor both have simultaneous access to other programs (e.g., PowerPoint, word processor, Web browser, spreadsheet) with ability to move among programs and discussion during live discussion
4. Have the accomplishment of creative tasks as their goal	• Collaborative discussion (an intrinsically creative action) led by students is explicit goal of IM activities in this situation • Archived discussion contents in text form are automated, readily distributable and extensible
5. Require many hours to discover full potential of the software or software-based activity	• Full repertoire of IM-based discussion techniques (e.g., interweaving other resources live, employing private side conversations) takes significant time to master

discussion, over which he or she would have retained control in the same sense. The teacher in this context is "first among equals" with regard to power over the discussion environment.

As the class discussions were simply one group conversation taking place in the IM environment, students were able not only to participate in other online discussions at the same time, but also to enter into private "side conversations"—either with other class members, or with other individuals present in the IM environment. Obviously, this is not entirely positive, but it *is* a clear indication that students retain a high degree of control over the learning environment. The instructor has the same capability, and it was often used for private conversations between instructor and student "on the fly"—a sort of ad hoc online office hours in mid-discussion.

It is clear that in this IM-based learning environment, students and instructor shared an almost equal level of control over the learning environment, freeing students from the traditionally passive role of information recipient and shifting the instructor into a facilitator role.

Type II Activities Provide the Learner with Control Over the Interaction Between the User and the Machine, with Extensive Repertoire of Acceptable User Input

This third characteristic focuses on what happens *within* the context of IM-based learning. Formatted text, essentially limited to

the characters available on a computer keyboard plus a limited selection of standardized icons (e.g., "smiley faces"), is the primary medium of IM communication. While this sounds limited, in skilled hands a surprising variety of techniques is possible, ranging from the use of emoticons to convey body language or emotional content (e.g., ";-)" to indicate a winking) to the use of URLs within IM to allow immediate links to Web pages containing images or auditory content that can be incorporated into an IM discussion. Each participant in IM retains control over these components, as well as other related variables such as text color, size, font, and style. In this respect, control over form of expression within IM is absolutely equal between student and instructor; each has the same tool set.

Since the IM client is simply one program among many on a computer's desktop, each participant retains access to other software on his/her computer while the IM discussion is in progress. One may move freely among the programs, and use information from these other programs to inform the discussion. For example, if numbers and calculations enter the discussion, any participant can fire up Excel on the side and check a set of figures, bringing the results back into the IM environment via copy and paste. Another common example: in mid-discussion, a participant may launch a Web browser and conduct a quick Google search for relevant Web pages. This information is promptly pasted into the IM environment, and all other participants are enabled to link immediately to the relevant source in mid-discussion. These capabilities were actively used by the students, who also regularly used PowerPoint and Word during IM discussions to refer back to information provided by each student discussion leader in advance of each discussion.

It is clear that through activities such as using different modes of expression within the IM environment and navigating among varied programs simultaneously during IM discussions, the IM-based environment can provide learners with control over the interaction between the user and the machine, allowing for an extensive repertoire of acceptable student input.

Type II Activities Have the Accomplishment of Creative Tasks as Their Goal

A fundamental concept underlying Type II activities is that they are intended for the accomplishment of a creative task. A collaborative discussion, properly conducted, is an intrinsically creative task. As implemented in this particular case, each discussion was led by a student who was required to prepare intensively for the event, creating and distributing in advance to classmates materials dealing with a particular set of concepts. This preparation was itself a creative activity, but the real point was the discussion itself as it evolved online in the IM environment. Such a discussion incorporates unique and highly individualized perspectives on the topic(s) at hand from the viewpoint of each student in the class, resulting in a tapestry of ideas that is different each time such a discussion occurs.

This would be true of a high-quality class discussion, even if technology were not involved—but the incorporation of the IM environment brings an additional set of properties to the process that strengthens and enhances student interaction with the content of the discussion. When such a discussion takes place using IM, the entire discussion in text form is automatically archived, readily distributable and extensible, forming the basis for further elaboration at a later time. This concurs with Ligorio's (2001) statement that providing chances for re-reading and reflecting on what has been written facilitates the immediacy of the synchronous online chatting process. The result is that an IM-based discussion—as a creative act—can continue over an extended period of time following the original discussion, producing a continuously expanding and evolving creative dialogue to address the original discussion topics.

Type II Activities Require Many Hours to Discover Full Potential of the Software or Software-Based Activity

Using this characteristic to describe IM-based discussions is a slight departure from Maddux, Johnson, and Willis's (2001) use of "Type II" to characterize specific pieces of software (e.g., the "Sim" series). As a piece of software, IM is not a complex program that requires long hours of discovery—but it does in fact require many hours of use for an instructor (and students) to discover all the ways in which a rich, deep, multi-faceted, and technologically interwoven group discussion can take place in an IM environment. The skills necessary for a student to simply

participate in an IM discussion are easily mastered, but experience shows that the IM environment has the potential for surprising depth through the incorporation of specific techniques that extend the range of the discussion to incorporate far more than simply verbal statements from individuals. Two techniques that were used heavily during these discussions were individual side conversations (both between instructor and student, and between pairs of students) and the incorporation into the discussion of information gleaned from the use of other programs running simultaneously on a student's or instructor's computer (e.g., URLs from concurrent Web searches). Clearly, full mastery of all the discussion-related potential of the IM environment requires considerable time and practice to master.

Limitations

In both traditional and IM-based discussions, there are certain commonalities. In both cases, the instructor has an opportunity to prepare students for the discussion ahead of time, and to establish expectations and parameters intended to guide the discussion. In both cases, all students have the potential to participate in the discussion, albeit via two different media (voice or keyboard). In both cases, the instructor can check attendance for all students participating. In both cases, the instructor can be present and can respond directly to student questions either privately or in such a way that the entire group can be aware of the question and answer.

The IM environment itself has certain limitations that are not present in a more traditional class setting, and it is important to acknowledge those; many are due to IM's reliance on text-based communication. Although most students type more slowly than they speak, IM requires individual expression to take place via the keyboard—and although some students comprehend (and compose) the spoken word more readily than the written word, all IM communication uses the written word. Non-verbal cues (e.g., body language, tone of voice) are largely absent in the IM environment, and when present are done using artificial means such as emoticons, which do not come naturally to new users. Unlike a traditional discussion in which protocol dictates that only one person speak at a time, IM discussions allow many simultaneous "speakers"—which can result in the phenomenon of "flooding," in which one's screen fills rapidly with too much content in too many threads from too many participants and rapidly overwhelms novice users. IM software accepts only a limited number of text characters in each posting, resulting in a need to break long statements into multiple postings, which may become separated by content from other participants and thus rendered less intact conceptually. All in all, the attributes of an entirely text-based exchange of ideas are sufficiently unfamiliar to some students to serve as a discouraging factor, potentially reducing their participation.

Two other limitations of the IM environment are due to its highly technological roots. It relies heavily on a reliable Internet connection for all participants, and it requires an instructor or moderator able to "think fast" and act on his/her feet due both to simultaneity of student response and to a need to troubleshoot occasional software or equipment difficulties in mid-discussion.

Conclusion

This paper is rooted in the concept of Type II technology applications; as Maddux, Johnson, and Willis (2001) have noted, such activities go beyond simply automating traditional learning applications and enable learning activities that would not be feasible without technology. Since this paper is also focused on class discussion, and since class discussion can be a very traditional learning application, the burden placed upon this paper is that of demonstrating that, when correctly planned and implemented, the use of an IM environment for class discussion does in fact go beyond simply automating what would take place in a traditional classroom, even though it takes place synchronously and covers much of the same course content.

Moving class discussions into IM causes the discussion to become logically independent of the participants' physical location. While useful and perhaps even essential in the case of distance education courses, it is doubtful whether this property alone is sufficient to warrant a Type II descriptor. Simply holding class discussions using IM does not in and of itself constitute a Type II technology application; it is the *way* in which class discussions are held using IM that can make the difference.

This paper has documented the instructor's methodology for moving IM-based classroom discussions solidly into the Type II arena. First, the instructor required all students to take on the role of discussion leader, and provided structure for the actions required of the discussion leader in advance preparation and discussion moderation. The instructor also made quantity and quality of participation in the online discussions part of the class evaluation scheme, and followed up by taking roll online and monitoring student participation. These actions stimulated relatively active intellectual involvement.

Second, the instructor chose to use the IM environment (as opposed to other possible text-based synchronous environments, such as IRC or WebCT chat), which preserved a high level of individual student control over the environment in which the discussions took place. This placed the learner in charge of the learning environment, including providing students with the ability to carry on multiple parallel communications or activities during the class discussion.

Third, rather than imposing a limited and formal structure for communication within the discussion, the instructor embraced the variety available within IM, welcoming student use of colors, styles, and icons and actively encouraging students to make use of multiple programs during class discussions in order to provide deeper and more complex fuel for the conversation at hand. This gave learners a large degree of control over the interaction within the IM environment and encouraged a maximum richness of content.

Fourth, the instructor built student-led chapter discussions into the structure of the course, including the active distribution of archived discussions to all participants and an individual *e*Portfolio area where students posted their reflections, observations, and questions about discussions after the fact. The resulting discussions and associated communications came to constitute an extended, group-authored creative task and were one of the main goals of the class.

Finally, the instructor chose to forego a strictly limited tool or implementation in favor of a relatively complex tool that may be quickly and easily used for simple activities but that requires many hours to master, and to directly encourage students to pursue the deepest and most complex ways of using the chosen tool—thus fulfilling the final Type II characteristic of requiring many hours to discover the full potential of the activity.

In summary, the type of IM-based class discussions and their attendant online interactions described herein fully embody the characteristics of Type II technology applications, and as such provide a powerful learning tool that can be used with traditional classes but has particular application to distance learning courses. It is the experience of the instructor that these activities empower students to use technology to create their own learning environments filled with enthusiasm and self-motivation—one of the best settings for teaching and learning success.

References

Brand, S. (1988). *The media lab: Inventing the future at MIT.* New York: Penguin Books.

Bullen, M. (1998). Participation and critical thinking in online university distance education. *Journal of Distance Education, 13*(2) [Online]. Retrieved February 20, 2004, from http://cade.athabascau.ca/vol13.2/bullen.html

Eastmond, D. (1994). Adult distance study through computer conferencing. *Distance Education, 15*(1), 128–152.

Eastmond, D., & Granger, D. (1998). Using Type II computer network technology to reach distance students. *Distance Education Report, 2*(3), 1–3 & 8.

Harasim, L., Hiltz, S., Teles, L., & Turoff, M. (1995). *Learning networks: A field guide to teaching and learning online.* Cambridge, MA: MIT Press.

Lauzon, A. C. (1992). Integrating computer-based instruction with computer conferencing: An evaluation of a model for designing online education. *American Journal of Distance Education, 6*(2), 32–46.

Ligorio, M. B. (2001). Integrating communication formats: Synchronous versus asynchronous and text-based versus visual. *Computers & Education, 37*(2), 103–125.

Maddux, C., Johnson, D., & Willis, J. (2001). *Educational computing: Learning with tomorrow's technology* (3rd ed.). Boston: Allyn & Bacon.

Wang, L. C., & Beasley, W. Integrating Instant Messenger into online office hours to enhance synchronous online interaction in teacher education. *International Journal of Instructional Media, 33*(3).

LIH-CHING CHEN WANG is Associate Professor of Educational Technology, Department of Curriculum and Foundations, College of Education and Human Services, Cleveland State University, Cleveland, OH 44115-2214 (E-mail: l.c.wang@csuohio.edu).

WILLIAM BEASLEY is Associate Professor of Educational Technology, Department of Curriculum and Foundations, College of Education and Human Services, and Director of the University Center for Teaching & Learning, Cleveland State University, Cleveland, OH 44115-2214 (E-mail: w.beasley@csuohio.edu).

From *Computers in the Schools,* Vol. 22, issue 1/2, 2005, pp. 71–84. Copyright © 2005 by Haworth Press. Reprinted by permission.

UNIT 4

Teacher Training

Unit Selections

Key Points to Consider

- Will communication technology such as an e-mail, threaded discussion groups, and chat rooms become a major part of teacher education? Why or why not?

- Will schools of education focus on structuring telecommunications to create a distributed learning environment for student teachers? Explain your answer.

- What will the classroom of tomorrow look like? How will it be equipped? What are the benefits of such a classroom to teachers and students?

- What effect do the implementation of instructional design and the use of application software have on teacher education?

Student Web Site

www.mhcls.com/online

Internet References

Further information regarding these Web sites may be found in this book's preface or online.

Boulder Valley School District Home Page
http://www.bvsd.k12.co.us

Canada's Schoolnet Staff Room
http://www.schoolnet.ca/home/e/resources

Teacher Support
http://quest.nasa.gov/services/teacher.html

Teachers Guide to the Department of Education
http://www.ed.gov/pubs/TeachersGuide

The History Channel
http://www.historychannel.com

The goal of teacher education should be to advance all aspects of education, including fundamental research, technology, curriculum, and professional development. However, the most important product derived from teacher education over the past two decades has been the emergence of a vision of what technology has to offer education. Earlier thinking focused on technology as supporting the rote and mechanical aspects of learning (drill and practice). The new vision focuses on using technology to support excellence in learning (searching, inferencing, deciding). In this vision, students tackle much harder projects, work on larger-scale and more meaningful projects, have a greater and more reflective responsibility for their own learning, and are able to work in a variety of styles that reflect differences in gender, ethnicity or simply individual personality. This new vision shows that creative use of technology by skilled teachers offers a promise to quickly and effectively restructure education as we know it. The new vision will ensure that students are afforded classroom or at-a-distance instruction at a pace that suits their learning styles and in a way that gives them

a more active role in the learning process. Schools must provide adequate teacher training, at both preservice and inservice levels, that enables teachers to become fully aware of and skilled in using the vast resources that today's technology offers.

The articles presented in this unit provide evidence that action is being taken to bring the benefits of technology to teachers as well as students. In the first report, Tugba Yanpar Sahin presents a new course for elementary student teachers that has been developed at the Zonguldak Karaelmas University in Turkey. This article reports on a study of the course during the academic year 2000-2001 and concludes that a *constructivist approach* should be adopted.

In "Accessing and Monitoring Student Progress in an E-Learning Personnel Preparation Environment" the authors draw upon their personal online teaching experience in addressing strategies for assessing student performance and using electronic portfolios in e-learning environments. Both aspects are presented as integral parts of the e-learning instructional process. Perspectives from the literature and lessons learned from authors are also shared.

Next, McCannon and Crews found that computers are prevalent in schools but they are being used for administrative tasks instead of part of the student learning process. The researchers recommended that teacher educators offer staff development courses in curriculum integration—presentation software and research—using the World Wide Web and CD-ROMs.

This unit brings home the fact that teaching multimedia to computing majors is no longer new. The multimedia course experiences reported on herein, however, put a new slant on the topic—because of the target audience. The course pedagogy and target audience interests are outlined with only passing mentions of specific software. This is based on the belief that university computing professors should strive to understand K-12 problems before they offer technology solutions. Some fresh classroom challenges for teachers and professors, as well as possible far-reaching benefits, are also noted.

Student Teachers' Perceptions of Instructional Technology: Developing Materials Based on a Constructivist Approach

A new course for elementary student teachers has been developed at the Zonguldak Karaelmas University in Turkey. This article reports on a study of the course during the academic year 2000–2001 and conclude that a constructivist approach should be adopted.

TUGBA YANPAR SAHIN

Introduction

Teacher education programmes need to incorporate technology for teaching and learning across the curriculum. Students on such programmes must have opportunities to apply these new technologies in a classroom setting and must also be shown that the use of technology can be more efficient and effective than traditional methods (Brennan, 2000, 2). The goal of many teacher education programs is to help future teachers to perceive technology as meaningful, authentic and necessary for their work (Duran, 2000, 5).

Betrus (2000) studied the content and emphasis of the introductory technology course for undergraduate pre-service teachers and found that the current version of the course was focused primarily on computer based content, entailing a decreased emphasis on traditional audiovisual technologies compared to such courses in the past.

Duran (2000) looked at the integration of technology integration into an elementary teacher education programme. His findings indicated that the preservice elementary teachers were not provided with the experiences they needed to use information technology in their future classrooms. He recommended that, in order to increase new teachers' technological proficiency, the institutions should increase the level of technology integration in their own programmes so that information technology should be integrated into methods and curriculum courses rather than being limited to stand-alone technology classes.

Shuell and Farber (2001) studied students' perceptions of technology use in college courses. Seven hundred twenty-eight undergraduate and graduate students completed a questionnaire on the use of technology in one of their courses. The respondents were generally very positive about the use of technology, with no major differences across class-level (freshmen to graduate). Computer-based technologies are increasingly being used in classroom teaching at all levels and student teachers have to become familiar with them.

In Turkey, teacher education progammes include a course on instructional technologies and material development, and in the Higher Education Centre at the Zonguldak Karaelmas University, College of Education the course is given in the 5th semester. The course includes (YÖK, 1998):

- the characteristics of different instructional technologies
- uses of these technologies
- the development of instructional materials (including overhead transparencies, video and computer based materials
- the evaluation of different materials

The teaching-learning process was not taken into account in developing the course and all of the instructors' teaching methods are different. Dome instructors use computer based methods while others use a range of different media. Since these courses are important, standards covering process as well as content, have been determined by The Higher Education Centre. This article examines the constructivist perspectives for this course.

Constructivism has been the subject of many research studies over the last decade. A central tenet is that learning is an active process and that learning is determined by the complex interlay among learners' existing knowledge, the social context, and the problem to be solved (Tam, 2000). Constructivism has encouraged teachers and curriculum developers to alter their perceptions of children from individuals who are irrational and unknowing to cognisant beings with well-developed theories. Constructivists have rightly turned their attention to the learner arguing correctly that he or she is responsible for their own learning (Osborne and Wittrock, 1985; Novak and Gowin, 1984; Pope, 1985; White, 1988). The evidence from research on learning styles would suggest *that there is no single effective method* for teaching and learning since students differ in their preferences (Osborne, 1996).

Students are active participants in the process of learning, with multiple learning styles, employing group activities, brain storming, interpretive discussion etc. The constructivist teacher encourages students to connect and summarise concepts by analyzing, predicting, justifying, and defending their ideas. The teacher produces opportunities for students to test their hypotheses, especially through group discussion of concrete experiences. The constructivist approach involves students in real-world possibilities, then helps them generate the abstractions that bind phenomena together. In a Constructivist Classroom student autonomy and initiative are accepted and encouraged. The teacher asks open-ended questions and allows time for responses: higher-level thinking is encouraged. Students are engaged in dialogue with the teacher and with each other, and in experiences that challenge hypotheses and encourage discussion. The class uses raw data, primary sources, and physical, and interactive materials (Brooks and Brooks, 1993). The assessment is based on process rather than product. Evaluation in this culture is rigorous and multidimensional. It is focused on the quality of the learner's understanding, its depth, and its flexible application to related contexts (Lindschitl, 1999; Hu, 1997; Yen, 1999).

Constructivism provides ideas and principles about learning that have important implications for the construction of technology supported learning environments (Tam, 2000). One of these implications is the need to embed learning into authentic and meaningful contexts. Another is that learning is a personal, as well as a social activity. There can be more individual learning in a student sitting in front of his or her computer but the technology also allows much more diversified and socially rich learning contexts: for example peer tutoring via computer, computer networks, e-mail, and telecommunications.

In general, constructivist instructional approaches are criticised because they:

1. Are costly to develop (because they are inefficient)
2. Require technology for their implementation and
3. Are very difficult to evaluate (Tam, 2000).

The aim of this study was to explore the student teachers' perceptions of the Instructional Technology and Material Development course based on a constructivist approach and to build constructivist perspectives for teaching and learning process of this course.

Method

The study used a sample of 80 student teachers who took the instructional technologies and material development course in an elementary teacher education program at Eregli College of Education in Turkey. The course was scheduled to take 4 hours each week. Thirty of the students were in the 3rd grade and the remaining fifty were in the fourth grade at the beginning of the spring semester in 2000–2001. The learning process was different for the 3rd and for the 4th grade students. The former were taught in small groups while the 4th grade students, who had taken the original version of the course the previous year, were dealt with as individuals. Both sets were in their fifth semester.

A qualitative research methodology was used: eight open ended questions were used to determine student perceptions:

1. What was your score on the instructional technologies and material development course?
2. What the process of the course? What did you do?
3. When were you active? How? While you were active, what kind of prior knowledge did you use?
4. Were you happy in this course? What do you think about student activity in this course?
5. What were the advanteges of this course?
6. How was the assessment? If you were an instructor for this course, how would you assess it?
7. What other process could be used in the course?
8. If you didn't take this course, what would you think about your competency?

Inductive coding techniques (described by Strauss and Corbin, 1990) were used for the analyses. The responses were collected and encoded and then reviewed line by line, typically within a paragraph. Beside or below the paragraph, categories or labels are reviewed and, typically, a slightly more abstract category is attributed to several incidents or observations. The incidents can then be assigned a qualitative data category. Starting with a working set of codes that describe the phenomena in the transcribed field notes we then move to a second level that is more general and explanatory.

However, just naming or classifying the responses is usually insufficient: we need to understand the patterns and the underlying reasoning. Pattern codes can be explanatory or inferential, identifying an emergent theme, configuration, or explanation, and groups those summaries into a smaller number of sets, themes, or constructs (Miles and Huberman, 1994). The process is thus to:

- Underline key terms in the students' responses for eight open-ended questions
- Restate key phrases
- Coding key terms in the students' responses for questions
- Pattern coding
- Construct themes
- Summaries for themes
- Integrating theories in an explanatory framework

Procedures

The group of third grade students first observed and researched the elementary school, interviewing the elementary teachers in their city. They then acquired theoretical knowledge from textbooks, articles and their lecturer before forming groups of four to five students. In these groups they discussed and researched different learning-teaching materials and technologies, each group producing three or four different sets of materials (for example, some computer based materials for an elementary school course unit, a video, a three dimensional map and a set of transparencies). After showing and discussing the materials they used them in role play and subsequently discussed the process of the lesson and the quality of the materials. Each group was evaluated, both by students from another group and by the lecturer.

The fourth grade students worked as individuals in the preceding year. Each student prepared one or two sets of teaching materials for a course in elementary education but did not visit a school, observe or carry out interviews. Each student was evaluated, both by other students and by the lecturer.

Results

The perception of 3rd grade students is given in Table 1 which shows some of the codes for the students' responses in the elementary teacher education programme.

The codes, derived from prior research (Chung, 1991; Copley, 1992; Brooks and Brooks, 1993; Osborne, 1996; Lindschitl, 1999; Windschitl, 1999) focus on two themes. The responses indicate that 9.2% perceived themselves as being active and preferred group preparation of the materials. Factors that were important for success were enjoyment (80%), group lecturing (72%) and effort (72%). The production of original materials was rated as 68%, followed by research and observation at 56%.

Some of the third grade students' comments were:

"Effective teaching occurs when effective course materials are used. Being active can be defined as active production. We studied as a group. We made different materials. I learned by seeing, making and living. I like my score. Scores were objective."

"Being active is fine. We completed our materials and I was pleased with our production."

"We made research, material. I used my skills, I used computer, video etc other technologies. I enjoyed being active. We have to be active as the teachers of future."

"Learning is important rather than scores. I learned a lot of knowledge. Concrete materials are important for effective learning I learned concrete activities. I studied as a teacher. We evaluated our friends."

We can infer from these results that students liked this approach with group activities that supported cooperation and active learning. The constructivist learning process builds upon their prior knowledge and enables them to construct their materials and activities.

The perception of the fourth grade students is given in Table 2.

The results imply that the students were in complete agreement with the active lesson process (100%). The individual

Table 1 The Perceptions of 3rd Grade Students (N:50)

Code of Perceptions	Frequencies	%
The development of theoretical knowledge	20	40
The preparation of materials in a group	46	92
Lecture in a group	36	72
Research and observation	28	56
Being active	46	92
Prior-knowledge is needed from curriculum development and educational psychology courses	18	36
Lessons are pleasant and enjoyable	40	80
Producing original materials	34	68
Meaningful learning of teaching for elementary students	22	44
Assessment of the group with scores of this lesson were given to individuals	26	52
The process is important for assessment	18	36
The lesson must be learned by the individual	8	16
This course is useful for teaching development	24	48
Instructor is a guide for the student teacher	18	36
Make proposals and critiques on course materials prepared by the students	16	32
Sharing and cooperation within the group	16	32
This lesson must be group learning	16	32
Effort is very important for success in this lesson	36	72

Table 2 The Perceptions of 4th Grade Students (N:30)

Code of Perceptions	Frequencies	%
The development of theoretical knowledge	12	40.0
The preparation of materials by an individual	28	93.3
Lecture by an individual	26	86.6
Materials exhibition	10	33.3
Being active in this lesson	30	100
Prior-knowledge is needed from curriculum development and educational psychology courses	22	73.3
Lessons are pleasant and enjoyable	26	86.6
Producing original materials as an individual	26	86.6
Meaningful learning of teaching for elementary students	22	73.3
Scores of this lesson were given as process	28	93.3
Assessment was objective	18	60.0
This lesson must be learned by the individual	10	33.3
This course is useful for teaching development	18	60.0
Instructor is a guide for student teacher	18	60.0
Make proposals and critique on course materials prepared by the students	22	73.3

preparation of materials and the feedback of scores were seen as important by over 93% of the students. Other factors are the enjoyment of the lesson, the individual production of materials and the individual tutorials (all at 86.6%) with other high scores for the meaningful learning of the teaching process and prior knowledge of curriculum development and educational psychology (73.3%).

Some of the fourth grade students' comments were:

"I made my material. I was an active learner. After I made my material, I presented it to my friends as an example elementary course. I learned the preparation of different materials with different technologies. Also, I observed my friends and evaluated their materials with my class and my lecturer."

"Students can be evaluated according to the usefulness of their materials and their active participation. I learned curriculum development before the lesson. But these lessons are better than before, because, I learned different materials and technologies in instructional technologies and materials development course."

"I was active throughout this lesson. Being active is useful for academic self concept and positive attitudes. The students were evaluated with their efforts, their original products and uses of these materials and technologies for the lesson of the elementary school."

These results show that active learning is important for an instructional technology and material development course. The candidate teachers like the approach because it helped them to prepare different materials in the future. Both group and individual work can support active learning.

These qualitative findings support the notion of a direct link between active learning and students' positive perceptions of instructional technology and material development course based on constructivist learning.

Conclusion and discussion

A new course, using a constructivist approach, in instructional technology and material development for students in elementary teacher education programs in Turkey has been investigated and provided some insights into the constructivist learning process. The data collected on two groups were coded in a search for evidence of an active approach, the development of materials, and enjoyment of the lesson.

In general, students perceived the use of the constructivist approach to be very beneficial. Over 90% said that being active is important for this course and those students who were actively engaged were more likely to perceive positive effect of constructivist approach as a learning process, reflecting the importance of active learning. Students in this course were more likely to indicate that the constructivist approach increased the quality of interaction with their peers when studying or developing materials together. The students who agreed strongly that they learn more when the instructor guides course activities responded more favorably to the learning benefits associated with constructivism.

A theme that developed through the open-ended items was the appreciation for learning by many students. The major outcomes from the research were:

- That both the interview and writing data appear to confirm that the constructivist practices had a highly positive impact on the way the student teachers perceived the teaching learning processes in the instructional technology and material development course.

- A suggestion that constructivist learning activities foster active learning. The research provided strong indications for implementation of constructivism in the teacher education.

- Prior knowledge is very important for a student's subsequent achievement. A constructivist approach can be used because student teachers have prior knowledge and extensive experience. Active participation should be provided continuously. The students can either study in groups or individually. The instructors should be co-learners and guides for the students. Assessment should be based on the lesson process. The efforts of the students, active participation and material development process, cooperation, etc should be evaluated by the other students and instructor.

- Uses of technology are important for teacher education and so student teachers must learn about technology and its effect on education—and about technology and constructivism. A comprehensive technology laboratory must be available in teacher education facilities to enable students to produce their own materials.

This study presents a qualitative study for the teacher education program but the generalization of the results may be limited because, the pre-service teacher candidates who participated in the study were enrolled in a single university. Future studies may be carried out on different samples.

References

Betrus A K (2000) The content and emphasis of the Introductory Technology course for undergraduate pre-service teachers *PhD.* Indiana University.

Brennan J P (2000) Preservice teachers and administrators' perceptions of instructional technology infusion *EdD.* The University of Southern Mississippi.

Brooks J G and Brooks M G (1993) *In search of understanding: the case for constructivist classrooms* Association For The Supervision and Curriculum Development, Alexandra, VA.

Chung J (1991) Collaborative learning strategies: the design of instructional environment for the emerging new school *Educational Technology* **31** (6) 15–22.

Copley J (1992) The integration of teacher education and technology: a constructivist model in D Carey, R Carey, D Willis and S Willis (eds) *Technology and teacher education,* AACE Charlottesville, VA, 681.

Duran M (2000) Examination of technology integration into an elementary teacher education program: one university's experience *PhD.* Ohio University.

Hu C W (1997) Research on elementary teachers' views about constructivist teaching *Educational Information and Research* **18** 21–25.

Lindschitl M (1999) A vision educators can put into practice: portraying the constructivist classroom as a cultural system *School Science and Mathematics* **99** (4) 189–197.

Miles M B and Huberman A M (1994) *Qualitative data analysis* Sage Publications Inc.

Novak J D and Gowin D B (1984) *Learning how to learn* Cambridge University Press.

Osborne, R J and Wittrock M (1985) The generative learning model and its implications for science education *Studies in Science Education* **12** 59–87.

Osborne J F (1996) Beyond constructivism *Science Education* **80** (1) 53–82.

Pope M (1985) Constructivist goggles: implications for process in teaching and learning. Paper presented *at the annual conference of the British Educational Research Association.*

Shuell T J and Farber S L (2001) Students' perceptions of technology use in college courses *Journal of Educational Computing Research* **24** (2) 119–138.

Strauss A and Corbin J (1990) *Basics of qualitative research: grounded theory procedures and Techniques* Sage, Newbury Park, CA.

Tam M (2000) Constructivism, instructional design, and technology: implications for transforming distance learning *Educational Technology and Society* **3** 2.

White R T (1988) *Learning science* Blackwell, Oxford.

Windschitl M (1999) The challenges of sustaining a constructivist classroom culture *Phi Delta Kappan* 751–755.

Yen R Y (1999) A study of exemplary elementary science teachers's beliefs, practices, and views about constructivist teaching *http: www.narst.org/conference/yenhsiung.htm.*

YÖK (Higher Education Foundation in Turkey) (1998) *Programmes for educational faculty* Ankara, Turkey.

Address for correspondence: **TUGBA YANPAR SAHIN,** Zonguldak Karaelmas University, College of Education, Kdz. Eregli, 67300 Zonguldak, Turkey. Email: tusahin@karaelmas.edu.tr, or tyanpar@yahoo.com

From *British Journal of Educational Technology,* Volume 34, Number 1, January 2003, pp. 67–74. Copyright © 2003 by British Educational Communications and Technology Agency (BECTA). Reprinted by permission. www.blackwellsynergy.com

Assessing and Monitoring Student Progress in an E-Learning Personnel Preparation Environment

EDWARD L. MEYEN, RONALD J. AUST, YVONNE N. BUI AND ROBERT E. ISAACSON

E-learning has emerged as a form of pedagogy and as a delivery system with broad implications for meeting personnel needs nationally in special education. At present, it is important to make investments in research and development to ensure that this new pedagogy becomes fully developed and is appropriately applied. Assessment and monitoring of student progress in e-learning environments is an important element of this new form of pedagogy that requires research attention to maximize the effectiveness of e-learning when applied to teacher education. The authors draw upon their personal online teaching experience in addressing strategies for assessing student performance and using electronic portfolios in e-learning environments, both presented as integral aspects of e-learning instructional process. Perspectives from the literature and lessons learned from the authors are also shared.

With the advent of the Internet a new form of pedagogy has emerged that has unprecedented potential for expanding access to and improving the effectiveness of personnel preparation programs in meeting national needs in special education. This new form of instruction has spawned many questions related to effectiveness, responsiveness of adult learners, appropriateness for teacher education, and viability for the future. A brief look at what is occurring will help build a perspective on e-learning in personnel preparation.

In the United States, 97 percent of full-time faculty and staff at two- and four-year institutions of higher education have access to the Internet, and 40 percent use Web sites to post course-related information (U.S. Department of Education, 2001). In recent years, virtual universities, with no prior education histories, have come into being, attracting large enrollments. This has contributed to universities responding by placing courses and degrees online. For example, the Online Academy, a project funded by the Office of Special Education Programs (OSEP), produced 22 online modules for teacher education that were adopted by over 160 universities (Meyen, 2000). Nearly 710,000 students in 1998 were enrolled in at least one online course, and that figure is predicted to reach 2.2 million by 2002. (Financial Times-Business Education, April 3, 2000). In the general-use market some industry estimates predict that the number of users worldwide will pass the one billion mark by 2005 (United States Internet Council, 2000). Similarly, the corporate e-learning market is expected to surpass the $23 billion mark by 2004, up from $2 billion in 1999 (IDC, 2001).

Questions related to the capacity to deliver e-learning and the acceptance by adult learners in the professions of this new mode of instruction have been sufficiently validated to warrant investing in research and development of e-learning in teacher education. The growing need for special education teachers and for professional development on the part of practicing professionals in special education is well documented (Higher Education Consortium for Special Education, 2001). What is not clear is the level of commitment by agencies and teacher education programs to research and development as a way to build on what is known about teaching and learning in maximizing the power of e-learning for adults. This is essential if we are to leverage this new capacity in meeting national personnel needs. While funding agencies such as OSEP have demonstrated leadership by supporting e-learning projects, they have tended to support initiatives that result in content-based programs. However important these programs are, support is needed of work targeted at improving instructional designs, expanded features, e-learning teaching/development tools, maximizing emerging technologies to personnel preparation applications, instructional management options for e-learning environments, and research on matching the attributes of adult learners with the instructional and assessment features of e-learning.

We are not talking here about replacing traditional approaches to personnel preparation with e-learning strategies. Rather, we are proposing that major attention be paid to exploring how to make this new form of pedagogy, with all its potential and shortcomings, maximally effective in the shortest period of time while also generalizing the best features to face-to-face instruction. Since it may become the dominant methodology for adult learners in the future, it should be made as powerful as possible. This requires attending to what we know about the principles of teaching and learning and determining how these principles generalize to e-learning as well as focusing on techniques that are unique to e-learning. In these efforts, it is important that the knowledge base and experimentation with applying this knowledge base in e-learning environments drive new designs and applications in personnel preparation rather than allowing technology alone to do so, which currently seems to be the case. Unless research and validated practices drive the use of technology in personnel preparation, we risk the development of models that are less than optimal or, even worse, that fail to achieve their potential. E-learning is a very young pedagogy and warrants the benefits of reasoned inquiry and controlled experimentation that comes with research.

> **... e-learning holds instructors to the validity of their assessments. There is also no denying what has been taught in e-learning due to its public and replicable nature.**

The present article on assessing performance and monitoring student progress via electronic portfolios is based on the authors' personal experience. Meyen has taught asynchronous online courses employing streaming media full time since 1996. Aust has been using Web-based supports and varied versions of enhancing access to and management of student work in his courses for an equal period of time. In addition, both served in leadership roles when creating the instructional design and the development tool for the Online Academy (Meyen, Skrtic, Deshler, Lenz, Sailor & Chaffin, 2000). They are now part of the e-Learning Design Lab involving researchers from the departments of engineering and education. Examples will be used to illustrate the practices described. The intent is to focus on experiences in online instruction and web-based supports in providing examples of how the pedagogy of e-learning accommodates good teaching practices and the contributions of employing sound assessment practices and the use of electronic portfolios in building a more powerful pedagogy of e-learning.

A Literature Perspective on E-Learning Assessments and Student Performance

The following discussion of assessment of student performance in e-learning environments for personnel preparation is based on our conviction that assessment is integral to instruction, and that it must be continuous and maximize feedback.

Principles of Assessment

While the underlying principles of assessing the performance of adult learners do not change when applied to e-learning, the e-learning environment does differ significantly from traditional modes of instruction. The e-learning environment creates opportunities for and possibly demands more intensive assessment. That is, while technology adds a level of efficiency to assessment in e-learning environments, it must also compensate for the lack of easy access to personal observation. Pennsylvania State University (1998) has developed a set of principles to guide assessment of e-learning in distance education and has published a guide for translating them into practice. These principles reinforce the importance of integrating assessment with instruction. They are as follows:

1. Assessment instruments and activities should be congruent with the learning goals and skills required of the learner throughout a distance education program or course.
2. Assessment and management strategies should be integral parts of the learning experience, enabling learners to assess their progress, to identify areas of review, and to reestablish immediate learning or lesson goals.
3. Assessment and measurement strategies should accommodate the special needs, characteristics, and situations of the distance learner.

In discussing assessment of student performance online, Kibby (1999) sees assessment as central to the teaching learning process and as part of the management system. Assessments should measure student performance and result in feedback to students about their performance. Kibby goes on to detail nine decisions to be made when developing assessments for Web-based instruction.

1. Which perspectives of learning are going to be assessed, cognitive (acquisition of knowledge), behavioral (skill development), or humanistic (values and attitudes)?
2. Who is going to make the assessment, the student, their peers, or the instructor?
3. Will assessment strategies be learning experiences in themselves?
4. Is the assessment to be formative (providing feedback during learning) or summative (measuring learning at the end of the process)?
5. Are judgments of performance made against peer standards (norm referenced) or established criteria (criterion referenced)?
6. How can assessment provide a balance between structure and freedom?
7. Will the assessment be authentic, related to real life situations?
8. Will the assessment be integrated, testing a range of knowledge and skills?
9. How can reliability and validity of assessment be assured?

Related to networked learning, McConnell (1999) observes that assessment may be one of the last remaining bastions of academic life in that in a formal course it is usually the one element where the learner has no, or very little, say or control. The instructor usually carries out the assessment unilaterally with the final decision about learner performance being their personal perspective. While this may be driven by the professional responsibility of the instructor for determining proficiency in skills or knowledge of the subject matter, assessment can be made a more integral part of the e-learning teaching/learning process. In doing so, it becomes feasible to design assessments that permit the learners to allow their performance to influence subsequent assessments. This is particularly true in e-learning where technology allows for frequent and varied assessments. The key in assessing the performance of students in e-learning is to remain focused on the learner's attainment of the instructor's stated goals and objectives. In doing so it is important to resist opportunities to impose assessments merely because technology facilitates the process.

E-Learning Design Implications

Because e-learning largely requires that courses are designed in advance of teaching, the instructor as the developer has an opportunity to not only plan situations to embed assessments in the instruction, but also to review the instructional content and planned experiences prior to implementation of the e-learning program. This can ensure the validity of the assessments. The development requirement of e-learning requires that the instructor (assuming he or she is also the course content developer) employs the full range of instructional skills in the teaching e-learning process. They cannot rely on interpersonal skills during teaching to compensate for weaknesses of organization in the course or the lack of substance or timeliness of the content, as is possible in a traditional course. Nor can well-structured learning experiences compensate for a lack of communication skills in the e-learning teaching process. All elements of the instruction must be in place in advance. For this reason there is no excuse for assessments not coinciding with the content or the emphasis of the instruction. Thus, e-learning holds instructors to the validity of their assessments. There is also no denying what has been taught in e-learning due to its public and replicable nature. This increases accountability from the perspective of the consumer (i.e., the student). Additionally, the communications capabilities of asynchronous e-learning allow for greater sampling of student performance, thus opening the door to opportunities for learners to influence the type and range of assessments made of their performance.

... it is the capacity for timely and frequent feedback that transforms an assessment experience into an instructional opportunity.

We must move away from viewing assessment from the perspective of periodic exams and graded activities, the results of which may or may not be discussed with the class, to considering it in the context of e-learning where students come to view their relationship with the instructor as one-on-one instruction. As this occurs, assessment can become a continuous process, much like formative evaluation in improvement of a course. It has been our experience that students truly value the personal focus on their work and the obvious efforts to enhance their performance as they progress through the instructional experiences at their own pace. The flexibility of time and place valued by students in asynchronous e-learning facilitates the use of assessment strategies as integral aspects of instruction. In face-to-face instruction, the same level of assessment may be viewed by instructors and/or students as excessively time consuming and even detracting from instruction.

Assessment Options

In viewing the range of assessment options available through e-learning, it is easy to say that they are little different from those routinely employed in face to face instruction. For example, Morgan and O'Reilly (1999) describe five different types of assessment activities that are familiar:

1. Ungraded activities and feedback built into study materials
2. Self-assessment quizzes and tests that allow learners to check their own learning
3. Formal feedback on assignments from instructors, peers, or work place colleagues or mentors
4. Informal dialogue with instructors, peers or others
5. Ungraded tests that prepare learners for formal graded assessments

While these are familiar and not unique to e-learning the difference is in how technology makes them more feasible and possibly more effective to plan and execute.

Feedback

In the online courses taught by Meyen (Meyen, Lian & Tangen, 1997) assessments typically include a mid-term plus a final exam, a literature review exercise, a collaborative project, and approximately 30 activities, all embedded or strategically placed in the course. With the exception of the exams, these are constructivist activities that engage students in demonstrating continuous progress, and each provides the instructor an opportunity to intervene, as necessary, via reinforcement, directions, and/or correction through feedback. By comparison, when teaching the same course in a traditional format one day a week, Meyen was unable to provide the same level of feedback or strategically deliver the feedback at a time when the student was engaged in the activity. The submission of activities as independent learning experiences or as a vehicle for the structuring of collaborative projects and the return of responses by email is seen by students as adding significantly to the usefulness of feedback.

Indeed, it is the capacity for timely and frequent feedback that transforms an assessment experience into an instructional opportunity. Wiggins (1998) defines feedback as providing a person information on how he or she performed in light of what he or she attempted. A critical factor in providing meaningful feedback is the closeness of the feedback to the task that is the focus of the feedback. That is, if students are to maximally benefit from the feedback they must be able to relate the feedback to the logic they employed in generating their response. In discussing instructor support for facilitating feedback in a Web environment, Collis, De Boar, and Slotman (2000) refer to the practical implications of feedback in the context of time expenditures, clarity of expectations for students, and efficiency of managing the overall submission and feedback process. Collis and colleagues go on to describe Tele TOP, a Web-based, support system. Inherent in the system is the capability to link to types of responses, thus reducing demands on the instructor while maintaining effective feedback to the students. Examples of links include:

1. Personal feedback by the instructor to an individual assignment
2. Model-answer provided by the instructor
3. Peer evaluation provided by the student(s)
4. Automatic direct feedback provided by the computer

If assessment is to be integral to instruction, feedback is central to the assessment process. E-learning makes this more achievable than traditional forms of instruction when factors of time and access to information are concerned.

> **Students are informed in advance that their reviews will be shared with all other students in the course ... the mutual benefit is that each student has access to a large number of reviews developed by peers in the course.**

In discussing continuous assessment in Web-based environments, Kerka and Wonacott (2000) stress the importance of pacing, feedback, and learning quality, arguing that pacing and feedback directly affect whether learners study and learn and how effectively they do so. These are features that are central to e-learning and easily accommodated in e-learning environments due to the ease of using electronic communications.

Lessons Learned from Assessing Student Performance in E-Learning Environments

In assessing student performance through e-learning we have capitalized on the capabilities of e-learning in integrating assessments into the instructional process. Electronic communications combined with the development processes required to place a course in an e-learning format facilitate the integration of assessments into the structuring of the content, assignments, collaborative projects, creation of products and evaluation procedures. We have found that in e-learning assessments can be made less obtrusive and transformed to instructional strategies in a manner that causes students to view assessments as opportunities to demonstrate what is being learned rather than as evidence for grading.

Following are examples of assessment techniques that have been employed successfully over 12 consecutive semesters in fully online asynchronous graduate-level courses. The courses are structured around 16 lessons in which the instruction primarily consists of multimedia lectures involving streaming media in combination with access to selected resources in the form of readings, research summaries, and lists of URLs. Each lesson is accompanied by at least one activity requiring a response from students to demonstrate their understanding of the lesson content. Formative data are also collected on each lesson as input for the instructor in improving the lessons and the course. Finally, at the completion of the course students provide feedback via an instrument designed to assess teaching effectiveness. This is the same instrument as used institutionwide to assess instruction. These formative techniques encourage students to view assessment as a cooperative enterprise in that the instruction is being evaluated in addition to their performance. The lesson and course evaluations are returned anonymously to a third-party email address. The following section includes examples of assessments that have been employed in fully online asynchronous e-learning courses by the authors.

Activities

An example of a lesson activity in the course on curriculum development entails the creating of a design for a curriculum project the student is working on. Specifically, the student is required to illustrate the design graphically and provide a narrative explanation. If a student lacks the necessary skills to submit the response in a graphic form he or she is allowed to fax the responses. This is a complex activity, in most cases necessitating two or three exchanges of communications via email between the instructor and the student before the student achieves a functional design. In addition to helping the student, the process allows the instructor to observe the level at which the students are in the initial activity and how they respond to the feedback provided. The feedback is provided within 24 hours to enhance the student's work in the refinement process.

This is a critical activity for the course being (on curriculum development), as it is important to observe the student's incremental progress in addition to the final product. In experimenting with grading we have found that it does not appear to make much difference in students' performance whether an activity is graded or not, as long as they are held to applying what is being learned through the activity in either exams or in projects. What is important is that the students clearly know if they have fully satisfied the instructor's expectations for their performance on a given activity.

Literature Review Activity

As a way to expand students' knowledge of the literature on the subject of the course, each student is assigned to do what is referred to as Focus Presentations—basically reviews of the published literature. Students are informed in advance that their reviews will be shared with all other students in the course. The result is that each student is creating resources for other students and the mutual benefit is that each student has access to a large number of reviews developed by peers in the course. Selections must be approved in advance and cannot replicate any resource included in the structured part of the course. Knowing that their reports will be shared contributes to the quality of students' work and adds meaning to both the assignment and the assessment of their work. The instructor is provided a sample of the students work as well as their perspective on what they consider literature that is relevant to the course. The quality of the writing and the substance of the review are considered in the grading.

Collaborative Projects

Each course also includes a collaborative team project. Students are required to form teams by communicating with peers from the course roster and subsequently select their own team leader. Team membership and project topics are subject to approval by the instructor, who clearly defines how the project relates to the course. The project results in a product such as a curriculum prototype for the curriculum development course. Instructions on the projects are embedded in five to six sequential multimedia lessons with accompanying activities. Teams work through the lessons and complete the activities as a collaborative effort. The instructor provides feedback to the team leader, who is responsible for sharing the feedback with team members.

Each activity response is reviewed by the instructor as an independent element of the project. Teams may follow up with the instructor on feedback pertaining to any activity response to ensure that they understand the respective element of the project covered in the activity. After completing the activities associated with the project, the team integrates the feedback into a revision of the project and then submits it as a cohesive product for evaluation. The number of email communications between the instructor and the team leader averages about 15 plus feedback on the graded project. Since team work is one of the goals of the course, each student receives that same grade on the project. This approach to assessing performance works well when an e-learning course involves a substantive outcome that is applied in nature and to be effective in real life involves a group process. Evaluation is based primarily on how effectively the team meets the requirements of each element of the project and the extent to which they use the instructor's feedback to improve on the final project as a useful product.

In e-learning courses where the project assignment has been used, the evaluation of the project contributes about 30 percent to the course grade. In only two incidences have students reported that a team member did not contribute equally to the group effort. Students largely use electronic resources to carry out the project, but they also meet face to face if circumstances permit but it is not required. The response to the collaborative projects has been very positive. The most difficult aspect of the project process appears to be searching out team members and reaching an agreement on the project topic. This is viewed as an important outcome in itself.

Exams

Viewing assessment as integral to instruction opens up many opportunities for sampling student performance. Minimum use is made of quizzes, and exams are limited to the traditional midterm and final exams. Exams are given online, with students having the option of submitting their responses online, by fax or delivering them to the instructor. The exams are a mixture of essay and objective items depending on the nature of the course content. Since the courses are self-paced, students take the exams at different times. To maximize the instructional value of the exams, detailed feedback is given on each item. Exams are graded in sets to help the instructor maintain a frame of reference for the expected performance.

In teaching online, there is always the issue of security and whether the student enrolled is actually the person completing the exams. In the future technology will help solve that problem. The courses reported here include an average of over 30 samples of student performance apart from the exams. Given the large number of opportunities to respond, it is unlikely that the probability of cheating is any greater than they would be in a traditional course. Nevertheless, instructors need to be alert to indicators suggesting cheating. This can be controlled partially in the design of the course and in the structuring of what is assessed via exams and other samples of student work. Proctored exams represent another option.

Student Reports in Real Time

A vehicle for assessing student performance that has proven to be helpful in evaluating performance in e-learning is the team report. To be effective, this requires a synchronous experience. For that reason, we have not used it in the asynchronous courses but have tried it in an online seminar that mixes synchronous with asynchronous techniques. Teams are formed to research a particular topic on which they are to prepare a narrative report. A Power Point presentation and use of an audio resource are used to make a live presentation. The PowerPoint presentation is posted in advance of the scheduled report time so other students enrolled in the class can review it prior to the session and also have the presentation on their desk top when the team reports. Students need not be at the same place to participate, but arrangements are made for group sites if members wish to be in small groups; otherwise they can participate individually from wherever they are able to access a computer and a telephone. It is important for team members to participate in all aspects of preparing and presenting the report. Creating the PowerPoint display is one exception as some team members may be more experienced in the use of PowerPoint.

This technique not only allows instructors to observe behaviors that are not evident when assessing text- and product-type responses, it also allows the instructor to probe individual team members using the audio capabilities. The key is to structure sufficient time for the interaction versus the presentation. We have allowed the final narrative report to be submitted following feedback on the report. We have experimented with peer evaluations with varied results. Students do differentiate in their assessments of peers. One concern has been students' varied background knowledge on the topics of the reports. It is not clear that more knowledge necessarily contributes to a more objective assessment. Our approach to the peer evaluations has been to play down the quality of the presentations and to focus on the substance of the reports as students tend to be impressed with the quality of presentations, often overlooking weaknesses in the substance. However, we believe that peer evaluations in the right context can be effective and can add to the instructional value of the experience. In this situation the emphasis is on reviewing and reporting research so the organization and presentations of information as perceived by others in a reasonable aspect of performance assessment.

Journal Entries

Because e-learning is still a new experience for most students, we have found that it is beneficial to engage them in reflection. Thus, students are asked to maintain a journal of their experiences as they progress through the course. The guidelines are very general—they are instructed merely to record their thoughts about the instructional experience. This need not occur each day but should happen on a regular basis. The entries may range from comments about an activity, to the lack of clarity of a lecture, the time required to access a resource, or students' personal reaction to the mode of instruction. The intent is to make them aware of the different features of e-learning on the assumption that they personally may me become engaged in developing e-learning in the future and/or will be enrolled in additional e-learning classes. The reaction has been especially positive from first-time students, whereas students experienced in e-learning find the process less useful. While this does not contribute to assessment from the perspective of judging performance in the realm of grading, it contributes to knowledge of student performance and thus serves as a formative feature for the instructor. These journal entries are best shared at the conclusion of the course following grading.

Literature Perspective on Electronic Portfolios in Monitoring Student Progress

The monitoring of student progress via electronic portfolio development facilitates two primary types of evaluation,

formative and summative. Formative evaluation can be used to identify strengths that can be built upon and weaknesses that need prescriptive feedback that will encourage both instructor and student reflection on ways to improve professional development and training. Summative evaluation serves more of a retrospective function in that it is a documentation of achievements and professional skills. Traditionally, portfolios have been widely used in both the visual and performing arts as a means to provide a showcase of select pieces of an artist's work. The use of portfolios and performance-based assessments have become a standard practice in business and various professions in recent years. Portfolios usually contain select samples of work that represents the student's or job candidate's strengths and weaknesses. In addition, when used in this manner, portfolio assessment provides a more accurate means of measuring academic and professional skills. Essentially, portfolio and performance based assessment are both ways of evaluating activities or products that are representative of skills applied to a performance task, whether that task is job related or associated with a series of instructional goals and objectives. In addition to providing evidence of depth and breadth of knowledge and skills, the professional portfolio when done thoughtfully, can serve as a "knowledge resource" for future reference. With the emergence of e-learning, the portfolio has evolved as a management tool for instructors and students. Thru the use of technology, the electronic portfolio in hypermedia format can become a "personal/professional information management" system that contributes significantly to the pedagogy of e-learning in higher education in addition to professional development and as a tool for K-12 students.

One of the recent trends in the field of professional development for teachers has been the use of the professional teaching electronic portfolio. The electronic portfolio is a way to encourage and showcase the professional development of teachers and their teaching skills. For pre-service students, it provides an excellent addition to a resume or curriculum vitae and is a valuable tool for marketing oneself to future employers. The portfolio is an excellent format for presenting one's professional goals and philosophy of teaching to others. Additionally, and most exciting, the portfolio can be used as a personal information management system during pre-service education that can ultimately provide an index of resources that will be used in one's future teaching practice such as lesson plans, multimedia presentations, bookmarks of favorite educational websites, handouts, and various other professional development resources. In this context it becomes a tool for use in courses to record and organize examples of what is being learned while generalizing to a product that can be employed when they begin teaching. In this sense, an electronic portfolio transforms from a management system while a student to later being a "teaching toolbox" that allows all of ones professional resources to be indexed into one self-contained system that can be stored in a variety of formats, whether CD or DVD-ROM or on any number of external hard disk storage devices. It is also an excellent way to develop and showcase one's knowledge of the use of technology for instructional purposes. By using electronic portfolios, students are developing their technology skills.

Electronic portfolios, like traditional portfolios, are selective representational collections of student work that are made available in electronic form, on CD-ROM or on the World Wide Web in the form of hypermedia (Barrett, 1994). What makes electronic portfolios more engaging is the use of various forms of multimedia that can include audio, graphics, photographs, text, and video. Recently, a number of software packages have been developed for use in both K-12 and higher education, which allow teachers and students to create electronic portfolios that help to document student classroom achievement. One such program is Aurbach's "Grady Profile" (Grady, 1991) that provides a template that allows various items to be entered and stored including work samples, test scores, and oral presentations. Other commercially available software programs such as Roger Wagner (1993) Publishing's "HyperStudio" and Claris' "FileMaker Pro," (Brewer, 1994) provide the means for teachers to develop their own templates for portfolio assessment. While these software programs can be used to create customized portfolios they are all proprietary solutions and therefore the trade off is ease of use for the costs associated with the initial purchase of the software program. The open standards of hypertext mark-up language (HTML) offers the most flexible and least costly approach to the creation of electronic portfolios.

The use of HTML format allows users to take full advantage of the community publishing capabilities of the World Wide Web. User friendly HTML authoring tools are available that make web page creation simple, even for the most novice computer user. Advantages of bringing portfolios into the web environment include the ability to create media rich records of accomplishments or performances such as a video of a dance recital or sports event. Moreover, the web facilitates the seamless integration of the portfolio's media components into a cohesive and readily accessible framework. Instead of creating a "portfolio box" with papers photos video and audio cassettes that require several days to mail, students can now create personal web portfolio sites that can be accessed and updated instantly by anyone at anytime with all media components of the portfolio only a click away.

Lessons Learned from Using Electronic Portfolios

In several of our courses students are required to create and manage their own personal course portfolio web site. At our university, students gain access to 10 megabytes of free server storage when they register to receive their email account. Their web address is based on their email so it is easy to locate. For example, a student with the email patsmith@ku.edu website would also have a website called http/people.ku.edu/~patsmith. We provide basic HTML templates that students can use in creating their web site. The students then use readily available web development tools such as DreamWeaver and to create their portfolio website.

Student Owned Electronic Portfolios

There are several advantages to the approach of students who use general web development tools to manage their own portfolio development and maintenance. Information technologies are continuing to evolve at an exponential rate and new or improved web development tools are emerging every few months. Some universities are using HTML and or XML as the primary underlying technology while others are using Adobe's Acrobat, Flash, MediaPlayer or RealPlayer. It may be too early in the evolution of these technologies to lock in to proprietary portfolio management tools if they restrict access to emerging information technologies.

Another advantage to student owned portfolio website is that each student learns to control the use or misuse of the server space. At one time we provided space for student work within the course's server space. The problem with this approach was that students would continue to deposit version 1, 2, 3 ... of their media projects on the course's web server and quickly fill up available space. When students own their web site they are more rigorous in controlling what is on "their" space.

With the student owned portfolio approach the students are developing lifelong skills for managing their personal web space. They choose which work from their course portfolio to carry forward in their general portfolio and which work to exclude. The students are also responsible for managing accessibility to sensitive personal and academic information. This is a liability better left in the hands of the student than with the instructor or educational institution.

The Structure of Content in Online Course Portfolios

For many of our courses we provide generic HTML templates that list contact information including the student's name (required), email (required), photo, telephone and address. Students are asked to write a brief (less than 150 word) descriptive statement that vary depending on the course content. For example in a research seminar students write a belief statement or philosophical perspective that provides the foundation for their research agenda. In other courses students provide a brief description of their current employment course expectations and/or career goals.

Other content varies with the course goals and pedagogy. Tailoring the course portfolio's structure is a matter of requiring additional links on the portfolio web site. In some cases these links are to other student created web sites. For example, some of our courses incorporate project base activities where students are creating media rich stories or reports that link to web sites. These projects integrate a wide variety of media including photos, diagrams, animations, streaming audio and video. For these project base activities we post the project requirements and assessment rubric. Students then develop the project and provide a link to the project web site from their course portfolio web site.

Some of the content for courses is best revealed in progressive manner. For example the course might involve a journaling activity where students are adding new information to a report each week that describes field observations, or new information that they have discovered. Ancillary web site development also works well for these progressive activities where students provide a link from their course portfolio web site to a web page that is updated each weak.

Exams and Portfolios

Many of our examinations take the form of written documents that are most easily saved as a Microsoft Word (.doc) or Rich Text Format (.rtf) document. In these case the exams are posted at a given time and students are required to post or email their responses on or before the due period. Examinations provide somewhat more involved security requirements than other information in the students' course portfolio. In many cases the students simply email their exams to the instructor and refrain from posting the link to their course portfolio until after the due period. We have recently explored the use of electronic keys to provide access to sensitive materials. In this case the instructor creates a password for each student that the student uses to provide the instructor with access to the sensitive material in their web site.

Our courses often involve students working together in group activities to develop artifacts that reflect what they have learned. The artifacts for these activities may take the form of papers, PowerPoint slides, group presentations and/or media rich websites. Each member contributes to the artifacts in unique and group roles. The online environment has proven particularly productive for these type of group activities. Many of our students are practicing professionals who live at considerable distance from each other. Student controlled web sites provide these students with an environment where they can contribute to product development from anyplace at anytime. For these group projects activities we ask each students to create a link from their course portfolio web site to a page that describes their role and how they benefited from the development of the group product. This page then links to their groups project.

Summary

The newness of e-learning as a mode of instruction in personnel preparation makes reliance on shared personal experiences important in furthering the development of best practices. While the literature on instruction in e-learning environments is emerging through traditional forms of scholarly dissemination and web sites, much of what is occurring has not yet found its way into accessible sources. This is largely due to the time required to develop, employ and validate practices prior to sharing them. In the space available we have tried to provide perspectives on the literature while at the same time sharing from our personal experiences in e-learning over the past seven years. While the applications have been subjected to repeated use and evaluation over several years, they may not generalize to all e-learning environments. They are presented here in the context of the position that the emerging e-learning pedagogy enhances the opportunity to fully integrate assessment into the instructional process and

implement instructional management systems for instructors and students in the form of electronic portfolios.

We would like to close with a list of web sites that we have found useful (see Table 1). They are a sample of the various web-based resources for specific assessment needs or models.

References

ADEC (2001). *American Distance Education Consortium Home Page.* Retrieved February 1, 2002, from http://www.adec.edu/

Barrett, H. C. (2001). *Using technology to support alternative assessment and electronic portfolios.* Retrieved February 1, 2002, from http://transition.alaska.edu/www/portfolios.html

Center for Effective Teaching and Learning, University of Texas at El Paso, (1998). *Teching portfolios.* Retrieved February 1, 2002, from http://www.utep.edu/~cetal/portfoli/index.htm

Collis, B., De Boar, W., & Slotman, K. (2001). Feedback for web-based assignments. *Journal of Computer Assisted Learning, 17,* 306–313.

Grady, M. P. (1991). Grady Profile [Computer software]. St. Louis, MO: Aurbach & Associates, Inc.

Higher Education Consortium for Special Education. (2001). *Policy, program, and funding recommendations for the preparation of qualified personnel under Part D of IDEA.* A position paper of the Higher Education Consortium for Special Education. University of Kentucky. Lexington, KY.

IDC. (2001). *IDC's worldwide corporate e-learning market forecast and analysis, 1999–2004.* Retrieved February 1, 2002, from http://www.idc.com:8080/Services/press/PR/GSV022701pr.stm

Kerka, S., & Wonacott, M. E. (2002). *Assessing learners online: Practitioner file.* Columbus, OH: The Ohio State University, ERIC Clearing House on Adult, Career, and Vocational Education Center on Education and Training for Employment. (ERIC Document Reproduction Service No. ED448285)

Kibby, M. (1999). Examining a collaborative assessment process in networked lifelong learning. *Journal of Computer Learning, 15* 232–243

McConnell, D. (1999). Examing a collaborative assessment process in networked lifelong learning. *Journal of Computer Learning, 15,* 232–243.

McCormack, R. (1997). Creating multimedia/interactive tests for the Internet in 10 minutes. Retrieved February 1, 2002, from http://www.aln.org/alnweb/magazine/issue2/rob.htm

Meister, J. C. (2000, April 3). The case for corporate universities. *Financial Times.* Retrieved February 1, 2002, from http://globalarchive.ft.com/globalarchive/article.html?id=0004030000245&query=Business+Education

Meyen, E. L. (2000). Using technology to move research to practice: The online Academy. *Their World 2000.* New York: National Center for Learning Disabilities.

Meyen, E. L., Deshler, D., Skrtic, T. M., Lenz, B. K., Sailor, W., & Chaffin, J. D. (2001). *An academy: Report on linking teacher education to advances in research.* Lawrence, KS: Author. (USDOE Office of Special Education Programs PR/Award no. H029K73002).

Meyen, E. L., Lian, C. T., & Tangen, P. (1997). Developing online instruction: One model. *Focus on Autism and Other Developmental Disabilities, 12* 159–165.

Morgan, C., & O'Reilly, M. (1999). *Assessing open and distance learners.* London: Kogan Page.

Table 1   Online Resources for Student Assessment

Title or Topic	Description	Location
1. Using Technology to Support Alternative Assessment and Electronic Portfolios	This Web site provides information regarding the use of technology to support alternative assessment and electronic portfolio development. It is maintained by Dr. Helen Barrett, Assistant Professor, Educational Technology, School of Education, University of Alaska Anchorage.	http://transition.alaska.edu/www/portfolios.html
2. Assessing Students Online	This Web site focuses on various aspects of online assessment including the purpose of assessment, the advantages and disadvantages of online assessment, as well as providing links to resources for creating online assessments.	http://www.newcastle.edu.au/department/so/assess.htm
3. Creating Multimedia/Interactive Tests for the Internet in 10 Minutes	This paper explains ways that instructors can create multi-media/interactive tests, surveys, and assignments for the Internet using QuizPlease software.	http://www.aln.org/alnweb/magazine/issue2/rob.htm
4. Rubrics for Web Lessons	This site focuses on authentic assessment and the use of rubrics with examples, templates, and links to other related resources.	http://edweb.sdsu.edu/webquest/rubrics/weblessons.htm
5. Assessment/Testing/Evaluation Issues	This page is the Module 5—Evaluation checklist from the instructional design section of the Parkland College Online Faculty Handbook.	http://online.parkland.cc.il.us/ofh/Assessment/Mod5Issues.htm
6. MVCR Course on Student Assessment in Online Courses	This is an online course that focuses on various assessment formats and theories that can be used for evaluating students in online courses. Topics include: alternative assessment strategies, linking assessment with curriculum and instruction, assessment reliability and consistency, creating scoring rubrics, and strategies to minimize cheating online	http://www.mvcr.org/catalog/showcourseinfo.asp?courseID=4
7. ADEC Distance Education Consortium	This is the website for the American Distance Education Consortium. This site provides a comprehensive list of general resources for distance education.	http://www.adec.edu/
8. Center for Effective Teaching and Learning	The University of Texas at El Paso. This site provides information and tools for developing and assessing teaching portfolios.	http://www.utep.edu/~cetal/portfoli/index.htm

Parkland College. (2001). *Assessment/evaluation issues.* Retrieved February 1, 2002, from http://online.parkland.cc.il.us/ofh/Assessment/Mod5Issues.htm

Pennsylvania State University (1998). *Management team for innovations in distance education.* State College, PA: Pennsylvania State University

Pickett, N., & Dodge, B. (2001). *Rubrics for web lessons.* Retrieved February 1, 2002, from http://edweb.sdsu.edu/webquest/rubrics/weblessons.htm

United States Department of Education, National Center for Education Statistics. (2001). *The condition of education 2001.* Washington, DC: U.S. Government Printing Office.

United States Internal Council. (2000). *State of the Internet 2000.* Washington, DC: U.S. Government Printing Office.

University of Illinois, MVCR Project. (2002). *MVCR course on Student assessment in online courses.* Retrieved February 1, 2002, from http://www.mvcr.org/catalog/showcourseinfo.asp?courseID=4

Wiggins, G. (1998). *Educative assessment: Designing assessments to reform and improve group performance.* San Francisco: Jossey-Bass.

EDWARD L. MEYEN is a Professor at the University of Kansas; **RONALD J. AUST** is an Associate Professor at the University of Kansas; **YVONNE N. BUI** is an Assistant Professor at the University of San Francisco; & **ROBERT E. ISAACSON** is a Media Production Manager at the e-Learning Design Lab, University of Kansas

From *Teacher Education and Special Education,* Vol. 25, No. 3, 2002. © 2002 by the Teacher Education Division of the Council for Exceptional Children. Reprinted by permission.

Assessing the Technology Training Needs of Elementary School Teachers

MELINDA MCCANNON
Georgia College and State University

TENA B. CREWS
State University of West Georgia

Computers are not just for use in secondary and post-secondary institutions any longer. Elementary teachers must be prepared to use the computer in their classrooms also. Teacher educators are preparing future educators for classrooms with computers. However, current teachers must depend on staff development courses to help train them in the area of computer technology. The purpose of this study was to assess the technology and its current use in Georgia public elementary schools and to also assess the teachers' technology training needs.

This study found that computers are prevalent in the elementary schools. Teachers are using them. However, teachers are using them largely for administrative tasks instead of using them as an integral part of the student learning process. Staff development courses only reinforced this administrative use because the majority of classes offered were word processing. The researchers recommended that teacher educators offer staff development courses in curriculum integration, presentation software, and research, using the World Wide Web (WWW) and CD-ROMs. In addition, it is recommended that follow-up studies be conducted to assess future technology training needs.

As computer use continues to increase in society, educators must also prepare for the use of computers within the classroom. This involves all levels of education, including elementary school. As a result, current and future elementary educators must remain up-to-date with new computer technologies in an effort to provide meaningful educational experiences for their students.

Research indicates that one of the largest factors which determines computer integration in elementary schools is the amount of computer knowledge the teacher possesses. Teachers with average to below average computer knowledge have considerably limited utilization of computers in instruction when compared to teachers with higher levels of computer skills (Larner & Timberlake, 1995).

According to Shick (1996), limited computer knowledge can also lead to high levels of anxiety for elementary teachers. This anxiety then hampers these teachers' computer-related instruction. Research shows that anxiety associated with computer use in elementary instruction can be reduced through proper training and education for teachers. This training includes teaching elementary teachers how to implement computers in the educational setting by teaching basic computer concepts and providing hands-on computer experiences (Barker, 1994). Additionally, computer training has been used to assist elementary teachers in lesson planning which has also reduced the amount of anxiety related to computer technologies (McCormack, 1995). Some Texas universities encourage and even require their pre-service elementary teachers to purchase laptop computers to reinforce the importance of computers in lesson planning and instruction (Smith, Houston, & Robin, 1995).

Unfortunately, computer training has often been inadequate or nonexistent for many elementary educators. The focus has frequently been on showing teachers how to operate the equipment but not how to integrate the technology into instruction. Moreover, technical support in elementary schools is considerably limited, with only 6% of these schools employing a full-time computer coordinator to provide teachers with the support they need to fully use the technology they have in their schools (Feil, 1996). Feil (1996) concluded that reality often is that teachers must educate themselves with regard to computer instruction, and while teachers should be proactive in their own educational training, more formal training should be provided to give adequate preparation in this area.

For those schools that do use computers in elementary instruction, there are a number of ways technology can enhance learning experiences for students. Numerous elementary teachers who have experience in computer-aided instruction have found that mathematics, writing, and reading instruction can be enhanced with the use of computers. Upper grade level elementary teachers use increased amounts of technology, when compared to lower grade level elementary teachers, in a variety of ways. These include presentations, communications through networked systems, and newspaper publications (Mergendollar et al., 1992).

According to a study conducted by the Appalachia Educational Lab and the Tennessee Education Association (1991), a major factor in determining computer use is the location and availability of computers. This report found that elementary teachers favored a single computer within the classroom to a computer lab of multiple computers. One difficulty that arose from a computer lab setting included scheduling problems and it was concluded that students and teachers could be better served with computer availability in the classroom due to the fact that such technology would more likely be used because of convenience.

Purpose

Teacher educators have made excellent strides in changing the teacher education curriculum so future teachers graduate with computer expertise. However, many of the current teachers graduated before these changes took place. Therefore, they are dependent on staff development classes to train them in the area of technology. The purpose of this study was to assess the technology and its current use in Georgia public elementary schools and to also assess the teachers' technology training needs. A number of issues were examined including availability of computers, how the computers were used, and training availability and participation.

Research Questions

1. Where are computers available in the elementary school (classroom, lab, media center)?
2. How do teachers use the computers in the elementary school?
3. What staff development courses have been made available to the elementary school teachers?
4. Of those available staff development courses, which ones did the elementary teachers choose to participate?
5. What staff development classes were considered most beneficial to the elementary teachers?

Scope and Method

Teachers from the state of Georgia were chosen for this study because the recent influx of lottery funds earmarked for education has greatly increased the number of computers bought for schools; however, training teachers to use those computers in the classroom has not been funded as heavily. Elementary school teachers were chosen because the literature reveals that they have shown anxiety and reluctance in using those computers (Barker, 1994; Shick, 1996).

The survey instrument was created by the researchers and pilot tested by a group of teachers. After revisions to the instrument, 250 instruments were mailed out to randomly selected Georgia elementary school teachers from kindergarten through fifth-grade. One hundred and twenty-seven usable instruments were returned for a response rate of 50.8%.

Findings

Respondents

One hundred percent of the respondents were female. The highest percentage of the respondents were veteran teachers with 29% of them having 16–20 years of teaching experience; 11–15 years (23%); and 21–25 years (20%). Sixty-one percent of the respondents teach in suburban schools, and they were evenly distributed among grades kindergarten through fifth.

Computer Availability and Use

Ninety-eight percent of the respondents had computers in their classroom, and they all used them. The 2% who did not use a classroom computer indicated that they were hampered by the computers not working properly and inadequate software. Ninety-eight percent also had access to computers in their media center/library but only 73% chose to use them. The ones who did not use them indicated that they preferred using the ones in their classroom. Ninety-four of the 127 people surveyed (74%) also had access to a school computer lab; however only 58% chose to use the lab. There were various reasons given for not using the computer lab. The two reasons cited most often were that they preferred using the computers in their rooms, or the computers labs were not used by their grade level. Table 1 shows the percentages of specific computer use in the classroom, lab, and media center.

Classroom Computer Use

The respondents were asked to review the ways they could use the computer in the classroom and mark all answers that

Table 1   Teachers' Use of Computers

Uses	Class	Lab	Media Center
Tutorial (introduction of information)	28%	21%	17%
Administrative (tests, electronic gradebook, parent letters, etc.)	78%	24%	24%
To enhance lectures and presentations	31%	15%	21%
Research using CD-ROM	37%	13%	35%
Research using the Internet/WWW	17%	13%	29%
Other	11%	4%	13%

applied. Seventy-eight percent of the respondents used the computer for administrative tasks such as creating tests, correspondence, and gradebooks. Only 31% used the computer to enhance their lectures or presentations, and only 28% used it to introduce new material. The respondents were categorized into veteran (16 years of experience or more – $N = 78$), non-veteran (15 years of experience or less – $N = 43$), and nonrespondents ($N = 6$). It was noted that veteran teachers used computers in the classroom approximately the same way as non-veteran teachers except for Internet usage. Twenty-six percent of the non-veteran teachers used the computer to access the Internet whereas only 12% of the veteran teachers used the computer for Internet purposes.

The respondents were also asked how they had the students use the classroom computer. Eighty-nine percent said they allowed the students to use the computer to explore the material more in-depth. Seventy-four percent said they had students use the computer to review previously learned material. Sixty-nine percent indicated that the computer was a reward. Students were allowed to play educational games. The veteran and non-veteran teachers had the students use the classroom computer in approximately the same ways.

Lab Computer Use

The respondents used the computer lab computers for administrative tasks (24%). Twenty-one percent used the computers for introducing new material while 15% used it for enhancing their lectures and presentations. The main difference between veteran and non-veteran teachers use of computers in a lab setting was that 23% of the non-veteran teachers used these computers mostly for administrative tasks, to enhance lectures and presentations, and to complete research using CD-ROMs almost twice as much as veteran teachers did.

Forty-seven percent of the respondents had the students use the computer lab computers to review previously learned material. Forty-five percent of the respondents allowed the students to use the computers to explore material in more depth. The veteran teachers had students use the lab computers much more than non-veteran teachers for enrichment purposes and research using CD-ROMs. The veteran teachers also had the students use the lab computers 6% more than non-veteran teachers for classroom presentations.

Multimedia Center/Library Computer Use

Thirty-five percent of the respondents used the computers in the multimedia center/library computers to conduct research using CDs. Twenty-nine percent used the media center/library computers for Internet/WWW research. However, 24% of the respondents used the computers for administrative tasks. The veteran and non-veteran teachers used the computers in the media center for basically the same purposes.

Forty-four percent of the respondents had the students use the computers in the multimedia center/library for research using CD-ROMs. Thirty-nine percent of them allowed the students to use the computers to explore material in more depth. Thirty-two percent used the computers as a reward for the students to play games or explore. The veteran and non-veteran teachers had the students use the media center computers basically for the same purposes.

Availability of Participation in Technology Staff Development

Ninety-seven percent of the respondents had been offered staff development courses in technology. Ninety-one percent of the respondents had participated. The respondents were asked to mark all the staff development classes that they had been offered and those in which they had participated.

Software. The two staff development classes offered the most were word processing (69%) and operating systems (65%). Fifty-four percent of the respondents had participated in the word processing training, but only 47% had participated in training on various operating systems. Training on presentation software had only been offered to 22% of the respondents but 17% participated. Software staff development classes which were mentioned in the "Other" category included classes in *Accelerated Reader, Writing to Write, and Gradebook.* (Table 2)

Hardware. Few of the respondents had been offered training in hardware issues. Only 21% of the respondents had been offered

Table 2 Software Staff Development Courses

Software	Available	Participated
Word Processing (WordPerfect, Word, etc.)	69%	54%
Database (Access, dBase, etc.)	34%	22%
Spreadsheet (Lotus 1-2-3, Excel, etc.)	34%	22%
Presentation (PowerPoint, Lotus Freelance, etc.)	22%	17%
Drawing/Painting (Corel Draw, Paint, etc.)	32%	21%
Software Troubleshooting	36%	21%
Operating Systems (Windows, DOS, Mac)	65%	47%
Other	28%	18%

Table 3 Hardware Staff Development Courses

Hardware	Available	Participation
Hardware Troubleshooting/Maintenance (Printer problems, monitor freezing up, etc.)	21%	19%
Networking (Connecting computers to each other, printers, scanners, etc.)	22%	17%
Other	5%	2%

training in hardware troubleshooting/maintenance but 19% had participated. Twenty-two percent had been offered training in networking problems and 17% participated. Hardware staff development classes which were mentioned in the "Other" category were classes in *Osiris* and *Laser Disc*. (Table 3)

Miscellaneous. Fifty-two percent of the respondents had been offered courses in how to integrate the computer into the curriculum but only 46% participated. Thirty-four percent had been offered training in using the computers for administrative work and 32% participated. Forty-three percent had been offered courses in using computers to conduct research using the Internet/WWW and 40% participated. Miscellaneous staff development classes which were mentioned in the "Other" category were classes in e-mail, web page design and the software program *Attendance*. (Table 4)

Most Beneficial Classes

Word processing classes were ranked as the most beneficial staff development classes by the majority of the respondents. Using the computers for curriculum integration was ranked second. Training in operating systems was ranked as being the third most beneficial.

Increased Computer Usage

Ninety-two percent of the respondents indicated that their computer use increased after participating in technology staff development classes. The respondents were asked to mark all the areas in which their computer usage increased. Sixty-one percent indicated that they used the computer more for administrative tasks. Forty-eight percent indicated that they can now solve more software problems. Thirty-five percent indicated that they did more research using CD-ROMs. Only 19% indicated that they used the computer more to enhance their lectures or presentations.

Discussion

Computers are prevalent in the elementary schools of Georgia. However, the computer is still being used as a tool (administrative tasks, student review of material) and not as an integral part of the student learning process (curriculum integration, presentation enhancement). Though staff development training has been offered and teachers have participated, it is training issues that need to be addressed.

Word processing staff development was frequently offered, had good participation, and was ranked as beneficial by the teachers. But it appears that word processing is most popular because the teachers use the computer for administrative tasks. Though administrative tasks are necessary, staff development training should now start to move from word processing and move more toward presentation software and curriculum integration to enhance student learning.

Curriculum integration is the heart of infusing technology into student-learning. Curriculum integration would finally allow the computer to become part of the teacher's repertoire instead of it being just a machine which allows students to play games and explore. However, studies have shown that integrating technology into the curriculum has met with many barriers. In his study, Hoffman (1997) cited such barriers as not having enough computers to in the classroom, no reward for the teachers making the extra effort to integrate technology, and no training to support their effort. He recommended that administrators make a concentrated effort to reward teachers who take the time to learn how to integrate technology into the curriculum, more staff development courses be offered, and more computers be placed in the classroom. Bailey, Ross, and Griffin (1995) offered another solution to overcome the barriers. They recommended that every school district "develop a vision of how technology should be utilized in every aspect of teaching and learning." Only then will technology be fully accepted as a vital part of the curriculum.

However in this study, there were plenty of computers available and integrating technology into the curriculum was seen by these teachers as beneficial. They appeared to have a high interest in attending courses in curriculum integration. The barrier in this study was that staff development courses in curriculum integration were offered only to half of those responding. To help overcome this obstacle, teacher educators should offer summer courses on these issues or work with the school systems to insist that current teachers get this training. Administrators should reward the teachers who participate in this type of staff development with financial incentives and opportunities for more professional development.

In addition, more classes on how to use the computers for research using CD-ROMs and the Internet/WWW should be offered. The elementary teachers are using the computer for research and appear to want to participate in these classes. Teachers could then use that research material to enhance their courses. Current teacher educators should volunteer to present training on this skill because conducting research is an integral part of a professor's professional life.

Another type of training that elementary teachers are interested in is training on hardware issues. Hardware staff development was offered to less than a fourth of the participants but

Table 4   Miscellaneous Staff Development Courses

Miscellaneous	Available	Participation
Curriculum integration (how to use a computer to teach math, language arts, etc.)	52%	46%
Keyboarding techniques (proper finger and wrists positions, etc.)	26%	17%
Administrative (test banks, grades, etc.)	34%	32%
Research using CD-ROM (encyclopedias, almanacs, etc.)	39%	35%
Research using the Internet/WWW	43%	40%
Other	3%	1%

had good participation from those who had the opportunity. It is possible that this training is not offered because the school systems employ technicians to repair hardware problems; however, it is important for the teachers to have hardware training to help keep the machines running and reduce down time.

Technology-based staff development courses are essential to enhance teachers' ability and confidence in using computers. However, staff development simply being offered is not enough. There are many reasons why teachers cannot or will not participate in the staff development courses offered. Some of the reasons stated by teachers in this study as to why they have not participated in staff development (SD) courses include the following.

1. I have not taken the time.
2. The SD courses are a great distance to travel after school.
3. No time was given to take the SD courses during the school day.
4. No stipends have been offered to take the SD courses.
5. Major traffic in the areas where the SD courses are offered.
6. Learning from someone else (computer teacher) on a one-to-one basis.

These are all noted reasons and include items for those who plan staff development courses to consider.

One way administrators may overcome these problems with staff development courses is to enlist the help of their newest teachers. Because technology is now being emphasized in many teacher education programs, new teachers can play a vital role in bringing innovative ideas for using technology in the classroom. Administrators should encourage the new teachers to take this leadership role. With the right training, all teachers can enhance their instruction with computers. The students will be the beneficiaries.

Recommendations for Future Research

This study was a first step in determining computer training needs for teachers at the elementary school level. Recommendations for future research include:

1. Conduct the study using a larger geographic area to compare and contrast Georgia with other states.

2. Conduct the study using teachers from middle schools and high schools to compare and contrast their responses with elementary teachers.
3. Conduct follow-up studies periodically to examine what the technology training needs will be in the future.

References

Appalachia Educational Lab, Charleston, W. VA & Tennessee Education Association, Nashville, TN (1991). *Bits, bytes, and barriers: Tennessee teachers' use of technology.* (ERIC Document Reproduction Service No. ED 343 580)

Bailey, G., Ross, T., & Griffin, D. (1995). Barriers to curriculum-technology integration in education—are you asking the right questions? *Catalyst for Change, 25*(1), 16–20.

Barker, F.G. (1994). *Integrating computer usage in the classroom curriculum through teacher training.* Nova Southeastern University. (ERIC Document Reproduction Service No. ED 372 751)

Feil, C. (1996). Teacher, teach thyself! *Learning, 24*(5), 59–61.

Hoffman, B. (1997). Integrating technology into schools. *Education Digest, 62*(5), 51–55.

Larner, D.K., & Timberlake, L.M. (1995). *Teachers with limited computer knowledge: Variables affecting use and hints to increase use.* (ERIC Document Reproduction Service No. ED 384 595)

McCormack, V. (1995). *Training preservice teachers in applying computer technology to lesson planning as a component of the elementary school methods curriculum.* Nova Southeastern University. (ERIC Document Reproduction Service No. ED 382 190)

Mergendollar, J.R.; and Others (1992). *Instructional utilization, teacher training and implementation of Utah's educational technology initiative in school districts and colleges.* Beryl Buck Institute for Education, Novato, CA; Utah State Office of Education, Salt Lake City. (ERIC Document Reproduction Service No. ED 370 533)

Schick, R.W. (1996). *Implementation of technology in the classroom.* Nova Southeastern University. (ERIC Document Reproduction Service No. ED 394 516)

Smith, R.A., Houston, W.R., & Robin, B.R. (1995). Preparing preservice teachers to use technology in the classroom. *The Computing Teacher, 22*(4), 57–59.

From *Journal of Technology and Teacher Education (JTATE)*, Vol. 8, no. 2, 2000, pp. 111–121. Copyright © 2000 by Association for the Advancement of Computer Education (AACE). Reprinted by permission via Copyright Clearance Center.

An Investment in Tomorrow's University Students:

Enhancing the Multimedia Skills of Today's K-12 Teachers*

DR. JOHN MINOR ROSS

Teaching multimedia to computing majors is no longer new. The multimedia course experiences reported on herein, however, put a new slant on the topic—because of the target audience. Instead of narrowly focusing on traditional students, this course was designed, in addition, to develop the multimedia skills of classroom teachers, both inservice and preservice. The course pedagogy and target audience interests are outlined with only passing mentions of specific software. This is based on the belief that university computing professors should strive to understand K-12 problems before they offer technology solutions. Some fresh classroom challenges for teachers and professors, as well as possible far-reaching benefits, are also noted.

Educating the nation's children has remained one of the prime societal concerns for generations. Yet, regardless of lessons learned, every generation remains susceptible to both cries of concern and promises of fixes for various troubles in the classroom. Today, even back-to-the-basics advocates are often advocating various computer technologies based, inpart, on the allure of multimedia. Clearly, hardware in classrooms does not, by itself, improve the skill levels of college-track students. One way to improve the skill levels students attain in school may hinge on improving the classroom computing skills of their schoolteachers. A number of programs are already being implemented in order to accomplish this goal[6,7,11], but they appear to require more resources than may be supported by a small college. The course developed over the last five years and outlined here is seen as a low-cost, easy-to-manage approach that any size university should be able to implement successfully. Further more, it may serve to expand cooperation between the CS/IS and Education departments.

Multimedia Over-Hype?

Because any newer computer purchased to connect to the Internet has the potential to harness the power of sound and pictures, multimedia demonstrations have likely already generated excitement among the stakeholders in many schools. Parents see computer skills as essential to the future success of their children. School boards see technology as a patch for district image troubles. Students of any age embrace computers since they can be novel and fun.

Among teachers, however, the excitement is likely tinged with cynicism. Teachers who have dedicated much of their lives in pursuit of what 'really works' in the classroom have been disappointed by various fads over the years. Many of these fads are remembered as having been forced upon them by people that were distant from the pressures of the front line. As part of the overall dream for classroom technology that promises "improved student learning, less stress for the teacher, and lower instructional costs"[2], multimedia probably sets off the skepticism alarms in many such teachers.

Adjusting Expectations

The biggest problem with successfully using multimedia technologies in the classroom is not the hardware or software suitability. Rather, the largest flaw, perhaps, is some people's expectation that technology will improve learning by itself. Used inappropriately, inadequately, or to treat every learning ill, multimedia can only lead to disappointment. Teachers remain the key part of the student learning equation. What is needed before embarking on a multimedia push in a school is establishing reasonable expectations among all parties involved. If expectations are too high, even good results are viewed as disappointing.

Parents should be apprized early on about the role planned for multimedia classroom technology. Unfortunately, Dede[4] suggests some people see a computer in the classroom similarly to people warming themselves by a campfire: "Students benefit just by sitting near these devices, as knowledge and skills radiate from the monitors into their minds." Parents need to be told clearly that while multimedia may inject some excitement into learning, learning will still be a task for most students, rather than a game.

For teachers, the instructional promises of multimedia are many. The risks, however, can be great. Coffee[3] worried that the development of "multimedia courseware threatens to confuse students more than ever, though with the dubious benefit of doing so at lower cost and with greater interactive flexibility than traditional methods." While everyone needs to understand what multimedia may realistically accomplish, teacher training is the often-overlooked key to using the potential of multimedia effectively.

Teachers need to be prepared to use technology effectively to garner the desired benefits. As O'Donnell[9] points out, "teachers must perceive the value of the computer's efficacy in the classroom before they invest time, effort, and funds gaining the complex skills necessary for the integration of computers into the instructional process." Furthermore, classroom management expectations about student interaction while sharing computers with other students will require an adjustment for many teachers.

Teacher Multimedia Education

Hands-on work has remained an important component since we first offered a three-week, twelve-session, three-credit multimedia course embracing K-12 educators in the summer of 1998. The course could be taken for graduate Education credit or undergraduate Arts and Science credit. Students learned the essentials of using a different multimedia hardware and software. The final projects were individual PowerPoint presentations incorporating audio clips and images. In addition, graduate students had to do presentations restricted to educational topics. The goal was to equip these educators with sufficient knowledge to select and use multimedia products and to create their own multimedia presentations for use in the classroom. Of course, they did not become experts in the short time period, but the experience helped them climb the learning curve far enough to see into the promising future.

No prerequisite skills beyond knowing generally how to use a PC were required. Not surprisingly, therefore, there was a wide-range of computer skill levels among the students. The class members were grouped[5] into teams of three or four as they worked with each hardware/software component. Such teamwork helped level the playing field and increased the odds of getting everyone through the new material. To avoid the temptation of students keeping too low of a profile in the team huddle, though, each student was quizzed individually over every component.

Although getting hands-on experience, students also read a textbook intended to provide the terminology foundations of multimedia literacy. For example, the educators learned that resolution has several terms associated with it. Resolution is expressed in pixels (picture elements) for screens and dpi (dots-per-inch) for printing and scanning. The students covered such topics as disk file name extension meanings: WAV and AU for sound files; BMP (uncompressed bitmap) and JPEG (Joint Photographic Expert Group image compression) for still images; along with MPEG (Moving Picture Expert Group compression) and AVI (Microsoft's audio/video interleaved) for movie clips. No time was spent on the intricacies of how compression is done, but rather on why most web pictures are JPEGs instead of BMPs—compressed pictures are much smaller in size and, therefore, transmit faster.

The educators used a digital camera to capture images and transfer the pictures into an editing program where they could then alter the image in numerous useful or even humorous ways. A flatbed scanner provided similar capabilities for printed materials. For video capture, for example, another computer with a video capture board and Adobe Premier software, allowed students to put short full motion clips on disk and transition between multiple clips by adding graphical fades between them. Audio capture grabbed music clips from CDs and enabled students to fade-in and out for smoother sounding bites in their PowerPoint presentations. Since the release of FrontPage 2000, web page development basics are also covered. The quiz requirements and software used are noted in Appendix A.

The educators gave the course high marks overall, but many reported a high stress level during the first week when confronted with the wealth of new information and terminology. In her journal notes, one student highlighted the impact of the course in the following journal entry.

> This class has given me a better appreciation of what it's like to learn material that seems very overwhelming and foreign at first. I promise to have a whole new level of patience with my students who struggle through their math.

Another teacher/student reported a change in her home-life while taking the course.

> Here is a real sign of progress. For the past week or two my children [at home] have *not* been able to give me answers to my computer questions. I am delving into areas where they have not trod. How about that! I've had fun saying to them, "Do you know what a _____ is?" It feels so good!

The educators also learned that basics should still come first in multimedia presentations. Fonts should be easy to read and everything placed on a screen should be tied to the educational needs of the topic. Flashy pictures and audio are wasted if students are lost during the lesson. Participants were reminded to have an introduction, a body, and a conclusion. In other words, a presentation needs to tell students what it is going to be about, show them the content, and then remind them what was covered. A more complete listing of the presentation guidelines is shown as Appendix B.

Another issue facing a university considering a multimedia course of this nature is what will it cost in terms of hardware and software? Here is more good news. We run the first half of the course with a traditional lecture and demonstration format followed by the second half as group work—one week, two days on each system. As such, we are able to operate the course with one system each for scanning, audio capture, video capture, and one for digital camera work with a color printer. The PowerPoint and FrontPage group work is done in the main computer lab (in the same building). To stay up-to-date, we are on our third camera, second scanner, and purchased a new video capture system last year. Software costs? Basically nothing. Most programs, including Adobe Photoshop, Adobe PhotoDeluxe, and Adobe Premiere, came free with the purchased hardware. Furthermore, the Microsoft products are very inexpensive through direct licensing agreements.

Lights, Camera, Action

Once a teacher is ready, he or she needs to be sure that there is an acceptable level of support available. Ideally, schools would have technology directors who are familiar with the needs of education, as well as computer networking and operating systems. Unfortunately, such people are in short supply. In schools that already have networks in place, it may be no surprise to teachers that they suddenly know more about using multimedia after on college course than their network specialist. The guru may know many techie buzz words, but know little useful about putting a digital camera to good use in a science class. Nevertheless, technology gurus who hold the same core goal as the teachers—student learning—are still an essential resource.

After deciding the time is right and support issues are under control, teachers new to using multimedia in the classroom must be careful not to "become involved in the trappings of multimedia and lose sight of the real goal"[1]. Multimedia presentations should be clearly focused and the teacher must avoid using multimedia programs as fancy class time filler. More media does not equal more learning, and while student attention to presented material may be necessary for learning, it is unlikely to be sufficient.

Another associated risk evolves if the instructor starts developing overly complex multimedia products for classroom use.

This takes the teacher into the perhaps unfamiliar water of television, radio, speech, media design, art, and instructional design. Whitten[12] warns, "People are notorious for underestimating the amount of work it will take to achieve success when dealing with new technology. It is not uncommon to miss the estimate by 100 to 200 percent." Teachers should be wary of getting bogged down in developments that are too expensive for their resources or too expansive for their available time. A stunning ten-minute multimedia presentation on a single civil war battle will not make up for being unprepared for the rest of the week's history lessons.

Setting Achievable Goals

Those putting together the plans and goals for multimedia in the classroom should clearly state objectives expected for student leaning and avoid plans that McKenzie[8] suggest "wax eloquent on lofty goals that relate to the millennium. The workplace and the society at large. These goals translate poorly into daily class realities." Schools should be wary of letting computer hardware and software vendors establish specific objectives at the classroom level. Rather, the teachers who have been trained in the rudiments of multimedia should be active participants in establishing their objectives.

Also, teachers should not be pressured to use multimedia equipment someone else thought would be good for them. It is better for educational leaders to simply support the diffusion of technologies into classrooms where a teacher wants to use multimedia and can present a plan with the potential for improving student learning. After getting multimedia equipment for classroom use, teachers (and administrators) should stay vigilant for the possibility of new equipment slipping into the shadows, unused, as teachers get caught up in their old duties and ways of teaching.

Assessing the Value of Change

After multimedia systems are put to use, the next big step is to determine how to show results—assessment. Teachers and staff will need to identify (1) that what was done was what was really needed and (2) that students really benefitted. Such assessment is necessary as feedback on grants, to school boards, and to parents. Without valid assessments of whether multimedia technologies have met the agreed upon goals, multimedia equipment provided for a specific purpose should be channeled elsewhere.

Assessment results should remind the interested parties of what the classroom needs were, of what were the anticipated benefits of using multimedia to address those needs, and of where the project is currently. Such analysis should note what worked, unexpected problems, and unanticipated benefits. Old student projects or teacher presentation materials can be presented side-by-side to show what changed after implementing new technologies. Done correctly, assessment should give parents and taxpayers an opportunity to see that their money was used wisely.

Multimedia should be an inviting door into the classroom instead of presenting a sinister technological fog. According to Bob Brock, a principal and student in one of the multimedia courses, one of the main things the principal needs to do is to see that the goals of the community and the school mesh well and that the actions taken to achieve the goals are visible to the stakeholders. This makes the next funding request easier when everyone has confidence that the school is using its resources effectively. The varied groups controlling the school purse strings should become vested in the decisions made.

Supporters of multimedia should be sure to consider the role equipment will play in the classroom, not just what it can do from a technology viewpoint. As noted by another principal, "the objective is not to increase the number of computers in the school. It is not to educate teachers in the use of technology. The objective is to increase student achievement"[13] Certainly we hope teachers will avoid developing classroom multimedia that is just "a dull approximation"[10] of the status quo.

While the impact of this type of multimedia course on future university students will take years to unfold, there are some clear short-term results for the IS department in our commuter campus. We started with two sections of twenty-five students a year—majors and interested non-majors. Now, since the Education department decided to require this course for their majors, we are up to six sections of twenty-five students, including the two summer sections scheduled to fit the needs of inservice teachers.

References

1. Anderson, V., & Sleezer, C.M. Getting started in multimedia training: Cutting or bleeding edge? *Performance & Instruction, 34,* 9 (1995), 4–8.
2. Carroll, W.M. Technology and teachers' curricular orientations. *Educational HORIZONS, 75,* 2, (1997), 66–72.
3. Coffee, P. Courseware authoring tools are no substitute for teachers. *PC Week,* (June 29, 1992), 108.
4. Dede, C. Rethinking how to invest in technology. *Educational Leadership, 55,* 3 (1997), 2–6.
5. Grissom, S. & Van Gorp, M.J. A practical approach to integrating active and collaborative learning into the introductory computer science curriculum. *Journal of Computing in Small Colleges, 16,* 1 (2000), 95–100.
6. Hornung, C.S. & Bronack, S. Preparing technology-based teachers: Professional lessons from a K-12/university collaborative. *Tech Trends, 44,* 4 (2000), 17–20.
7. Kalmbacher, S. & Maxson, D. Instructional technology academy: Empowering teachers to lead instructional change. *NASSP Bulletin, 84,* 616 (2000), 42–48.
8. McKenzie, J. Technology's webs. *The School Administrator, 55,* 4 (1998), 6–10.
9. O'Donnell, E. *Integrating computers into the classroom: The missing key.* Lanham, MD: Scarecrow Press, 1996.
10. Schank, C. The computer isn't the medium, it's the message. *Communications of the ACM, 44,* 3 (2001), 142–143.
11. Swain, C. Predicting sunny skies: The improved forecast of K-12 technology integration in the State of Florida. *Tech Trends, 44,* 2 (2000), 25–28.
12. Whitten, W.B., II. The hurdles of technology transfer. In D.M. Gayeski (Ed.), *Multimedia for learning: Development, application, evaluation.* Englewood Cliffs, NJ: Educational Technology Publications, 1993, pp. 29–42.
13. Winter, R. (1998, September) Don't know much about technology planning. *The High School Magazine, 6,* 1 (1998), 26–28.

Appendix A

*Multimedia Skill Demos   Name:*_____

Points: 4 – smooth and accurate, practiced (perfection not required)
      3 – good but some mouse/menu fumbling; seemed to lack practice
      2 – fair, but reads prompts or slow completion/comprehension
      1 – poor, able to complete only with instructor support
      0 – failure, unpractical, and unprepared

Points ____.____ Date _____	*Points ____.____ Date _____*
Audio Capture / Manipulation	Video Capture / Manipulation
start SoundBlaster software	start Premiere
run / explain mixer and CD	capture motion video and audio
capture / edit audio from CD	place captured AVI clip in project
start Microsoft audio software	add MOV clip to project
run / explain mixer and CD	add a transition between clips
capture / alter audio from CD	preview audio
Points ____.____ Date _____	*Points ____.____ Date _____*
Digital Camera Use	Scanning
attach cable at correct times	start scanner from PhotoDeluxe
take and transfer picture to PC	crop image / do final scan
apply instant fix	rotate image
insert and place text over	apply Glowing Edges then undo
apply Watercolor in Photoshop	show how to save as JPG file
delete picture in camera	do soft edges in PhotoDraw
Points ____.____ Date _____	*Points ____.____ Date _____*
PowerPoint Operations	FrontPage Webpage Creation
new pres; apply template	create a new web page
change font, size, color	add text content
add / rearrange slides	apply a theme
do text animations	add a scrolling marquee
do transitions between slides	add a photo-quality picture
insert photo picture from file	create a second page with words
insert and setup sound from file	put links between pages

Appendix B

Multimedia Final Presentation Grading

Your topic (you must have my topic approval) should be something that you know about already. Pick something of relatively small scope (NOT the history of France.) I will not pre-grade the presentation—my requirements are listed below. For development problems, I am available as needed before the last minute. The penalties below are not exact or inclusive, just guidelines.

    a.   Must submit <u>6-to-page handout</u> before starting – 5%
OBVIOUS presentation organization required
    <u>introduction</u> to topic with your name on the first slide – 5%
    <u>body</u> usually with three main points – 10%
    <u>summary</u> slide of the main points – 5%
    take question on topic or presentation development

use captured pictures
    <u>at least five pictures, NOT clipart</u> – 10%
    must support topic and be recognizable – 5%
    may be scanned, still-camera, motion captured, downloaded

    full-motion clips NOT required

use captured voice or music
    <u>at least three different audio clips (usually 1 to 10 seconds)</u> – 10%
    NOT PowerPoint, Office, or other "noises" – 5%
        From any source as appropriate; may be just background
    music at start or at end but must not detract from topic

multimedia presentation
    <u>not a formal speech, nor rambling, nor read</u> – 5%
    you seem able to run PowerPoint – 5%
    consistent, legible colors and fonts – 10%
    avoid random transitions and animations – 10%
    bullets; **not** text for reading by the audience – 10%
    <u>FOUR minutes</u> – if under 3 or over 6 minutes – 10%
        you **MUST** stop after 6 minutes with no credit for the rest.

From *Journal of Computing in Small Colleges*, October 2001, pp. 52–61. Copyright © 2001 by Consortium for Computing Sciences in Colleges - CCSC. Reprinted by permission.

UNIT 5

Multimedia and Technology

Unit Selections

Key Points to Consider

- What is ROI? How would you perform a return-on-investment analysis? How would you determine what is a cost and what is a benefit?

- Can we create virtual classrooms with interactive Internet multimedia? What are the problems involved in implementing such technology? Can such classrooms provide instruction that is as good as the best of today's classroom instruction?

Student Web Site

www.mhcls.com/online

Internet References

Further information regarding these Web sites may be found in this book's preface or online.

CNN Interactive
   http://www.cnn.com/
Mighty Media
   http://www.mightymedia.com
MSNBC Cover Page
   http://www.msnbc.com
NASA Aerospace Education Services Program
   http://www.okstate.edu/aesp/AESP.html
The Science Learning Network
   http://www.sln.org

Multimedia is important to education because of its potential to improve the quality of classroom and at-a-distance learning. It can pull together text, pictures, and even moving video, in any combination to provide a richer environment that will engage all the senses. It provides a new means of communicating, an easier way to illustrate difficult concepts, and a way to entice the learner to become actively involved in controlling and manipulating information, anytime and anywhere.

Because of the nature of multimedia systems, it is easy to provide a variety of choices to the learner. This capability enables designers and developers to build systems that fit the requirements of interactive problem solving instructional systems. Such systems are called multimedia inference engines. The engines provide learners with three types of buttons that include the following functions: navigation, access, and manipulation. The inference engines are used in conjunction with knowledge base that is related to a subject matter area. The computer can then assess the learner's data and decide whether the learner has collected an adequate sample and if the conclusion is justified. Such systems will allow learners to develop their problem-solving skills. Without multimedia, instructional problem-solving systems would not be feasible, nor would we be able to enrich the problem-solving facilities within schools at a fraction of the cost of physical laboratories. Such applications of multimedia provide a cost-benefit ratio that is quite favorable, and return-on-investment analysis is one of the side benefits provided by powerful technology.

The articles in this unit review some of the issues emerging from widespread interest in designing, developing, implementing and publishing multimedia titles. In the lead article, Mott and Granata discuss the difficulties of demonstrating benefits of ROI for money and time spent building, implementing, and supporting a teaching and learning infrastructure. They propose an alternative method for accounting for the costs and benefits of investments made in teaching and learning technology. They recommend that institutions focus on measuring the value on investment (VOI) of their instructional technology programs and initiatives. For reasons detailed in the article, the authors believe this approach is both more realistic and more helpful in terms of prioritizing and assigning scarce resources to maximize institutional effectiveness.

In the next article, Diana Oblinger states that an essential component of facilitating learning is understanding learners. The learning styles, attitudes and approaches of high school students differ from those of eighteen to twenty-two year-old college students. The styles, attitudes and approaches of adult learners differ yet again. How well do college and university faculty, administrators and staff understand these differences? How often do they take the differences into account when designing programs or courses? Diana answers these questions in this article.

Next, Lucille Renwick discusses creating E-Books, Interactive Prairies, Science Up Close, and Virtual Field Trips that can be brought into the classroom using today's emerging multimedia technologies. Many teachers are using technologies such as computers, scanners, and digital cameras to motivate and excite their students. Whether studying ecosystems or the solar system, teachers have found super and simple ways to embed technology in their science lessons. This article provides examples of these exciting uses of multimedia.

In the next essay, Richard B. Speaker, Jr. introduces a set of papers focusing on the issues and practices in using technologies for teaching and learning science and mathematics in the K-12 schools in the Southern United States where the digital divide between technology rich schools and technology poor schools is growing wider despite attempts to provide funds and standards to bring the schools up to national standards. In particular, the paper discusses the current political and theoretical stances that entangle the schools, methodological issues in the collection of data on technology integration in science and mathematics classrooms, a framework for technology integration into the various levels of education, and the governance and funding structures of the schools.

Next, Kopec, Whitlock, and Kogen discuss SmartTutor—a comprehensive web-based peer-tutoring service geared to the needs of urban commuter college students. The new system is based on SmartBooks, a multi-media educational technology that was developed just prior to the emergence of the World Wide Web. This technology has provided a user-friendly, self-paced, easy to modify, software environment intended to serve the user's learning needs—particularly in an urban commuter college environment.

The Value of Teaching and Learning Technology: Beyond ROI

Measuring the value of an investment instead of dollar-for-dollar return provides a clearer picture of benefits and costs

JONATHAN D. MOTT AND GARIN GRANATA

Given the hundreds of millions of dollars spent each year on technology initiatives in higher education, questions about the value of these expenditures almost seem moot. However, virtually every CIO at every institution of higher education is asked to report the return on investment (ROI) of technology spending on his or her campus. Making such an accounting is a daunting challenge. Applying a strict business-school definition of ROI would require providing evidence of a dollar-for-dollar return on hardware, software, and infrastructure projects. The desired return in question, however, is not always so obvious. Should technology investments save money? Increase institutional capacity? Improve throughput?

In the face of such ambiguity, many CIOs throw up their hands in frustration. Bob Weir, vice president of Information Services at Northeastern University in Boston, asserted that technology ROI is "impossible to reliably calculate, compare, or claim" in higher education.[1] This is so, he argued, because there is no universally recognized "coin of the realm" for assigning value to IT investments.

While the academic community has become accustomed to the "ROI question" as it relates to IT in the broad sense, the burgeoning scope and expense of instructional IT raises the question in new, more targeted ways. Virtually every university and college in the United States has implemented a course management system (such as Blackboard, Desire2Learn, Sakai, or WebCT). At the same time, most institutions have ramped up their support for instructors interested in developing online courses or multimedia enhancements for traditional courses. As a consequence, institutions now face the dilemma of storing and managing terabytes of teaching and learning content. Together with expenditures on e-portfolio solutions, online assessment and evaluation tools, and increasingly sophisticated classroom technologies, colleges and universities are spending a growing percentage of their overall IT budgets on what might be termed the teaching and learning infrastructure.

Just as it is difficult to demonstrate ROI for broad IT initiatives, it is difficult to show ROI for money and time spent building, implementing, and supporting a teaching and learning infrastructure. In this article, we propose an alternative method for accounting for the costs and benefits of investments made in teaching and learning technology (hereafter TLT). More specifically, we recommend that institutions focus on measuring the *value* on investment (VOI) of their instructional technology programs and initiatives. For reasons detailed below, we believe this approach is both more realistic and more helpful in terms of prioritizing and assigning scarce resources to maximize institutional effectiveness. A focus on VOI allows institutions to begin with the end in mind—that is, to design, build, and implement a teaching and learning infrastructure that demonstrably and consistently contributes to the realization of desired institutional outcomes. We believe that using the approach recommended here not only makes it possible to demonstrate the value of teaching and learning investments but also makes the value more obvious and easier to communicate to others.

VOI versus ROI

Perhaps because most colleges and universities have departments or schools of business, higher education has a powerful tendency to demand evidence of dollar-for-dollar returns for time and money expended on IT. While this seems a straightforward proposition, such efforts generally falter in the face of competing definitions of "return." Indeed, the lack of consensus about how to measure ROI has led many to give up on precise, quantitative measures of the value of IT investments. Similar frustration in the corporate world prompted Gartner to challenge organizations to focus on the VOI of so-called soft initiatives that do not obviously or directly add to the bottom line.[2] While value can be had from investing in organizational competencies, new methodologies and capabilities, and better organizational collaboration, the dollar-for-dollar return on such investments is difficult to measure.

Stated in the simplest terms, VOI differs from ROI in its focus on intermediate rather than final outcomes. A VOI approach to

IT, for example, emphasizes the contributions of new hardware or software to institutional competencies. Targeted competencies are those shown by experience, evaluation, and research to contribute to an institution's performance—its ability to produce key deliverables.

A VOI-driven resource allocation and evaluation process promotes a broader, more strategic view of project consideration and prioritization. ROI might offer greater precision, but it also creates a tendency to emphasize narrowly tactical IT.[3] Although tempting, this approach is a mistake because ROI is much more difficult to demonstrate for strategic investments aimed at broad organizational competencies and capacities. Because these soft improvements are critical to the success of institutions of higher education, however, we believe that it is at least as important for organizations to account for VOI as to account for ROI.

A focus on value instead of return promotes more meaningful measurement of the benefits of investments in TLT, but measuring VOI is not without pitfalls. The most significant problem stems from the fact that VOI is not a direct measure of an investment's impact on the bottom line. For institutions of higher learning, the most important measurable results are things like the number of students served, time-to-completion, graduation rates, and success of graduates (initial job placement, career performance, and so forth).

Adopting a VOI-centered approach to TLT is particularly appropriate given the difficulties associated with consistently measuring teaching and learning outcomes. For example, one possible indicator of student success is average GPA. However, with grade inflation and inconsistent grading standards across disciplines and institutions, this is not an entirely valid or reliable measure. Using exit exam scores, job placement statistics, or other measures would be similarly problematic. Each institution and each program within each institution has its own set of success criteria for students, a reality reflected in current accreditation standards. Investments in TLT do not always contribute to these things in an obviously direct way. Rather, these investments contribute to institutional capacity to produce these results more effectively and consistently.

It might not be obvious how a CMS, for example, contributes to an institution's time-to-completion or graduation rates. While an ROI model would require demonstrating exactly how a CMS contributes to these things, VOI simply requires that we show how a CMS contributes to important institutional competencies (Gartner's soft infrastructure). Appropriately used, a CMS can promote better teacher-student communication, enhance large lecture courses, make classes more flexible for students, and so forth. These things can, in turn, improve time-to-completion and graduation rates.

The more realistic (though messier) reality of VOI is illustrated in Figure 1. If we think of the inputs and outputs of a university, the inputs are dollars, faculty, and enrolling students. The outputs are graduates, research results, and general community improvement. In between, however, are thousands upon thousands of decisions about what to do with inputs to get the desired outputs. Focusing on VOI is synonymous with focusing on how to use inputs more effectively to promote better (both in quantity and quality) outputs. The middle of the diagram depicts this as a process of prioritizing the use of inputs to increase competencies and capacities in areas that contribute to desired outputs. When inputs are used to increase the ability of an institution to produce desired outputs, we can say that the inputs (investments) have been used to add value to the institution.

Pursuing VOI at Brigham Young University

The late 1990s saw considerable administrative support for infusing technology into teaching and learning at Brigham Young University (BYU). Behind this support was a desire to make teaching and learning more effective, to provide learning opportunities for more students, and to save money. There were

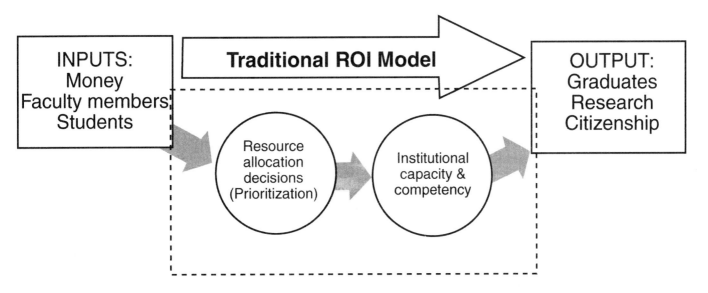

Figure 1 Using inputs to promote desired outputs.

significant points of disagreement, however, about which goals were most important and how they should be pursued. From an instructional technology perspective, difficult questions were raised about resource allocation and project prioritization. Should we focus on online course development? Building a sophisticated learning management system? Buying and implementing a less sophisticated (but more practical) CMS?

University leaders decided it was important not just to answer these questions but also to create a framework for answering them consistently in the future. Several key stakeholders and a new teaching and learning with technology "czar" (the TLT Czar) were assigned to tackle these issues. The brief retrospective of this effort provided here might give the false impression that we had a clear idea of the steps we would take from the day the journey commenced. That is simply not the case. Rather, we began by focusing on what seemed to be the most important first question—What is it that we really value?—and then moved on from there. The process is represented in Figure 2.

Identifying and Agreeing on Teaching and Learning Values

The first step in strategically mapping an institution's teaching and learning infrastructure is to reconcile current activities and projects with the institution's mission and objectives. While it might seem grandiose and pedantic to make such a connection, doing so is vital in establishing a successful VOI process.

Our process began with a year-long project to define the university's distributed learning strategy, starting with revisiting the university's founding documents. Through extensive conversations with stakeholders from across campus and with input from an outside higher education consulting group (Collegis Eduprise), we articulated a strategy for teaching and learning improvement at BYU.

The strategy consisted of five specific goals:

1. Develop and support faculty instead of courses, enabling faculty members to effectively integrate technology into their teaching and learning efforts.
2. Develop and refine distributed learning models to promote wider adoption of technology-mediated instruction.

3. Encourage and empower departments to take strategic advantage of available models, tools, and resources.
4. Unify production and delivery of instructional materials across campus.
5. Effectively manage teaching and learning resources.

These objectives have since been amended and fine-tuned. We incorporated the Sloan Consortium's *Elements of Quality in Online Education*[4] standards into our evaluation of a TLT initiative's value, for example. Changes made collaboratively have contributed to the maintenance of a commonly agreed upon, unifying statement of TLT value.

Note that none of our TLT value objectives refers explicitly to university outputs (graduation rates, for example). Rather, the strategy emphasizes areas of opportunity where effective TLT integration can improve the university's capacity to achieve its loftier goals.

Coordinating Support Organizations

Once articulated, these objectives became a common touchstone for organizations across campus that support teaching and learning. This in turn prompted a willingness to coordinate and collaborate in new and important ways. Under the direction of the TLT Czar, a loose federation of support organizations was established, called the Teaching & Learning Support Services (TLSS) Group. Group membership consisted of leaders or decision makers from the library, the IT office, independent study, copyright, and the Center for Instructional Design. At first, the group focused almost exclusively on learning about member organizations—what they did, how they did it, and why they did it. As areas of overlap or common purpose emerged, group meetings rapidly evolved into coordination and collaboration sessions.

The power of the TLSS was not simply open communication, however, but communication with a purpose. Each member group had bought in to the five objectives of the distributed learning strategy, so the communication (and subsequent collaboration) of the TLSS focused on better achieving these goals as an institution. Most importantly, the strategy provides a consistent, shared definition of value and serves as a foundation for

| Step 1: Identify and agree on teaching & learning values | | Step 2: Get various support organizations on the same page | | Step 3: Create capacity & environment for collaboration & coordination | |

OUTCOME: Consistent process for prioritizing and completing projects that add measurable value to the university

Figure 2 Creating a process for pursuing VOI at BYU.

a consistent framework for evaluating, approving, and prioritizing new TLT initiatives.

Creating an Environment for Collaboration and Coordination

Supported by a unified strategy statement and consistent goals, the TLSS organizations collaborated and coordinated in ways not possible a few years earlier. Strategic budget plans were shared and reviewed openly at group meetings; resources (budgets and personnel) were transferred to address institutional priorities; old programs were altered to foster better coordination; and new programs were created to take advantage of new organizational synergies.

One of the most significant accomplishments of the TLSS was the establishment of a unifying TLT infrastructure blueprint (see Figure 3). The schematic represents the group's efforts to accomplish goals 4 and 5 in the distributed learning strategy: "Unify production and delivery of instructional materials across campus" and "Effectively manage teaching and learning resources." The blueprint serves as a basis for rationalizing the teaching and learning systems the university adopts and supports. It also provides various groups a common framework for thinking about components of the infrastructure and how they affect other organizations. This significantly reduces the temptation to freelance and build or buy applications that meet local needs but tend to thwart enterprise interoperability and collaboration.

This blueprint has the virtue of focusing on the functions necessary to extend and improve teaching and learning, not specific applications. For example, it is critical to manage curriculum at the university and program levels. Technology solutions can make this a more efficient and effective undertaking, certainly, but the key functional needs are the most important variables in the analysis, development or acquisition, and implementation process—not specific applications or tools.

Similarly, the blueprint identifies content management, content transformation and publication, course content delivery, and other functions that must be supported by the teaching and learning infrastructure. This non-application-specific approach keeps the focus on adding value to teaching and learning activities at the university and mitigates inevitable tendencies toward tunnel vision and vendor-induced myopia. The blueprint thus serves as a teaching and learning strategy reinforcement mechanism, constantly returning focus and attention to the value (defined by shared goals) of current and potential teaching and learning applications and tools.

Again, note that the common framework for TLT investments (as represented in BYU's schematic) does not explicitly focus on the university's key outcomes or results. The purpose of a common framework is instead to focus resources and efforts on improving the institution's capacity to deliver these results. The VOI of a TLT expenditure is measured by its direct contribution to the institution's statement of teaching and learning competencies.

Institutionalizing a VOI-Driven Process for TLT

These three steps (agreeing on common values, getting organizations on the same page, fostering better collaboration) were essential preconditions for implementing a VOI-driven process

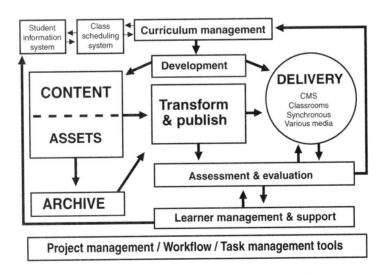

Figure 3 Teaching and learning infrastructure schematic.

for identifying, prioritizing, and completing TLT projects that consistently add measurable value to the university. All of these efforts would have been for naught, however, if we had not also implemented a new process for evaluating, approving, prioritizing, implementing, and evaluating TLT projects. We recognized the necessity of creating a commonly adhered to, consistent framework for assessing the value of TLT efforts and expenditures at all stages of a product's life-cycle.

In our experience, a disciplined, rigorous process is essential to the institutionalization of a VOI-driven approach to TLT decision making. At BYU, we instituted three specific support disciplines to create and sustain a culture of VOI: product management, priority management, and project management.

Product Management

Each application and tool in the TLT infrastructure is a product defined by function, not vendor. Each product has a natural life-cycle that must be carefully managed. Product management oversees all aspects of a product to ensure it meets immediate user needs as well as the university's long-term goals and objectives. Product managers work closely with key stakeholders to evaluate the potential or current value of each product in the TLT portfolio. Product managers function most effectively when integrated into the organizations that implement the products they manage.

A product portfolio manager takes the larger view of several product managers' products, the interactions of those products, and the value the portfolio adds to the university. Both product managers and product portfolio managers monitor the TLT environment, the effectiveness of the current configuration of products, and the value the products individually and collectively add to the university. Product managers initiate project proposals when existing products need to be upgraded or replaced or new products need to be acquired to fill gaps.

Product management is an essential support discipline because university executives responsible for TLT generally lack the time and often the product-specific expertise to monitor product spaces and make detailed recommendations about them. BYU leaders rely heavily on product managers to help them identify needs and solutions in the TLT infrastructure.

Priority Management

The number of good TLT ideas will always outstrip the resources available at any institution of higher education. Consequently, decisions must be made about the comparative value of competing TLT product proposals. The centerpiece of an effective VOI-driven process is a disciplined, value-focused priority management team (PMT). This team evaluates, approves, and prioritizes TLT project proposals. These decisions are based on a well-defined set of objective scoring anchors that allow the team to assign quantitative scores to projects based on the value they will add to the university. The scoring anchors are derived from the objectives of the distributed learning strategy, the TLT infrastructure schematic (Figure 3), and the Sloan standards. The PMT not only evaluates and approves work on specific

TLT projects but also ranks and prioritizes projects to allocate resources to the most important projects first.

A PMT should consist of university and organizational leaders responsible for realizing institutional objectives affected by the product portfolio for which the team makes decisions. For example, the TLT PMT at BYU consists of the director and associate directors of the Center for Instructional Design and the TLT product manager from the Office of Information Technology. The associate academic vice presidents for Undergraduate Education and Faculty are also ex officio members of the PMT. These individuals provide executive input and endorsement of the TLT team's decisions.

Project Management

Projects differ from products in that projects have clear start-and-stop dates and target specific, limited, product-related outcomes. For instance, a CMS is a product, but the effort to bring a CMS online in a specific hardware and software environment is a project.

Once TLT projects have been approved and prioritized, project management makes possible successful execution of initiatives in priority order. Project managers employ a set of principles, practices, and techniques that help project teams stay focused on priorities established by the PMT. In particular, project managers enforce decisions about project schedule, cost, and scope. At the task level, project managers carefully track the progress of each project and report regularly to the PMT. Project managers also optimize resource allocation and use and facilitate effective planning and collaboration for project teams.

Putting It All Together

In addition to the three specific support disciplines, a successful VOI-driven process also depends on executive-level sponsorship and participation with the PMT. Each product and project needs a sponsor—someone who has the authority to approve the product or project and to assign resources to it. Most importantly, the sponsor also confirms that a proposed product or project adds value by improving key university competencies and capacities.

The product or project sponsor may be a department chair, a vice president, or another institutional leader who champions the product or project in the context of all other competing demands for resources and attention. The TLT project prioritization framework provides the sponsor with a consistent, objective rationale for supporting specific initiatives. The sponsor anchors the product or project in the VOI-driven evaluation, approval, implementation, and evaluation process.

In addition to working closely with the organization supported or served by specific products, a product manager achieves success through his or her working relationship with a designated sponsor or sponsors. This is especially true for product portfolio managers. It is critical that these individuals partner effectively with the appropriate sponsor or sponsors having institutional stewardship for their product portfolios.

As product managers maintain a value-focused eye on each product in the portfolio, they continually consider how an established product can be optimized within the context of other university systems. Working closely with product sponsors, the product manager helps create and implement value-driven product strategies.

The product manager also works with product implementers, users, evaluators, vendors, and user communities to keep up with current local and market trends, emerging deficiencies, and opportunities. Based on these observations, product managers initiate proposals for product enhancements or replacements. As institutional requirements change (as defined by the sponsor), the product manager adjusts accordingly.

Product managers play a critical role in the VOI evaluation and reporting process by carefully analyzing the performance and financial aspects of each product, including end-user evaluations, profit and loss statements, and total cost of ownership. At BYU, product managers also work closely with TLT support organizations to conduct thorough evaluations of each product's contributions to key institutional competencies (as delineated in the prioritization process). This process assesses the past, current, and projected future value of each product in the portfolio.[5] Channeling this information back into the process permits measuring and refining the value-effectiveness of products.

Does It Really Work?

The process described above might seem too good to be true. After two years of implementing this process, however, we can declare that it does, in fact, work. An example is in order. Like many institutions, BYU has grappled with the ROI of our CMS. In the past, this question focused on the kinds of difficult-to-measure factors we have cited—does our CMS improve student GPA, job placement, exit-exam performance, and so forth? By changing the focus to VOI, we instead seek to measure the value of our CMS by measuring its contributions to our institutional capacity for effective teaching and learning.

Through surveys, focus groups, and interviews, faculty and students overwhelmingly report that our CMS enhances their teaching and learning activities. Using this data, we have been able to "count" the value of our CMS. In the context of our distributed learning strategy objectives, we can say that we have:

1. Developed and supported faculty members who are transforming teaching and learning by using a CMS.
2. Developed and refined our distributed learning models (although this remains a work in progress).
3. Encouraged and empowered academic departments to use technology strategically to address curricular challenges and opportunities.

Considering the Sloan Consortium's *Elements of Quality in Online Education*, we can also objectively demonstrate that the implementation of a CMS at BYU has:

1. Improved learning effectiveness—a claim backed by rigorous studies of key hybrid courses where the CMS is used to free up instructor time to pursue higher-order learning objectives in the classroom and in one-on-one student consultations.
2. Improved student access to learning materials and learning opportunities.
3. Improved student and faculty satisfaction with the learning process.

We do not have space here for a detailed discussion of each of these assertions or the data collected to support them. Our focus on VOI, however, has allowed us to objectively evaluate the value added to the university by licensing and implementing a CMS. Through this exercise, we have determined that the value gained is worth the dollars and time required to get it. Among other things, our faculty and students report that the CMS improves their ability to communicate (particularly outside of regular class or office hours times) and to organize and manage their courses more effectively.[6] Additionally, students are using the CMS to collaborate, share ideas, and complete group projects more consistently and effectively than in the past. Perhaps most significantly, growing numbers of faculty use the CMS to manage the didactic elements of their courses and low-stakes assessment (quizzes) so that they can spend in-class time on more intensive discussion, analysis, and synthesis. During the past four academic semesters, students at BYU have completed an average of more than 20,000 quizzes a day using the CMS. These and other kinds of activities are occurring on our campus at significantly higher rates because we have implemented a CMS.

A significant caveat is in order, however. While a VOI approach can help institutions avoid the pitfalls of vainly trying to measure ROI, value judgments must still be made. VOI does not promise a purely objective evaluation and decision-making process with regard to TLT. For example, we have debated (and likely will continue to debate) the dollar and time value of the benefits derived from our CMS. Are our CMS benefits worth $100,000? $500,000? $1,000,000? Another obvious factor is that wise administrators will seek to get as much value from their CMS (and other teaching and learning technologies) for as little money as possible. Consequently, we are constantly evaluating and considering alternatives to our current CMS that might return the same or similar value at a lower cost. In the end, though, a VOI approach has enabled us to make more rational, well-informed decisions about the real, measurable value of our CMS and the resources the university is willing to commit (now and in the future) to a product that produces that value.

Conclusion

We have outlined a replicable VOI process for making decisions about TLT in higher education. We readily admit, though, that no process or set of guidelines can yield a perfectly objective framework for evaluating the relative value of TLT projects. However, we believe BYU's VOI process provides a much more consistent and objective framework than many TLT decision makers believed possible.

As you contemplate implementing a VOI process at your institution, we reiterate the importance of broad, open communication and patience. It will take time to get the right people involved in the conversation (at multiple levels both in the administration and the faculty). It is also critical to articulate and build consensus around a framework of goals against which products (and associated projects) can be evaluated and prioritized. We do not believe it is necessary to adopt the same structures and processes that we have at BYU. Nonetheless, you will need discipline, rigor, and consistency to define, implement, and sustain a VOI process that will enable decision makers to look at the same data through the same set of lenses and make widely agreed upon decisions about TLT.

Our experience tells us that with the right people involved and with a commitment to follow accepted objectives and processes, it is imminently possible for institutions of higher learning to consistently measure the relative value of potential and existing TLT products and projects. Doing so enforces a consistent focus on adding value to the core business of the university and mitigates against arbitrary and less-effective resource allocation.

Endnotes

1. R. Weir, "IT Investment Decisions that Defy Arithmetic," *EDUCAUSE Quarterly*, Vol. 27, No. 1, 2004, pp. 10–13, <http://www.educause.edu/apps/eq/eqm04/eqm0412.asp>.

2. K. Harris, M. Caplan Grey, and C. Rozwell, "Changing the View of ROI to VOI—Value on Investment," Gartner Research Note, SPA-14-7250, Nov. 14, 2001.

3. D. M. Norris, "Value on Investment in Higher Education" (Boulder, Colo.: EDUCAUSE Center for Applied Research, Research Bulletin, Issue 18, 2003). According to Norris, "tactical" investments also tend to anchor organizations in the status quo because they usually focus on incrementally improving the efficiency and probability of existing processes and practices.

4. J. Bourne and J. C. Moore, eds., *Elements of Quality in Online Education: Practice and Direction* (Needham, Mass.: The Sloan Consortium, 2003).

5. TLT support organizations also work with university leaders and the Office of University Assessment to evaluate the connection between these competencies and key university outputs.

6. Data from our CMS studies about increases or decreases in faculty time spent on teaching is inconclusive. Some faculty members report spending less time managing their course with a CMS while others report spending slightly more time. Still others report no change in the amount of time they spend teaching with a CMS. On average, the CMS does not appear to increase or decrease the amount of time faculty spend managing their courses. We anticipate that this will change over time as faculty members become more familiar with the CMS and use it more efficiently.

JONATHAN D. MOTT (jonmott@byu.edu) is Director of the Center for Instructional Design, and Garin Granata (garin_granata@byu.edu) is Enterprise Product Manager, Teaching & Learning, at Brigham Young University in Provo, Utah.

Boomers and Gen-Xers Millennials

Understanding the New Students

DIANA OBLINGER

An essential component at facilitating learning is understanding learners. The learning styles, attitudes, and approaches at high school students differ from those of eighteen- to twenty-two-year-old college students. The styles, attitudes, and approaches of adult learners differ yet again. How well do college and university faculty, administrators, and staff understand these differences? How often do they take the differences into account when designing programs or courses?

More students attend college part-time than in previous years; a higher proportion of students are women; and more students are over age twenty-five.

What do we know about today's "new students"? Perhaps most obviously, we know that these students have been heavily influenced by information technology. The "new" student may be a seventeen-year-old high school student (a "Millennial") who uses instant messaging to contact peers and teachers. The "new" student may be a twenty-six-year-old college student (a "Gen-X") whose expectations of customer service are radically different from those of previous generations. Or the "new" student may be a forty-year-old working mother (a "Baby Boomer") who is completing a degree via e-learning so that she can balance work and family responsibilities. One of the greatest challenges facing American higher education is how to deal with such a variety of "new" students.

Changes in the Student Population

Current higher education administrators, as well as many faculty and staff, represent a different generation from the majority of the student population. With an average faculty age of over fifty, many decision-makers in higher education graduated in the 1970s.[1] The experiences of a 1970s generation of students are likely to be quite different from those of the current student body. A comparison of student data from 1970 and 1999 illustrates some of these differences (see Table 1).[2]

It is no surprise that enrollment has increased in the last thirty years. The data illustrate that enrollment growth in two-year institutions has exceeded the pace of growth in four-year colleges and universities. There are other trends worth noting: more students attend college part-time than in previous years; a higher proportion of students are women; and more students are over age twenty-five.

The National Center for Education Statistics (NCES) has reported that three-quarters of all undergraduates are

Table 1 Student Data in 1970 and 1999

	1970	1999
Enrollment	7.4 million	12.7 million
Two-year enrollment	31%	44%
Attend part-time	28%	39%
Women	42%	56%
Older than age twenty-five	28%	39%
Nontraditional	N/A	73%
Have dependents	N/A	27%
Employed	N/A	80%

Source: National Center for Education Statistics, "The Condition of Education 2002".

"nontraditional!"[3] Nontraditional students are defined as having one or more of the following characteristics:

- *Delayed enrollment*, and did not enter postsecondary education in the same year that he or she graduated from high school
- *Attend part-time,* for all or part of the academic year
- *Work full-time,* thirty-five hours or more, while enrolled
- *Are financially independent*, as defined by financial aid
- *Have dependents,* other than a spouse, including children or others
- *Are single parents,* having one or more dependent children
- *Lack* a *high school diploma*

Many of these characteristics were not measured in earlier studies, presumably because they were relatively rare. The implication is that campus populations today are quite different from those in the days when college and university decision-makers were students.

Not only is the profile of today's student body different, but the life experiences that shaped today's students are quite different from those of previous eras. Each generation is defined by its life experiences, giving rise to different attitudes, beliefs, and sensitivities. The "Depression generation" experienced World War II and the Cold War. "Baby Boomers" grew up with the space race, the civil rights movement, Vietnam, and Watergate. "Generation X" saw the fall of the Berlin Wall and the emergence of AIDS and the Web. Consider some of the other defining experiences of Generation X students:

- The Chinese government killed protesters in Tiananmen Square.
- The U.S. stock market crashed.
- The Chernobyl nuclear accident occurred.
- The *Exxon Valdez* caused an oil spill.
- The *Challenger* space shuttle exploded.
- The first computer disk was sold.[4]

But Gen-Xers do not necessarily represent current college and university students. A new group is entering higher education—a group called the "Millennial generation:" The Millennials were born in or after the year 1982. Millennials exhibit different characteristics from those of siblings just a few years older. Millennials

- gravitate toward group activity;
- identify with their parents' values and feel close to their parents;
- spend more time doing homework and housework and less time watching TV;
- believe "it's cool to be smart";
- are fascinated by new technologies;
- are racially and ethnically diverse; and
- often (one in five) have at least one immigrant parent.

When asked about problems facing their generation, many Millennials respond that the biggest one is the poor example that adults set for kids.[5]

Along with differences in attitudes, Millennials exhibit distinct learning styles. For example, their learning preferences tend toward teamwork, experiential activities, structure, and the use of technology. Their strengths include multitasking, goal orientation, positive attitudes, and a collaborative style.[6]

View of Technology

Some general trends are emerging about how learners view technology. Not surprisingly, technology is assumed to be a natural part of the environment. The younger the age group, the higher is the percentage who use the Internet for school, work, and leisure. This comfort with technology often leads to a perception that the use of technology in schools is inadequate.

In a study of how those age twelve to seventeen use the Web, researchers found that 94 percent use the Internet for school research and that 78 percent believe the Internet helps them with schoolwork. Among teens, instant messaging and e-mail seem to be natural communication and socialization mechanisms: 70 percent use instant messaging to keep in touch; 41 percent use e-mail and instant messaging to contact teachers or schoolmates about classwork. An even higher percentage (81 percent) use e-mail to stay in touch with friends and relatives. In fact, a slight majority (56 percent) prefer the Internet to the telephone.[7]

Perhaps because of the contrast between their comfort with technology and the technology comfort level of teachers, many students find the use of technology in schools to be disappointing. Students consider themselves more Internet-savvy than their teachers. They indicate that their teachers' use of technology is uninspiring. Students report seeing better ways to use technology than do their teachers. They also state that administrative restrictions, older equipment, and/or filtering software inhibit their in-school use of technology. Their greatest use of technology is outside of schools.[8]

A few years their senior, today's college and university students were born in the years immediately following the introduction of the PC. Among this group, 20 percent began using computers between the ages of five and eight. Virtually all students were using computers by the time they were sixteen to eighteen years of age.[9] Another measure of the ubiquity of technology to current college and university students is the percentage who own computers. In a recent survey, 84 percent reported owning their own computer, with 25 percent owning more than one computer. Twenty-eight percent own a notebook computer. And in 2003, more students plan to buy a notebook (47 percent) than a desktop (43 percent). Students spend an average of eleven hours per week online. Other indicators of their comfort with technology include the percentage who make online purchases (54 percent, with $1.6 billion in sales) and the percentage who bank online (43 percent).[10]

When asked about the impact of the Internet on their college experience, 79 percent said the Internet has had a positive influence: 60 percent believe the Internet has improved their relationships with classmates; 56 percent believe it has improved their relationships with professors. Contrary to fears expressed by some in academia, students are not using e-mail as their sole mode of communication. Only 19 percent communicate with professors more by e-mail than face-to-face. However, 55 percent use e-mail to arrange face-to-face meetings. They also tend to use e-mail to clarify information: 75 percent use e-mail for explanation of assignments. Even more (89 percent) have received class announcements via e-mail. In addition, students report that the Internet allows them to express ideas that they would not have voiced in class. Finally, 73 percent of students say they are more likely to conduct research by using the Internet than by going to the library.[11] When students were asked, two-thirds indicated that they know how to find valid information from the Web. However, they added that they realize the Web does not meet all their information needs.[12]

One way to describe these trends is the emergence of an "information-age mindset." The attitudes—and aptitudes—of students who have grown up "with technology (or who have spent significant amounts of time with it) appear to differ from those of students who rarely use technology. Jason Frand has described ten attributes of an information-age mindset:

- *Computers aren't technology.* Students have never known life without computers and the Internet. To them the computer is not a technology—it is an assumed part of life.
- *The Internet is better than TV.* In recent years, the number of hours spent watching TV has declined, being supplanted by time online. Reasons for the change include interactivity and the increased use of the Internet for socializing.
- *Reality is no longer real.* Those things that appear real over the Internet may not be. Digital images may have been altered. E-mail sent from someone's address may not have come from that person. And the content may or may not be accurate.
- *Doing is more important than knowing.* Knowledge is no longer perceived to be the ultimate goal, particularly in light of the fact that the half-life of information is so short. Results and actions are considered more important than the accumulation of facts.
- *Learning more closely resembles Nintendo than logic.* Nintendo symbolizes a trial-and-error approach to solving problems; losing is the fastest way to mastering a game because losing represents learning. This contrasts with previous generations' more logical, rule-based approach to solving problems.
- *Multitasking is a way of life.* Students appear to be quite comfortable when engaged in multiple activities simultaneously, such as listening to music, sending instant messages, doing homework, and chatting on the phone. Multitasking may also be a response to information overload.
- *Typing is preferred* to *handwriting.* Students prefer typing to handwriting. Many admit their handwriting is atrocious. Penmanship has been superseded by keyboarding skills.
- *Staying connected is essential.* Students stay in touch, via multiple devices, as they move throughout the day.

Cell phones, PDAs, and computers ensure they remain connected anyplace and anytime. As the network becomes more ubiquitous, increasing numbers of students participate in real-time dialogues from anywhere using a variety of devices.

- *There is zero tolerance for delays.* Having grown up in a customer-service culture, today's students have a strong demand for immediacy and little tolerance for delays. They expect that services will be available 24x7 in a variety of modes (Web, phone, in person) and that responses will be quick.
- *Consumer and creator are blurring.* In a file-sharing, cut-and-paste world, the distinctions between creator, owner, and consumer of information are fading. The operative assumption is often that if something is digital, it is everyone's property.[13]

For today's learners, customer service is an expectation, not an exception. Yet it is rare that students and institutions have the same expectations for service.

Implications

What do the differing learning preferences and views of technology of the "new students" mean for colleges and universities? There might be few implications if students were passive consumers and did not use their "purchasing power." However, there are many indications that students actively compare programs, evaluate institutions based on the characteristics they consider to be important, and make choices. Beyond the tuition provided by students, many institutions actively seek out the "light" individuals to be part of their student body in the belief that the caliber of the student body in part determines the quality of the institution. As a result, colleges and universities may find that understanding—and meeting the expectations of—the "new students" is important to their competitiveness.

A number of current programs exemplify a good match between expectations and services. A few examples will illustrate some of the options available to those institutions that seek to modify their programs to address the needs of the "new students."

Elimination of Delays

In a 24x7, customer-service culture, delays cause dissatisfaction and disengagement. Institutions are finding ways to eliminate delays in processes that range from admission to academic support.

The University of North Carolina at Greensboro utilizes online personal assistants, automated e-mail responses, dynamically created Web portals, and customized Web-mail to provide instant responses to students. Through their Virtual Information Station (http://infostation.uneg.edn/), students can get answers to a range of questions that often begin with "How do I . . . ?" "Where do I . . . ?" or "When do I . . . ?" The Web site covers topics from admission to graduation. For example, an online chat tool allows staff to respond to Web-based queries in real time. Prompt responses make a difference in the decision-making process of prospective students.[14]

At many institutions, financial aid is a chronic source of dissatisfaction for students. Confusion over the process, complicated paperwork, and data-entry errors cause delays and even rejections. Compliance with federal guidelines further complicates the situation. To provide better service, the University of Phoenix, with 152,000 students and more than 120 campuses, created the Financial Aid Paperless Project (FAPP). Prospective students can complete an online application, then link to the Free Application for Federal Student Aid Web site to obtain a federal financial aid application, including a master promissory note. A student may then file the application online with the lender of his or her choice. If the lender participates in the university's FAPP project, the lender's system communicates with the FAPP computers at the university and pulls data from the student's application for enrollment. The lender uses the information to complete the student's master promissory note, eliminating the need to rekey data and ensuring that data is consistent across the two applications. The university then retrieves the completed master promissory note, enabling the university to validate the information and process the application. The student is informed almost immediately that his or her application is complete and has been received for processing. The time to fill in and process an application has also been cut by several days, so students get faster responses to their applications.[15]

Customer Service

For today's learners, customer service is an expectation, not an exception. Yet it is rare that students and institutions have the same expectations for service.

At Athabasca University, service expectations are clearly spelled out on a Web site (http://www.athabascau.ca/misc/expect/) as well as in print material provided to entering students. Whether provided by the registrar, counseling service, academic support, or library, each service is accompanied by a standard as well as a contact person's e-mail address and phone number. This practice helps set expectations for students as well as for staff. How well units meet service expectations is measured, as is also the level of student satisfaction.[16]

Adult learners bring customer-service expectations to the institutions they attend. In many cases, customer service is more than a preference—it is a prerequisite to retention and effective learning. One reason often cited by adult learners for abandoning their studies is the lack of timely support. As an institution focused on serving adult learners, Rio Salado College has adapted its approach to ensure that learners have the services they need. A "beep-a-tutor" program, available seven days a week, guarantees students that tutors will respond to

their question within one hour. With beepers, the tutors receive questions no matter where they are.

Two other Rio Salado programs focus on being sure the right person responds to queries. Online students often seek help from instructors when they encounter problems, whether these are related to technical issues or to the subject matter. To ensure that instructors are not deluged with technical questions—and to ensure that students get the best responses—Rio Salado created a technical help desk. Staffed by noninstructional personnel, the help desk is specifically tasked to help students resolve technical issues.

Also, because instructors cannot be online at all times, Rio Salado has an instructional help desk staffed by generalist faculty who answer questions about the logistics of a course at times when the class instructor is not available. The instructional help desk personnel, available seven days a week, also provide e-learning orientations to students and serve as a liaison between the instructor and the student. By reducing the number of non-learning-related inquiries, this service assists students who need immediate answers and also maximizes the amount of time an instructor can spend on activities directly related to learning.[17]

> **The aging infrastructure and the lecture tradition of colleges and universities may not meet the expectations of students raised on the Internet and interactive games**

Experiential, Interactive, and Authentic Learning

The aging infrastructure and the lecture tradition of colleges and universities may not meet the expectations of students raised on the Internet and interactive games. Several programs address this problem.

Laboratories represent a traditional approach to providing learners with experiential, interactive, and authentic learning. However, many institutions feel that they do not offer enough laboratory experiences due to expense pressures, safety concerns, and lack of space. While not diminishing the importance of hands-on labs, online laboratories enable learners to have rich learning experiences without some of the limitations of traditional labs. At MIT; a microelectronics laboratory, called WebLab, enables the characterization of microelectronic devices at any time of day or night, allowing students substantial flexibility. A remote instrument (in this case, the Agilent 4155B Semiconductor Parameter Analyzer) is accessed by students via an application that uses the circuit language of electrical engineering to specify the measurements to be performed. Students can program the instrument and collect data through the Web, download it to their computers, and then complete the analysis and laboratory reports. Students can remotely select the device to be characterized and specify the variables to be measured. Because of the design, the lab is available 24x7. In an estimate of its capacity, WebLab can handle more than 2,000 users per week and more than 15,000 experiments per week. In fact, excess lab capacity is being made available to students in Sweden and Singapore.[18]

Likewise, rather than telling students the conclusions of history, a University of Virginia interactive Web site, "The Valley of the Shadow" (http://jefferson.village.virginia.edu/vshadow2/), allows students to draw their own conclusions about the Civil War through original records taken from two similar counties in Virginia and Pennsylvania—similar except for the fact that one allowed slavery and the other was free. Utilizing census data, agricultural records, newspaper articles, church records, and letters from soldiers and their families, the site allows individuals to explore authentic information via multiple paths. Students report the experience to be highly engaging and more effective for learning than being told about history. In fact, according to Google, the site is the most heavily trafficked Civil War site on the Web, attracting students from other institutions as well as millions of informal learners.[19]

Simulations can be used to help learners visualize complex systems as well as to turn text or numbers into more readily comprehended forms. A simulation can magnify an environment (e.g., the inside of a cell), making it easier for learners to understand the environment. In other cases, events can be slowed down (e.g., a chemical reaction taking place), sped up (e.g., the moving of tectonic plates), or re-created to help learners visualize a process. The Columbia Center for New Media Teaching and Learning and the School of Public Health have developed a simulation in which students can become epidemiologists in the town of Epiville. The students gather facts from newscasts, interviews, and Web sites to deal with outbreaks of disease (http://lester.rice.edu/browse/lstprojectbrowse.aspx?ord=378).

Game systems, such as Nintendo, were a common part of growing up for the majority of today's college and university students. A number of attributes of games make them good educational environments. Games often involve problem-solving and decision-making. They provide rapid feedback and can adjust the level of difficulty to the expertise of the player. Speed and a sense of urgency can contribute to learner motivation. For example, games such as *Gettysburg* let users re-create military engagements using different assumptions. Would the battle have gone differently if General Lee had been there? Users can ask questions, explore situations, and create unique scenarios to explore history.[20]

Staying Connected

Many students carry multiple electronic devices and use various communication protocols to be sure they are always connected to friends, events, and information. If they are at home or in the dorm, instant messaging dominates. On campus or around town, they use their cell phones.

Drexel University has developed the capability to allow users to stay connected no matter which device(s) they choose to connect with—Blackberries, Web phones, PDAs, laptops, or other devices. The program, DrexelOne Mobile, enables students to retrieve personalized information from virtually any Web-enabled handheld device. Users who have registered their mobile devices may choose to have relevant personal announcements pushed out to them automatically, without having to browse to find the information. For example, students can get grades as soon as they are posted, learn about last-minute classroom changes, get updates to their schedules, and find out about holds placed on their records (e.g., for late tuition payments). The advantage is that information reaches users when and where they need it, rather than requiring users to wait until they are at their desks. And the university can send news to the entire campus community quickly and easily. The headline news service is updated every ten minutes with the latest sports, entertainment, and general news. In addition, users have access to a searchable university phone directory that operates phonetically so that users don't need to know correct spellings of names.[21]

Conclusion

A growing body of evidence reveals that today's college and university students have developed new attitudes and aptitudes as a result of their environment. Although these characteristics may provide great advantages in areas such as their ability to use information technology and to work collaboratively, they may also create an imbalance between students' expectations of the learning environment and what they find in colleges and universities today. As a result, institutions may find it valuable to ask how well they know and understand their "new students." How are learners' views represented in institutional decisions about courses, curricula, programs, and services? Does the institution have a mechanism that balances students' preferences with the opinions of faculty and administrators? Where can IT be used most effectively?

Beyond balancing the interests of students and institutions, colleges and universities should also consider other implications of the "new students" and their learning styles:

- Is instant messaging a fad, or should it be incorporated into how institutions work with current and prospective students?

- Do the educational resources provided (e.g., textbooks, reference materials) fit the needs and preferences of today's learners? Will linear content give way to simulations, games, and collaboration?

- Does the current definition of "anytime, anywhere" equate to students' expectations that any device (laptop, PDA, cell phone) will be able to access the Web at any time and from any place?

- Do students' desires for group learning and activities imply rethinking the configuration and use of space in classrooms, libraries, student unions, and residence halls?

Colleges and universities are finding a variety of ways to meet students' expectations for service, immediacy, interactivity, and group activities. There is no single formula, particularly since students often span broad ranges of ages, learning styles, and communication preferences. Though each institution will find its own answers, a common set of principles may emerge that will help guide decisions and directions. The first step will almost undoubtedly be to better understand the "new" learners—Boomers, Gen-Xers, Millennials, and those still to come.

Notes

1. According to the National Center for Education Statistics (NCES), 35.5 percent of faculty were under forty-five years of age in 1998. NCES, "Teaching Undergraduates in U.S. Postsecondary Institutions: Fall 1998," August 2002, <http://nces.ed.gov/pubs2002/2002209.pdf > (accessed April 22, 2003).

2. 1999 is the most recent year for which data is available. The source for Table 1 is National Center for Education Statistics (NCES), "The Condition of Education 2002," June 2002, <http://nces.ed.gov/pubsearch/pubsinfo.asp?pubid=2002025> (accessed April 22, 2003).

3. NCES, "The Condition of Education 2002."

4. Arthur Levine and Jeanette S. Cureton, *When Hope and Fear Collide: A Portrait of Today's College Student* (San Francisco: Jossey-Bass, 1998).

5. Neil Howe and Bill Strauss, *Millennials Rising: The Next Great Generation* (New York: Vintage Books, 2000).

6. Claire Raines, "Managing Millennials," 2002, < http://www.generationsatwork.com/articles/ millenials.htm> (accessed April 22, 2003).

7. Amanda Lenhart, Maya Simon, Mike Graziano, "The Internet and Education: Findings of the Pew Internet and American Life Project," September 2001, <http://www.pewinternet.org/reports/pdfs/PIP_Schools_Report.pdf> (accessed April 22, 2003).

8. Douglas Levin and Sousan Arafeh, "The Digital Disconnect: The Widening Gap between Internet-Savvy Students and Their Schools," August 2002, <http://www.pewinternet.org/reports/pdf/PIP_Schools_Internet_Report.pdf> (accessed April 22, 2003).

9. Steve Jones, "The Internet Goes to College: How Students Are Living in the Future with Today's Technology," September 1002, <http://www.pewinternet.org/reports/toc.asp?Report=71> (accessed April 22, 2003).

10. For statistics on computer ownership and time spent online, see the Student Monitor Web site: <http://www.studentmonitor.com>.

11. Jones, "The Internet Goes to College."

12. Online Computer Library Center (OCLC), "How Academic Librarians Can Influence Students' Web-Based Information Choices," June 2002, OCLC White Paper on the Information Habits of College Students, <http://www2.oclc.org/ocle/pdf/printondemand/informationhabits.pdf> (accessed April 22, 2003).

13. Jason Frand, "The Information Age Mindset: Changes in Students and Implications for Higher Education," *EDUCAUSE Review 35,* no. 5 (September/October 2000): 15–24.

14. Jim Black, Associate Provost for Enrollment Services, University of North Carolina, Greensboro, e-mail, April 4, 2003.

15. Robert A. Carroll, Chief Information Officer, University of Phoenix, e-mail, May 1, 2003.

16. Dominique Abrioux, President, Athabasca University, e-mail, April 4, 2003.

17. Carol Scarafiotti, Dean of Instruction, Rio Salado College, e-mail, April 5, 2003.

18. J. A. del Alamo, J. Hardison, G. Mishuris, L. Brooks, C. McLean, V. Chan, and L. Hui, "Educational Experiments with an Online Microelectronics Characterization Laboratory," 2001, <http://science.donntu.edu.ua/koni/konf7/0102.pdf> (accessed April 12, 2003).

19. Edward Ayers, Dean, Arts and Sciences, University of Virginia, e-mail, April 4, 2003.

20. J. C. Herz, "Gaming the System: What Higher Education Can Learn from Multiplayer Online Worlds," in Maureen Devlin, Richard Larson, and Joel Meyerson, eds., *The Internet and the University: Forum 2001* (Boulder, Colo.: EDUCAUSE, 2002) <http://www.educause.edu/ir/library/pdf/ffpiu0l9.pdf> (accessed April 22, 2003).

21. Drexel University Deploys Mobile Web Portal Based on Microsoft .NET Technology," March 6, 2003, Microsoft Higher Education Web site: <http://www.microsoft.com/education/?ID=DrexelUniversity> (accessed May 6, 2003).

DIANA OBLINGER is the Executive Director of Higher Education for Microsoft Corporation. She has served as a Senior Fellow for the EDUCAUSE Center for Applied Research (ECAR) as well as Vice-President and Chief Officer for the University of North Carolina.

Science and Technology:
It's a Perfect Match!

Lucille Renwick

When Katie Long wants to excite her students about science, she turns to her digital camera and her computer. Long is among many teachers who are using technology—computers, scanners, and digital cameras—to motivate and excite students. Whether studying ecosystems or the solar system, teachers have found super and simple ways to embed technology in their science lessons.

Creating E-Books

Technology Needed: Digital camera. At least one computer with PowerPoint. Printer.

How It Enhanced Learning: "Students are thrilled to be the authors of their own work and to explore for themselves the difference between living and non-living things."

For a lesson on living and non-living things, invite students to publish an e-book and create a slide show presentation about their findings and research. After discussing the characteristics of living vs. nonliving things with students, divide the class into groups and assign each group a short project on the subject, such as guided reading, working on a collage, drawing pictures, and so on. One of the projects will be to create an e-book. As groups complete their assignments, they will rotate on to the next, continuing until each group has had an opportunity to try each project. For the group working on e-books, ask a parent volunteer or student teacher to take students on a short (15-20 minute) field trip in the schoolyard to scout for living and non-living things. Have students use a digital ccamera to photograph what the find, and take notes about whether or not—and why—it is a living or non-living thing. When students return to class, help them import their pictures from the digital camera into a PowerPoint file. Then have students write short sentences describing each of their pictures from their notes.

Create a special cover in PowerPoint for each of the groups to make an e-book. Be sure to write the name of each author and to specify if there was a "photographer" in the group. Create a separate PowerPoint file for each group. Once all the PowerPoint books are done, print them out and laminate them. You can also show the e-books as a PowerPoint slide show for all students to see what each group discovered on their field trips. These e-Books can be created for almost any science topic.

—Katie Long, Grade I, Eaton Park Elementary School, Abbeville, LA

Interactive Prairies

Technology Needed: An Internet-connected computer. PowerPoint. Projector.

How It Enhanced Learning: "Students gained a wonderful understanding of all aspects of life on prairies."

To teach students all about prairie life (plants, animals, people, etc.), try combining PowerPoint slides and interactive Web sites to make the lesson come alive. First, create a PowerPoint presentation explaining prairies by incorporating images of various prairies, and even information about Laura Ingalls Wilder's life on a prairie, found on various Web sites. You can also integrate vocabulary about prairies in each slide of the presentation. Show the presentation to your class using a projector connected to the computer. Keep the presentation going during discussions about prairies to refer to if students have questions. Use the Web site TrackStar (http://trackstat.hprtec.org) to develop a list of interactive Web sites on prairie habitats. See Kimberly Etie's Web site for inspiration: (http://trackstar.hprtec.org/main/display.php3?track_id=115333).

After discussing the basics of prairies with students, give each a packet of information that includes research assignments they can do using the Web sites you've located. Have students use information they gather from the Web sites to complete other hands-on activities on the topic. For example, students can locate prairie states on a map, create paper murals with the various animals and plants about which they learned, build a model prairie homestead, or create life-size prairie plants on newsprint.

—Kim Etie & Natalie Hebert, Grade 4 Eaton Park Elementary School, Abbeville, LA

Science Up Close

Technology Needed: A digital video microscope. A projector or a TV with a large screen. An Internet-connected computer.

How It Enhanced Learning: "Students' interest in details was piqued by seeing enlarged images of animals."

While digital video microscopes can be costly (around $700), it is possible to get them through grants. Once a school has one microscope, it can be shared among teachers. Digital microscopes allow teachers to zoom in on minute details of specimens and magnify them onto a projector or TV monitor for the entire class to view.

For a lesson on the differences between frogs and toads, gather small frogs and toads from nearby ponds or swamps, or order them from a local pet store or pond supplier, such as Carolina Biological Supply (www.carolina.com). Have students examine the amphibians in a tank, taking notes of the differences they see with the naked eye. Then aim the microscope on one section of the frog, such as the eye, and project that on to the TV screen for the class to view. Have students take notes on what they discover. Continue to magnify different parts of the frog for students to note the similarities and differences.

In addition, create a checklist of comparisons for frogs and toads from any Web site about the amphibians (http://allaboutfrogs.org/weird/general/frogtoad.html or www.thelily-pad.org). Students can refer to the checklist as they examine all the different aspects of frogs and toads while the animals are in the tank and magnified on screen.

—Laura Lombas, Grade 3 Glendale Elementary School, Eunice, LA

Virtual Field Trips

Technology Needed: An Internet-connected computer.

How It Enhanced Learning: "Since we can't get to the Galapagos Islands, this is the next best thing."

Virtual field trips allow teachers to take students on an exploration to far off places without ever leaving class. For example, for a lesson on evolution, students can visit a Web site about the Galapagos Islands to research the life cycles and characteristics of wildlife species, such as the giant tortoise. Provide students with a written assignment to find specific information from the Web site. Once students have gathered all of their information, have them compile it in a written report with graphs, charts, diagrams, images, and details about the island, which they can gather from the Web sites. Students can also create PowerPoint presentations to share their work with classmates.

—Judith Meier, Grades 7 & 8, Vassar Junior High School, Vassar, MI, jfmeier@svsu.edu

Tips from Teachers

Here are some classroom-tested ideas for incorporating technology into your science lessons.

- Understand your objectives for the lesson. That will help you use the technology more effectively to meet those objectives.
- Take time to search the Internet for the best Web sites for students. Look for the most appealing (as well as educational) sites from a kid's perspective. Do some research over the summer to give yourself a head start.
- Don't try to do it all by yourself. Collaborate with other teachers to share great Web sites and information.
- Don't limit yourself to computers and Web sites. Try using every piece of technology at your disposal.
- Take some time to instruct students on how to conduct basic Internet searches, navigate Web sites, and properly care for a computer.

From *Instructor,* March 2003. Copyright © 2003 by Scholastic Inc. Reprinted by permission.

Technologies for Teaching Science and Mathematics in the K-12 Schools: Reviews, Observations and Directions for Practice in the Southern United States

RICHARD B. SPEAKER, JR.

This paper introduces a set of papers focusing on the issues and practices in using technologies for teaching and learning science and mathematics in the K-12 schools in the Southern United States where the digital divide between technology rich schools and technology poor schools is growing wider despite attempts to provide funds and standards to bring the schools to national standards. In particular, the paper discusses the current political and theoretical stances that entangle the schools, methodological issues in the collection of data on technology integration in science and mathematics classrooms, a framework for technology integration into the various levels of education, and the governance and funding structures of the schools. The individual presentations focus on the following levels: K-3rd, 2nd-5th, 5th – 8th, and 9th-12th. Teachers and students at every grade level are gradually entering more and more technological environments as our societies have jumped into highly technological workplaces. These environments produce a variety of concerns for teachers related to the appropriateness of designing instruction that uses communications technology, multimedia and various hands-on technologies. In the United States, learned societies, professional organizations and accrediting agencies include a variety of technological skills in their standards and benchmarks, although many practicing teachers have had no training in using current multimedia technologies.

Introduction and Post-Modern Apology

In our post-modern world, the schools must serve many masters and theoreticians as they develop learners' abilities in science and mathematics. These masters include the political, the civic, the social and the economic engines that drive transnational economies in a technological age. Theoreticians provide us with lenses into the meanings we construct in our interpretations of complex sociopolitical institutions like the school. In this brief introduction, I mention only a few of the issues facing the schools in the southern United States of America as they incorporate current science and mathematics standards in their curriculums. A discussion of the current political and theoretical stances which entangle the schools, methodological issues in the collection of data on technology integration in science and mathematics classrooms, a framework for technology integration into the various levels of education, and the governance and funding structures of the schools are included.

The schools of our republic (the United States of America) are governed by a tangle of regulatory agencies, entities and individuals, including the federal bureaucracy (under the control of executive departments like the U.S. Department of Education), the judicial fiats of the Supreme Court, and the legislative milieu of Congress with its changing political control structures; the sovereign powers of the state (e.g., Louisiana with its contradictory controls of Code Napoleon and common law) that mirror the structures of the federal government with policies purveyed by legislatures and appointed state school boards; local governance from counties, cities and elected school boards; administrative structures of the school systems with superintendents, teams of curriculum specialists and bureaucratic functionaries like the overseers of the payroll computers and data collectors; professional accrediting agencies like the Southern Association of Colleges and Schools and the National Council for the Accreditation of Teacher Education; learned societies purveying standards for teacher, school and student performance (i.e., the International Society for Technology in Education (2002), the National Council of Teacher of Mathematics (NCTM, n.d.) and a host of science organizations (e.g., National Science Education Standards; n.d.; Science for All Americans, n. d.)); text book publishers; religious organizations; nongovernmental funding agencies (e.g., the Bill and Melinda Gates Foundation), and teachers, parents and students. Using a variety of industrial, behaviorist accountability standards, public schools are now ranked and graded based primarily on data from standardized tests with minimal regard for the nature and cultures of the learners who attend as if they were to become interchangeable performers in the postindustrial economy.

The theoretical lenses on the schools are equally complex. Behaviorism (Bandura, 1969), social cognitive learning theory (Bandura, 1986), social interactionism (Vygotsky, 1978, 1986), social/cultural reproduction (Bourdieu & Passeron, 1977), pragmatisim (Dewey, 1909/1975,1916/1966, 1927, 1934, 1938), the various flavors of constructivism from radical to social to methodological (Bereiter, 1994; Phillips, 1995; Steffe & Kieren, 1994; von Glaserfeld, 1995), feminisms (Belenky, Clinchy, Goldberger, & Tarule, 1986; Gurian, 2001), liberation theology (Freire, 1985, 1993), postcolonialism and multicultural/race theories (Banks, & McGee-Banks, 2001; Gibbs, & Huang, 1997; Ladson-Billings, 1997), multiple intelligence theory (Gardner, 1993), complexity theory (Briggs, & Peat, 1990; Gleick, 1988), and critical theory (Apple, 1995; Giroux, Lankshear, McLaren, & Peters, 1996) play their parts as we tell the stories of teachers' work in classrooms where the instructional content is mathematics and the sciences and where technologies provide some students with almost unlimited access to the virtual multimedia world while others rarely venture beyond traditional textual representations of classroom realities (LeBaron, & Collier, 2001; Means, Penuel, & Padilla, 2001; Schofield, & Davidson, 2002; Zucker, & Kozma, 2002). Experiences of mathematical and scientific thought (the experiential, the multimedia and the textual) can be supplemented, enhanced and interpersonally corroborated with teaching environments rich in hands-on, manipulative, socially communicated experiences in laboratories where teachers guide inquiry, problem solving, hypothesis testing and data-driven interpretations of appropriate content for the learners situated in their schools laboratories and field-based actions in diverse local communities where communication technologies can throw local activities into international communicative environments of the web.

These multifaceted influences on the modern educational system lead to four guiding questions for the papers in this symposium: What aspects of multimedia and communications technologies are appropriate for teaching science and mathematics concepts and practices at different developmental levels? What technologies are teachers using to teach science and mathematics at different developmental levels in the United States? What inequities or divides still exist in technological access for science and mathematics teachers and their students at different developmental levels, especially in schools dealing with diverse students and children of poverty? In the current standards and achievement test driven educational situation, how are individual schools and teachers of science and mathematics integrating technology into their instructional practices? I will now provide some notes on the methodologies used in the papers which follow, a brief discussion of a technological framework for communicating and teaching science and mathematics in the K-12 schools, and then set the stage for the four papers in the symposium with which we hope to open the debates about how teachers can improve teaching and learning with technology and developmentally appropriate practices in their local schools.

Some Notes on Methodology and the Technology Framework

The authors of the papers for this symposium have long standing interests in technology integration into instruction. Most of them have participated in the New Orleans Consortium for Technology Integration and Implementation in Teacher Education (NOCTIITE, Speaker, 2002) and have been active in studying and observing teaching with technology in the schools. As part of this process we have collected various streams of evaluation data related to NOC-TIITE and analyzed it for technology integration in the teaching of sciences and mathematics. In general this data is qualitative in nature, leading to narrative analysis (Bruner, 1990, 1996; Clandinin, & Connelley, 1999), case study methods (Merriam, 1999), and portraiture (Lawrence-Lightfoot, & Davis, 2001) within a postmodern, interpretivist stance (Foucault, 1972). Each observer acts as a tool recording and interpreting the situated events in classroom contexts. The goal of the evaluation system for NOCTIITE was to provide both formative and summative information about the ongoing and cumulative effect of the project. Thus, the system was designed to summarize, analyze, and interpret data collected systematically within and across the three years of the project itself by various stakeholders and the follow-up years beyond the scope of the project.

NOC-TIITE had as its goal to make ubiquitous the use of various modes of technology in teaching in two separate, but interrelated, spheres—university teacher education and K-12 classrooms—with the added expectation that a mutually beneficial transactive relationship that would occur between these spheres as a result. A guiding belief of the project was that students educated in Teaching with Technology (TWT) will, themselves, make use of many modes of technology in their K-12 field experiences and will, in turn, stimulate university faculty to increase the sophistication of the technology presented in subsequent methods classes; concurrently, university faculty in the TWT project will become increasingly able and willing to embed technology in methods classes and will, in turn, stimulate student teachers to higher levels of sophistication in using technology; further, K-12 children will benefit from interdisciplinary instruction that is project-based and technology rich. The data streams are complex and nuanced and cannot be adequately evaluated by a focus on any single participant group. Furthermore, two recent dissertations have looked at aspects of TWT among faculty in higher education (Wang, 2002) and high school biology teaching (Malone, 2002).

In examination of the situations of TWT, two kinds of data were collected:

1. *Portrayal Data.* These data are concerned with the landscape and focus on documentation of the classroom and school profiles from the beginning of the study and throughout. What do classrooms and schools look like? What is going on in them? What is taught and learned? How is it taught? Who are the stakeholders? What is the profile of each stakeholder group? What are the expectations of each group from the others? What is the effect of TWT on each stakeholder group over time? Field interviews, questionnaires, observations, videotaped lessons and events, and other documentary information (e.g., numbers of computers in classrooms, time spent engaged with technology, etc.) will be used as evidence for the portrayal data. Data collection occurred throughout the course of the project, for the purpose of documenting change over time. Portrayal data included university faculty, their students/student teachers, K-12 teachers and students in whose classrooms the students/student teachers work, and the university and K-12 classes and classrooms themselves.

2. *Perception and Satisfaction Data.* These data are concerned with value added to university and K-12 instruction that already exists; in other words, what has the TWT project experience added to the quality of teaching and learning in university methods and K-12 classrooms? What do graduates of the TWT teacher education programs offer to K-12 schools that graduates of other programs do not? What do university faculty participants in TWT offer to teacher education programs that other faculty do not? How sustainable are the benefits of TWT? How does the TWT project experience affect the conversation between stakeholder groups? Journal entries, e-mail and on-line fora conversations were used in addition to field interview, questionnaire, and observation as evidence for the perception and satisfaction data. Data collection occurred at significant points in the project events—end-of-semester, end-of-institute, end-of-year, end-of-project—to allow sufficient time for value added to be perceived.

For the purposes of these symposium papers, these rich qualitative streams of data collected for the project and by the authors of various papers were mined for contexts and narratives of TWT which illustrate the uses of technology in the teaching of mathematics and science at various levels.

Out of the streams of data on various levels a framework of technology use gradually emerged. This framework is represented in the table below. This framework emerged from our discussions of the various data streams and cross-referencing with technology standards from International Society for Technology in Education (ISTE, 2002) and other organizations.

The framework, developed under the auspices of the New Orleans Consortium for Technology Integration and Implementation in Teacher Education, examines equipment, software, ease of software use, keyboard use, internet use, level of learner activity with technology, multimedia, web site evaluation, e-mail for students, communication with parents and the school community, trouble shooting and ethical and legal issues at each age/developmental level. It will receive further explication in each of the papers of the symposium.

Setting the Stage for the Descriptive Papers: Contexts and Directions

The specific schooling contexts in Louisiana, where our data were collected, provide an extreme example of the educational division present in the Southern United States. Louisiana has a tripartite educational structure consisting of the public school systems, the Catholic systems, and individual private schools. The Louisiana State Department of Education enforces different rules for each of these categories of schools and for the small fourth educational division, the charter schools. Each public school system is governed by an elected board of local members from the citizens of the district, which is contiguous with the governmental unit within the state (this is called a parish in Louisiana but is called a county in all other states). The chief executive officer of each public school system is a superintendent, appointed by the board and usually someone with considerable educational and management experience,

although recently retired military officers have taken the post. The public school systems range from sprawling urban systems with over a hundred schools to small rural ones with only a few. In Louisiana, only about 40% of students attend the public schools. The Catholic systems have a board and superintendent but the membership of the board is selected in various ways according to the policies of the particular diocese. The private schools have a variety of organizational and governance structures and are only loosely affiliated through professional organizations. The final category of schools, charter schools, is made of public schools receiving a special charter and governed minimally by the public school board and the State Department of Education. Most of these schools are also supported by parents' organizations that contribute advice, funds and projects to support the learners and the schools.

All of the schools receive some public funds for books, record keeping and equipment, but their funding structures and accountability measures are very different. Public schools receive most of their funding from the state; however, for districts with populations of students from high poverty areas, substantial federal funds are supplied through the U.S. Department of Education under programs such as Title I. Individual public schools have been funded in various ways through grants and parents' organizations. Teachers, administrators, parents and alumni have written grants to supply technology to schools from various state, federal and non-governmental sources. In some cases, parents' organizations have build entire computer laboratories and in one case, school buildings have been funded by this means. The Catholic school systems receive support from the state, from the church and from tuition. Tuition for most of these schools is moderate, ranging from about $1200 to $4000 per year; however, special programs for learners with difficulties and special needs can cost up to $8000 per year. The private schools tend to be expensive and most of their funding comes from tuition and endowments from alumni. The annual cost for private schools can be as high as $12,000 per student. Because of this higher level of funding, private schools tend to be well staffed and technology rich, displaying a dramatic Matthew Effect (the rich get richer while the poor get poorer).

Current reform efforts in education have been directed primarily towards the public school systems. Politicians have promulgated the idea that these schools are failures because test scores show that learners from poverty do not perform as well, on average, as learners from middle class or wealthy backgrounds. This performance problem seems inherent and widely recognized internationally by such scholars as Bourdieu and Passeron (1977), but, in the U.S., it has become a marker of systemic failure, despite the complex needs of educating a very diverse, multicultural population. This problem has generated three major trends in reform: 1) standards-based science and mathematics teaching revisions promulgated by professional organizations of science and mathematics teachers and accrediting agencies for higher education units preparing teachers; 2) accountability systems with corrective actions for school not meeting new test standards; and 3) major redesign of teacher preparation mandated by state legislatures. The effects of these reform efforts have included: 1) an emphasis on inquiry, problem-based learning, technology integration and collaboration in science and mathematics learning and teaching without funding for supplies, equipment and retraining of practicing teachers while general teaching has increased emphasis on test taking practices; 2) punishment

Table 1   Framework of Technology Use in K-12 Classrooms

Levels U.S. Grades Descriptor	Early Elementary K-3	Upper Elementary 3-6	Middle School 6-8	High School 9-12
Equipment	Computers, projection device, printer, floppy drives, CD-drives, web connections, scanner; Issues about the number of computers in the classroom	Computers, projection device, printer, scanner, laptops, probes, floppy drives, CD-drives, web connection; Issues about the number of computers in the classroom	Computers, projection device, printer, scanner, laptops, probes, floppy drives, CD-drives, web connection, CD burners; Issues about the number of computers in the classroom	Computers, laptops, projection device, printer, scanner, laptops, probes, floppy drives, CD-drives, web connection, CD & DVD burners; Issues about the number of computers in the classroom
Software	KidPix, Hyperstudio, Word, Simple graphically-oriented simulation software	PowerPoint, Word, Excel, image editing, initial web design, complex graphically-oriented simulation software	PowerPoint, Word, Excel, image editing, video editing, full web design packages, HTML	PowerPoint, Word, Excel, image editing, video editing, programming languages, full web design packages, systems, scripts, Java
Ease of Software Use	Very easy, intuitive software	Basic packages with intuitive interfaces, Initial web design (pages and links), placing images	Sophisticated use of Office, full web design, image editing, and browsers	Personal and project webpages incorporating images, forms, animations, digital video, cookies
Input System Use	Initial activities with easy beginning software for typing, mouse control and various touch pads (To be replaced with word recognition systems in the future)	Advanced activities with the full range of software for teaching typing and other input devices	Proficient with most input devices	Proficient with all input devices
Internet Use	Directed by the teacher	Webquests, Simple searching, using selected webpages	Full search and research capabilities, Understanding of web hosting	Security of web sites and initial business concepts
Level of Learner Activity with Technology	Slight, mostly viewing selected activities and participating with selected multimedia software	Moderate, initial choices of software, viewing and constructing multimedia for small presentations	Consistent, wide range of choices and occasional construction of multimedia for presentations	Full, extensive range of choices and regular construction of multimedia for presentations
Multimedia	Digital still camera for collecting images, CD's, floppies	Digital Video for collecting images with minimal editing, CD's, floppies, DVD's, DV cassettes	Digital Video with editing and webpage insertion, CD's, floppies, DVD's, DV cassettes	Digital Video with software enhancements like Flash, sound dubbing, CD's, floppies, DVD's, DV cassettes
WebSite Evaluation	Topic appropriate for learners	Websites for use with peers about particular topics	Accuracy, currency and appropriateness of the websites for peers	Appropriateness of websites and links for different learner groups
E-mail for Students	Teacher controlled and filtered	Mentored keypals and e-mail through teacher	Forums, full use of e-mail, chat	Personal webpages with chat, forums, forms and e-mail facilities, wireless connectivity control
Communication with Parents and the School Community	Webpage about school and classroom, activities for parenting and support of learning, and special activities; occasional e-mail contact	Webpage about school and classroom, homework, and special activities; newsletter from the class by members of the class; regular e-mail contact	Webpage about school and classroom, homework, and special activities, segments maintained by the children in the class; moderated class forums and groups; e-mail contact for special purposes	Webpage about school and classroom, homework, and special activities, segments maintained by the children in the class; moderated class forums and groups; e-mail contact for special purposes
Trouble Shooting	Basic connections to power & internet, basic parts	Connecting drives and setting up internet connections	Control panels and preferences	System trouble shooting and compatibility issues, wireless communication control
Ethical and Legal Issues	Sharing, Discussions of Appropriateness for the classroom	Noting sources from the web, Discussions of Appropriateness for the classroom	Full attribution and knowledge of fair use, Discussions of Appropriateness for the classroom	Security and appropriateness of pages for different groups

and disruption of school cultures where students do not show annual growth as measures by standardized tests; and 3) costly, time-consuming and technologically demanding systems to control the preparation of teachers, including mandated follow-up and support of new teachers by their university programs, a plethora of new tracks for teacher preparation, and on-line electronic portfolio systems for constant progress evaluation which do not yet function (all without funding or staff increases).

Conclusions

The descriptive papers which follow (Buxton, Hall, & Speaker, 2003; Germain-McCarthy, Haggerty, Buxton, & Speaker, 2003; Kieff, & Speaker, 2003; Willis, Longstreet, & Speaker, 2003) and their presentations are designed to bring readers up to date descriptions on the issues and practices in using technologies for teaching and learning science and mathematics in the K-12 schools in the Southern United States where the digital divide between technology rich schools and technology poor schools is growing wider despite attempts to provide funds and standards to bring the schools to national standards. The individual papers focus on the following levels: K-3rd (Kieff, & Speaker, 2003), 2nd-5th (Buxton, Hall, & Speaker, 2003), 5th-8th (Willis, Longstreet, & Speaker, 2003), and 9th-12th (Germain-McCarthy, Haggerty, Buxton, & Speaker, 2003). Teachers and students at every grade level are gradually entering more and more technological environments for their teaching of mathematics and sciences as our societies have jumped into highly technological workplaces. These environments produce a variety of concerns for teachers related to the appropriateness of designing instruction that uses communications technology, multimedia and various hands-on technologies. In the United States, learned societies, professional organizations and accrediting agencies include a variety of technological skills in their standards and benchmarks, although many teachers have had no training in using current multimedia technologies. Each paper addresses the issues from the current theoretical social constructivist viewpoint, providing portraits of practices that incorporate technology in at least two schools, one technology rich and the other technology poor. Despite efforts at reform on all levels of education in the United States, Matthew effects (the rich get richer) are rampant in our observational data, even as individual teachers make use of available technology in schools that are technologically poor.

References

Apple, M. W. (1995). Education and power (2nd Edition). New York: Routledge.

Bandura, A. (1969). Principles of Behavior Modification. New York: Holt, Rinehart & Winston

Bandura, A. (1986). Social foundations of thought and action: a social cognitive theory. Englewood Cliffs, NJ: Prentiss Hall.

Banks, J. A., & McGee-Banks, C. A. (Eds.). (2001). Handbook of Research on Multicultural Education. Somerset, NJ: Jossey-Bass.

Bereiter, C. (1994). Constructivism, socioculturalism, and Popper's world 3. Educational Researcher, 23, 21-23

Belenky, M. F., Clinchy, B. M., Goldberger, N. R., & Tarule, J. M. (1986). Women's ways of knowing: The development of self, voice and mind. New York: Basic Books.

Bourdieu, Pierre, & Passeron, Jean Claude. (1977, trans. Richard Nice). Reproduction in education, society and culture. London: Sage.

Briggs, J., & Peat, F. D. (1990). Turbulent mirror: An illustrated guide to chaos theory and the science of wholeness. Grand Rapids: Harper & Row.

Bruner, J. S. (1990). Acts of meaning. Cambridge, MA: Harvard University.

Bruner, J. S. (1996). The culture of education. Cambridge, MA: Harvard University.

Buxton, C. A., Hall, F. R. & Speaker, R. B. Jr. (2003, July). Striving for Relevance: Elementary Grade Teachers Exploring Uses of Technology to Promote Science Learning. Paper to be presented at the conference of Computer-based learning in Sciences (CBLIS). Nicosia, Cyprus.

Clandinin, D. J., & Connelley, F. M. (1999). Narrative Inquiry: Experience and Story in Qualitative Research. Somerset, NJ: Jossey-Bass.

Dewey, J. (1909/1975). Moral principles in education. Carbondale, IL: Southern Illinois University Press.

Dewey, J. (1916/1966). Democracy and education. New York, NY: The Free Press.

Dewey, J. (1927). The public and its problems. Athens, OH: Swallow Press Books.

Dewey, J. (1934). Art as experience. New York: Perigee Books.

Dewey, J. (1938). Experience and Education. New York: Macmillian.

Foucault, M. (1972). The archaeology of knowledge. [Trans. M. Smith.] New York: Pantheon.

Freire, P. (1985). The politics of education: Culture, power, and liberation. South Hadley, MA: Berginand Garvey.

Freire, P. (1993). Pedagogy of the oppressed. New York: Continuum Publishers.

Gardner, H. (1993). Multiple intelligences: The theory in practice. New York, NY: Basic Books.

Germain-McCarthy, Y., Haggerty, D., Buxton, C. & Speaker, R. B. Jr. (2003, July). Crafting the Technological Solutions in High School Science and Mathematics Teaching and Learning: Matthew Effects and the Digital Divide. Paper to be presented at the conference of Computer-based learning in Sciences (CBLIS). Nicosia, Cyprus.

Gibbs, J. T., & Huang, L. N. (1997). Children of Color: Psychological interventions with culturally diverse youth. Somerset, NJ: Jossey-Bass.

Giroux, H. A., Lankshear, C., McLaren, P., & Peters, M. (1996). Counternarratives: Cultural Studies and Critical Pedagogies in Postmodern Spaces. New York: Routledge.

Gleick, J. (1988). Chaos: Making a new science. New York: Penguin.

Gurian, M. (2001). Boys and Girls Learn Differently! Somerset, NJ: Jossey-Bass. International Society for Technology in Education (ISTE). (2002). http://www.iste.org/.

Kieff, J. & Speaker, R. B. Jr. (2003, July). Teaching Sciences and Mathematics Concepts in the Early Grades: K-3 Teachers Engaging Developmentally Appropriate Practice which Incorporates Technologies. Paper to be presented at the conference of Computer-based learning in Sciences (CBLIS). Nicosia, Cyprus.

Ladson-Billings, G. (1997). The Dreamkeepers: Successful Teachers of African American Children. Somerset, NJ: Jossey-Bass.

Lawrence-Lightfoot, S., & Davis, J. H. (2001). The Art and Science of Portraiture. Somerset, NJ: Jossey-Bass.

LeBaron, J. F., & Collier, C. (Eds.). (2001). Technology in Its Place: Successful Technology Infusion in Schools. Somerset, NJ: Jossey-Bass.

Maloney, R. S. (2002, December). Virtual Fetal Pig Dissection as an Agent of Knowledge Acquisition and Attitudinal Change in Female High School Biology Students Unpublished dissertation. University of New Orleans.

Means, B., Penuel, W. R., & Padilla, C. (2001). The Connected School: Technology and learning in high school. Somerset, NJ: Jossey-Bass.

Merriam, S. B. (1999). Qualitative research and case study applications in Education. Somerset, NJ: Jossey-Bass.

National Science Education Standards. (n.d.). Available: http://stills.nap.edu/readingroom/books/intronses/, http://www.allstar.fiu.edu/aerojava/nasci912.htm.

NCTM (n.d.). National Council of Teachers of Mathematics. Standards. Available: http://www.nctm.org/standards/.

Phillips D. C. (1995). The good, the bad, and the ugly: The many faces of constructivism. Educational Researcher, 24(7), 5-12.

Schofield, J. W., & Davidson, A. L. (2002). Bringing the Internet to School: Lessons from an urban district. Somerset, NJ: Jossey-Bass.

Science for all Americans. Available: http://www.project2061.org/tools/sfaaol/sfaatoc.htm.

Speaker, R. B., Jr. (2002). NOCTIITE Webpages. Available: http://tec.uno.edu/NOCTIITE.

Steffe, L. P., & Kieren, T. (1994). Radical constructivism and mathematics education. Journal for Research in Mathematics Education, 25, 711-733.

Von Glaserfeld, E. (1995). Radical constructivism: A way of knowing and learning. Washington, DC: Falmer Press.

Vygotsky, L. S. (1978). Mind in society: The development of higher psychological processes (M. Cole, V. John-Steiner, S. Scribner, & E. Souberman, Eds.). New York, NY: Plenum.

Vygotsky, L. S. (1986). Thought and Language (A. Kozulin, Trans., Ed.). Cambridge, MA: The M.I.T. Press.

Wang, L. (2002, May). Investigating How Participation in a technology-based Project Has Influenced Education Faculty Members' Beliefs and Practices with Technology Integration: Factors that Influence Faculty Technology Integration and Implications for Faculty's Integration of Technology. Unpublished dissertation. University of New Orleans.

Willis, E., Longstreet, W. S., & Speaker, R. B., Jr. (2003, July). The Middle School Teacher Faces the Technological Generation: Digital Divides in Sciences and Mathematics Teaching and Learning with Adolescents. Paper to be presented at the conference of Computer-based learning in Sciences (CBLIS). Nicosia, Cyprus.

Zucker, A., & Kozma, R. (2002). The Virtual High School: Teaching Generation V. New York: Teachers College Press.

RICHARD B. SPEAKER, Jr. University of New Orleans Department of C&I, Ed 342J New Orleans, Louisiana, USA 70148 Email: rspeaker@uno.edu

SmartTutor: Combining SmartBooks™ and Peer Tutors for Multi-media On-Line Instruction

SmartTutor is a comprehensive web-based peer-tutoring service geared to the needs of urban commuter college students. The new system is based on SmartBooks, a, multi-media educational technology that was developed just prior to the emergence of the World Wide Web. This technology has provided a user-friendly, self-paced, easy to modify, software environment intended to serve the user's learning needs, particularly in an urban commuter college environment. A model for the student creation of the SmartTutor web site is discussed as well as the ongoing evaluation of the emerging software for the project. The assessment of the usefulness of the site is just beginning and its development is an ongoing process. We believe that consistent experimentation with iterative refinements will lead to an effective website for delivery of peer tutoring. In time, this approach will also lead to a more sophisticated and intelligent system.

Danny Kopec, Paula Whitlock, Myra Kogen

Introduction

The Brooklyn College Learning Center has had a long history of providing effective on-site peer tutoring for an urban college campus in New York City. Brooklyn college is a four-year liberal arts institution whose students are a blend of many cultures and languages: 38% speak English as a second language, 70% receive financial aid and many are the first in their families to attend college. These students are often highly motivated but they need help to achieve their goals. At Brooklyn help is provided by trained undergraduate tutors who assist students in understanding course concepts and assignments. Each year about 4000 of the College's 15,000 students visit the Learning Center to work with their peers on assignments in writing, mathematics, science, and the twelve required core curriculum courses. However, a serious problem has developed in that demand for help has exceeded the Learning Center's ability to provide assistance. Budget constraints limit the number of tutoring staff that can be hired and the number of hours that the Learning Center can be open. Brooklyn's commuter students, most of whom work many hours to support their college education, need additional help available at the times when they are free to address their coursework.

The solution to these problems has been the development of an interactive website that offers information about on-campus Learning Center programs and selected tutoring services on-line[1]. On-line tutoring is not intended to replace peer tutoring, but to work hand in hand with peer tutoring by creating customized out-of-class web-based instruction for students. Our new approach for offering on-line tutoring involves the use of SmartTutor, a multimedia, educational technology based on the SmartBooks system first developed more than a decade ago[2]. SmartTutor innovates in its use of the heuristic technique of concept mapping[3] designed to be flexible and facilitate the individual learning preferences of each student user. The user reinforces his/her understanding of new information by navigating through the web-based material. The system is designed to meet the needs of students who have different levels of understanding of course content. Of major importance in the development of the SmartTutor system is the input of peer tutors, students, faculty and advanced computer and information science majors.

Background

SmartBooks, which is the foundation for SmartTutor, provides a technique for allowing users to navigate through complex domain specific material in a non-linear fashion designed to meet their own cognitive stages. The model has been used in the last decade for the development of prototypes of educational software for sexually transmitted diseases including AIDS[2b] and training materials in navigation for U.S. Coast Guard Academy Cadets[4].

The driving force of the SmartBook approach is the use of "concept mapping," which has been demonstrated to be a sound paradigm for learning and education[5,6]. Concept maps are a graphical form of knowledge representation whereby all the important information in a domain can be embedded in the form of nodes and links (connecting the nodes). At any time during the use of the system a user can view how they arrived at where they are (the path taken through the SmartBook) and where it can lead. This is indicated by a pictorial representation on the top of each section illustrating how the shaded topic (node) was reached and what circle(s) (nodes) it can lead to.

Unlike static conventional textbooks where the traversal is sequential, rigid and unchangeable, an advantage of a Smart-Book is flexibility, the fact that it can be developed for any domain using a sound educational methodology [2a,4]. It can be used and explored in many ways. The order in which material is covered is the choice of the user. In essence, the SmartBook represents a road map through a knowledge base. Transparency in form and function is fundamental to SmartBooks. In addition to existing pop up windows, there is the potential for linking to a glossary of terms, synonyms for key words, a retrace facility, expert advice, and video-based presentation of graphical information. As any good knowledge base, it is easy to modify, expand, and refine.

SmartTutor

SmartTutor applies all the useful, student-learner oriented features of SmartBooks in a web-based environment. We are currently planning the design of SmartTutor for a number of domains which can be used to enhance the undergraduate curriculum. Modules for courses in Computer Science, Biology, Mathematics, Physics, and Social Science are being constructed using essentially the same paradigm we have detailed above. The new technology provides instant access for the student at all times to the tutoring facility. It is intended to provide *all* students with access to the best possible content, and to provide an alternate path for students who may otherwise be too intimidated to seek help.

In addition, the more knowledge a tutoring environment has about the domain in which it is presenting educational material, that is the more domain-specific expertise the system has, the more effective it will be. For example, excellent baseball video games know everything that needs to be known about the subtleties of the baseball environment, including the rules, the playing fields, the idiosyncrasies of the players, etc. The same is true for effective educational environments. They must have rich and deep domain knowledge and must be able to ask the right follow-up questions to the learner in order to deliver effective instruction. They must embody rich multimedia-based curricula, assimilated tutoring knowledge, and have the ability to assess the level of the learner. They must know how

to test, evaluate, and improve the knowledge of the learner. The aim of the SmartTutor system is to capture and mimic the knowledge and the experience-based intuition of the effective teacher. In this case, the peer tutor working with faculty members and senior computer science students provides the knowledge base.

In our initial implementation of the SmartTutor system we have focused on a key gateway course for computer science majors (this course has a 50% drop-out/failure rate). Aiming to reproduce the best qualities of one-on-one peer tutoring, Smart-Tutor tries to predict and answer the most typical student questions by focusing on the most frequently misunderstood topics, for example, control structures. The student, upon entering the CIS tutoring site, is presented with a concept map which graphically represents the relationships between basic course topics (Figure 1). The student can access further material on any of the topics on the concept map (students come for tutoring with different levels of subject knowledge). Once students have entered the system they can choose their own path through the material by referring back to the concept map which records where they have visited. For example, they can access further material on "The *for* loop" and then on "The *if* statement" and then back and see in the map the record of their visits. To further help clarify concepts for students, at any point they can query the database about keywords and concepts or visit links for further information. An innovative feature of SmartTutor, now under development, is that students will be able to give themselves a self-test at any time, based on the particular subtree (path) of learning they have selected through the SmartTutor site. The quiz can refer learners back to the appropriate sections of SmartTutor where the relevant material is presented.

The page on the **for** loop (see Figure 2), enables the student to view the coding paradigm, watch real-time execution and modify the coding example. Since students have difficulty in knowing when a loop will terminate, the webpage provides both actual code and a flow diagram of the code. As each line of the C code is executed it is highlighted, and the relevant portion of the flow diagram lights up as well. The user has the choice of stepping through the flow diagram one statement at a time, or viewing an animated trace of the complete execution of the code," the **for** loop.

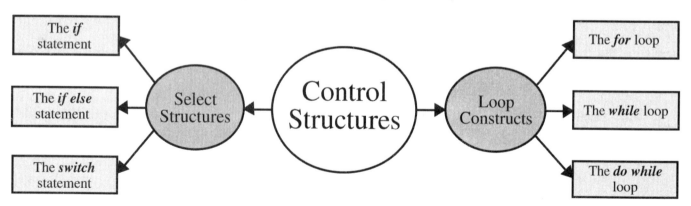

Figure 1 Concept map of some topics on the introductory C programming language SmartTutor prototype. This map distinguishes between the various control structures available in the language. A user clicks on one of the nodes to obtain further information on the topic.

Finally, as an important added feature, future plans call for SmartTutor to store and categorize students' most frequently asked questions and to provide links to pages that answer these questions. On campus tutors often answer the same questions over and over again, but once online, answers will always be accessible. A student will be able to scan topics, discover what other students have asked, and will be able to access the answers (just being aware of other students' questions can sometimes help clear up confusion.). The peer tutors are not equally qualified in their abilities, so some studies receive better help than others, but with SmartTutor, only the best answers will be available to all. Consequently, faculty will also become more aware of the kinds of questions their students are asking.

The model that we are evolving to facilitate the addition of new SmartTutor domains, employs the pairing of an advanced computer and information science (CIS) undergraduate working on a senior project with a master (peer) tutor for the course. The peer tutor is responsible for identifying the key material that students request assistance with. Since additional material can always be added, the initial development focuses on the areas that students claim are most difficult. The CIS student then transforms the tutor's material into a concept map for the domain. The two work closely together to design the appearance and the content of the nodes within the domain. Implementation is the responsibility of the CIS student doing a senior project supervised by a CIS faculty member. New ways to carry out tutoring are discussed at group meetings and input is regularly solicited from the larger community at Brooklyn College.

It is important to note here that to prepare an effective SmartTutor system requires the input of a number of major college constituencies—in this case students, tutors, faculty and computer experts. The purpose of the Brooklyn College Learning Center web site is not to replace instructors but to assist students who are having trouble and need extra help. Peer tutors are considered the experts on student learning since they have had considerable experience in identifying the concepts that are giving students the most difficulty, but faculty have deeper understanding of course content. Early in the development of SmartTutor packages, peer tutors consult extensively with faculty. For example, a recent preparation of a concept map for the college's core curriculum course in physics (required of all students) had to be modified when physics faculty disagreed with the tutors' analysis of how topics should be categorized. The faculty members suggested that inertia and kinematics be split into two separate sections. On the other hand, tutors were aware that students often have difficulty distinguishing between conservation of energy and conservation of momentum, so they decided to alter the original concept map to help students solve this problem. Then when advanced computer science students work on the SmartTutor system, decisions are made about formatting, basic design, associating information, and highlighting of key words that correspond to database entries, in addition to such decisions as whether to include animation and sound. And finally the packages must be tested by student users in order to identify potential strengths and problems.

At our online tutoring website, the basic web pages are programmed in HTML. We are using MySQL, an open source SQL database system, that the college had installed for use with Blackboard. Most interactive activities are implemented using the PERL scripting language. Also, database access from the webpages is carried out via PERL. Javascript and PHP are also used when necessary to provide animation and other multimedia features.

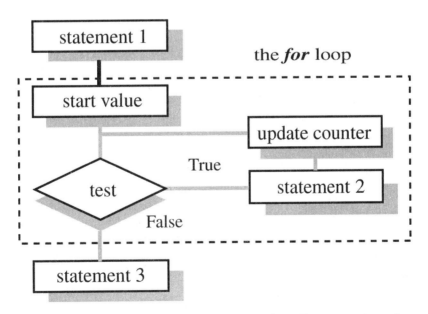

Figure 2 Example of the *for* loop node from the SmartTutor concept map from the introductory C programming system. In addition, there are animated traces of for loops on the webpage.

Future Developments and Assessment

The Brooklyn College Learning Center project aims to: 1) design an on-line tutoring program that recreates the advantages of person-to-person tutoring and works hand-in-hand with on-site services; 2) create effective on-line tutoring strategies that support the learning needs of nontraditional urban students; 3) make use of faculty, peer tutor and student input to design a program that reflects institutional needs; 4) continually assess and revise the program so that it will be useful and usable; 5) create a prototype that other institutions can use to develop on-line tutoring programs that suit their own needs.

Site usefulness is always a major concern[7,8]. According to Davis[9], though lack of human friendliness can hinder user acceptance, perceived usefulness is not primarily about design choices—it's about cognitive understanding and retention: "No amount of ease of use can compensate for a system that doesn't do a useful task." As more content is added to the web site, more formal testing and evaluation will be done. Focus groups of students in the targeted courses will also be formed to more thoroughly evaluate the usefulness of the site.

Our aim in creating SmartTutor is to give students the feeling that they are filling gaps in their knowledge, that they have a greater ability to move forward in a class, and that they have more understanding of how successful students approach difficult problems. If SmartTutor can provide these things then that would be a real mark of success. It is important that SmartTutor's effectiveness as a learning tool be carefully tested and evaluated. We can give pretests and post-tests evaluating subject matter knowledge. For example, performance of students in courses delivered with and without the SmartTutor (which can reside on the web with a special course password) would be one way to measure their effectiveness. Traces of nodes visited can also be helpful in evaluating learning styles of the students using SmartTutors.

Evaluation will also examine whether students who use SmartTutor return to use it again, whether certain webpages seem to be more effective than other pages, whether the online program works hand in hand with on-site tutoring, whether students, tutors and faculty feel that the program sufficiently supports coursework, and, eventually, whether students who use the on-line system perform better in gateway courses than those who do not use tutoring services, or better than those who use only on-site tutoring services, or those who use a combination of both services.

The SmartTutor system is designed to formulate a model for an on-line resource that will support students working on their own initiative and out of their own interest to integrate and synthesize knowledge and methodology outside the classroom. The model combines collaborative learning techniques (social interaction, access to peer tutors) with SmartBooks technological advances (individualized learning paths, coaching controlled by the learning) to create an integrated package for the student. While the goal of providing 24/7 tutoring for core curriculum and other courses has not yet been fully achieved, much has been learned and the web site is viewed as an ongoing experiment that can only become more comprehensive and better with time.

Acknowledgements

Two of the authors (P.A.W. and M.K.) gratefully acknowledge support from the U.S. Department of Education, FIPSE Grant # P116D990181.

References

1. Whitlock, P.A. and Kogen, M. (2002), "Creating a Useable Peer-Tutoring Site On-Line," *J. of Computing in Small Colleges,* **55**, #3, 143–156. URL: http://lc.brooklyn.cuny.edu

2. a). Kopec, D, Brody, M., Shi, C., and Wood, C. (1992), "Towards an Intelligent Tutoring System with Application to Sexually Transmitted Diseases" in (Kopec, D. and Thompson, R.B. eds) *Artificial Intelligence and Intelligent Tutoring Systems: Knowledge-based systems for learning and teaching,* Ellis Horwood Publishers, Chichester, England, pp. 129–51.
   b). Kopec, D. and Wood, C. (1994) *Introduction to SmartBooks.* Booklet to accompany interactive educational software AIDS SmartBook, Jones and Bartlett Publishers, Boston, MA. Also published as United States Coast Guard Academy, *Center for Advanced Studies Report No. 23–93,* New London, CT., December, 1993.

3. Novak, J.D. and Gowin, D.B. (1985), *Learning How to Learn,* Cambridge University Press, Cambridge, England.

4. Kopec, D. (2001), "SmartBooks: A generic methodology to facilitate delivery of post-secondary education." in *Proceedings AMCIS 2001 (Association for Information Systems) 7th Americas Conference on Information Systems.* Boston, August 2–5, 2001, Curriculum and Learning Track; (CDROM).

5. Kopec, D., Wood, C. and Brody, M. (1991), "An Educational Theory for Transferring Domain Expert Knowledge Towards the Development of an Intelligent Tutoring Systems for STDs," *Journal of Artificial Intelligence in Education,* Vol. 2 (2), pp. 67–82.

6. Wood, Carol L. (1992), "Use of Concept Maps in Microcomputer Based Program Design for an AIDS Knowledge Base," EDD Thesis, University of Maine, Orono.

7. Venkatesh, V. and Davis, F.D. (1996), "A model of the antecedents of perceived ease of use: development and test." *Decision Sciences,* Vol. 27, 951-481. Abstract: http://dsi.gsu.edu/DSJ/vol27_3/27_3_451.htm.

8. Mahmood, M.A., Burn, J.M., Gemoets, L.A. and Jacquez, C. (2000), "Variables affecting information technology end-user technological advances (individualized learning paths, satisfaction: ameta-analysis of empirical literature," *International Journal of Human Computer Studies,* **52**, 751–771. URL: http://www.idealibrary.com/links/toc/ijhc/52/4/0

9. Davis, F. (1993), "User acceptance of information technology: system characteristics, user perceptions and behavioral impacts," *International Journal of Man-Machine Studies,* **38**, 475–487.

DANNY KOPEC completed his undergraduate work at Dartmouth College obtaining a degree in Psychology modified with Math (1975).

His Ph.D. at the University of Edinburgh, was in Machine Intelligence (1983) with a thesis entitled *Human and Machine Representations of Knowledge.* There, under the supervision of Donald Michie, he first learned about "advice languages" and knowledge engineering. At the University of Maine (1988–1992), Dr. Kopec helped develop the SmartBook paradigm which was subsequently implemented for AIDS education, for a "Rules of the Road SmarkBook" to help US Coast Guard Cadets learn ship navigation rules (1995), and most recently at Brooklyn College (Summer, 2001) for delivery of CPR. Dr. Kopec's general interest is in identifying the knowledge necessary for expert performance.

PAULA A. WHITLOCK received her Ph.D. from Wayne State University in engineering where she studied elementary combustion systems using computer modeling. Subsequently, she joined the Courant Institute of Mathematical Sciences at New York University where she worked on the development and application of Monte Carlo methods to solve the Schroedinger Equation for ground state and finite tempera-ture systems. Since joining the Computer Science faculty at Brooklyn College in 1990, Professor Whitlock has studied parallel pseudorandom number generators and continued Monte Carlo investigations of quantum mechanical systems. She has also been active in improving the undergraduate computer science curriculum.

MYRA KOGEN is the Director of the Brooklyn College Learning Center, which has a national reputation in the field of collaborative learning in a college setting. Learning Center projects have been funded by the U.S. Department of Education, the National Science Foundation, the Fund for the Improvement of Post-Secondary Education (FIPSE), and the Howard Hughes Medical Institute. Kogen's Ph.D. is in modern American literature, and she has written on writing across the curriculum, peer tutoring and college composition. She is an advisory editor of the *Journal of Basic Writing* and is co-editor of *Dialogue on Writing: Rethinking ESL, Basic Writing, and First-Year Composition,* a collection of articles recently published by Lawrence Erlbaum.

From *2002 Proceedings of the International Conference on Engineering Education,* August 18–21, 2002, pp. 1–5, by Danny Kopec, Paula Whitlock, and Myra Kogen. Published by the International Network for Engineering Education and Research (iNEER). Reprinted by permission of the authors. www.ineer.org

UNIT 6

Learning Management Systems and Learning Objects

Unit Selections

Key Points to Consider

- How would you justify the installation of a learning management system?

- Describe the process and the justification for moving from a learning management system to a course management system.

- What are the major assessment aspects that need to be examined in order to determine the effectiveness of management systems on learner performance and learner autonomy?

Student Web Site

www.mhcls.com/online

Internet References

Further information regarding these Web sites may be found in this book's preface or online.

Consortium for School Networking
http://www.cosn.org

Educators Net
http://www.educatorsnet.com

ERIC Clearinghouse on Teaching and Teacher Education
http://www.ericsp.org

Over the past five years we have witnessed a mushrooming of learning management systems and many educators have received these developments enthusiastically. During the years 2001 through 2006, the method of delivery and assessment shifted from cognitivist-oriented to social-constructivist orientation. In addition there was a shift in the mode of assessment from cumulative to more formative measures. Determining just how moving conventional instruction to online learner management systems improves or detracts from learning is still an open question. In addition to the fundamental challenge of defining learning and how we implement learner managed instruction, we need to pay attention to the dynamics of the teams of learners and their interactions with each other and the online managed instruction.

Online managed delivery and assessment engenders opportunities for learners to grow as intelligent agents as part of a team of learners working within their disciplines. Within the learning community, we gauge success through formal and informal feedback to the participants. This is no less true of the group experience. The group project is a popular way for online educators to mimic social exchanges similar to those that might emerge in traditional classroom environments when individuals are compelled to work together to achieve a common outcome. The delivery and assessment of managed online collaborative study presents new opportunities and challenges, both in terms of separating the process and product of collaboration, and in support of skills development. We must explore the role of learner management systems with respect to the process and products of online collaborative study. The implementation of online managed instruction and the science and art of online assessment are evolving daily.

Although the immediate future looks very bright, questions remain. Administrators are concerned with how to measure the productivity factor that learning management delivered instruction may provide. Policy makers wonder how to get educators to form consortiums so they can access joint educational facilities and thus increase the usage of the facilities while decreasing the per-unit cost of delivery. Teachers wonder how technology can best be used with existing educational programs in a distance learning environment. The public is concerned with the level of return on investment that will be realized from the new technologies in the home and classroom.

The articles in this unit shed some light on the promises and areas of concern. In the first article, Kathy A. Smart and Katrina A. Meyer describe the process of converting a Blackboard course to Desire2Learn. The process taught them some of the hazards and benefits of changing course management systems. A system-wide committee—including faculty, technical staff, and CIOs from all campuses—was formed to evaluate moving the North Dakota University System (NDUS) to one CMS. The task of moving all of the learning management systems to one CMS was difficult and costly. They were successful in making the conversion and the article describes how they did it and the benefits of their efforts.

Next, Xin Liang and Kim Creasy investigate the dynamics of WebCT classroom assessment by analyzing the perceptions and experience of the instructors. Grounded theory method was employed to generate a "process theory." The study included 10 faculties who taught WebCT classes, and 216 students in the College of Education in an urban university in the Midwest. Interviews and classroom observations were undertaken online. The findings indicated that, performance-based assessment, writing skills, interactive assessment, and learner autonomy were major assessment aspects to inform teaching and enhance learning. If one of the major roles of online instruction is to increase self-directed learning, as part of the pedagogical mechanism, web-based classroom assessment should be designed and practiced to impact learner autonomy.

Finally, Zuhal Tanrikulu describes the development of an electronic support system that was developed specifically to provide Web-based support for students and instructors in the Management Information Systems (MIS) Department at Bogaziçi University in Turkey. Because of its flexibility, the resulting system, called MISESS, could easily support other departments and other universities wanting to offer course materials, exams, and tutorial services online.

Changing Course Management Systems: Lessons Learned

Converting a Blackboard course to Desire2Learn taught us some of the hazards and benefits of changing course management systems

KATHY A. SMART AND KATRINA A. MEYER

During 2003, the North Dakota University System began to be concerned about the cost of supporting multiple course management systems. Since 1997, the 11 NDUS institutions had used 9 different course management packages,[1] including one homegrown product (HTMLeZ) and such proprietary products as Blackboard, WebCT, and e-College. The University of North Dakota (UND), for example, uses both Blackboard and HTMLeZ.

During the fall of 2003, a system-wide committee including faculty, technical staff, and CIOs from all 11 campuses was formed to evaluate moving the North Dakota University System (NDUS) to one CMS. While this effort went forward, staff at UND's Center for Instructional and Learning Technologies wondered what might happen if the 300 faculty who used Blackboard needed to transfer their courses to a new CMS. This concern generated a search for research from other institutions that were studying a move to another CMS or had done so.

We found several other universities or systems that were considering consolidating on one CMS or transferring existing courses to a new CMS. The State University of New York (SUNY), University of Buffalo, University of Notre Dame, Minnesota State Colleges and Universities System, and University of Wisconsin System had completed studies of multiple CMS products. Recent EDUCAUSE Center of Applied Research (ECAR) research bulletins by Gallagher[2] and Hanson and Robson[3] are useful guides for selecting a CMS and ensuring it supports the institution's future goals and needs. In addition, several evaluation tools help institutions or systems choose a CMS, including the Committee on Institutional Cooperation's guidelines,[4] the Lguide,[5] and EduTools.[6] The interactive, Web-based EduTools site helps institutions compare more than 65 CMS products—some open source and others proprietary—on 42 different functions or characteristics ranging from whether the product offers chat functions, to testing, to compliance with disability standards. Neither EduTools nor other sources had

information on whether a course in one CMS could be converted to another CMS or how complete and accurate that conversion might be. We were unable to determine whether and to what extent a course in Blackboard could successfully be converted to another CMS.

This lack of research on how well courses converted from one CMS to another was surprising, largely because other institutions were clearly contemplating or implementing a change in CMS. The NDUS was not the only system facing constrained budgets and the increasing cost of CMS licenses and supporting multiple products. In 2003, 56 percent of public universities experienced a decrease in their academic computing budgets,[7] which prompted a reexamination of CMS costs on many campuses. According to results of the 2003 EDUCAUSE Current Issues Survey, IT funding was the number one issue EDUCAUSE members felt must be resolved for institutional success, and course management systems were ranked sixth in the category of requiring the most institutional resources.[8]

Several CMS providers claim to provide accurate transfer of course materials from another CMS, although such claims do not appear to have been tested by conducting a course-to-course conversion. Furthermore, what would such a transfer mean to faculty, in terms of time and effort taken to evaluate the accuracy of their transferred course? After several months of deliberations, the NDUS selected Desire2Learn as the system-wide CMS. Thus, Desire2Learn became our target CMS product, and the research questions became the following:

- Would all course content of a Blackboard course convert to Desire2Learn?
- If course material converted and for those portions of the course that did convert, how intact and accurate would the content be? In other words, was anything lost in the conversion/transition, or was any material garbled or otherwise made unintelligible or inaccurate?

- How would faculty assess the ease of Desire2Learn, and would they be willing to convert their courses and use another system?

Method

Ten faculty in the Academic Affairs Division at UND evaluated the transition of a Blackboard course to Desire2Learn. These faculty represented five of the seven Academic Affairs colleges and schools and the Honors program. All were users of Blackboard, one for one year and several for four years. We chose faculty for this study for two reasons. First, faculty would need to determine what had converted successfully from their earlier course, what had not, and what had but was inaccurate. Second, it was important to ask faculty's views of the new CMS after they had gained some experience with the new tool.

The Center for Instructional and Learning Technologies contacted Desire2Learn to request assistance with this study. In summer 2004, Desire2Learn transferred a UND Blackboard course into Desire2Learn using their proprietary conversion tool and provided access to their product for each faculty member participating in the study. The course had been created by center staff and was commonly used to train faculty on how to use Blackboard, and it included content in all feature areas of Blackboard. We used this course so that no intellectual property issues would arise as a result of sharing the materials with Desire2Learn.

The faculty were briefed on how to access the Desire2Learn system, issued user names and passwords, and shown where the course was located via a test log in. Faculty assessed the course in their offices or the center's faculty lab. While technical support was available to troubleshoot problems, the purpose of the test was to have faculty assess the operation of Desire2Learn, so no more assistance was provided than needed to get to the course or the evaluation instrument.

An Instructional Content Screening Instrument (ICSI) was constructed to capture all the features and content in the original Blackboard course. The ICSI helped faculty determine which content of the Blackboard course converted to the Desire2Learn course and, if the material converted, to what extent it appeared to be intact and accurate. For this study, "intact" meant "the content appears whole or unchanged with no missing parts or elements," while "accurate" meant "the content appears to be precise and free from error."

After completing the ICSI, faculty were asked about their (admittedly modest) experience with Desire2Learn, including questions about its ease of navigation, its effect on teaching, the accuracy and completeness of the conversion process, their willingness to move to a new CMS, and their assessment of students' willingness to move to a new CMS. Given the small number of participants, responses are reported by frequency and percent only. Because this study may be the first of its kind and because it used few faculty, it is at best a preliminary exploration to be followed by studies that include more subjects and delve into these issues more deeply. Despite these qualifications, the study produced some interesting data and intriguing questions for further study.

Results and Lessons Learned

Figure 1 presents the data on which Blackboard content converted and which did not. Content in the Blackboard course that did convert were Web resources (90 percent of faculty thought this was converted), assignments (80 percent), course documents (75.17 percent), and the syllabus (100 percent). Parts of the Blackboard course that did not convert were the gradebook (86.67 percent of faculty found this did not convert), control panel (74.44 percent), library connections (100 percent), communications (97.89 percent), tests and surveys (95 percent), faculty name (100 percent), and announcements (80 percent). Summarizing across all parts of the course, faculty indicated that 46.91 percent of the course content converted and 53.09 percent of the course content did not convert. This might lead one to a "glass half empty or half full" conclusion, but in fact the parts of the course that did not convert are often time-consuming to reconstruct (for example, test surveys and the gradebook).

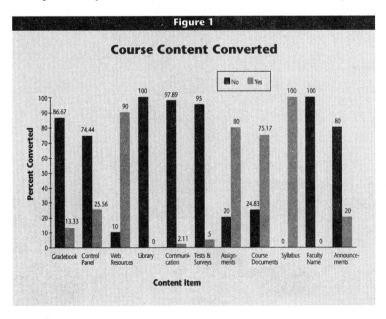

Figure 1

Course Content Converted

Concerning the course content that converted, faculty were asked if it converted "intact." A total of 70 percent of faculty reported that content converted "intact," while 5 percent reported the content converted "partially," and 24 percent reported content did not convert "intact." When asked if the converted material seemed to be "accurate," 80 percent of faculty indicated that the content appeared to be accurate, 5 percent indicated the conversions were partially accurate, and 15 percent indicated the conversions were not accurate. This means that faculty—who would need to restore course content that did not convert intact and accurately—will face increased workloads and frustration should an institution choose to change from one CMS to another.

However, it is important to contrast the faculty answers to the next five questions to these findings. When asked if they felt the Desire2Learn interface was familiar or easy to navigate,

- 20 percent of the faculty indicated the design was familiar/easy,
- 50 percent felt the interface design was moderately familiar/easy, and
- 30 percent indicated it was minimally familiar/easy.

In answer to the question on how changing to the new CMS might affect teaching,

- 50 percent of the faculty viewed the CMS as a tool, having no effect on their teaching,

- 10 percent felt the CMS might improve their teaching,
- 10 percent felt the switch might lose work, and
- 30 percent felt it would be too much effort for too little gain.

As for their impression of how well Desire2Learn converted the Blackboard course,

- 40 percent of the faculty reported it was not intact and somewhat accurate,
- 20 percent reported it was moderately accurate and intact,
- 20 percent reported it was somewhat accurate and intact, and
- 20 percent reported the conversion not acceptable.

Surprisingly, when asked to indicate their willingness to change to another CMS, 80 percent of the faculty reported a willingness to change, while 20 percent were not willing to change or opposed to it (see figure 2). This is intriguing, since it captures the willingness of faculty to switch to another CMS despite the work of ensuring materials in the new CMS are intact and accurate. And, these faculty had already seen how well (or poorly) the conversion process worked, so their willingness to change is doubly interesting.

Faculty were also asked how willing they thought students might be to change to a new CMS, and their answers were again

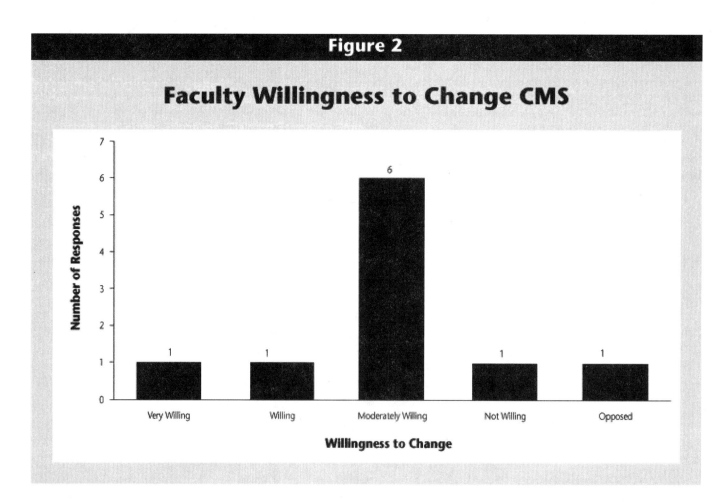

Figure 2

Faculty Willingness to Change CMS

largely positive: 70 percent of faculty felt the students would be willing, and 30 percent felt students would be unwilling or opposed to the change. In other words, despite some negative comments, the faculty seem to be open to a change in CMS. What lessons can we learn from this exploratory study?

- First, institutions and systems seeking to save money by consolidating with one CMS need to factor in the time and effort of faculty who will need to review, correct, and revise content once the course has been converted. Since this preliminary examination revealed half of the course might not convert to the new CMS, the decision by institutional leaders to move to a new CMS represents a real cost to the faculty member, department, and college.

- Second, institutions and systems need to investigate and evaluate the conversion tools of potential CMS products.

- Third, CMS providers need to improve and market their ability to convert material from one CMS to their own product, since this could well be an important selling point to institutions already invested in a particular product.

- Fourth, these considerations also may apply to the new, emerging world of free or open source CMS products.

- Fifth, despite the work of fixing partially converted courses, faculty were not averse to trying a new product, and they felt students would be willing to change too.

Faculty may not be the brakes to change that some make them out to be, but they are legitimately concerned about the time and effort needed to make the transition a success for their courses and students.

Endnotes

1. North Dakota University System Online, "History of Learning Management Systems in the NDUS," 2003, <http://www.nduso.org/history.htm>.

2. S. R. Gallagher, "The New Landscape for Course Management Systems" (Boulder, Colo.: EDUCAUSE Center for Applied Research, Research Bulletin, Issue 10, 2003).

3. P. Hanson and R. Robson, "Evaluating Course Management Technology: A Pilot Study" (Boulder, Colo.: EDUCAUSE Center for Applied Research, Research Bulletin, Issue 24, 2004).

4. L. E. King et al., "CIC Course Management System Evaluation Guideline," poster presented at the 2002 EDUCAUSE Annual Conference, Atlanta, Ga., <http://www.umich.edu/~leking/cic-cms.pdf>.

5. C. Zeiberg, *Lguide: Ten Steps to Successfully Selecting a Learning Management System* (Tacoma, Wash.: Lguide, 2001).

6. See <http://www.edutools.info/course>.

7. K. C. Green, *Campus Computing 2003* (Claremont, Calif.: The Campus Computing Project, 2003), <http://www.campuscomputing.net>.

8. G. Crawford and J. A. Rudy, "Fourth Annual EDUCAUSE Survey Identifies Current IT Issues," *EDUCAUSE Quarterly*, Vol. 26, No. 2, 2003, pp. 12–26, <http://www.educause.edu/ir/library/pdf/eqm0322.pdf>.

KATHY A. SMART (kathy.smart@mail.und.nodak.edu) is Director of the Center for Instructional and Learning Technologies and Assistant Professor in the Teaching and Learning Department, College of Education and Human Development, at the University of North Dakota in Grand Forks. **KATRINA A. MEYER** (kmeyer@memphis.edu) is Associate Professor of Higher and Adult Education at the University of Memphis in Tennessee.

Classroom Assessment in Web-Based Instructional Environment: Instructors' Experience

XIN LIANG
University of Akron

KIM CREASY
Slippery Rock University

While a great deal has been written on the advantage and benefits of online teaching, little is known on how assessment is implemented in online classrooms to monitor and inform performance and progress. The purpose of this study is to investigate the dynamics of WebCT classroom assessment by analyzing the perceptions and experience of the instructors. Grounded theory method was employed to generate a "process theory". The study included 10 faculties who taught WebCT classes, and 216 students in the College of Education in an urban university in the Mid west. Interviews and classroom observations were undertaken on line. The findings indicated that, performance-based assessment, writing skills, interactive assessment and learner autonomy were major assessment aspects to inform teaching and enhance learning. If one of the major roles of online instruction is to increase self-directed learning, as part of the pedagogical mechanism, web-based classroom assessment should be designed and practiced to impact learner autonomy.

The unique features, especially the synchronous and asynchronous communication, web search, online resources and technical support, allow teaching and learning to be place and time independent. Although educators at all levels have embraced using online technology as a teaching tool, the issue of assessment of student learning in an online course has not been thoroughly addressed (Robles & Braathen, 2002). As an instructional delivery method, online instruction should be designed to facilitate teaching and promote learning. As (Meyer, 2002C) pointed out "It is irrelevant to speak of the effects of using Web without understanding how it is entwined with instructional design". As instructors reflect upon online learning as an instructional delivery mechanism, they must also examine their assessment delivery method. They should ask

questions about how assessment practice as part of the instructional design is related to the quality of online teaching.

Black and Wiliam (1998b) define assessment broadly to include all activities that teachers and students undertake to get information that can be used diagnostically to alter teaching and learning. Under this definition, assessment is not limited to just assigning grades to students in the form of paper-pencil exams. Assessment should permeate many aspects of teaching and learning activities, encompassing teacher observation, classroom discussion, group collaboration, and analysis of student work. This form of assessment used as a regular element in classroom work, holds the key to better learning (Broadfoot et al., 2001).

Web-based instruction takes place on line, with different modes and resources for retrieving class content, subject related information, and student-teacher interactions (Sherry, Bilig, & Jesse, 2001). Without a teacher being physically present, web-based teaching requires new instructional practices built on a unique relationship between learners and instructors. As the mechanism of learning paradigms are changed, so should the assessment delivery method. As a different instructional practice, online teaching should practice a systematic assessment that embraces and reflects the nature to this type of teaching and learning environment. If we acknowledge that assessment impact student learning, it is likely that assessment will be at the center of the curriculum design to ensure the quality of online instruction. It is very important for educators to examine the existing assessment practice, and seek guidelines applicable to the design of assessment in online environment (Mcloughlin, & Luca, 2001, p. 417). Penn State University in association with Lincoln University (Innovation in Distance Education, 1999) provided some benchmarks for distance education environment. Recommendations on assessment process are as follows:

- Enable students to self-monitor progress;
- Give regular feedback to students;
- Support peer learning and assessment;
- Design self-assessment practice.

These recommendations on assessment process capitalized on the unique characteristics and situations of online learners. Laurillard (1993) believed that one of the major roles for distance learning is to promote self-directed learning and increased learner autonomy. Collis and Moonen (2001) used the term pedagogical re-engineering to describe the change in online pedagogy from one that is teacher centered to one that is focused on learner activity. However, no research has been focused on the interpretation of pedagogical reengineering to online classroom assessment. The purpose of this study was to generate a theory that explains the "process" of how assessment, as part of instructional practice in web-based environment was implemented to promote learning from instructor's perspectives. The research questions that guided the exploration were:

1. How assessment is designed and implemented to reflect online instructional paradigm to facilitate teaching and promote learning?
2. What are the effective assessment strategies available to support learning process on line?
3. What is perceived to be the most important assessment component(s) to obtain and process the information on teaching and learning?

Assessment as Part of Instructional Practice

Findings from research on student learning indicate that pedagogical techniques influence how well students learn to apply concepts (Michlitsch, & Sidle, 2002). Achieving higher academic standards for all students depends not only on a thorough knowledge of pedagogical content, but also teachers' ability to determine what students really know and can do, and where the learning gaps are, so that they can target instruction to fill the gaps. As Stiggins (1997) pointed out "good education encompasses good assessment". Rather than being an event at the end of a course or period of learning, good assessment is an instructional event that describes, and promotes students' best performance across time and uses a range of methods. Two experimental studies have shown that students who understand the learning objectives and assessment criteria and have opportunities to reflect on their own work show greater improvement than those who do not (Frederikson & White, 1997). Elwood, & Klendowski (2002) believe there is a distinction between *"assessment of learning"* (assessment for the purposes of grading and reporting with its own established procedures) and *"assessment for learning"* (assessment whose purpose is to enable students, through effective feedback, to fully understand their own learning and the goals they are aiming for). Assessment for learning requires

teachers to never take a student's grade in and of itself as the only central goal of the assessment. Rather, assessment performance is taken as a proxy for the student's status with respect to target instructional domain (Popham, 2002). No doubt, there is a vital link between assessment, learning, and teaching. Instructors can build in many opportunities to include students in the assessment of learning and then use the information to make beneficial changes for both learning and instruction. How to make it happen places a challenge for instructors, especially for online instructors when the instructional environment and communication devices are different. At the same time, the unique features of web-based instructional environment also open up a new frontier for online instructors to practice a more student-centered pedagogy.

Challenges and Opportunities for Online Classroom Assessment

Moving courses from the traditional classroom to an online setting fundamentally shifts human interaction, communication, and learning paradigms (Robles & Braathen, 2002). Jung (2001) characterized three key components of Web-based instruction different from traditional face-to-face classroom instruction as 1) content expandability, 2) content adaptability, and 3) visual layouts. And also three types of interaction were identified as essential for the success of online teaching. They were: 1) academic interaction, 2) collaborative interaction, and 3) interpersonal interaction (Jung, 2001). The characteristics of online instruction present special challenges for assessment. As online instructors can no longer monitor and react to student questions, comments, asides, body language, and facial expressions, they must employ other techniques to acquire the same information (Alessi & Trollip, 2001). The absence of low level of social cues and emotions may minimize the richness of communication, limit and impede a more interactive cyber learning community (Robels & Braathen, 2002). The verbal and written communication enjoyed in f2f classrooms has been limited to written text with static images, slower because the student cannot type as fast as he can talk and may be inexperienced in written communication (The Institute for Higher Education Policy, 2000). It is often more difficult to identify online cheating and student authentication as student has access to various course materials, and impersonation is perceived as a greater risk (Kerka & Wonacoot, 2000).

These same features in online classes can offer a unique communication environment in which texts, pictures, video and audio are integrated into one system. This system allows a much easier access to huge database for students, and more flexible interactions (Jung, 2001). The flexibility of communication to be time and place independent increased the opportunities for dialogues, and more thoughtful reflections. The unique features of online communication allows more interactive assessment to not only accurately measure learning outcome, but also to nurture peer feedbacks, and encourage participation. As more and more educators and researchers realized that effective instruction with technology must be driven by sound pedagogical principles (Daugherty & Funke, 1998), it is very important to ask such questions as how this could be achieved, and what aspects should be concerned for a more effective assessment to ensure the quality of web-based instruction.

Method

WebCT Learning Environment

WebCT is a type of online teaching software that was prevalent in the studied university. The WebCT classes included in the study were web-based courses (over 50% of the course content delivered online) offered by the college of education in a Midwestern university. There was no restriction for students to register WebCT courses in the university. Instructors were required to send in application and curriculum proposal to move a course from traditional or web-enhanced (less than 50% online) to web-based instruction. In the curriculum proposal, instructors were expected to explain the rationales to move a course online, and a detailed teaching plan. The proposal was reviewed by the department, the college council and, approved by the provost office. The starting and ending dates of WebCT classes were the same as f2f courses offered in campus. The course web page functioned as the major setting for instructors to post class related materials. Students log onto the class web to retrieve materials, interact with the instructors and other classmates. Students and instructors usually did not meet f2f throughout the whole semester. Some classes in the study did meet once or twice when issues came up, and the instructors were needed to meet with students. Most classes (13 out of 16) did not have a fixed "meeting" time (synchronous communication). Each week, the instructor posted certain amount of content materials for students to study by the form of class note, unit module or studying materials of the week on the web. Instructors also posted assignments, projects, cases analysis, and questions to help students understand and exercise the content. Students were required to log onto WebCT to retrieve materials, and to do self-study at their own convenience. Usually, the class interactions between learners and instructors were asynchronous on individual bases. Three classes required once a week (synchronous discussion for two hours). Each member of a WebCT class was able to contact other members privately or publicly via the WebCT mail list, or posting messages via threaded or unthreaded discussions. Students were able to send in assignments, projects or exams electronically to the instructors. Students were also able to obtain both formal and informal assessment from the instructors on the web.

Participants

University faculties who teach course content over 50% online were the target population. After sending out consent forms, ten instructors (who taught 16 WebCT classes) agreed to participate the study. The WebCT classes included in this study were both at undergraduate and graduate levels in the College of Education. Among the ten instructors, four were males and six were females. Two hundred and sixteen students enrolled in the 16 WebCT classes were indirect participants, whose classroom participation, discussion, and assignment were observed and recorded.

Data Collection Procedures

The major avenue for data resources included in the study were 1) field notes of WebCT classroom observation, 2) transcription of on-line interview with the instructors, 3) transcription of threaded and unthreaded discussions, 4) record of classroom assessment activities, and virtual artifacts (assignment, project, presentation, etc.). The virtual classroom observation was carried on for nine months (three semesters, Spring, Summer, and Fall, 2003). The online observation data were the base line to understand how assessment as an instructional process was incorporated and operated in WebCT classes. Observation foci entailed 1) general instructional procedures of web-based classroom, 2) classroom interactions between learners and learners, between instructors and learners in the web, 3) classroom assessment activities. The observation was recorded in forms of field notes, journals, and memos for further analysis. Particular attention was given to observe the dynamics of classroom interactions with a cyclical process of content, input, procedures and product to inform and direct teaching and learning. Two independent observers were present to conduct online observation of the same WebCT classes to control the reliability and accuracy of the data. Discussions were held routinely between the two observers to exchange field notes, and observation findings. The discrepancy between the two observers was resolved by reviewing the field notes, and by comparing with online interview transcripts.

After the observation of WebCT classrooms was finished, data was sorted, categorized, and compared. The ten instructors were interviewed via e-mail with both structured and open-ended questions. The purpose of online interview was to obtain the instructors' reflections and experiences of their own teaching. Besides observation and interview data, other data resources, such as syllabi, class notes, discussion notes, individual projects, group projects, quizzes, tests and exams were used with the observation and interview data to develop themes and build a chain of evidence. The documentation started with the observation. As the observation moved along, documentation began to accumulate, diverge by topics, categories and themes. The different data resources were also merged and compared together as a way to triangulate the truthfulness of the research outcome.

As the study focused on understanding the process of implementing classroom assessment in relation to the unique features of online instructional environment, it seemed appropriate to use qualitative research method. It was decided to take a Straussian approach to grounded theory, in which a "process theory" was generated to explain an educational process of events, activities, actions, and interactions that occurred over time (Creswell, 2002, p. 441). It is believed that the "process theory" discovered during data collection "fit" the situation being researched and will work when put into use (Glaser & Strauss, 1967, p. 3). The major characteristics of grounded theory study are the three stages of coding procedures, which are open coding, axial coding, and selective coding (Creswell, 2002, p. 441–442). In open coding, online observation, and class activity documentation were sorted, categorized and compared. Concepts or themes with similar properties were grouped together. During the interview transcription analysis, data were considered in terms of their match to the existing categories. This was a contrast to the initial data analysis. In order to clarify the issues emerging from initial data analysis, another set of informal interviews took place to discuss and obtain feedbacks from instructors about the emerged themes. Three final themes derived from the open coding process. In axial coding, we specifically compared each theme to explore the interrelationships between one another. Selective coding whereby all data are related to one single category for theory generation was not undertaken.

Findings

Descriptive of Online Assessment Design and Implementation

From all the classroom activities and assignments we observed in the WebCT classes, instructors tend to have a heavy focus on enhancing student's ability to knowledge application. Among the 16 classes, 3 WebCT classes included quiz and exam to assess student learning. Mostly, assessment activities were designed to help students to analyze and demonstrate proficiency in solving real world problems. Collaboration and peer learning were also clearly emphasized in the assessment design and practice. Table 1 listed WebCT assessment design and implementation in the study.

Table 1   WebCT Classroom Assessment Design and Implementation

Assessment Type	Assessment Name	Assessment Method
Test and exam	Module quiz	Numeric score
	Exam	
Written assignment	Reaction paper	Evaluation rubrics
	Evaluate an instructional software	Assessment guidelines
	Personal reflections	Work guideline
	Description of a program	
	Journal writing	
	Lesson plan	
Proficiency demonstration	Electronic portfolio	Rubrics (Content coverage and showmanship. Practicality and creativity)
	Create slide show	
	Create an online brochure	
	Create a database	
	Create and deliver a multimedia presentation online	
	Submit a syllabus online	
	Create an evaluation instrument	
	Online mini teaching	
	Online case analysis	
	Electronic project presentation	
Collaboration	Group research project,	The amount of time and contribution to learning Rubrics
	Research method presentation	
	Peer reflection	
	Peer facilitation	
	Research scenario strategies	
	Leading panel discussion	
Participation	Threaded discussion (n times/week)	The amount of time and response quality
	Unthreaded discussion (n times/week)	
	Questions posted	
	Answers posted	

Integration of Instructional Objectives with Performance-Based Assessment

From the syllabus collected from online observation, we found that all instructors claimed that they relied heavily on "performance" assessment. The most commonly used assessment tasks for the courses were writing projects, visual presentations, threaded or unthreaded group discussions of a particular topic, and group work. The instructors we interviewed told us they wanted to create a cyber arena for their students to "show" their competency. One of the instructors, Jane said, "*All the assessments are directly tied to the course competencies (objectives) to demonstrate proficiency*". David told us about his assessment strategy as "*Each of the product documents (Word product, PowerPoint, Excel, Inspiration) were to access the learners ability to follow structured instructional task-aids to develop product and master the ability to utilize that particular software effectively and efficiently*". The instructors felt that the unique features of online environment made it possible for them to design performance oriented assessment model. They felt they could preset very concrete performance assessments in the course content, course objectives, and course activities. Ben commented, "*I only assesses what I teach, and try to make sure there is an explicit and direct link between what I believe is important to assess, and the learning activities that I provide*". According to the instructors we interviewed, one of the reasons the online instructors relied so much on performance-based assessment is the elimination of assessment bias. Becky told us "*My grades are based strictly on performance. The course and assessments are structured to allow learners to authentically represent their proficiency.*" Linda also expressed the same feeling "*The way they look, speak and socialize with me or other members of the class did not affect me in grading student work in this type of class. The only thing I need to make comments on was the answer to the quizzes, project and visual display of the presentation. These factors allowed me to evaluate student more objectively*".

Writing Skill as a Confounder in Online Assessment

A closer examination of the data pointed out that the seemingly straightforward performance assessment model applied by the instructors was far more complicated than it appeared to be. One of the major issues that drew the instructors' attention was that writing and the assessment of one's writing skill was confounded with performance-based assessment. This made the seemingly objective assessment model problematic. In an online environment, the most essential media to "demonstrated" competency is writing competency. Angie admitted "*I basically assess growth and work production on students' own writing*". Tom agreed, "*The student presence is usually written which can influence student performance as well as student evaluation*". Some instructors we interviewed felt that the nature of relying heavily on writing to demonstrate competency allowed them to be more objective to evaluate student work. David shared his experience with writing process in online class "*One big*

difference is that in an online course I tend to remain unbiased in my informal assessments of students much longer than in a classroom because of the writing process this type of course is required". But these instructors also felt that the absence of f2f interaction did seem to problematic, especially for students with poor writing skills. Some instructors felt they need to rethink students' abilities to accurately demonstrate in writing how actively engaged students were with assignments and discussions since the major part assessment involved in evaluating how students wrote. They were concerned that some students might not be accurately assessed because the way they wrote. David admitted students with poor writing skills were put in a disadvantaged position to demonstrate their performance. He said, "*Students who are poor writers may be at a greater disadvantage in an online classroom, not because of their learning, but because of their writing skills*". Angie also noticed that the writing skills intertwined made her objectively evaluate students' performance questionable, because "*In an online class I can't as easily identify students from those who are engaged, prepared, etc from those who are engaged, but simply have poor writing skills. Sometimes it took me a while to distinguish a student from lack of preparation or engagement and poor writing skill. Sometimes, I never distinguished the two*". Obviously, the essential role of writing skills in online communication has drawn the instructor's attention in their assessment design and instructional practice.

Interestingly, these same instructors did not seemed to concern their own ability to accurately express expectations and concerns to students in writing. There was an absence in the faculty's responses, of any level of concerns for the students' need to clearly understand instructors' assignments, directions, and writing style. From our online observation, students would go off the topic originally posted by the instructors for a chat room discussion. It would usually take half of the discussion time before the instructor jumped in and pull the topic back on track. Obviously, there was miscommunication between and among learners and instructors. We suspect in many cases it might be because of the writing process, or writing style that caused the miscommunication. Even though one instructor did indicate, "*The instructor needs to frame their comments in a way that does not stifle the discussion*", the general sense was still not there. Very few instructors recognized that the instructor's writing and writing style might have influenced interaction and learning.

Role Shift Between Learners and Instructors

The observation of online class and discussions with the instructors also revealed a role shift between instructor and learner's in web-based environment. The instructors tended to see themselves as a facilitator, consultant and promoter to self-directed learning in online classes. Jackie pointed out that her course is designed to be "extremely interactive and requires learners to be independent and use peers as a resource". As a result of this design, "Students do "talk" to each other (online), help each other, and give direction to each other. Through the shared environment students learn to constructively give comment and reflect on their work" (Jackie). Our nine months observation also indicated that there were many designed activities that focused on the process of learning, and the student-student interaction. Linda indicated in the interview that in her class "the questions should be posed first to peers and the instructor is contacted when peer interaction cannot resolve the question or issue". She thought, "My primary role is a moderator and "expert" in times when the discussion is going nowhere". Tom allowed his students in charge of their own learning. "Students select a primary study from a list provided, work in collaborative groups to discuss the article, and may choose to work collaboratively or independently to write a scholarly critique of the article". From the courses we observed, instructors usually spent considerable amount of time for self-introduction, and networking at the beginning of the classes. Most often the online dialogue tended to be more in depth and personal than a regular first class introduction. Almost all the online classes we observed spent the first and second threaded discussions for just self-introduction. The instructors would use first class introduction to learn and assess student's learning style, and personality. They also overtly told students to use the first and second period introduction to familiarize with the basic computer skills essential for studying online, and to reinforce the comfort level in cyber classrooms where there was not a classroom to serve as a meeting place and a warm body to give guidance. From our observation, we noticed that some instructors made a substantial move to incorporate collaboration as part of the classroom assessment to encourage teamwork and participation. These instructors recognized the importance of collaborative learning and peer feedbacks. They also found that it was relatively easier to document participation and involvement in online learning environment. When Wendy expressed her experience of using assessment to encourage students' participation, she said, "In a f2f classroom I would not consider grading participation. I believe there are too many constraints in a f2f classroom to grade on participation. In an online classroom, many of those constraints are lifted, and grading on participation or discussion is more appropriate".

Learner autonomy was a noticeable factor to practice a more interactive assessment in online instructional environment. According to Moor & Kearsley (1996), learner autonomy refers to the extent to which learners make decisions regarding their own "learning", and "construct" their own knowledge based on their own experience. The observation data in the present study indicated that in an online environment, learners were more often put in charge to initiate the learning process. For example, students must be responsible to read the material, explore the links, partake in the discussion, ask questions, chose to learn the objectives, set aside the time to learn, and select an layout for presenting learning outcome. Web provided access to information, databases and course notes, but learners had a control on all these sources. In this information sorting process, learner autonomy became essential to ensure the quality of learning outcome. Learners also had much more autonomy to choose the visual interface and screen layout in online classes to fully express themselves, and to "show" what best present them as an individual person. Vickie commented, "My role should be seen as the facilitator, allowing the learners to construct their learning". Tom also told us, "In the year that I have taught online I see that I am putting students more "in charge" of directing aspects of the discussion". Our observation to the threaded and unthreaded group discussion also repeated learner autonomy as an important feature for online teaching and learning.

However, learner autonomy was also a learning process for online students to adopt and develop as the course moved on. A lot of these students from various educational backgrounds brought in different knowledge base and life experience. To some extend, they all needed to take some time to adjust their role to be in charge of their own learning. Instructors also had to spent considerable amount of time to identify and encourage such a shift of learning. Vickie told us that her students were "very concerned about "doing it right" and "getting it the way I want it." I had to spent some time to have them get used to the shift that I do not have a specific way of "doing it right". The assigned written papers, projects, and presentations we observed in the WebCT classes repeatedly demonstrated the learners' ways of "doing things right" when instructors recognized that learner autonomy could be included as an important aspect of assessment.

It was obvious that the instructors sensed the importance of learner autonomy, and learner control for an interactive learning community. The performance based assessment model embraced the unique features of web communication and interaction such as writing skills and learner autonomy. From our observation, the instructors had a general sense of satisfaction about the online teaching environment and assessment delivery system. Wendy contended, "My expectations are so clear (in writing) that I see no reason for noncompliance". Vickie admitted, "By the end of the course, I think the various assessment activities worked pretty well to keep us on track and got my goal accomplished". However, when these instructors indicated "Expectations", " Goal accomplishment", they were more often referring to "my" expectation, and "my" goal accomplishment. There was still a gap for a shared ownership in goal setting, criterion setting for a more interactive assessment to increase learner autonomy.

Conclusion

The study examined how assessments were designed and implemented to reflect online instructional paradigm to facilitate teaching and promote learning, identified assessment strategies available to support on line instruction, and explored major components of classroom assessment to obtain and process information in online learning environment by studying WebCT classrooms and the instructor's experiences. The findings in the study indicated that as the mode of communication shifted, assessment in online instructional environment should practice a different assessment model to direct teaching and promote learning. The pedagogical reengineering process may indicate the greatest effort for innovation and departure from traditional practices by modifying and developing effective and reliable assessment to maximize online learning (Ryan, 2000).

The unique nature of web-based learning put learners up in the front to be responsible for their own learning. Consequently, web-based classroom assessment should be practiced to reflect this nature. Assessment should be centered on "assessment for learning" to increase learner autonomy. The theory derived from the study is reflected in this shifting "process" different from traditional assessment in the following aspects:

1. Due to physical absence, test security, student authenticity reasons, performance-based assessments were found to be prevalent to describe learning and guide teaching for online instruction. The traditional paper-pencil tests were rarely used in the 16 WebCT classes we observed. The flexibility of space and time in online classroom environment provides instructors with a choice of many different assessment designs for students to demonstrate what they have learned. The absence of all the visual elements to favor one student over another allowed online instructors to evaluate student performance more objectively. The use of web expands the range of channels available to learners to demonstrate proficiency. Instead of using narrowly defined learning outcomes tested by examinations, technology offers a rich environment where skills such as written communication, collaboration, team work, reflective thinking can be assessed by giving learners multiple channels, unlimited space of expression. Technology can be used to create environments for assessment of learning.

2. The transformation of time and space in online learning environment has changed the traditional role between learners and instructors. The findings in the study indicated that the instructors were more of facilitators than teachers in online classes. Without physically interact with students, what the instructors actually did was to provide learners with resources and information. Learners were responsible to make decisions to when, where, what, how much, with whom they wanted to learn. Consequently, online classroom assessment activities should reflect this aspect. The experience of self-directed learning, and interactive assessment played an important role to increase learner autonomy (Frederiksen, & White, 1997). The data from our study revealed that the online instructors recognized the shift of roles in online instructional environment. They put an effort to practice a more student-centered pedagogy. The computer-mediated communication tools also supplied online instructors with options to document, facilitate and nurture active involvement, collaborative learning, and learner autonomy. However, no observable strategies were found in the instructional practice to include learners in the goal setting and assessment design process. Future assessment should encompass not only measurement of learning objectives, self-assessment, but also interactive assessment in a cyber learning community.

3. Instructors and learners relied heavily on writing communication and visual layout to carry out the task to assess learning and instructional effectiveness. One of the major issues that drew our attention in the study was that writing and the assessment of writing skill was confounded with performance-based assessment. This finding has several implications relating to online classroom assessment. The absence of lower social cues such as body language, physical appearance, voice, etc. allowed instructors and learners to be more focused on writing, and visual layouts. Without other social interference, instructors may feel they can evaluate student "performance" more objectively. To put everything in writing also encourages both learners and instructors to give more thoughtful reflection. It's much easier for instructors to document, thus give a more accurate assessment to student participation and collaboration. The instructors and learners also feel more comfortable and relaxed in writing up the questions, and answers because no one is watching them, and they don't see other people's physical response right away.

On the other hand, there exists wide range of variability of writing skill among the students, and among the instructors themselves. The lack of facial interaction also requires more time for instructors to know their students, especially if the students are not good writers. For the same reason, learners would have to spend more time on self-exploring how the class is managed, how to communicate efficiently with the instructors and other classmates simply because of the way each person writes. Both instructors and learners must be aware that a very important component of classroom interaction, and classroom assessment is heavily dependant upon the assessment of writing. During the course of assessment design and practice, it is very important for web-based instructors to distinguish the assessment of the course objectives and the assessment of writing. To better understand students in online learning environment depends very much on the understanding of the writing styles, and this can only be achieved by large amount of interactive writing. Instructors need to preset the objectives and goals for a course explicitly and precisely in writing. The assessment criterion and assessment procedures also need to be accurately written to clarify the goals and objectives. Even though, web-based assessment is heavily dependent on writing and the assessment of writing, very few instructors have any background in assessment of writing. More empirical study is needed to explore the impact of writing in web-based instruction and web-based classroom assessment.

Angelo and Cross (1993) defined assessment as the multidimensional process of appraising the learning that occurs in the classroom before and after assignments are graded, with the feedback used to improved teaching and, hence student learning. As such assessment is not an end in itself but a vehicle for educational improvement (Banta, Lund, Black, & Oblander, 1996), assessment is most effective when it reflects an understanding of learning as multidimensional and integrated and when it effects change in specific student performance outcomes. Brookhart (1997) called for motivating student effort and achievement with the vehicle of classroom assessment. Her theory is also applicable for online classroom assessment. The findings in the study demonstrate that moving courses online shifted the traditional meaning of teaching and learning paradigm, and classroom assessment is no exception. As an important pedagogical component in teaching and learning dynamics, classroom assessment in web-based learning environment can be practiced to reflect the shift. Technology has provided opportunities for online assessment to be more learner-centered to promote self-directed learning, and to increase learner autonomy. Practicing "assessment for learning" can cultivate student ownership, and will impact effort and achievement eventually.

Acknowledgment

The research was generously funded by the University of Akron Faculty Research Grant (UA FRG 1568), Spring 2003.

References

Alessi, S. M. & Trollip, S. R. (2001). *Tests. Multimedia for learning: Methods and development, 3rd*. pp 334–368. Boston: Allyn & Bacon.

Anglo, T.A. & Cross, K. P. (1993). *Classroom assessment techniques: A handbook for college teachers (2nd ed.)*. San Francisco: Jossey-Bass.

Banta, T. W., Lund, J. P., Black, K. E., & Oblander, F. W. (1996). *Assessment in practice: Putting principles to work on college campuses*. San Francisco: Jossey-Bass.

Black, P., & William, D. (1998b). Inside the black box: Raising standards through classroom assessment. *Phi Delta Kappan*, 80(2): 139–148.

Broadfoot, P., Osborn, M., Sharper, K. & Planel, C. (2001). Pupil assessment and classroom culture: a comparative study of language of assessment in England and France, in Scott, D. (Ed.): *Curriculum and assessment*. Westport, CT: Ablex Publishing.

Brookhart, M., S. (1997). A theoretical framework for the role of classroom assessment in motivating student effort and achievement. *Applied measurement in education*, 10(2), 161–180.

Collis, B. & Moonen, J. (2001). *Flexible learning in digital world*. London: Kogan.

Creswell, W. J. (2002). *Educational Research-Planning, Conducting, and Evaluating Quantitative and Qualitative Research*. Merrill Prentice Hall, Upper Saddle River, New Jersey.

Daughterty, M., Funke, B. (1998). University faculty and student perceptions of web-based instruction. *Journal of Distance Education*, 13(1), pp. 21–39.

Elwood, J. & Klendowski, V. (2002). Creating of shared practice: the challenges of assessment use in learning and teaching. *Assessment & Evaluation in Higher Education*, Vol. No. 3, pp. 243–256

Frederiksen, J. R., & White, B. J. (1997). Reflective assessment of students' research within an inquiry-based middle school science curriculum. Paper presented at the annual meeting of the American Educational Research Association, Chicago, IL.

Glaser, B. & Strauss, A. (1967). *The Discovery of Grounded Theory*. Chicago: Aldine.

Innovations in distance education (1999). An emerging set of guiding principles for the design and development of distance education. Pennsylvania: Pennsylvania Sate University. Retrieved from (September 24 2002): http://www.outreach.psu.edu/de/ide.

Jung, I. (2001). Building a theoretical framework of web-based instruction in the context of distance education. *British Journal of Educational Technology*, Vol 32 No 5, 2001, pp. 525–534.

Kerka, S., & Wonacoot, M. E. (2000). Assessing learners online: Practitioners file. Washington, DC: Office of Educational Research. (ERIC Document Reproduction Service No. ED448285).

Laurillard, D. (1993). *Rethinking university teaching*. London: Routledge.

Mcloughlin, C., & Luca, J. (2001). Quality in online delivery: What does it mean for assessment in e-learning environment. (ERIC document, ED 467 959).

Meyer, K. A. (2002C). *Quality in distance education: focus on on-line learning*. San Francisco, Ca: Jossey-Bass.

Michlitsch, J. F., & Sidle, M. W. (2002). Assessing Student Learning Outcomes: A Comparative Study of Techniques Used in Business School Discipline. *Journal of Education for Business*, January/February 2002.

Moor, M.G., & Kearsley, G. (1996). *Distance education: a system view*. Wadsworth, New York.

Popham, W. J. (2002). Classroom Assessment—What Teachers Need to Know. Allyn and Bacon, Boston.

Robles, M., & Braathen, S. (2002). Online Assessment Techniques. The Delta Pi Epsilon Journal, Vol. XLIV No. 1 Winter 2002.

Ryan, R. C. (2000) Student assessment comparison of lecture and online construction equipment and methods classes. *THE Journal*, 27(6), 78–83.

Sherry, L., Bilig, S., Jesse, D., & Watson-Acosta, D. (2001). Instructional technology on student achievement. *THE Journal*, Feb 2001 Vol. 28 Issue 7, p. 40.

Stiggins, R. (1997). *Student-Centered Classroom Assessment (2nd edition)*. Upper Saddle River, N.J.: Merrill.

MISESS: Web-Based Examination, Evaluation, and Guidance

The Management Information Systems Electronic Support System (MISESS) gives teachers and students access to courses, related content, and exams on the Web

ZUHAL TANRIKULU

Many universities are reevaluating their traditional educational methods and providing pedagogical material through the Internet.[1] Some Web-based systems offer a constructionist learning environment, for example, where students can learn by designing their own objects.[2] Providing effective, convenient technology to support learning is important, and the Web offers multiple opportunities for the academic who wants to take advantage of its capabilities in teaching and engaging students.

The most popular support tools are Internet chat applications. They exist in endless variations, such as Internet Relay Chat (IRC). Chat is used for education and pleasure and sometimes replaces the phone as a means of communication.[3]

An electronic support system was developed specifically to provide Web-based support for students and instructors in the Management Information Systems (MIS) Department at Bogaziçi University in Turkey. Because of its flexibility, the resulting system, called MISESS, could easily support other departments and other universities wanting to offer course materials, exams, and tutorial services online.

Objectives and Benefits

The MISESS project aimed to facilitate the work of the department's teachers and students and to enrich educational content by ensuring that they would have access to all classes, related subject matter, and examinations electronically. Students should be able to access the system from anywhere and at any time, and instructors should be able to upload course documentation, handouts, exams, class notes, and questions without constraints.

The MISESS online environment lets students study materials from a large database of course subjects and take exams constructed from questions provided in a question database. MISESS also creates Web pages that ensure feedback and assessment, and the system produces instructions to help students understand subjects more deeply.

MISESS requires user authentication. Each user is given a username and a password as defined by the system administrator. Registered students have rights granted by the system administrator to read course documentation and participate in specified exams. Registered instructors can add and update class notes, upload questions, delete questions, prepare exams, and upload exams. Instructors can set exam criteria such as duration, difficulty level of the questions, or date by which students must take the exam. Some types of questions and their answers are evaluated by the system, while the instructor evaluates other types manually. At the end of an exam, students can see their grades and the relevant class notes with reference to their mistakes.

The expected benefits from this system can be summarized as follows:

1. Making classrooms more geographically and demographically available.
2. Providing a mechanism for distribution of the courses over the Internet.
3. Accessing all the MIS courses at the students' request.
4. Converting all types of classical exams to electronic types in a short period, including

   - creating the most efficient examination system on the Internet, and
   - minimizing the time spent to prepare an exam.

5. Increasing the students' knowledge of the course material.

Methodology

A structured methodology underlies the building of MISESS. Structured methodologies are top-down, progressing from the highest, most abstract level to the lowest, detailed level. "Structured" refers to the step-by-step techniques employed, with each step building on the previous one.[4] The MISESS development procedure relied on two major types of analysis: system users' requirements and system components.

System Analysis 1: System Users

MISESS was designed according to the use requirements determined by examining the following groups:

1. Students
2. Instructors
3. System administrators
4. Net surfers

The resulting requirements were defined based on literature surveys, meetings with the instructors, and the developer's personal experiences in undergraduate and graduate teaching.[5]

Analysis of Students' Requirements. The system originally was intended for MIS students to use in their courses, midterms, quizzes, and final exams. The following functions are needed to satisfy students' requirements:

- *Log in.* Registered students log in to the system to reach the course contents or take exams.
- *Change password.* Students can change their passwords on request.
- *Read course content.* After the username and password are verified, students can see content of the courses for which they have registered.
- *Take exams.* Authenticated students take the exams open to them.
- *See exam results.* Authenticated students can see the results of the exams they have taken.
- *Log out.* Students log out of the system to end a session.

Analysis of Instructors' Requirements. Instructors' primary purpose in using this system is to provide lecture notes and give students online exams, which they create using the system itself. The following system functions satisfy these requirements:

- *Log in.* To create and offer content or exams to students, the instructor must first log in to the system.
- *Change password.* Instructors can change their passwords on request.
- *Add course content.* Instructors add content, including course notes, for students to read and study. They prepare a database for all course subjects.
- *Add questions.* Authenticated instructors add questions to the question database for later use.
- *Update course content.* Instructors can update (write or delete) the content, lecture notes, and handouts they created previously.
- *Update questions.* Instructors can update (write or delete) the questions they created.
- *Create exams.* Instructors can create exams from the questions they entered into the part of the database allocated for a specific course, or they can add new questions and create an exam using them.
- *Update exams.* Instructors can make any changes on exams they created previously.
- *View exam results.* Authenticated instructors can see the students' results on the exams given in their courses but not in other instructors' courses.

- *Evaluate questions.* Instructors must manually evaluate essay questions and assign a score.
- *Log out.* Instructors log out from the system to end their session.

Analysis of System Administrator's Requirements. The system administrator plays an important role in keeping the system working. Every semester, students take and instructors teach different courses. Considering that each student enrolls in four to five courses in the MIS department every semester, a huge amount of data must be updated at the beginning of each semester. With an average of 50 students in each of four classes and an average of five courses per student, 1,000 course records must be entered into the system, along with records for 30 masters students taking an average of four courses each semester.

System functions, which an administrator will require, follow:

- *Log in.* The system administrator logs into the system as needed.
- *Enter student data.* At the beginning of each semester, student data must be entered for every departmental course offered. All students who take a course must be entered in the system database. When students log in, they may see the list of courses in which they have enrolled and access the course content. At the beginning of a semester, the administrator enters the enrollment time and course codes for the courses offered during that semester. These transactions could be combined with the course management system.
- *Enter instructor data.* At the beginning of each semester, instructor data must be entered for every course offered. Each course must be assigned an instructor. The administrator can add new courses, new students, and course matching information for instructors and students. These transactions can be combined with the course management system. Course rights are determined at this point, giving instructors access only to the courses they are giving that semester.
- *Log out.* The administrator logs out at the conclusion of each session.

Analysis of Net Surfers' Requirements. Net surfers can be described as users who, although not registered in the MIS department, are allowed to take sample exams and test themselves on their knowledge of MIS-related topics. Functions of the system that satisfy their requirements follow:

- *Study basic MIS concepts.* Net surfers can self-study main MIS subjects, which they can access without getting additional approval. The main subjects differ from individual courses offered during each semester.
- *Take sample exams.* Net surfers can take sample exams in the main subjects only. The sample exams consist of questions selected by instructors responsible for the prerequisite courses. The instructors prepare questions for the courses they give, then each instructor selects two or three questions related to her or his courses to go

into the sample exam. The system administrator puts the sample exam on MISESS for access by net surfers, who may not access regular course exams.

- *See sample exam results.* Net surfers can see the results of the sample exams they took. Because they are not official students enrolled in the department, nobody else—including the system administrator and the course instructors—may view their exam results.

System Analysis 2: Key System Components

MISESS was divided into subsystems by combining its functions into groups. In this step, each subsystem was analyzed separately.

Content Subsystem. The content subsystem includes documents from all the MIS courses. MIS department students can choose the courses for which they want to obtain relevant knowledge, whether officially registered for the course. The content is stored by the system after being converted into HTML format. Instructors can also upload graphics using the Content Interface Screen.

Question Subsystem. If instructors and students look in MISESS for the types of questions typically encountered in traditional exams, they will find them. However, it is not easy to word all types of questions for a Web-based examination system. To keep things simple, four types of questions are defined in MISESS:

- Multiple-choice
- True/false
- Fill-in-the-blank
- Essay

The instructor enters the question, specifies the course name and question type, and selects the difficulty assigned the question. Questions added to MISESS go into the course question pool instructors can consult in creating exams. Instructors can also update questions if needed.

Exam Subsystem. Several differences distinguish traditional from online examinations. First, a traditional exam requires only that students come to the exam location at a specific time and take the exam. Nothing prevents people from taking the exam other than health problems or catastrophic events such as natural disasters. In a Web environment, however, an Internet connection problem can result in missing the exam and getting a zero grade. Second, in a traditional exam environment, proctors observe students to prevent cheating. This inspection is very difficult in an online environment.

To solve these two potential problems, some guidelines regulate online exams:

- Each exam has a deadline after which students may not take the exam. In this way, students do not have to take an exam at a specific time but rather during a time interval, usually in terms of days. The MISESS interface screen lets the instructor set exam criteria including exam name, length of time the exam will last (in minutes), activation date, and end date for students to complete the exam.
- Students click on the exam name to begin the exam. Questions are presented one by one. When a student answers a question, she or he proceeds to the next question. Students cannot go back and change an answer.
- Students do not have to complete an exam in one session. For instance, a student can answer three questions and log out. The next day, the student can log in again and answer the rest of the questions. This way, if a student's Internet connection fails in the middle of an exam, the student can continue when the connection is restored.

Evaluation Subsystem. When instructors prepare questions, they assign each one a point value. In this context, a student receives the full point value for correct answers to multiple-choice, true-false, and fill-in-the-blank questions and zero for wrong answers. Essay questions are permitted in MISESS because student attainment of some course knowledge requires the instructor's subjective evaluation. For essay questions, instructors evaluate the answers manually and assign points to the individual students' answers.

Guidance Subsystem. The guidance subsystem provides course notes relevant to the questions answered incorrectly in an exam. The student sees the exam results with the specific course notes linked to the wrong answers, ensuring that the student can conduct a relevant search in the course content for information to address the indicated knowledge gaps. Students can thus find the right answers by themselves, leading to increased retention of knowledge about the course.

System Design

The design phase concerned how to classify the system requirements into subsystems, each with different functions, and how to present them to users. The steps in this process are determination of software and hardware, user interface design, and database design.

System Software and Hardware

Under the guidance of the analysis done, the MISESS software and hardware specifications were determined. System software specifications include:

- Operating system: Windows 98, 2000, NT, and XP supporting multitasking and multiprocessing; graphical user interface (GUI), and Internet connection
- Utility programs: virus protection
- Programming tools: MS FrontPage 2000, MS Access
- Programming languages: HTML and ASP as source code
- Servers: Web, database, FTP

System hardware specifications include:

- Processor: Pentium IV
- RAM type: SRAM for high speed
- Data representation: ASCII character set
- Expansion slots and board: modem
- Fax: external device

User Interface Design

User interface design is the most important stage because it builds the interaction between users and the system. User-program interaction has two aspects. First is how information from the user is entered in the system. Second is how information from the program is presented to the user.

In designing the interface, some basic principles were taken into account for presenting the MISESS Web site in the most usable and efficient way. The most common browsers must display the MISESS Web pages acceptably, for example, as colors, layout, and fonts might look very different from browser to browser.

MISESS, built mainly with FrontPage 2000, reflects the design of the MIS department's Web site. It lacks colorful images and animations because the system is designed to serve academic purposes. The main goals were simplicity and ease of use, so the menu designs for all users employ the same format. The menus appear on the left side of the screen and enlarge when the mouse passes over them. Menu items were carefully chosen for easy use.

Database Design

The MISESS database contains detailed records about users and courses. The database design incorporates the tables of records and the relationships among tables. Designed with MS Access, the database includes the following tables and relational queries:

- Content table
- Course table
- User table
- User course table
- Exam table
- Questions table (the questions pool)
- Exam questions table (contains questions selected from the question pool for possible inclusion in exams)
- Exam results table
- Student exam table (each student takes different courses and exams; this table shows the exams for one student)
- Find user title
- Find instructor's course
- Exam questions not taken
- Show selected exam questions (selected questions must be checked or changed before creating official exams)
- Wrong questions content (content of questions a student answered incorrectly on an exam)

The organization and linking of the tables give an idea of the database relationships.

Conclusions

Technical features are important to effective use of MISESS. If the right information cannot be provided at the right time, the system will not function efficiently, especially during the examination process. Therefore, coding received the strongest focus—to give instructors an efficient environment for creating exams, a question pool from which to draw, and options on setting exam duration and difficulty.

Successful functioning of MISESS also depends on content issues. Suitable content is vital for efficient, effective online course support and the online examination process. To achieve this goal, the MIS department instructors were interviewed to determine the right content to attract more students to the system and thus provide administrative relief to the instructors.

MISESS differs from other systems in the distance education area because of its content management. Unlike a course content system or an examination system, it allows instructors to add content related to the individual questions in the question pool, which are used in the exams. Students can see their mistakes and the content related specifically to the questions answered incorrectly. They can review the content and increase their retention of knowledge for the course. As result, MISESS can be used as a support for traditional education or as a tool for distance education.

In the future, the project manager and the instructors plan for MISESS to expand in a manner to include links to MIS departments in other universities around the world. The system also could be modified to support any academic department and its students by changing the content and questions entered by instructors to match the relevant subjects. The ease of use for instructors and students, combined with the content and exam features, makes MISESS an effective tool for supporting departmental coursework on campuses anywhere.

Endnotes

1. G.-Q. Zhang et al., "Roadmap for a Departmental Web Site," *EDUCAUSE Quarterly,* Vol. 28, No. 3, 2005, pp. 68–72, <http://www.educause.edu/ir/library/pdf/eqm05311.pdf>.

2. L. Neal, "Distance Learning," *CHI'99 Extended Abstracts on Human Factors in Computing Systems,* (New York: ACM Press, May 1999), pp. 157–158, <http://doi.acm.org/10.1145/632716.632810> (accessed November 9, 2005). See also L. Neal, R. Perez, and D. Miller, "Special Interest Groups: E-Learning and Fun," *CHI'04 Extended Abstracts on Human Factors on Computing Systems* (New York: ACM Press, April 2004), pp. 1590–1591, <http://doi.acm.org/10.1145/985921.986160> (accessed November 9, 2005).

3. Timothy J. Newby et al., *Instructional Technology for Teaching and Learning: Designing Instruction, Integrating Computers, and Using Media* (Upper Saddle River, N.J.: Prentice-Hall, 2000), pp. 57–60.

4. K. C. Laudon and J. P. Laudon, *Management Information Systems: Managing the Digital Firm,* 9th ed. (Upper Saddle River, N.J.: Prentice-Hall, 2006), pp. 511–512; and K. C. Laudon and J. P. Laudon, *Management Information Systems: Organization and Technology in the Networked Enterprise,* 6th ed. (Upper Saddle River, N.J.: Prentice-Hall, 2000), pp. 383–388.

5. See the unpublished project report *Web-Based Examination, Evaluation, and Guidance Systems,* June 2003, by MISESS project manager Z. Tanrıkulu and MIS department students U. Hosgelen and E. Yucel. Contact Tanrıkulu for information.

ZUHAL TANRIKULU (tanrikul@boun.edu.tr) is Assistant Professor, Management Information Systems Department, at Bogazici University in Istanbul, Turkey.

UNIT 7

The Internet and Computer Networks

Unit Selections

Key Points to Consider

- What do you believe is the future of the Internet? What effect will it have on education in this century?

- What is the role of telecomputing in the classroom, the library, the administration, or the home?

- What effect will hand-held technology have on educational programs and institutions?

Student Web Site

www.mhcls.com/online

Internet References

Further information regarding these Web sites may be found in this book's preface or online.

ADA Compliance Center
http://www.cast.org/bobby/
CAST
http://www.cast.org
Google
http://www.google.com
Online Internet Institute
http://oii.org
The Teachers' Network
http://www.teachers.net
WebCrawler
http://webcrawler.com
Yahooligans! The Web Guide for Kids
http://www.yahooligans.com

The history of humankind has been tied closely to the tools of each age and the conditions shaped by those tools. During the last sixteen years global implementation of the Internet tools has turned the global village, produced by television into a global mindset by enabling us to collectively process information. This collective processing is done by making each one of us an integral part of the processing. In this way we preserve in this our individuality, which is maintained while we enjoy the benefits of collective thinking. The Internet may be the most important tool since the invention of the printing press. It enables us to develop an international point of view without leaving our desktop.

However there is cause for caution. The torrential hype that has surrounded the Internet and the World Wide Web has created expectations high above current capabilities. We are just approaching the point where multiple gigabit connections are available to the masses.

The articles in this section address several issues about the Internet and other networks, including the need to build critical skills that enable learners to benefit from using the Web as a ready reference tool and inferencing engine.

The first article, by Diana Oblinger and Brian Hawkins analyzes the real IT competence of college and university students today who seem to be technologically competent. Whereas colleges and universities often focus on technology skills, it is actually *information literacy* that should be the concern. Information literacy is much more than knowing how to open a Web browser and type a search term into Google. Information literacy is the ability to recognize when information is needed and to locate, evaluate, and use information effectively. This article puts the focus on what information literate people need to know.

Next, Warschauer, Grant, Del Real, and Rousseau present case studies of two K-12 schools that successfully employ high-technology environments, including laptop computers for each student, toward the development of English language learners' academic language proficiency and academic literacy. In the first school, Latino fourth-grade students use laptops and other new technologies for a wide variety of pre- and post-reading tasks as part of their effort to transition from learning to read to reading to learn. In the second school, diverse immigrant and refugee students at the middle school level combine technology use with Expeditionary Learning to carry out community projects leading to the development of sophisticated products. In both schools, technology is used to engage students in cognitively demanding activity, motivate independent reading, and provide scaffolding for language development, while the researchers also made use of technology to document learning processes and outcomes.

The following article expresses the authors' concern about the preservation of academic integrity in the virtual classroom. They believe that websites and software now available to educators have the ability to detect and battle plagiarism and cheating. They also believe that the various types of online assessment tools, assignments, and activity available with a virtual course are a deterrent for cheating.

Finally, Katrina Meyer provides a good start on the research that is needed to ensure that the Web is used effectively for student learning.

The Myth about Student Competency

"Our Students Are Technologically Competent."

DIANA G. OBLINGER AND BRIAN L. HAWKINS

College and university students today seem so technologically competent. When they wake up in the morning, they don't turn on the TV to find out about the weather; instead they go to the Web site WeatherBug.com. For news, they use CNN.com, not channel 21. Of course, this is after they check to see what instant messages (IMs) they missed while sleeping. To learn about friends, they turn to Facebook.com. Going online for entertainment is normal for them. Computer games, massively multiplayer games, and music downloads are an assumed part of their environment (for example, 85% of 18- and 19-year-olds download music).[1] And when they want to communicate, sending IMs or text messages is as natural as picking up the phone. There is no question that students go online before they go to the library; Google has become this generation's reference desk.

Watch just about any college or university student. Whether it is taking pictures with a cell phone, downloading ring tones, searching the Web for information, or contributing to Wikipedia or a blog, today's students seem to have no hesitation about using technology. This is what we've come to expect from a generation that has never known life without the Internet. Among today's college and university students aged eighteen to twenty-two, 20 percent first used a computer when they were between the ages of five and eight; all of them had used a PC by the time they were in high school.[2] They continue to use the Internet daily. Surveys consistently put student computer ownership above 90 percent.[3]

Faculty, staff, and administrators see the facile use of technology by students and assume that students have more than adequate IT competency. After all, even senior IT professionals still feel the need to read instruction manuals, can't type text messages with their thumbs, and prefer to read rather than to listen to podcasts. But are students competent or just confident? Having no fear is not the same as having knowledge or skill.

Virtually 100 percent of students use word processors and utilize the Internet for coursework. But the impression of broad competence slips when percentages are revealed for use of other applications, such as those for presentation development (65%), spreadsheets (63%), graphics (49%), or creating Web pages (25%).[4] Using a variety of applications is just one possible definition of IT competency. Perhaps a more important question is, what is IT being used for? From the perspective of a college or university, *learning* must be part of that answer—learning that will continue well past graduation.

Part of a college or university's charge is to prepare students not only for today but also for tomorrow. Even graduates who are well qualified today will experience changes in their disciplines and their careers, requiring additional education. Although just about everything is on the Internet, will graduates have the skills they need to find the right information, assess its value, and interpret it? Will the information selected by students be legitimate? Historically, library collections have ensured quality control and have safeguarded the legitimacy of the material used by students. Beyond the quality of the collection itself, professional librarians have helped students hone their information searches and find information resources. What happens when students bypass the library and librarians entirely? Doing a Google search or exploring Wikipedia may be a start, but do students know where to go next?

Whereas colleges and universities often focus on technology skills, it is actually *information literacy* that should be the concern. Information literacy is much more than knowing how to open a Web browser and type a search term into Google. Information literacy is the ability to recognize when information is needed and to locate, evaluate, and use that information effectively. Moreover, information literacy is not just a skill required in college; there is "a lifelong need for being informed and up-to-date."[5]

Information literacy includes cognitive activities, such as acquiring, interpreting, and evaluating the quality of information. It is enabled by technical skills, such as using a computer to research, organize, analyze, and communicate. And it carries legal and ethical implications such as understanding intellectual property and copyright,[6] as well as understanding bias in the information itself.

Whether the focus is calculus or calorie counting, information-literate users should be able to use IT to scan the environment. This means the user must be knowledgeable about reliable information sources as well as the process of finding and using information. Beyond just searching for information, users must evaluate the legitimacy of the information, put it in context, and then apply problem-solving and decision-making skills. In fact, information literacy can be seen as using information wisely for the benefit of others. And because the world is changing constantly, users must be able to build up new knowledge bases—over and over again.[7]

In thinking about student IT competency, college and university executives should ask themselves the following strategic questions:

1. *What skills do students (and faculty) need in a digital world?* A college/university education is designed to develop subject matter expertise, among other competencies. As more and more material is made available in digital form, IT skills become necessary to access and manipulate those information resources. But a college/university education also implies that students acquire other critical skills, such as information gathering, analysis, critical thinking, and problem-solving. Each of those can be facilitated by technology. Is the institution providing students with the tools, guidance, and practice they need? Can the students tell a legitimate source from one that is biased? Not to be forgotten are the ethics associated with ideas, information resources, and communication. In an age of cut-copy-and-paste, music downloads, and pirated software, do the students have guidance in applying the principles of academic honesty and respect to the digital world?

2. *Do we have an operative definition of IT literacy?* It can be easy to oversimplify IT literacy as the ability to use a computer and a search engine. Does the quality of different information resources matter? Has the institution discussed the new media and communication forms that have become part of our culture—multimedia, podcasts, Web sites, IM, and avatars? Is the institution defining IT literacy based on today's tools (word-processing programs, spreadsheets) or on the activities they enable (communication, analysis)? As the world increasingly uses visualization, audio, and augmented reality, is the institution including these in the definition of IT literacy, or did it stop with keyboarding skills?

3. *Do we help students acquire the skills they need?* Although it was hoped that one day colleges and universities would be able to scale back their help desks because students would be able to handle all of their own IT problems, the fact is that students come to campus with uneven IT skills. Some are experienced Web-site builders, game players, and graphic designers. Others have never before had consistent access to a computer. The help desk may be here to stay. But what about the other types of assistance that students might require? Does the institution mention information literacy in freshmen orientation or in the library overview and then leave students to their own devices?

4. *Is IT literacy integrated across all units?* Although most of the advocacy for IT literacy has come from the library community, this is not just a library issue. Nor is it just an IT issue. Information literacy requires the cooperation of library, IT, and academic units. Like skills such as writing, information literacy is best learned in the context of a discipline. Developing these skills will not come from a single exposure to IT literacy but requires a cross-campus, long-term effort.

5. *Do we know how well we are doing?* Information literacy is a relatively new concept. There are few measures of students' IT needs, expectations, and skills. Does the campus have a definition of or metrics for information literacy? Are those measures shared for the purpose of improvement?

"Information literacy is a survival skill in the Information Age…. Information literate people know now to find, evaluate, and use information effectively to solve a particular problem or make a decision—whether the information they select comes from a computer, a book, a government agency, a film, or any number of other possible resources."[8] Colleges and universities must go beyond the visible IT skills that students possess to help students develop the skill that will support them in a complex, rapidly changing world—information literacy.

Notes

1. Judith B. Caruso and Robert B. Kvavik, "ECAR Study of Students and Information Technology, 2005: Convenience, Connection, Control, and Learning," *EDUCAUSE Center for Applied Research (ECAR) Research Study,* vol. 6 (2005): 35.

2. Steve Jones and Mary Madden, "The Internet Goes to College: How Students Are Living in the Future with Today's Technology," *Pew Internet & American Life Project,* September 15, 2002, <http://www.pewinternet.org/reports/toc.asp?Report=71>.

3. Based on studies such as ibid.; Student Monitor, "Computing and the Internet: Fall 2003," <http://studentmonitor.ecnext.com/coms2/summary_0246-38131_ITM>; and Caruso and Kvavik, "ECAR Study of Students and Information Technology."

4. Caruso and Kvavik, "ECAR Study of Students and Information Technology," 14 (table 1-3).

5. American Library Association, *Presidential Committee on Information Literacy: Final Report* (Washington, D.C.: ACRL, January 10, 1989), <http://www.ala.org/ala/acrl/acrlpubs/whitepapers/presidential.htm>.

6. Irvin Katz, David Williamson, Heather Nadelman, Irwin Kirsch, Russel Almond, Peter Cooper, Margaret Redman, and Diego Zapata, "Assessing Information Communications Technology Literacy for Higher Education," presentation at the Thirtieth Annual Conference of the International Association for Educational Assessment, Philadelphia, Pennsylvania, June 13–18, 2004.

7. Christine Bruce, "Seven Faces of Information Literacy in Higher Education," 1997, <http://sky.fit.qut.edu.au/~bruce/inflit/faces/faces1.php>.

8. American Library Association, *Presidential Committee on Information Literacy.*

DIANA G. OBLINGER is Vice President of EDUCAUSE, where she is responsible for the association's teaching and learning activities and for the EDUCAUSE Learning Initiative (ELI). **BRIAN L. HAWKINS** is President of EDUCAUSE. Comments on this article can be sent to the authors at <doblinger@educause.edu> and <bhawkins@educause.edu>.

From *EDUCAUSE Review,* March/April 2006, pp. 12–13. Copyright © 2006 by Diana Oblinger and Brian L. Hawkins. Reprinted by permission of the authors.

Promoting Academic Literacy with Technology: Successful Laptop Programs in K-12 Schools

MARK WARSCHAUER, DAVID GRANT, GABRIEL DEL REAL, AND MICHELE ROUSSEAU

Department of Education, University of California; Portland Public Schools, Maine; Newport-Mesa Unified School District, California; and University of California, Irvine

One of the main challenges that US schools face in educating English language learners is developing their academic literacy. This paper presents case studies of two K-12 schools that successfully employ high-technology environments, including laptop computers for each student, toward the development of English language learners academic language proficiency and academic literacy. In the first school, Latino fourth-grade students use laptops and other new technologies for a wide variety of pre- and post-reading tasks as part of their effort to transition from learning to read to reading to learn. In the second school, diverse immigrant and refugee students at the middle school level combine technology use with Expeditionary Learning to carry out community projects leading to the development of sophisticated products. In both schools, technology is used to engage students in cognitively demanding activity, motivate independent reading, and provide scaffolding for language development, while the researchers also made use of technology to document learning processes and outcomes. Taken together, the schools offer valuable lessons for utilization of technology to promote academic literacy among culturally and linguistically diverse students.

1. Introduction

The percentage of language minority students in US schools continues to grow, with nearly four million K-12 students receiving special instruction as English language learners (ELLs) (National Center for Educational Statistics, 2004). Many more non-native speakers of English graduate out of ESL programs to mainstream instruction, but have still not fully caught up with grade level instruction. Unfortunately, most language minority students never achieve academic success in the US, with great disparities between them and native English speakers in standardized test scores, graduation rates, college admission and completion rates, and adult wages (Noguera, 2001).

1.1. Academic literacy

Virtually everyone who is born in the US or who immigrates to the country by the age of 12 becomes conversationally fluent (Greenberg et al., 2001). The major challenge that schools face vis-à-vis ELLs is not conversational fluency but rather academic literacy. Academic literacy can be defined as the reading, writing, speaking, listening, and thinking skills, dispositions, and habits of mind that students need for academic success. It includes the ability to critically read and interpret a wide range of texts, to write competently in scholarly genres, and to engage

in and contribute to sophisticated academic discussion (Intersegmental Committee of the Academic Senates, 2002). While English learners develop basic interpersonal communication skills within a year or two, it takes them much longer to develop the knowledge of complex vocabulary, syntax, and genres that underpin academic literacy (Cummins, 1988). The development of this broader academic language proficiency requires five to seven years of instruction with several key elements, including large amounts of extensive reading, focused linguistic analysis of texts, and involvement of students in motivating and cognitively engaging learning activities and projects (Cummins, 1989a,b).

2. Laptops and Literacy

New technologies have been promoted as a potent tool for helping language minority students develop the kinds of reading, writing, and thinking skills that contribute to academic literacy (see, for example, Cummins and Sayers, 1995; Warschauer, 2003). However, studies suggest that the actual use of computers and the Internet with language minority students in K-12 schools leaves much to be desired, due in part to the complexity of integrating new technology in instruction when students have uneven access to computers at school and home (Warschauer et al., 2004). Increasingly, school districts are experimenting with one-to-one laptop computing to provide more consistent computer access to students. The number of laptops in US schools is growing at the rate of some 60% per year (Market Data Retrieval, 2003). In most cases, schools place laptops on mobile carts that are used by different teachers on an "as-needed" basis. However, an increasing number of schools are assigning laptops to individual students for daily use at school and home throughout the academic year (Johnstone, 2003). Relatively little research has been conducted to date on these one-to-one computing environments (for a summary, see Rockman, 2003), and virtually none of it focusing on language minority students.

3. The Study

In this paper, we provide case studies of two schools that have successfully made use of high-technology environments, including one-to-one laptop computing, with language minority students. As part of a national study of K-12 one-to-one computing, our research team identified two schools that demonstrated exemplary models of laptop instruction with ELLs toward developing academic literacy. Following that identification, educators from those schools were invited to assist us in further documenting the educational practices at those sites. The collective authorship of this paper thus represents the collaborative effort of "outside" researchers and "inside" educators in identifying and documenting exemplary practices.

The authors of this report used standard qualitative methods, including observations, interviews, and collection of artifacts, with an emphasis on digital documentation of best practices. This paper thus highlights presentation and discussion of student work and projects in order to give the reader a close-up look at the ways that digital technology can be deployed for development of academic literacy among ELLs. The two schools involved in the study were quite different in terms of location, level, populations served, and pedagogical approach, but both are highly effective in achieving their goals. We begin by first discussing Adelante Elementary School in California, and then turn to Urbania Middle School in Maine. Both school names have been changed for the purposes of this report.

4. Adelante Elementary School

Adelante Elementary School is located in a low-income Latino community of California. Some 96% of the students in the school are Latino and 75% are designated as ELLs. As a grade 4–6 school, Adelante deals with students at a critical juncture for the development of academic literacy. Students in upper elementary school must go through a transition from learning to read, with a focus on decoding skills, to reading to learn, with a focus on comprehension of increasingly challenging expository texts across a number of content areas (Chall, 1996). This represents a special challenge for language minority students, who often begin to fall behind due to their limited mastery of vocabulary and syntax and insufficient cultural background knowledge, leading to what is widely referred to as the "fourth-grade slump" (Chall et al., 1990).

Adelante has strongly emphasized the use of new technologies to help their students meet the challenge of reading to learn. For five years, the school has been implementing a computerized system, *Accelerated Reader,* for monitoring and evaluating independent reading activity (Renaissance Learning, Inc., 2004). Three years ago, a Technology Academy was developed in several classrooms, involving the use of interactive white boards (SMART Boards), access to two mobile laptop carts, wireless networking, and special professional development for teachers. This past year, the program was extended through the purchase of a third class set of laptops, which were assigned to one fourth grade language arts and reading class on a daily basis for use at school and home. Research for this study was carried out in that classroom, which meets 3 h per day and is taught by Mr. Molina. All but one of the 29 students in the class are Latino and native speakers of Spanish. Some 20 of the 29 are classified as English language learners, while the rest have reached the stage of fluency in English. The class is on the average six months to one year behind grade level in reading.

Mr. Molina was chosen by Adelante to teach their one-to-one laptop class based on his prior success in integrating technology into the reading and language arts curriculum. His class was selected for observation in this study as the one class at Adelante with one-to-one laptop computing. The school and district hope to expand the one-to-one laptop program through acquisition of additional equipment, so Molina's course was thus seen as a pilot effort. Molina is an exceptionally talented teacher—he was previously selected as Adelante's Teacher of the Year—so his results are not necessarily typical of what can be accomplished in any classroom with laptops, but they do demonstrate how technology can be combined with instructional excellence to promote academic literacy among non-native speakers of English.

4.1. Technology and language arts at Adelante

Technology is used in Molina's class as a complementary piece to the language arts curriculum. The success of the laptop program in Molina's class is due to a deliberate integration of technology into the reading/language arts curriculum. Students are not taught technology skills in isolation. Instead, the technology skills are infused into each of the projects that Molina's students complete through thematic literature units. In Molina's class a SMART Board, Renaissance Learning Programs, the Internet, digital cameras, and computer programs such as SMART Ideas cognitive mapping software, *Microsoft Word, Microsoft Excel,* and *Microsoft PowerPoint* are used as media for projects where students interact with text. The goal of these projects is to refine the students' process of constructing rich meaning from text. Coupled with this wealth of technology are extensive opportunities for students to practice reading. The reading practice is structured as guided independent reading where the students make decisions about what reading comprehension strategies to use based on explicit instruction and modeling of reading comprehension strategies. Students become proficient at applying reading comprehension strategies to a variety of text genres as a result of diverse guided reading experiences through teacher modeling and cross-age tutoring activities that promote thorough examinations of text organization. One final piece in the successful implementation of laptops in Molina's class is his ability to effectively manage behavior and promote elevated standards for student work through motivating literacy projects.

4.2. Pre-reading with Mr. Molina

Technology is used to complement and enrich the instructional experience, but it is a means to an end, with the collateral benefit of students developing technology skills in addition to their ability to engage in meaningful interactions with text. The interactive white board and Internet are integrated into pre-reading activities. Students come to the board to carry out vocabulary-picture matching activities, thus providing a foundation of background knowledge for the readings, as well as allowing students to employ vocabulary acquisition strategies that have more utility than pre-teaching a rigid definition of a word (see, for example, Picture1.jpg). Background knowledge is also built by drawing on the Internet resources relevant to literature themes, drawing on pedagogical sites such as *NetTrekker* (Thinkronize, 2003). Molina downloads content or images to the SMART Board to engage the whole class in a discussion of content, or the students visit websites individually through the use of a teacher created Webquest. These Internet experiences provide a platform for reflective discussions among students. Teacher led questioning about the Websites scaffolds the students' use of language by providing opportunities to practice using language with members of cooperative groups.

4.3. Independent Reading

Once background knowledge has been adequately activated, the literature is read as a whole class. Molina's students, like the students in the rest of the school, also engage in 60 min independent reading per day. The library has some 16,000 books for which computerized quizzes are available in the *Accelerated Reader* program, and once students finish a book they independently take the quiz on a computer, and, upon passing, receive recommendations of further books at their level. *Accelerated Reader* has come under much criticism for failing to teach reading skills (e.g., Oppenheimer, 2004). However, at Adelante, the program is not used to teach reading skills or strategies, but rather to encourage and evaluate students' independent reading, and in that it is highly successful. The students at Adelante check out an average of one book per day from the library, and their reading scores are well above the state average for students of similar demographics. Molina closely monitors students' independent reading, having them fill out special cards to indicate the reading strategies they used (such as predictions made) and actively discussing with them the books they will or have read (see, for example, MSWord1.doc Excel1.xls).

4.4. Post-Reading

The most focused use of technology occurs after the whole class reading of particular texts. Molina skillfully makes use of a variety of tools to help students deconstruct texts and understand their genres and structures, key elements of academic literacy. Students use cognitive mapping software to outline and interpret texts. In the process, the students reread to locate and clarify key points, while organizing their understanding of the text into a visual representation (see, for example, PPT1.ppt). Searching for images that match text has further positive effects on student vocabulary development, while also developing students' technological skills. In order to search for images in clip art and/or the Internet, the students are forced to articulate their understanding of the text in a one-word summary.

Another post-reading project that exemplifies the use of technology to teach academic literacy is an extension project that stemmed from the story, *Sadako and the Thousand Paper Cranes* (Coerr, 1999). After the story, the students developed their ability to read and follow written instructions by folding paper cranes as a class. To explore organization of written instructions through the reading–writing connection, the students were required to design their own origami models and to write instructions for modeling their figure (see, for example, PPT2.ppt). This project served as a catalyst to promote students' connections from the written instructions they had just read, to the instructions that they were writing, thus taking advantage of the principle of pushed output (Swain, 1985), in which learners are pushed or stretched to attempt new language forms as a necessary part of making themselves understood. The students wrote the steps for their folding instructions on slides in *Microsoft PowerPoint*. Included on each slide was a digital picture that the students took of the steps for folding their origami model. After completing their instructions, the students printed out the instructions and a class origami book was created.

One fascinating example of technology for apprenticeship into communities of practice involved students writing customer reviews of *Sadako and the Thousand Cranes* for Amazon.com. Students first viewed some other customer reviews of the book on the SMART Board, and collectively critiqued them, discussing the particular features of an effective book review, such as how to provide an effective title, how to gain readers' interest, and how to avoid giving away too much through "spoilers". In examining already-published customer reviews, the students also took careful note of grammatical or spelling errors, and reinforced their own commitment to do better. Students then wrote their own reviews of *Sadako and the Thousand Cranes* and saved them on the school file server. Molina then made suggestions to the students through the use of the comment feature in *Microsoft Word*, and students retrieved their files and revised their reviews. The students submitted their reviews for publication on Amazon.com, and checked back with great delight a couple of days later to see that they had been published (see, for example, GIF1.gif and GIF2.gif). The activity emphasized for students both the iterative nature of writing, as well as the mindset of composing for a particular real-world purpose and audience, and also helped them by default learn many technological skills. Following this activity, some of the students in the class continued to submit reviews to Amazon.com even when not assigned by the teacher. This example and the previous one both point to how literacy became much more of a public event in the class through the use of digital technology.

One final use of technology in Molina's class is the organization of information through the creation of matrices. One project employed a matrix as a semantic feature analysis to connect stories in a literature theme. In this project the students created a matrix in *Microsoft Word* and recorded the titles and common elements of the stories within a theme. The goal of this is to help ELLs make a literal connection between stories in a thematic unit through a graphic organizer. Another use of a matrix was to study character development across a novel. Students were able to explore how the author uses characters' actions to portray key personality traits and motivations. In this project the students created a workbook in *Microsoft Excel*. Each worksheet within the workbook was named for a character in the book. On the worksheets, the students logged the characters' most significant actions and evaluated if the characters' actions had a positive or negative effect on the development of the plot (see, for example, Excel2.xls and Excel3.xls). The log was then analyzed by the students and they looked for trends in character behavior. As a summative evaluation, the students selected characters with dissimilar personality traits and wrote an essay comparing and contrasting the characters citing specific evidence from the text.

Observations at the school, as well as interviews with students and their parents, indicated an extraordinarily engaged group of students with a joyous attitude toward school, literacy, and learning. These results are of course not solely attributable to the laptop program or other use of technology. Rather, Molina and the school were able to make use of new technologies to build on their previously successful approach, which involved promotion of academic literacy through extensive reading, intensive attention to texts, and involvement in cognitively engaging projects.

5. Urbania Middle School

Urbania Middle School represents a different, but we feel equally effective, approach to using laptops to promote academic literacy. Urbania serves the most economically, academically, and linguistically diverse neighborhoods in the state of Maine. Among a population of 520 students in grades six through eight, approximately 24% of students are from immigrant or refugee families, speaking some 25 languages. The largest groups of ESL students come from Somalia and Sudan, with others from Afghanistan, Southeast Asia, the Middle East, Eastern Europe, and Latin America. Since the school serves as a major refugee relocation center, many of these students have little educational background in their own country prior to their arrival in the US. A majority of the native-English speaking white students at the school also face educational and social challenges, with some 70% of children in the surrounding neighborhoods coming from single-parent households and a nearly equal number living in poverty. If students at Adelante are faced with the prospect of a fourth-grade slump, Urbania's students face a similar but more severe threat known as the "eighth-grade cliff" (de León, 2002). Simply put, students who do not gain sufficient academic literacy skills by the completion of Middle School face so many

challenges with increasingly difficult material that they often drop out.

Urbania has met this challenge with an ambitious educational reform effort that has actually raised test scores at the same time the school as become more culturally and linguistically diverse. Though Urbania has more English language learners than any other school in the state, its reading and writing test scores fall well above the state average. The educational reform at Urbania has developed in three stages. In the first stage, beginning in 1993, Urbania's principal and staff developed and implemented a Expeditionary Learning Outward Bound (ELOB) model (Expeditionary Learning Outward Bound, 2004), in which the main curriculum of the school is organized around 8–12 week interdisciplinary projects. In the second stage, beginning gradually in the mid-to-late 1990s, efforts by the school's technology coordinator and classroom teachers helped make new media central to many of the ELOB projects, with students using computers, the Internet, and other digital media to carry out their inquiry and develop products. In the third stage, beginning in 2002, the school issued laptop computers to all students at the seventh grade and eighth grade levels, and one-to-one computing further supported the reform effort.

The principal and staff's relentless commitment to overcoming educational inequity, conflict, and division in the school has been key to the overall reform effort. Before the reform effort began, Urbania was characterized by low test scores, deteriorating attendance and discipline, few extracurricular activities, low expectations for teachers and students, and a climate of hostility. The school ran on a master schedule with bells moving students among classes on 40 min intervals. Students were tracked in seven separate ability groups, and 24% of students were pulled out of classrooms for special education services. Today at Urbania, interdisciplinary teaching teams have authority to design their own schedules based upon the needs of their students and the curriculum. Passing bells have been eliminated. Students are no longer tracked, pullouts are reduced, and students are heterogeneously mixed in core subjects with the expectation that teachers would teach to all students. Teachers are encouraged and supported in developing and implementing thematic curriculum with effective middle level teaching practices. Related arts teachers, special education teachers, and reading specialists have been integrated into the teaching teams.

Teaching teams work together to develop the 8–12 week interdisciplinary units known as *Learning Expeditions* (Expeditionary Learning Outward Bound, 2004). In these units, teams of teachers and students collaboratively develop knowledge and skills around a set of guiding questions. Each expedition is composed of common segments including a kick-off (in which the context and the topic of inquiry for the expedition are introduced to students), a period of teacher and student directed learning, field work (visiting with experts both outside and inside the school), product development (developing a collective model of the knowledge and skills gained in the expedition), and a culminating event in which students share the final product with a significant audience. This integrative approach—of both students and curriculum—is implemented with the school's English language learners as well. Previously, all of the schools' ELLs were taught in self-contained ESOL classrooms. Today, the emphasis is on mainstreaming, with three-quarters of the ELLs integrated into the mainstream program, though receiving additional support for language and reading. The beginning ESL students who have not yet been mainstreamed either participate in their own Learning Expeditions or sometimes join the expeditions of other students at their grade level.

Technology and project-based learning are combined at Urbania to promote learning in four ways: developing models of knowledge and learning with students, creating opportunities for instructional differentiation within the context of learning expeditions, constructing real products as the outcome of learning of expeditions, and preparing students to be producers as well as consumers of media.

5.1. Developing Models of Knowledge at Urbania: Representing to Learn

The *Expeditionary Learning* model focuses on the relationship between learning and representation. This methodology is supported by research indicating that student's best master curriculum that they are required to represent, and consequently, that learning is extended by one's access to, and literacy and facility with, representational media (see discussion in Zemelman et al., 1998). In the last weeks of a learning expedition at Urbania, students and teachers typically finalize the design of the expedition product, create multiple drafts of individual student contributions, and assemble the work of all students in a single culminating product. Prior to the development of multimedia resources, products (and the learning processes for developing them) were limited to non-digital, largely linear, and difficult-to-edit media. Use of color artwork was limited due to expense of reproduction. Moving images, sound, and interactive models were limited to performance-based products. Though such products can play important roles in learning, many early student products at Urbania lacked the sophistication to represent non-linear systems of knowledge, and often emphasized form above content due the rigid nature of the media.

Through the introduction of multi-media production technology and strategies at Urbania, students and teachers have the means to construct appropriately sophisticated representations of curriculum. The use of new technologies enable students and teachers to create comprehensive representations of the processes and outcomes of learning expeditions through products that are rich in core content, connect discrete knowledge to broad concepts through hyperlinks, and include multiple forms of learning and expression.

5.2. Instructional Differentiation

Urbania's diversity and heterogeneous school design present obvious challenges to planning for the needs and potential of all students, especially English language learners. Teachers at Urbania use the time frame of expeditions and the design of multimedia final products to address questions of differentiation. A common technique involves developing a multi-tiered product in which each student is required to produce a discrete portion that demonstrates essential knowledge and skills. For many students, these requirements are appropriately challenging considering the duration of the project. Students who finish ahead of classmates, however, are expected to develop other portions of the product by carrying out additional research related to the expedition or developing documentary video, audio or other media chronicling the expedition.

5.3. Constructing Real Products

A brief discussion of one expedition product, *Fading Footprints*, is illustrative of this process (see also Grant, 2004). *Fading Footprints* is a 12 week science, art and technology expedition student project that has been conducted twice at Urbania, most recently in 2003. Over the course of the expedition, students acquired knowledge of broad concepts of ecology in relation to specific species in Maine. The product for the expedition was a CD-ROM field guide cataloguing Maine's endangered wildlife, rich in scientifically correct species illustrations, individual species pages (see, for example, HTML1.htm, HTML2.htm and HTML3.htm) and broad ecology concept pages, and a student-produced documentary video of the learning process (see Mov1.mov). The final product was presented to the Maine Audubon Society and made available to the other elementary schools in the school district. An expository species page and scientific species illustration were required of each student. Those who finished constructed concept pages covering the broad themes of ecology (see HTML4.htm). Near the conclusion of the expedition, all 80 students reviewed each of the 20 concept pages produced by peers, and subsequently created links from their species pages to the concept pages most clearly connected to their species.

5.4. Students as Producers of Media

Working in a representation and media rich learning environment has important advantages for the diverse students, and especially ELLs. The incorporation of visual artwork allowed students to develop and display multimedia skills while they simultaneously develop their writing ability. The creation of a multi-tiered final product created opportunities for all students to do their best work while contributing to a collective product. When one views the final product, all of the work looks equivalent on the surface. The extra work, though immediately accessible through hyper-links, lies beneath the surface and does not detract from the appearance of anyone else's work. Finally, students develop an ability to think critically about new media genres when they actually go through the process of producing new media rather than just consuming it.

Fading Footprints is just one of a number of Learning Expeditions student projects that students engage in at Urbania. Other recent expeditions have included Kings of Rhythm, a music and technology expedition in which all sixth graders film, edit and produce documentary video of their music classes (see Mov2.mov), and Four Freedoms, a mixed media humanities expedition about freedom of expression and social responsibility (see, for example, HTML5.htm, HTML6.htm, HTML7.htm, and HTML8.htm). An annual Celebration of Learning at Urbania showcases student work from these and other expeditions.

Though the approach at Urbania is different than that of Adelante, students similarly engage in all the practices that are considered critical for the development of academic literacy at the middle school level. First, the research for the expeditions involves extensive background reading, as students independently gather information for their contributions. Second, as students work to create their products, intensive work is done on editing and language scaffolding. Students are motivated to attend to issues of syntax, vocabulary, mechanics, and structure, knowing that their work is going to be made available to the public, while peer editors and teachers provide feedback to individual students and collectively. Finally, the projects involve students in motivating and cognitively engaging contexts, which maintains their interest level and pushes them to excel.

6. Conclusion

The promotion of academic literacy involves far more than "teaching English". Rather, it involves offering students "access to the ranges of knowledge, abilities, and forms of language" that will enable them "to lay claim to the social identities that afford them a participant status" in academic communities, and provide the scaffolding and supportive environment necessary for attainment of these (Hawkins, 2004, p. 23). New technologies are an extraordinarily valuable tool to facilitate this process. The use of computers and the Internet can provide support for extensive and independent reading and writing, assist with language scaffolding, and provide opportunities for authentic research and publication. Unfortunately, though, most K-12 teachers in the US have experienced great difficulty in effectively integrating new technologies in instruction of ELLs (Warschauer et al., 2004).

The two schools highlighted in this study represent very different instructional contexts. In the first case, a somewhat homogenous group of Latino English language learners focuses on language arts and reading at the fourth grade level. The underlying theme of the program is reading to learn. In the second case, a highly heterogeneous group of immigrant and refugee students take an interdisciplinary middle school curriculum, mostly in mainstream classes in a diverse urban school. The underlying approach of that program is *Expeditionary Learning* and representing to learn. Both schools make highly effective use of technology to promote academic literacy among their students, resulting in sophisticated student products, highly engaged learners, and high standardized test scores in relationship to school demographics. The keys in both cases are a school-wide commitment to excellence, equity, and development of classroom communities of inquiry. Technology is used to apprentice students into academic literacy through promotion of independent reading, support for language scaffolding, involvement in cognitively engaging projects, and student analysis and creation of purposeful texts in a variety of media and genres. Schools that look to technology as a magic bullet to transform education will be disappointed. Rather, new technologies serve as an amplifier that can magnify preexisting strengths and weaknesses (Warschauer, 1999, 2000). As these two cases show, schools that develop an effective approach for promotion of academic literacy will be able to amplify their efforts with the use of new technologies.

Acknowledgements

The research for this paper was supported by grants from the Ada Byron Research Center for Diversity in Computing and Information Technology at the University of California, Irvine (UCI), and the UCI Cultural Diversity Studies Program of the Council on Research, Computing and Library Resources. We are also grateful for the involvement in the broader laptop research project of LaWanna Shelton-Carrigan, Kelly Bruce, Melanie Wade, and Jorge Velastagui (http://www.gse.uci.edu/markw/ research.html). Finally, we thank the administrators, teachers, parents and students at the two schools sites for so generously welcoming us into their schools.

Appendix A. Supplementary data

Supplementary data associated with this article can be found, in the online version, at doi:10.1016/j.system.2004.09.010 .

References

Chall, J.S., 1996. Stages of Reading Development, second ed. Harcourt Brace College Publishers, Fort Worth.

Chall, J.S., Jacobs, V.A., Baldwin, L.E., 1990. The Reading Crisis: Why Poor Children Fall Behind. Harvard University Press, Cambridge, MA.

Coerr, E., 1999. Sadako and the Thousand Paper Cranes. Puffn Books, New York.

Cummins, J., 1988. Second language acquisition within bilingual education programs. In: Beebe, L.M. (Ed.), Issues in Second Language Acquisition. Harper & Row, New York, pp. 145–166.

Cummins, J., 1989a. Empowering Minority Students. California Association for Bilingual Education, Sacramento, CA.

Cummins, J., 1989b. Language and literacy acquisition in bilingual contexts. Journal of Multilingual and Multicultural Development 10 (1), 17–31.

Cummins, J., Sayers, D., 1995. Brave New Schools: Challenging Cultural Illiteracy Through Global Learning Networks. St. Martin's Press, New York.

de León, A.G., 2002. Moving beyond storybooks: Teaching our children to read to learn. Carnegie Reporter 2(1), Downloaded May 25, 2004 from http://www.carnegie.org/reporter/05/ learning/index.html .

Expeditionary Learning Outward Bound. 2004. Expeditionary Learning. Retrieved August 12, 2004, from http://www.elob.org.

Grant, D. 2004. Fading Footprints (SEED Packet). Retrieved May 27, 2004 from http://king.portlandschools.org/documents/ fprints/concepts/FootprintsPDF.pdf.

Greenberg, E., Macías, R., Rhodes, D., Chan, T., 2001. English Literacy and Language Minorities in the United States. National Center for Education Statistics, Washington, DC.

Hawkins, M.R., 2004. Researching English language and literacy development in schools. Educational Researcher 33 (3), 14–25.

Intersegmental Committee of the Academic Senates, 2002. Academic Literacy: A Statement of Competencies Expected of Students Entering California's Public Colleges and Universities. ICAS, Sacramento.

Johnstone, B., 2003. Never mind the laptops: Kids, Computers, and the Transformation of Learning. Universe, Lincoln, NE.

Market Data Retrieval, 2003. Technology in Education 2003: A Comprehensive Report on the State of Technology in the K-12 Market. Market Data Retrieval, Shelton, CT.

National Center for Educational Statistics, 2004. Overview of Public Elementary and Secondary Schools and Districts: School Year 2001-2002. Retrieved May 1, 2004, from http://nces.ed.gov/pubs2003/overview03/table_10.asp.

Noguera, P., 2001. Racial politics and the elusive quest for excellence and equity in education. Education and Urban Society 34 (1), 18–41.

Oppenheimer, T., 2004. The Flickering Mind: The False Promise of Technology in the Classroom and How Learning Can be Saved. Random House, New York.

Renaissance Learning, Inc., 2004. Accelerated Reader. Retrieved July 27, 2004 from http://www.renlearn.com/ar .

Rockman, S., 2003. Learning from laptops. Threshold Magazine, fall, pp. 24–28.

Swain, M., 1985. Communicative competence: Some roles of comprehensible input and comprehensible output in its development. In: Gass, S., Madden, C. (Eds.), Input in Second Language Acquisition. Newbury House, Rowley, MA, pp. 235–253.

Thinkronize, 2003. NetTrekker. Retrieved July 27, 2004 from http://nettrekker.com.

Warschauer, M., 1999. Electronic Literacies: Language, Culture, and Power in Online Education. Lawrence Erlbaum Associates, Mahwah, NJ.

Warschauer, M., 2000. Technology and school reform: A view from both sides of the track. Education Policy Analysis Archives 8 (4).

Warschauer, M., 2003. Technology and Social Inclusion: Rethinking the Digital Divide. MIT Press, Cambridge.

Warschauer, M., Knobel, M., Stone, L., 2004. Technology and equity in schooling: deconstructing the digital divide. Educational Policy 18 (4), 562–588.

Zemelman, S., Daniels, H., Hyde, A., 1998. Best Practice: New Standards for Teaching and Learning in America's Schools. Heinemann, Portsmouth, NH.

Probing for Plagiarism in the Virtual Classroom

Lindsey S. Hamlin and William T. Ryan

Virtual learning in higher education has seen enormous development in both public and private universities. In 2000, about 47 percent of U.S. colleges offered some form of distance learning. This figure will increase to almost 90 percent by the end of 2004 (Flisis, 2001).

Educators who are making the transition into online teaching are skeptical about the preservation of academic integrity in the virtual classroom. They often assume that Internet technology and online classrooms are providing students with additional opportunities to cheat. In reality, the probability that a student will cheat in an online course is about equal to the chances that a student will cheat in a traditional course (Carnevale, 1999). In fact, with the Web sites and software now available, educators have the ability to detect and battle plagiarism and cheating in virtual classrooms. Also, the various types of online assessment tools, assignments, and activities available within a virtual course (i.e. threaded discussions, virtual chats, quizzes, group presentations, etc.) are, by their very nature, a deterrent for cheating.

Virtual vs. Traditional Cheating

Unfortunately, cheating has always existed and will continue as long as there is temptation to do so. In 2002, 47 students at Simon Fraser University turned in nearly the same economics paper (Black, 2002). According to a 1999 study conducted by the Center for Academic Integrity at Duke University, of the 2,100 students surveyed on 21 campuses across the country, "more than two-thirds of the students admitted to one or more instances of serious cheating, such as copying from another student on a test, plagiarizing or submitting work done by another student" (Muha, 2000). Although these statistics show that cheating remains a serious academic problem, it is unclear as to whether the Internet has really changed the percentage of students who cheat.

Online Exams

While giving an exam in the traditional classroom, educators look for roaming eyes and cheat sheets to identify cheaters. Yet, in an online classroom instructors do not have the benefit of visually monitoring students during an exam. To compensate for this problem, instructors can place time restrictions on exams or require that exams be proctored by a college testing center or library. While creating an online exam, instructors have the option of restricting the amount of time the student has to complete the exam. When the time limit has expired, the exam is automatically submitted to the instructor. This technique is most successful at deterring cheaters when it is used in short, multiple-choice quizzes. For example, if an exam consists of 10 multiple choice questions and a student has nine minutes to complete the exam, the chances of the student looking up each answer is slim because of the time restriction. Instructors that require exams to be proctored are gaining the same benefit of the visually monitored exam in a traditional classroom. However, many testing centers charge students a fee of up to $15 per hour for use of their facilities. In addition, if the class perceives proctoring as an indication of the instructor's mistrust in his/her students, it can markedly damage the student/teacher relationship. Some educators have criticized proctoring as a "violation of the spirit of the honor code" (Young, 2001).

Discussion Boards

Virtual skeptics have criticized online education for worsening a student's sense of "isolation and anonymity" (Carnevale, 1999). From an outside perspective this may seem true, however, virtual learning offers ways of communicating with students and assessing their knowledge that extends beyond the traditional classroom. Threaded discussions allow instructors to post discussion-type questions to which students can respond. These discussions are not asynchronous, which allows students to chat their leisure within a given time period. Threaded discussions encourage students to communicate, discuss, and debate topics with each other. They also provide instructors with countless examples of a student's writing style, which can be very useful in determining if a student has plagiarized a paper. The benefit to these discussions, as opposed to live, in-class discussions, is that students have the time and opportunity to research and thoroughly structure their responses. Many times students will even provide Web links within the discussion for other students to view. Because of this continuous research that takes place during the threaded discussions, the quality of responses tends to be much higher than that of traditional, classroom-based discussions. Along with threaded discussions, instructors can assess students through virtual chat or synchronous discussions. By requiring groups of students to meet at a predetermined date and time in the online chat room and discuss a specified topic, students begin to form working relationships with their classmates and instructor. The time commitment required to participate in virtual chats and threaded discussions is also a deterrent to online cheating.

Selected Anti-Plagiarism Sites

Plagiarism.com

Three software programs from Glatt Plagiarism Services Inc. www.plagiarism.com

Plagiarism.org

Self-described "online resource for educators concerned with the growing problem of Internet plagiarism." www.plagiarism. org and www.turnitin.com

Plagiarized.com

"The Instructors Guide to Internet Plagiarism." www. plagiarized. com

EVE (Essay Verification Engine)

A downloadable application that performs complex searches against text, Microsoft Corp. Word files, and Corel Corp. Word-Perfect files. www.canexus.com

The Center for Academic Integrity

An association of more than 225 institutions that provides a forum for identifying and promoting the values of academic integrity. www.academicintegrity.org

What is Plagiarism?

Guidelines from the Georgetown University Honor Council. www.georgetown.edu/honor/plagiarism.html

Avoiding Plagiarism

Guidelines from the Office of Student Judicial Affairs at the University of California, Davis. sja.ucdavis.edu/avoid.htm

Online Plagiarism

With the increasing number of online term-paper mills, such as Schoolsucks.com and Cheater.com, students have an even greater temptation to plagiarize. Instead of copying text out of books or journals by hand, students can now find an array of term papers online and can copy and paste blocks of text right into their word processors (Heberling, 2002). Deceitful students may also copy papers from Web sites of conference proceedings or well-intentioned academics. As of March 2003, the Kimbel Library at Coastal Carolina University had identified 250 active Internet term-paper and essay Web sites (Fain, 2003). A national survey conducted by Donald McCabe, a professor of manage-

ment at Rutgers University, found that 54 percent of students admitted to plagiarizing from the Internet; 74 percent of students admitted that at least once during the past school year they had engaged in "serious" cheating; and 47 percent of students believe their teachers sometimes choose to ignore students who are cheating (Stricherz, 2001).

In the May-June 2002 issue of the *Journal of College Student Development*, Patrick M. Scanlon and David R. Neumann of the Rochester Institute of Technology reported their research findings on Internet plagiarism. Surprisingly, their research indicates that the proliferation of Internet plagiarism may not be as extensive as many may assume. The professors polled 698 undergraduate students at nine institutions of higher learning. Some 16.5 percent of the respondents reported plagiarizing "sometimes," while 50.4 percent claimed that their peers "often" or "very frequently" committed plagiarism. Slightly more respondents said they plagiarized conventional text more than online documents and almost 100 percent agreed that their peers plagiarized conventional text. Scanlon and Neumann concluded that more conventional plagiarism is occurring, while the growth of online plagiarism may not be significantly contributing to the growth of plagiarism in general (Kellogg, 2002). These statistics show that online access to papers has increased plagiarism in both the traditional and online classroom. However, because papers are submitted electronically in the virtual classroom, it is easier for online instructors to detect plagiarism by running student-submitted papers through plagiarism-detecting Web sites or software programs (Heberling, 2002).

Plagiarism-Detecting Web Sites

Plagiarism.org maintains a database of thousands of digitally fingerprinted documents including papers obtained from term-paper mills. According to Plagiarism.org, when an instructor uploads a student's paper to the site, the document's "fingerprint" is cross-referenced against the local database containing hundreds of thousands of papers. At the same time, automated Web crawlers are released to scour the rest of the Internet for possible matches. The instructor receives a custom, color-coded "originality report," complete with source links, for each paper. For a fee, this service will detect papers that are entirely plagiarized, papers that include plagiarism from different sources, or papers that have bits and pieces of plagiarized text (www. plagiarism.org). However, educators must remember that even though plagiarism-detecting software can identify plagiarized text, it may not highlight the quotation marks surrounding the text or the reference to the text within the paper. An overzealous professor could hastily accuse a student of plagiarism by running their paper through plagiarism-detecting software and then fail to revisit the paper to verify whether the identified text was referenced.

Internet detection services, both fee-based and non-fee-based, are on the rise. Many educators would find this growth positive, however, a March 2002 article in *The Chronicle of Higher Education* reported that two plagiarism detection Web sites, Plag-iServe.com and EduTie.com, appear to have ties to Web sites that sell term papers to students. Apparently, the companies that were checking student papers for plagiarism were then selling those same papers through its term-paper mills. Although the allegations were denied by both companies, the possible conflict of interest is a reminder to educators to be cautious in submitting student papers to unsubstantiated sites (Young, 2002).

Plagiarism-Detecting Software

Many software companies have developed innovative programs for detecting plagiarism. Glatt Plagiarism Services Inc. produces the Glatt Plagiarism Screening Program, which eliminates every fifth word of the suspected student's paper and replaces the words with a blank space. The student is asked to supply the missing words. The number of correct responses, the amount of time intervening, and various other factors are considered in assessing the final Plagiarism Probability Score. This program is based on Wilson Taylor's (1953) cloze procedure, which was originally used to test reading comprehension (www.plagiarism.com).

Internet Search Engines

Educators may also find the more popular Internet search engines to be a useful tool in plagiarism detection. Google, Yahoo, Excite, AskJeeves, HotBot, GoTo, AltaVista, and MetaCrawler are just a few of the search engines that can aid an instructor in detection. When an instructor suspects a student of copying text or notices an inconsistency in a student's writing style, he or she can enter the suspect phrase into the search engine. The search engine will return a listing of all websites that contain an exact match of the entered text. Instructors can broaden their results by searching a few different search engines (Heberling, 2002).

Preserving Academic Integrity

Educators are faced with the task of preserving academic integrity. Although it is nearly impossible to eliminate cheating in traditional or virtual classrooms, educators can deter it by using the tools available to them. Instructors who advise their students that writing samples will be collected, term papers will be through plagiarism-detecting software, pop-quizzes will be given throughout the semester, and that weekly participation in the discussion boards is a class requirement are setting up a virtual environment that will deter cheating.

References

Black, Barbara. "Universities Still Confronted By Student Plagiarism." *Concordia's Thursday Report.* Jan. 24, 2002. [Online]. Available from http://pr.concordia.ca/ctr/2001-02/ Jan_24/ 01-Plagiarism/index.shtml. Accessed Dec. 14, 2002.

Carnevale, Dan. "How to Proctor From a Distance." *The Chronicle of Higher Education.* Nov. 12, 1999. [Online]. Available from http://chronicle.com/cgi2-bin/printableverity.cgi. Accessed Dec. 13, 2002.

Fain, Margaret, and Peggy Bates. "Cheating 101: Paper Mills and You." March 10, 2003. [Online]. Available from www.coastal.edu/library/papermil.htm. Accessed April 4, 2002.

Flisis, Maximilian. "eLearning is Burgeoning." *IDC eNewsletter.* April 26, 2001. [Online]. Available from www.idc.com/getdoc.jhtml?containerId=ebt20010426. Accessed Dec. 14, 2002.

Heberling, Michael. "Maintaining Academic Integrity in *Online Education.*" *Online Journal of Distance Learning Administration,* vol. V, no. 1. Spring 2002. [Online]. Available from www.westga.edu/~distance/ojdla/spring51/ herberling51.html. Accessed Dec. 13, 2002.

Kellogg, Alex. "Students Plagiarize Less Than Many Think: A New Study Finds." *The Chronicle of Higher Education.* Feb. 1, 2002. [Online]. Available from http://chronicle.com/free/ 2002/02/2002020101t.htm. Accessed Dec. 14, 2002.

Muha, Dave. "Cheating: When Students Cheat." Rutgers Focus. March 17, 2000. [Online]. Available from http://ur.rutgers.edu/focus/index.phtml?Article_ID=88&Issue_ID=12. Accessed Dec. 14, 2002.

Stricherz, Mark. "Many Teachers Ignore Cheating, Survey Finds." *Education Week.* May 9, 2001. [Online]. Available from http://www.edweek.org/ew/ewstory.cfm?slug=34cheat.h20&keywords=Internet,%20Plagiarism. Accessed Dec. 14, 2002.

Young, Jeffrey. "Anti-Plagiarism Experts Raise Questions About Services with Links to Sites Selling Papers." *The Chronicle of Higher Education.* March 12, 2002. [Online]. Available from http://chronicle.com/free/2002/03/2002031201t.htm. Accessed Dec. 14, 2002.

Young, Jeffrey. "The Cat-and-Mouse Game of Plagiarism Detection." The Chronicle of Higher Education. July 6, 2001. [Online]. Available from http://chronicle.com/free/v47/i43/43a02601.htm. Accessed Dec. 14, 2002.

The Web's Impact on Student Learning

A Review of Recent Research Reveals Three Areas That Can Enlighten Current Online Learning Practices

KATRINA A. MEYER, PH.D.
University of North Dakota

Recently, I set out to find an answer to the question of what current research was saying about how, if at all, the Web impacted student learning. My recently released monograph, *Quality in Distance Education: Focus on Online Learning,* is a compilation of more than 100 studies drawn from several online journals, conference Web sites, as well as some interesting sites maintained by associations and institutions. (The one maintained by the Asynchronous Learning Networks organization at www.aln.org/ is an especially rich source of studies.) One of the unintended lessons learned from this project was discovering how easy it is to locate good research on the Web and how many studies there actually are. My search focused on current research and studies—usually no earlier than the mid-1990s—completed on college students. I think many of the findings also will be applicable to K-12 students. In any case, the search sent me on a circuitous route to a number of answers, some of which I think are very sound and will stand up over time, while others are more tentative, although intriguing.

Anyone who has been around distance education for a while is familiar with the compilation of 355 research studies by Thomas L. Russell of North Carolina State University (1999), who coined the phrase, "no significant differences phenomenon." Many of the studies in Russell's report were comparison studies, comparing the new mode of education—be it telecourse, interactive video or satellite—with traditional education. Subsequent writers have faulted these studies for poor research design and inadequate controls, a naive understanding of what affects learning, and a lack of recognition that online students are different from their on-campus counterparts.

Therefore, it may surprise you to know that more than 30 of the studies I found were a comparison of Web-based courses against traditional ones. Better studies have been done, of course, some of them attempting to repair the deficiencies of earlier research, while others opt for a case study approach to Web-based learning. While it is difficult to summarize all of the findings, there are three areas of the studies worth mentioning:

- The role of individual differences;
- Instructional design; and
- Specific skills that are enhanced by online environments.

Individual Differences

No educator will be especially surprised to learn that success in a Web-based learning environment is heavily influenced by what the student brings to the learning situation. There is evidence that students with certain learning styles (e.g., visual) or behavioral types (e.g., independent) do learn better in the Web environment. Conversely, aural, dependent and more passive learners may not do as well. It is this sort of insight that leads some to propose that the potential for maximal learning results when instructional approaches are matched to student learning styles and are supported by appropriate technologies.

Furthermore, students with a high motivation to learn, greater self-regulating behavior, and the belief they can learn online do better; as do students with the necessary computer skills. These are not particularly profound insights, although they do tend to explain why online learning will work as well as other forms of education for good students, but may not work as well for students who struggle because of a lack of motivation or self-confidence.

Interestingly, gender differences appear in online exchanges just as they would in regular situations. Based on content analyses of exchanges in Asynchronous Learning Network (ALN) courses, Blum (1999) found differences in male and female messages that mirror traditional face-to-face communication. Males were more likely to control online discussions, post more questions, express more certainty in their opinions and were more concrete. Whereas females were more empathetic, polite and agreeable. The females also supplied the niceties that maintain relationships such as "please" and "thank you." This finding may only indicate that we take our normal personalities, judgments and beliefs about others into the online setting. In other words, we are consistent in our online interactions, despite expressing ourselves in a different form.

There is another interesting development along generational lines. Now, it's true that students are arriving at college with greater abilities in online learning and an expectation to learn that way. But, what is even more intriguing is that these students also arrive with brains that are more likely to have been shaped by very visual, rapid movement, hypertexted environments (Healy 1998). This has led some to suggest that these younger brains are different from those of faculty, who are more likely to have brains formed by reading—a largely linear and slow activity.

Our brains may also be the reason why we can become so involved with our computers. As a result of 35 laboratory studies, Reeves and Nass (1996) concluded that it is the psychology of the relationship between us and the computer that is important, not the fact that one member of this so-called relationship is a piece of technology. They came to this conclusion after experiments where subjects were asked by the computer to critique its work. Subjects responded politely and seemed not to want to hurt the computer's feelings. But, when asked by one computer to critique another's work, subjects were more likely to offer criticism.

Asked to explain their behavior, subjects said they knew the difference between a computer and a person, and argued vehemently that technology is a mere tool without feelings. Yet, their responses belied an underlying belief that the computer is real, implying that the relationship of humans to media may be unconscious and perhaps innate. The authors hypothesize that this relationship may be due to the brain's slow evolution over the ages, as well as its inability to distinguish between rapidly advancing media and real life.

In addition, if humans cannot distinguish between computers and real people, then this might imply that technology could not independently influence the quality or quantity of learning. It would also argue that failures of learning are more likely to be due to other factors, such as inadequate instruction or a poor match between the individual and the learning situation.

Instructional Design

If there is one major boon resulting from the advent of online learning in colleges and universities, it is the renewed focus on pedagogy and instructional design. Higher education faculty, who are hired and trained for expertise in a discipline, are not trained in these matters, and often adopt a teaching style that is either modeled on how they were taught or how they prefer to learn. In any case, introducing the Web into college teaching has generated an enormous upswell of attention on the aims and various methods for achieving student learning. I can say this without hesitation, having read several articles by faculty who write about what they learned by using the Web, what they learned about instruction and student learning, and how they are translating their newfound knowledge to on-campus courses.

Much of the early research on Web-based learning focused on the technology and ignored the instructional design imbedded in the course. This is unfortunate, and has given people the impression that the Web produced learning, when it is more likely to have resulted from the instructional design and the pedagogies chosen to help students learn. Smith and Dillon (1999) call this the "media/method confound," and it continues to confuse researchers and practitioners alike. This is not to say that unraveling the media and method—separating the effects of the Web from its instructional uses—can be done; in fact,

I found no such research attempting to do this. Regardless, to say the Web affected learning may be inappropriate unless the powerful effect of instructional design has been isolated from the technology used to deliver it.

However, if there is one strong area where the Web is used to consistent effect, it is by making ample interaction feasible, including students interacting with the course material, faculty or other experts, as well as other students. This interaction, if consciously programmed into the course, allows students to discuss ideas online, ask questions, share information, tackle group projects, develop joint understandings and even forge friendships. If someone complains that online learning is passive, the problem isn't the Web, it is the use that is made of it.

There is growing work around whether e-learning communities can be achieved and how. Palloff and Pratt (1999) provide an excellent primer on how community may be defined and created online. And research about online learning communities has followed. Wegerif (1998) found that the ALN model increased interaction, self-discipline, a sense of community, communication, reflection and shared space among students. Brown (2001) describes a three-stage process by which a community is formed in a computer-mediated asynchronous distance learning class:

- Stage 1: Making friends
- Stage 2: Community conferment or acceptance
- Stage 3: Camaraderie

Each stage represents a greater degree of engagement "in both the class and the dialogue" over the previous stages, and greater levels of interpersonal bonding or affiliation. The consequences for students of building community include improved confidence expressing oneself, learning from others, and feeling connected and accepted.

Improved Skills

The research conducted so far on Web-based learning has focused on evidence of critical thinking and writing skills. While these two skills are not solely or uniquely the result of Web environments (since you can improve these skills by various means), it is good to know that the Web supports the acquisition of these important skills.

To do this research, one method that may be especially useful for analyzing online exchanges—be it a threaded discussion or chat—is content analysis. Newman, Webb and Cochrane (1995) used content analysis of online messages to look for critical thinking indicators in computer conferences. They found that online students were more likely to make important statements and link ideas, although they contributed fewer novel ideas than to face-to-face comparison group. This may indicate that online conversations are less suited to functions like brainstorming, or that working online encourages respondents to work in a more linear fashion by linking comments to earlier ideas.

Garrison, Anderson and Archer (2001) also looked at critical thinking in computer mediated communications using a four-stage analysis of the critical-thinking process:

1. Triggering—posing the problem
2. Exploration—searching for information
3. Integration—construction of a possible solution
4. Resolution—critical assessment of the solution

Transcripts of online discussions were coded, resulting in 8% of the responses coded as triggers, 42% as exploration, 13% as integration and 4% as resolution. The authors hypothesize that the low numbers for integration and resolution were due to the need for students to take more time to reflect on the problem, and that individuals were reluctant to offer solutions that would be scorned by others in the class. The opportunity for reflection is especially suited to asynchronous learning environments, as well as for students whose learning styles require some time and reflection to make sense of information.

There is also ample evidence from a variety of sources that suggests having students work online improves writing skills. Wegerif's (1998) study found that the ALN model improved writing skills by having students write more and more often, as well as by increasing the public visibility of student writing. (It is there for others—especially their peers—to see and, presumably, critique.)

Being able to express one's personality, or "presence," is another intriguing skill that may impact the creation of satisfactory learning communities, and could become a necessary new skill for online conversations. Certainly, with the loss of facial expressions, voice intonations and gestures, important nonverbal meaning and shadings of meaning are lost. Yet, there is evidence that a personal presence—as captured by one's written expression—is important in Web-based classes.

Gunawardena and Zittle (1997) found that "social presence" (i.e., the degree to which a person is perceived as real in an online conversation) is a strong predictor of satisfaction with computer mediated communications. Arbaugh (2001) calls this skill the production of "immediacy behaviors," since they reduce the "social distance" between teachers and students. In this study, these types of behaviors were positive predictors of student learning and course satisfaction.

The issue of presence was also addressed in a study by Anderson et al. (2001) that reviewed transcripts of course discussions held over computer conferencing systems. The authors developed the concept of "teaching presence," expressed by faculty comments, in three categories:

- Design and organization ("This week we will discuss …");
- Facilitating discourse ("I think we are getting off track"); and
- Direct instruction ("Bates says …").

Faculty who are adept at expressing their unique personalities through e-mail or other Web-based communications may be at an advantage in connecting with students, which may help students bond to the instructor or learning environment. This idea of presence may soon be a skill not only well-suited to Web-based exchanges, but also a requirement for student and faculty success in online coursework.

Looking for Answers

This is a good start on the research that is needed to ensure that the Web is used effectively for student learning. However, there are some holes in our understanding; not least of which is determining whether and how the Web might have an independent effect on learning, separate and apart from the instructional method imbedded in the application. The focus of those who criticize using the Web in education—worrying that technology may affect us negatively—is worth addressing with well-designed research studies.

And if there are differences in effectiveness, can we determine as Barbules and Callister (2000) put the challenge: "Which technologies have educational potential for which students, for which subject matters, and for which purposes?" In other words, is there an optimal match possible between student, learning and technology? Furthermore, we need to continue to collect good information on what works and why. This is because answers to these questions will likely be more helpful to educators than asking whether or not the Web affects learning, which presumes that it can and does, and initiates a search for answers to the wrong question.

References

Anderson, T., L. Rourke, D. Garrison and W. Archer. 2001. "Assessing Teaching Presence in a Computer Conferencing Context." Journal of Asynchronous Learning Networks 5 (2). Online: www.aln.org/publications/jaln/v5n2/pdf/v5n2_anderson.pdf.

Arbaugh, J. 2001. "How Instructor Immediacy Behaviors Affect Student Satisfaction and Learning in Web-Based Courses." Business Communication Quarterly 64 (4): 42–54.

Barbules, N., and T. Callister. 2000. "Universities in Transition: The Promise and the Challenge of New Technologies." Teachers College Record 102 (2): 271–293. Online: www.tcrecord.org/PDF/10362.pdf.

Blum, K. 1999. "Gender Differences in Asynchronous Learning in Higher Education: Learning Styles, Participation Barriers and Communication Patterns." Journal of Asynchronous Learning Networks 3 (1). Online: www.aln.org/publications/ jaln/v3n1/v3n1_blum.asp.

Brown, R. 2001. "The Process of Community-Building in Distance Learning Classes." Journal of Asynchronous Learning Networks 5 (2): 18–35. Online: www.aln.org/publications/jaln/v5n2/v5n2_brown.asp.

Garrison, D., T. Anderson, and W. Archer. 2001. "Critical Thinking, Cognitive Presence, and Computer Conferencing in Distance Education." The American Journal of Distance Education 15 (1): 7–23.

Gunawardena, C., and F. Zittle. 1997. "Social Presence as a Predictor of Satisfaction Within a Computer-Mediated Conferencing Environment." The American Journal of Distance Education 11 (3).

Healy, J. 1999. Failure to Connect. New York: Simon & Schuster.

Newman, D., B. Webb, and C. Cochrane. 1995. "A Content Analysis Method to Measure Critical Thinking in Face-to-Face and Computer Supported Group Learning." Interpersonal Computing and Technology Journal 3 (2). Online: www.qub.ac.uk/mgt/papers/methods/contpap.html.

Palloff, R., and K. Pratt. 1999. Building Learning Communities in Cyberspace. San Francisco: Jossey-Bass.

Reeves, B., and C. Nass. 1996. The Media Equation. Cambridge: Cambridge University Press.

Russell, T. 1999. "The No Significant Differences Phenomenon." International Distance Education Certification Center: Montgomery, Ala.

Smith, P., and C. Dillon. 1999. "Comparing Distance Learning and Classroom Learning: Conceptual Considerations." The American Journal of Distance Education 13 (2): 6–23.

Wegerif, R. 1998. "The Social Dimension of Asynchronous Learning Networks." Journal of Asynchronous Learning Networks 2 (1). Online: www.aln.org/publications/jaln/v2n1/v2n1_wegerif.asp.

UNIT 8
Distributed Learning

Unit Selections

Key Points to Consider

- What will be the role of interactive technologies within a distance learning environment during this century?

- To what extent will higher education provide distance learning to business and the community?

- Is the intent of distance learning to allow students to work alone, or is it to bring them closer together? Provide reasons for your answer.

Student Web Site
www.mhcls.com/online

Internet References
Further information regarding these Web sites may be found in this book's preface or online.

The Chronicle of Higher Education: Distance Education Page
http://www.chronicle.com/distance
Distance Learning on the Net
http://www.hoyle.com
Weblearning Resources
http://www.knowledgeability.biz/weblearning

One of the primary concerns facing distance learning today is finding ways to increase the level of student involvement and thus maintain students' interest in what they are learning. Fortunately, technology that can solve this thorny problem is now available. Over the past decade several technologies, such as networking advances, teleconferencing, wide-band communications, n-way digital video, high-definition video, and Internet2, have helped make the delivery of high-quality interactive instruction a reality. In addition, software advances such as compression software, and management systems are making the job of developing e-learning courseware and presentations more efficient and less time consuming.

However, when using these more sophisticated technologies, it becomes essential that an adequate infrastructure is constructed and high-quality technical support is made available when learners and instructors need it. Technologies role in high-quality interactive distance learning to create an environment that will promote active learning using higher-order thinking skills such as evaluation, analysis, and synthesis, rather than rote learning and memorization. In addition, the technology can be used individually and through the social interaction of the student during the construction of knowledge and problem solving skills.

Within a technology-driven distance learning environment, there are two kinds of interaction with regard to learning. One is a student individually interacting with content. The other is social activity, a student interacting with others about content. Both types of interaction are necessary for efficient, effective, and affective learning. In distance education, it is particularly important to provide an environment in which both kinds of interaction can occur.

Technology advances such as phone mail systems, the Internet, teleconferencing systems, and online interactive multimedia can provide interaction and involvement. Today's technologies provide an electronic pipeline to reach students at a distance with an instructional delivery system that will involve and interest those who are using it. The articles in this unit demonstrate how educators are riding the crest of current technology and instructional design to meet the need for interaction and involvement in a distance learning environment.

The unit begins with a description of how "Software Agents to Assist in Distance Learning Environments." The authors investigated employing a software agent to act as a teaching assistant to the course coordinator by monitoring and managing course activities. The agents use data from the server hosting the course Website that contains a lot of data about students' learning progress and their behavior when interacting with the course Web site. The information was useful in providing timely and meaningful feedback on student progress and aids in early detection of problems in both the teaching and learning processes. The article provides the detail on how this was done in a distance learning environment.

Next, Greenway and Vanourek describe how their work with virtual schools has led them to a number of observations about their current practice that they believe can guide policymakers. First, the principles of quality education still hold. Just putting the word "virtual" in front of the word "school" doesn't make it good, bad, or even innovative anymore. What matters is the school's ability to educate children. The point of virtual learning is of course *learning,* not virtual technology. Without good curriculum, instruction, training, resources, support, and leadership, virtual schools will flounder. In good virtual schools, the technology is so powerful, well-designed, and intuitive that it becomes an afterthought. Read this article to get the history and details of how this is being accomplished.

Finally, Hardman and Dunlap state that a critical component of an effective retention program for online students is a learner support services program. While many factors contribute to attrition, at the top of the list are the levels of interaction and support. To this end, some students in distance learning programs and courses report feelings of isolation, lack of self-direction and management, and eventual decrease in motivation levels. This article describes the types of learner support services strategies that can effectively address these retention challenges. Examples from Western Governors University (WGU) are provided to describe these strategies in action.

Software Agents to Assist in Distance Learning Environments

Software agents can act as teaching assistants for distance learning courses by monitoring and managing course activities

SHEUNG-ON CHOY, SIN-CHUN NG, AND YIU-CHUNG TSANG

The Open University of Hong Kong (OUHK) is a distance education university with about 22,500 students. In fulfilling its mission, the university has adopted various Web-based and electronic means to support distance learning. For instance, OUHK uses a Web-based course management system (CMS) to provide students with a flexible way to obtain course materials. Apart from traditional print-based course materials and textbooks, the university staff and instructors use the Web to replace surface mail to deliver assignment files, supplementary study materials, and other correspondence with students. Online discussion forums provide students with a convenient place to ask questions and receive answers from the teaching staff.

An electronic assignment-handling system administers student assignments. Assignments, which are marked up and commented on, are considered an important element in the distance learning process. The assignment-handling system enables students to submit assignments electronically, apply for an extension, inquire about the status of their submitted assignments, and receive timely feedback on assignments from the teaching staff.

Clearly the Web-based CMS provides many benefits in the service of distance education. However, it is also fair to say that the current ways that we use and interact with the CMS are not ideal. Employing a human teaching assistant to relieve academic staff from manual monitoring and management of course activities is one way to improve the process, but not effectively and efficiently. We investigated employing a software agent to act as a teaching assistant to the course coordinator instead—the idea behind this article.

The Process Explained

The key players in the OUHK education process are students, tutors, and academic staff. Students normally spend much of their time studying alone. To complement the distance learning process, face-to-face sessions are provided, including tutorial, day school, and laboratory sessions. Part-time tutors conduct the face-to-face sessions. Students in a course are required to submit homework assignments to their tutors (usually four to five times during the course). Tutors then mark the assignments and provide feedback to students.

Every course at the OUHK has an academic staff member as the course coordinator. The coordinator's major responsibility is to supervise the teaching and learning process for that course. This includes making assignments and scheduling examinations, delivering the course materials and supplementary teaching notes, and monitoring students' learning progress, tutors' teaching performance, and the assignment-marking process.

The use of the Internet and Web-based technologies to support large-scale distance learning has led to a significant change in the working pattern of OUHK academic staff. In order to ensure smooth course presentation, improve adherence to procedures, and enhance students' comfort levels and retention, course coordinators expend a lot of time and effort in interacting directly with various Web-based systems and communicating with students and tutors over the Internet. The following list summarizes tasks that an OUHK academic staff member would usually do for a distance-learning course:

- Post course material and assignment files.
- Post course schedules and details of upcoming face-to-face sessions.
- Post announcements about the course, such as changes to the course material.
- Remind students of assignment submission and due dates.
- After the assignment due date, contact those students who did not complete their assignments.
- Monitor tutor progress in marking assignments to ensure

that submitted assignments are marked and commented upon within an established period of time.

- Identify inactive students and contact them for proactive consultation.
- Assist those students who are having problems completing the course.

Figure 1 illustrates the interactions of distance-learning students, part-time tutors, and the academic staff in an OUHK course that uses a Web site as a common interface for course presentation, communication, and student support. The server hosting the course Web site contains a lot of data about students' learning progress and their behavior when interacting with the course Web site. The information can be useful in providing timely and meaningful feedback on student progress and aids in early detection of problems in both the teaching and learning processes.

Unfortunately, acquiring information from the course Web server requires initiating all information retrieval tasks and interacting directly with the replies from the server. In other words, to manage the course and acquire useful information, the user must interact directly with the course Web server, initiate all tasks explicitly, and monitor and process all the server's responses. This direct-manipulation method of interaction[1] is labor-intensive, consuming a lot of time for unintelligent information retrieval and filtering. To check students' progress, for example, the user has to visit many Web pages regularly and use different tools within the server to verify student progress and participation. This includes regularly checking the course activity log to monitor students' online activities, visiting the assignment submission records to see if students have submitted their assignments, and reviewing the assignment marking records to identify students with problems.

Employing a human teaching assistant to interact with the CMS is one option, of course, but with most of the same problems as involved in having academic staff perform these functions. We propose creating a software agent to act as a teaching assistant to the course coordinator instead.

Software Agents

The term software agents originated from the field of artificial intelligence, back in the 1950s. Research on software agents started to proliferate in the mid-1990s, after several key agent-related papers appeared in the popular computing press, followed by several books. (See the sidebar for research publications on software agents.)

Research Publications on Software Agents

Bradshaw, J. M., ed., *Software Agents* (Boston: MIT Press, 1997).

Maes, P., "Agents that Reduce Work and Information Overload," *Communications of the ACM,* Vol. 37, No. 7, 1994, pp. 31–40, <http://www.acm.org/>.

Middleton, S. E., "Interface Agents: A Review of the Field," Technical Report Number ECSTR-IAM01-001, University of Southampton, August 2001.

Norman, D., "How Might People Interact with Agents?" *Communications of the ACM*, Vol. 37, No. 7, 1994, pp. 68–76.

Nwana, H., "Software Agents: An Overview," *The Knowledge Engineering Review*, Vol. 11, No. 3, 1996, pp. 205–244, <http://journals.cambridge.org/bin/bladerunner?30REQEVENT=&REQAUTH=0&116000REQSUB==&REQSTR1=KER>.

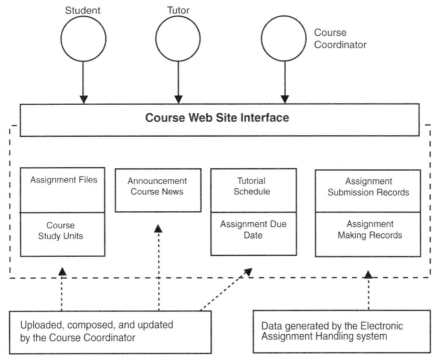

Figure 1 Interactions in the course web site

Nwana, H. S., and D. T. Ndumu, "A Perspective on Software Agents Research," *The Knowledge Engineering Review*, Vol. 14, No. 2, 1999, pp. 1–18, <http://journals.cambridge.org/bin/bladerunner?30REQEVENT=&REQAUTH=0&116000REQSUB==&REQSTR1=KER>.

Ovum Report, *Intelligent Agents: the New Revolution in Software* (London: Ovum Publications, 1994).

Reinhardt, A., "The Network with Smarts," *Byte*, October 1994, pp. 51–64.

Wooldridge, M., and N. R. Jennings, "Intelligent Agents: Theory and Practice," *The Knowledge Engineering Review*, Vol. 10, No. 2, 1995, pp. 115–152, <http://journals.cambridge.org/bin/bladerunner?30REQEVENT=&REQAUTH=0&116000REQSUB==&REQSTR1=KER>.

Software agents can be defined in a number of ways depending on the functions and context. A general and widely accepted definition is that software agents are computational autonomous entities capable of sensing (such as acquiring information) and acting (such as producing and sending information) in an environment (such as a Web server) to accomplish a set of designated goals.

The domain of software agents is divided into two types: autonomous *interface/information agents* (interface agents for short) and *multi-agent systems*.[2] The concept of interface agents involves the provision of agents that enable the user to advance from direct manipulation of systems to indirect human-computer interaction by delegation to autonomous software agents. Multi-agent systems are more complex. The goal is to create a system that interconnects separately developed agents and to enable the ensemble to function beyond the capabilities of any single agent in the system.[3]

Interface agents demonstrate great potential, as reflected in multiple developments in various application domains. Existing use includes auctions and electronic markets, entertainment, e-mail filtering, news filtering, expert assistance, matchmaking, recommendation systems, and Web domain management.[4]

In the context of this article, the term software agents refers to personal interface agents. We are interested in the application domain specific to teaching a distance-learning course within the OUHK setting. This article reports on the implementation and realization of software agents as personal teaching assistants in the distance-learning environment. The software agents work on behalf of academic staff and have the authority and autonomy to interact with the course Web server.

Related Work

A number of researchers have proposed the development of software agents in teaching and learning situations. Jafari[5] conceptualized three types of software agents to assist teachers and students:

- Digital Teaching Assistant—assists the human teacher in various teaching functions
- Digital Tutor—helps students with specific learning needs
- Digital Secretary—acts as a secretary to assist students and teachers with various logistical and administrative needs

Our work involves the first type of software agent.

Razek, Frasson, and Kaltenbach[6] proposed the application of software agents to provide distance learning students with timely and useful information in a group discussion. The software agent they built can observe conversations among a distance learning community, interpret the community's input, organize the information, and then present information useful to the students in their current activities.

Our work also proposes using software agents to make the communication in a distance learning community more effective. However, we focus on the communication between teachers and students. The software agent we built is designed to work on behalf of teachers, assisting them in communicating more effectively and closely with students.

Suzuki and Yamamoto[7] proposed an agent-based distance learning system for effective delivery of distance learning courses. Their system provides a personalization service to each set of courseware, allowing it to customize its content and present materials in a context-sensitive way.

Distance learning considered from a learner perspective basically involves four types of interactions:

- Learner-to-interfaces
- Learner-to-content
- Learner-to-learner
- Learner-to-instructor[8]

Suzuki and Yamamoto's work[9] focused on using software agents to enhance the first two types of interactions for a distance-education course. Razek, Frasson, and Kaltenbach's work[10] contributed to the third type of interactivity factor. Our work proposes applying a software agent to enhance the fourth type of interactivity factor in a distance education environment—learner-to-instructor interaction.

Software Agents as Teaching Assistants

As mentioned earlier, the main actors in the education process of an OUHK course are students, part-time tutors, and an academic staff member as the course coordinator. Most of the time, these three actors are geographically and temporally remote from each other, and they use the course Web site as the online environment for course delivery, assignment management, and communication. Therefore, the course Web server contains a lot of data about students' learning progress and their study behavior.

We propose a software agent working in the course Web environment to assist the course coordinator in performing the tasks requiring tedious and direct interactions with the course Web server. Figure 2 depicts how the proposed software agent would work. The agent can be configured through an agent configuration interface to perform its jobs on behalf of the course coordinator. It can retrieve information such as that about students' learning progress and study behavior, aggregate the information, and send e-mails to the coordinator to report status. When appropriate or necessary, the agent can represent the course coordinator in sending e-mails to tutors or students for timely alerts or reminders.

Based on the course coordinator's usual responsibilities (summarized earlier in the task list), we wanted the software agent to perform the following duties. Note that none of these tasks was new because of the availability of the software agent.

- Send alert e-mails to inactive students (those who have not accessed the course Web site for a long period of time). The course coordinator decides the length of the inactive period and instructs the software agent to send the alert e-mails based on the established time.
- Send e-mails to inform tutors about inactive students and advise tutors to have proactive consultation with those students.
- Send e-mail alerts to those students who have not downloaded a particular piece of course material or who have not read an important piece of course news since it was uploaded to the file server. This helps prevent students from missing information or forgetting to download an important item, such as an assignment file.

- Help the course coordinator keep track of students' progress, and send e-mails to the coordinator and tutors about those students whose performance is at a marginal level.
- Retrieve information from the course timetable and send reminder e-mails to students. For example, it might send a reminder to students five days before an assignment due date and one day before a face-to-face session.
- During the period when assignments are submitted, the agent will monitor the assignment submission status and send e-mails after the due date to those students who have not submitted the assignment. It will also inform the course coordinator and tutors about those students.

We did not follow a rigorous procedure in coming up with this list of tasks—we simply selected them from those of the course coordinators' list of tasks that can be clearly expressed without the need for further clarification or judgment. They are tasks that can be easily delegated to an autonomous software agent. In the absence of software agents, these tasks consumed massive human effort for unintelligent information retrieval and processing.

Development and Implementation

We first installed Red Hat Enterprise Linux (http://www.redhat.com/) as the operating system on a server connected directly to the Internet. This machine is used as the software agent's execution environment. We also installed an Apache Jakarta Tomcat

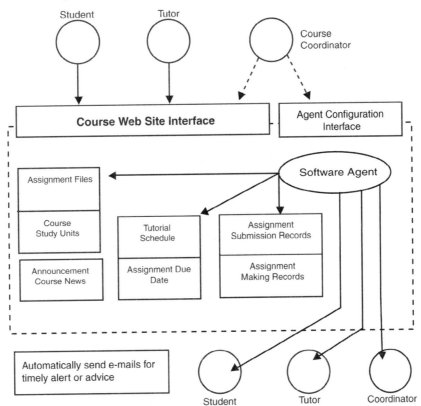

Figure 2 Software agent working in the course web site

175

(http://jakarta.apache.org/tomcat/) server in the machine as the Web server. The Tomcat server is a Web application container that can run Java Servlets and JavaServer Pages in Web applications. We chose it because our implementation of the software agent was based on these two Java technologies, and the Tomcat is an open-source, stable, Java-based Web server with good performance.

The software agent has to access course presentation information including the schedule of face-to-face sessions and assignment due dates. The agent also needs to access course news and announcements posted by the course coordinator. For this purpose, we developed a course Web interface for the coordinator to perform the following tasks:

- Enter or update course presentation information.
- Post course news and announcements.
- Upload assignment files and supplementary study material.

All this information is stored in the server's database, which the software agent can access to perform its duties. In particular, the agent can send e-mails to students and tutors to:

- Remind them about upcoming face-to-face sessions
- Remind students to submit their assignments before the due date
- Inform students that a new course item (such as a course announcement or an assignment file) has been posted on the course Web site for them to read or download

We also developed a Web interface for students to use in subscribing to the course reminder service. Students can also choose the frequency and quantity of those reminder e-mails. Figure 3 shows the interface we built for this service.

The software agent can access information relating to assignment submission, mark-up progress, and students' assignment scores. The agent needs this information to perform its analysis and reach some conclusions that may be useful for early detection of problems in either the teaching or the learning process. For this purpose, we developed the agent to the extent that it can log into the university's electronic assignment submission and recording system (ASRS), interact with the system to obtain the necessary information, filter the information, and send e-mails to the course coordinator to report its findings. The agent needs the coordinator's authorization (user name and password) before logging into the ASRS. For example, one task the software agent can do on behalf of the course coordinator is locate—after the due date—those students who have not submitted an assignment. The agent reports this to the coordinator by e-mail.

Next we describe implementation of the software agent at a more technical level. Figure 4 shows the main elements, which we implemented using Java servlets and the related technology. To start the process, we put the "ScheduleLife servlet" in the server to accommodate the agent. The servlet will start and initialize execution of the software agent when the server starts and stop the agent when the server shuts down.

To facilitate the software agent's performance in the server, we implemented several Java classes:

- *Schedule Control Class* is the program code to control the software agent's life and behavior in carrying out various tasks.
- *Job Listener Class*, which listens to Schedule Control Class, generates an error notification e-mail to report to the system administrator when exceptional events occur.
- *Data Retrieval Class* retrieves all required information at once for the Job Central Processing Class. The information includes students, tutors, the course coordinator, the schedule of face-to-face sessions, assignments, and course news.
- *Job Central Processing Class*, which is invoked by Schedule Control Class, accepts information provided by Data Retrieval Class. This class hosts the criteria to generate e-mail alerts to participants, composing e-mails and sending them to the appropriate recipients when the criteria are met.

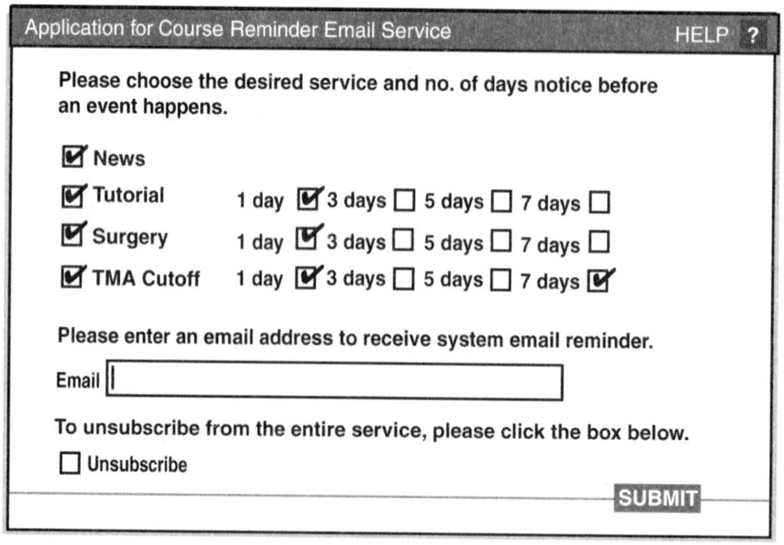

Figure 3 Reminder service interface

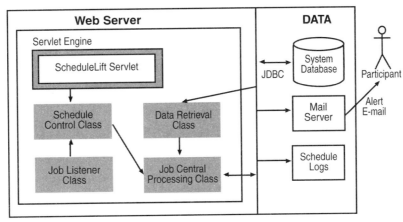

Figure 4   Agent architecture

The software agent is scheduled to run every day. It sleeps until the current server time meets the scheduled time defined in its configuration file. After it "wakes up," the agent retrieves all necessary data from the system database or from outside sources. In particular, it obtains information about the participants' (including the course coordinator, tutors, and students) e-mail addresses and their communication preference (when and what types of information). After all information has been prepared, the software agent composes e-mails and sends them to the corresponding participants using the system's mail server.

Figure 5 shows the software agent's operational flow. Monitoring Agent monitors the software agent's scheduled time. When the scheduled time arrives, the Scheduler Module invokes the Job Control Module, which looks into the Objectives defined previously. According to the Objectives defined, different tasks require handling that are governed by different conditions. When all the required conditions for a specific task have been fulfilled, the control module takes corresponding action(s) by using previously retrieved information to compose an e-mail alert and automatically send it to recipients on behalf of the course coordinator. At the same time, the Job Control Module updates the system database according to the information sent to recipients. After all tasks have been performed, the module records the total number of reminder e-mails sent out to all participants in each course. Then the Job Control Module returns control to the Execution Module, which invokes the Monitoring Agent again to monitor the next scheduled time.

Discussion

We have piloted use of the software agent as a teaching assistant in four OUHK distance learning courses, of which one commenced in April 2004 and three in October 2004. Choy and Ng are the course coordinators and the sole users to interact with the software agent to date. As mentioned before, the ultimate function of the implemented agent was to take over routine jobs handled by the course coordinators. Because the coordinators handle those routine jobs in the absence of the software agent, its existence was not noticed by students and tutors. When the agent sent reminder e-mails to students or tutors, it wrote on the coordinator's behalf. It also sent a duplicate e-mail to the coordinator for recording purposes. During the pilot period, all the software agent's operations, such as accessing course information, processing information, and sending e-mails to the course coordinators, students, or tutors, functioned properly.

Choy and Ng agreed that the software agent was helpful and concluded that course coordinators could save a lot of time by delegating those routine jobs, which involve direct interactions with the course Web site and tedious information processing, to the software agent. It is fair to say that students experienced no immediate impact, since, after all, the software agent worked as an administrative assistant to the course coordinators. Nevertheless, from time to time the coordinators received positive feedback. Students commented that their teacher was enthusiastic about their studies and aware of their learning progress

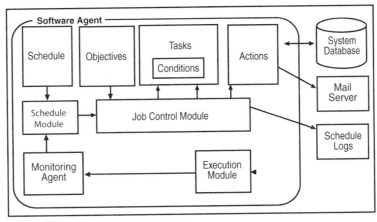

Figure 5   Software agent's operational flow

and performance in the course. They appreciated the close communication between coordinators and students—maintained by the software agent. This communication, in turn, helped create a good learning atmosphere—the indirect benefit of the software agent to students.

We developed the software agent to work as a software robot to assist the teaching staff in the OUHK distance learning environment. We can further increase the agent's capabilities in advancing the project. For example, the software agent could perform a number of useful tasks with the information stored in the assignment-management system. It would also be valuable to develop the agent to the extent that it can read the discussion messages among students and tutors in the online discussion forum, analyze them, and report its findings to the teaching staff.

At the time we wrote this article, the OUHK software agent had only been used by its advocates—us—in our courses. We are convinced, however, that software agents offer good support of distance education. Still, the developer of a tool no doubt finds it helpful and easy to manage when others might not enjoy the same experiences, so we know the potential difficulties facing us in promoting the use of software agents in our university. The institution-wide adoption of software agents to assist distance learning teaching requires institutional policy to emerge during the evolution of this new technology. We hope that further development of the software agent's capabilities will prompt the development of supportive institutional policies and increased adoption of this technology at OUHK.

Acknowledgment

The project described in this article was funded by Earmarked Research Grant Ref: 9004/03H. We would like to thank the Open University of Hong Kong and the Education and Manpower Bureau for funding that allowed the system to be developed.

Endnotes

1. P. Maes, "Agents that Reduce Work and Information Overload," *Communications of the ACM*, Vol. 37, No. 7, 1994, pp. 31–40, <http://www.acm.org/>.

2. S. E. Middleton, "Interface Agents: A Review of the Field," Technical Report Number ECSTR-IAM01-001, University of Southampton, August 2001; and H. S. Nwana and D. T. Ndumu, "A Perspective on Software Agents Research," *The Knowledge Engineering Review*, Vol. 14, No. 2, 1999, pp 1–18.

3. Nwana and Ndumu, op. cit.

4. Middleton, op. cit.

5. A. Jafari, "Conceptualizing Intelligent Agents for Teaching and Learning," *EDUCAUSE Quarterly*, Vol. 25, No. 3, 2002, pp. 28–34, <http://www.educause.edu/ir/library/pdf/eqm0235.pdf>.

6. M. A. Razek, C. Frasson, and M. Kaltenbach, "A Context-Based Information Agent for Supporting Intelligent Distance Learning Environments," *Proceedings of the Twelfth International World Wide Web Conference*, held May 20–24, 2003, in Budapest, Hungary, <http://www2003.org/cdrom/papers/alternate/P344/WWW2003-Razek-344/Razek-344.htm>.

7. J. Suzuki and Y. Yamamoto, "Building a Next-Generation Infrastructure for Agent-Based Distance Learning," *International Journal of Continuous Engineering Education and Life-Long Learning*, Vol. 12, Nos. 1–4, 2002, pp. 299–317, <http://www.cs.umb.edu/~jxs/pub/ijceell.pdf>.

8. D. B. Ehrlich, "Establishing Connections: Interactivity Factors for a Distance Education Course," *Journal of Educational Technology & Society*, Vol. 5, No. 1, 2002, pp. 35–47, <http://www.ifets.info/journals/5_1/ehrlich.html>.

9. Suzuki and Yamamoto, op. cit.

10. Razek, Frasson, and Kaltenbach, op. cit.

SHEUNG-ON CHOY (sochoy@ouhk.edu.hk) is a lecturer of Applied Computing in the School of Science and Technology at the Open University of Hong Kong. **SIN-CHUN NG** is an assistant professor, and **YIU-CHUNG TSANG** is a technical assistant, at the same institution.

The Virtual Revolution

RANDALL GREENWAY AND GREGG VANOUREK

No doubt the Internet has had a profound effect on our lives, our work and play, our politics, and our business. But in the middle of a revolution that seems so profound, no one is yet quite certain what the landscape will look like when the electronic dust settles. Some believe that schools have come late to the revolution; some would say late is good. For better or worse, though, the Internet is beginning to liberate education from the confines of traditional time and space.

According to the U.S. Department of Education (DOE), during the 2002–03 school year (the last data available), 36 percent of U.S. school districts (5,500 out of 15,040) had students enrolled in distance-education programs, and 38 percent of public high schools offered distance-education courses. The DOE study had 328,000 students in 8,200 public schools enrolled in distance-education courses. As of November 2005, the North American Council for Online Learning (NACOL) listed 157 unique online learning programs in 42 states in its database, including 32 virtual charter schools, 3 online home-school programs, and 53 public, non-charter virtual schools that offer programs. The DOE's 2004 National Education Technology Plan predicted that with the "explosive growth in the availability of online instruction and virtual schools … we may well be on our way to a new golden age in American education." Virtual schools have arrived—and with them, a host of challenges to our notions about school and schooling.

What will the new landscape look like? Will it be one without class periods, grade levels, six-hour school days, or 180-day school years? Will it even need school buildings, classrooms, or district boundaries?

Those questions are no longer the stuff of education science fiction.

Our Virtual Ancestors

Most accounts of the history of schooling take us from fee-based schools in ancient Athens, to the first tax-funded public schools in our land in Boston in 1635, to the compulsory education of Horace Mann's "common school" in the mid-19th century.

The modern mail-based "correspondence school" is said to have been invented at the University of Chicago in 1891. The delivery mechanism subsequently evolved from mail-based correspondence courses and radio programs to television and satellite broadcasts to today's Internet-based virtual schools, which were launched in the 1990s. There were a couple of important precursors. The federal Star Schools program began in 1988, with a focus on serving small rural schools through grants to advance distance-education technologies via telecommunications partnerships. In August 1993, Horizon Instructional Systems established a charter school in Lincoln, California, offering a range of innovative programs, including an "electronically assisted student teaching" program that blended home-based computers with distance learning and satellite technology.

The first incarnation of what we think of as a K–12 virtual school appears to have been launched in the summer of 1995, with the CyberSchool Project in Eugene, Oregon. Started by nine district teachers, it offered supplemental online high-school courses. By 1996 the virtual fire was beginning to blaze: an experimental WebSchool in Orange County, Florida (a precursor to the Florida Online High School), offered online courses to local students; Federal Way School District in Washington State founded the CyberSchool Academy with nearly 50 students (both elementary and secondary); the Concord Virtual High School (later to be called Virtual High School) was awarded a $7.5 million federal Technology Innovation Challenge Grant; and the University of Nebraska–Lincoln was awarded a combination of grants to research and develop Internet-based high-school courses (later marketed by a for-profit enterprise called Class.com). The growth of large, multistate programs such as Florida Virtual School and Virtual High School was especially important in putting K–12 virtual schools on the map.

Virtual schools are growing so quickly that a good count of them remains elusive. But the excitement is palpable, even if hyped. Mortimer Zuckerman, owner of *U.S. News & World Report*, has opined that, with distance learning and its accompanying "digital revolution … [w]e are on the threshold of the most radical change in American education in over a century.… Here with the Web is the way for America to use the marvels it created to end the regression in our competitive and academic performance."

In 1951, WFIL-TV in Philadelphia broadcast *The University of the Air* as one of the first educational television programs.

Mapping the Frontier

It is too early to know with much certainty how, or how well, the latest version of distance learning will serve the education needs of our children, but we can begin to map the territory in anticipation of studies to come. First, however, a note about terms. In Alaska and Pennsylvania, the programs are called "cyber" schools; in Minnesota and Colorado they are "online" schools; and Ohio prefers "e-schools." They are essentially the same: education delivered primarily over the Internet.

Some people confuse virtual schools with home schooling, or with charter schools. The truth is that virtual schooling is more like a hybrid of public, charter, and home schooling, with ample dashes of tutoring and independent study thrown in, all turbocharged by Internet technology.

Most attempts to define virtual schools sort them into categories based on their operating entity. The problem, though, is that they mix critical distinctions and miss the full array of elements. We have identified six defining dimensions of "virtual" schooling: comprehensiveness (whether the activity is complete or supplemental), reach (whether spanning a district or the entire globe or something in between), type (whether public, private, charter, contract, magnet, or even home school), location (in school, at home, somewhere else, or a combination), delivery (synchronous or asynchronous), and control (run by a school district, university, state, other provider, or combination). It is important for those who authorize and regulate these newfangled schools to fully understand the complexities in order to ask the right questions and review them against a set of rubrics that will ensure education quality while protecting the flexibility that is inherent in the virtual environment.

Perhaps the best way to think about a virtual school is to think of a regular school without the building. Students and teachers are at home—or anywhere there is an Internet connection, the equivalent of the cars and buses that take them to school. As with other schools, most virtual schools still have a central office, administrators, teachers, professional development, curriculum, daily attendance, grades, report cards, parent conferences, special-education and health services, field trips, rules, discipline infractions, state reporting, school board meetings, and even disgruntled parents. But they no longer have to be housed in big brick-and-mortar buildings.

Here is what several of the more-established virtual schools "look" like:

- The Florida Virtual School (FLVS) is a state-operated program founded in 1997 serving more than 33,000 students in grades 6–12. FLVS is a supplemental online program, with students averaging 1.7 courses, and it provides courses to public, private, and home-schooled students. Students receive some instructional materials, but not a computer or Internet access. Teachers and students interact through e-mail, telephone, and instant messaging (IM). Teachers are available from 8 a.m. to 8 p.m. weekdays. Students set their own schedule and can access all assignments, but must obtain teacher approval to access tests and quizzes. Students must submit a certain number of assignments each week as specified by the teacher, and each course includes a "pace chart"

with traditional, extended, or accelerated options. FLVS also provides courses to schools in other states through contractual tuition agreements with school districts and states.

- The Arkansas Virtual School (ARVS), where one of us works, is a pilot program for students in grades K–8 that has been operated since 2003 by the Arkansas Department of Education in partnership with K12 Inc., an online curriculum company. It offers only a full-time program. Upon enrollment, each student receives a computer (on loan), Internet access, and an array of school materials including textbooks, science equipment, math manipulatives, art supplies, maps, videos, and more. Working from home, its 430 students spend less than 20 percent of their time online in the elementary grades and about 40 percent in the middle-school grades. Teachers monitor student progress and attendance from their home offices and interact with parents and students via phone, e-mail, instant messaging, web conferencing, and occasional in-person visits. Students attend school-sponsored field trips (for example, museums, libraries, zoos, and family picnic outings) and participate in all state testing programs.

- The Cyber Village Academy (CVA) in Minnesota was originally set up in 1998 to be the first online learning charter school to serve seriously ill children (often home- or hospital-bound) and home schoolers—now a total of 140 students in grades 4–8. The school's founders devised a unique model to serve them: Most CVA students attend on-campus classes with licensed teachers two days a week and "attend" school from home three days a week, completing online learning activities via a Microsoft e-learning platform, a daily bulletin system, e-mail, and a synchronous classroom tool using an interactive whiteboard and an audio bridge. In other words, students at home actually "dial in" to the on-campus classroom and can hear the teachers (who use a wireless microphone) and see and interact with the lesson on their computer screen.

- The Delta Cyber School is a fully accredited charter school in central Alaska serving about 425 students statewide in grades K–12 since its inception in 1997. The school offers a combination of packaged online programs and teacher-created lessons supplemented by commercial online programs, all flowing through a Blackboard Learning System. It offers two foreign languages and courses in fine arts, auroras, NASA, oceanography, zoology, and botany. Students communicate via web conferencing and an internal messaging system and take self-grading quizzes online, conduct online research projects, and click through online reviews. About half the students access their classes from separate brick-and-mortar schools all over the state, while others log in from home, some from nearly a thousand miles away.

The delivery mechanism for virtual schooling subsequently evolved from mail-based correspondence courses and radio programs to televison.

Old and New

Though virtual schools, like traditional schools, have a central office, administrators, teachers, curriculum, daily attendance, grades, report cards, professional development, parent conferences, special-education, health services, field trips—even school board meetings (though often conducted remotely)—there are important differences from their nonvirtual cousins: greater dependence on technology; more individualized, interactive, and self-paced instruction; complicated logistical issues due to the dispersion of students; different kinds of socialization (some face-to-face, some virtual); no snow days.

One of the key differences relates to time and learning. In a traditional classroom, time is fixed and learning is variable (that is, classes are held for a set period of time, and when the bell rings the amount of learning that has occurred varies, sometimes dramatically, by student). In a virtual classroom, learning is fixed and time is variable (that is, the lesson continues until each student achieves mastery).

What does virtual schooling mean in practice for families, students, and teachers? Though the models vary, we can provide a basic snapshot. Families begin with the enrollment process—completing online forms and submitting the required residency documentation. Upon enrollment, students often receive a computer on loan from the school and reimbursement for Internet access—as well as the necessary books, supplies, and other instructional materials necessary for the program. (Some virtual schools are completely online while others rely heavily on physical materials.)

In a "typical" day (see sidebar), a student might take mostly core courses with some electives and log on to the computer for an hour or two, clicking through interactive lessons with text, audio or video clips, Flash animation, and links to related sites; completing an online math quiz; e-mailing the teacher; and "chatting" with classmates online. Students complete the majority of their work *offline* in many of these online schools, for example, reading assignments, drafting an essay, conducting an experiment with school-supplied materials, and studying for an exam. (Here we must pause to notice how much of what happens in virtual schools is so oddly "unvirtual.") A parent or other responsible adult is asked to supervise—and sometimes to assist with instruction and motivation, all under the direction of a licensed teacher. (Some virtual schools don't incorporate much parental involvement at all, but others, especially in the younger grades, rely on a close partnership among parents, teachers, and online lessons to facilitate student learning.) All students in public virtual schools take state tests. In addition, many students participate in extracurricular activities provided by their schools.

Depending on the school, teachers work out of a school office building or from their homes (with school-supplied computers, Internet access, and training). Teachers may develop courses; assign lessons and homework; monitor student attendance and progress; provide feedback through phone conferences, e-mail, instant messaging, or web conferencing; grade assignments; collect student portfolios; attend field trips; proctor state exams; and more. Sometimes teachers meet face to face with students. Teachers often design individual learning plans for their students based on placement tests, standardized test results, parental input, and student interests.

For Whom the Mouse Clicks

Virtual schools appeal to a wide array of students, attracting children from both ends of the achievement spectrum. Self-paced study allows struggling students to catch up without a classroom full of distractions and enables advanced students to accelerate their work according to their own abilities and without bogging them down in "busywork." Families choose virtual schools for many reasons: curriculum quality or focus, individualized instruction, flexible scheduling, interest in technology, and more. Most students in virtual schools transfer into them from traditional public schools, but many home-school students transfer into them to connect with other learners and professional staff or to access the credibility of accredited programs. Students with intensive acting or athletics regimens and children of high-mobility military families are served well by the flexibility. Urban parents may want to address safety or overcrowding concerns, while rural parents may seek advanced or specialized academic offerings not available locally. (According to the College Board, about 43 percent of U.S. high schools, many of them rural, do not offer Advanced Placement courses.)

Future Schooling Today: A "Day in the Life" of a 6th-Grade Virtual Student*

Time	Activity
7:00 a.m.	Wakes up, gets dressed, and eats breakfast
8:15	Logs on to his personalized school page and reviews his lessons scheduled for the day.
8:40	American History: reviews notes on the French and Indian War; writes a diary entry in his history journal from the perspective of an officer in the Virginia militia serving with General Washington; reads chapter 3 on the

Of course, virtual schools have their challenges. Surely, they are not for everybody. They often face difficulties in serving students with limited English proficiency, visual impairments, severe or multiple disabilities, and motivation problems. They also ask teachers to learn new technologies and approaches. According to the North Central Regional Educational Laboratory (NCREL), "It is likely that less than 1 percent of all teachers nationwide are trained as online teachers. The intensity, duration, and quality of staff development for online teachers appear to vary significantly." According to *Education Week*, only 11 states require at least some of their online teachers to receive training in online instruction. Virtual-school teachers need training on a variety of software applications, basic hardware maintenance, effective communication strategies (such as effective writing techniques for web-based lessons), information management skills, and instructional intervention strategies.

There are downsides to not having daily face-to-face interactions between students and teachers. Even though many virtual schools provide social opportunities, there is no denying the amenities of the comprehensive school: from jazz band, sports, and school plays to debate team, student councils, and proms. We have seen examples of chess clubs, sports teams, academic Olympiads, spelling bees, and science clubs organized by virtual schools, but rarely without logistical challenges.

Additionally, developing a high-quality virtual-learning program can be costly, requiring sizable capital expenditures on computers and servers, sophisticated instructional design (the orchestration of different media—such as online, offline, images, sound—into compelling and effective instructional units), content and course-management systems (computer systems for organizing and facilitating collaboration on documents and courses), course-authoring platforms (computer frameworks that allow educators to "post" their courses onto the Internet), and beta and usability testing (publishing test versions of new programs to eliminate the "bugs" and ensure ease of use). Too many programs simply load lessons developed for the traditional classroom directly onto the web without making adjustments for the new delivery methods; they are not likely to advance the "state of the art." We cannot assume that excellent teaching translates directly into excellent online lesson development.

E-teacher applicants complete an online seminar to be certified for the Alabama Online High School.

Evidence of Effectiveness

While there are hundreds of reports on distance education, the research on virtual schooling is newer and slimmer. There is a large base of research on postsecondary distance learning and a growing base of research on virtual high schools, but very little research on K–8 virtual schools.

What we do know is that many comparative studies suggest that the distance-learning model can be as effective as the classroom model. A 2004 NCREL meta-analysis of 116 effect sizes from 14 web-delivered K–12 distance-education programs between 1999 and 2004 found "no significant difference in performance between students who participated in online programs and those who were taught in face-to-face classrooms … in almost every comparison, students in distance education programs performed as well as students in classroom-based programs." A 2005 NCREL report draft (which we received special permission to cite for this article) finds "new evidence supporting the apparent effectiveness of online programs and schools and generally demonstrating the potential of online learning as a promising instructional intervention that can, when implemented judiciously, and with attention to 'evidence-based' practices, apparently improve student academic performance." However, it is clear that we need more data points and more rigorous methodological approaches. According to the 2005 NCREL report draft, "Only a small percent [of the hundreds of studies addressing distance education] meet established standards as experimental or quasi-experimental research."

What's more, the question about the comparative effectiveness of virtual schooling may be too blunt. We should also ask which *types* of virtual schools work, under what *conditions*, with which *students*, with which *teachers*, and with what *training*. Note also that most virtual schools receive significantly less funding than conventional schools—often 20 to 30 percent less (though there are no systematic and reliable data on funding rates or comparisons nationally)—leading to interesting questions about equity, parity, and productivity.

Reactions to This New Model

Not surprisingly, the rapid growth of virtual schooling has generated mixed reactions. Some parents and schools, as we have seen, seem to have voted with their virtual feet. But within the policy community, there is no clear consensus on how to "do virtual schools." In many cases, policies are being established after virtual schools are already up and running and by people without a good working understanding of how they operate. There is a seductive urge to regulate these schools using conventional bureaucratic protocols designed for physical schools. Not surprisingly, these approaches are outmoded in this new world and can end up hamstringing virtual schools by tying them to existing authorization regimes, salary schedules, certification requirements, textbook adoption processes, curriculum development processes, assessment procedures, and accreditation regimens.

Our own work with virtual schools has led us to a number of observations about their current practice that we believe can guide policymakers. First, the principles of quality education still hold. Just putting the word "virtual" in front of the word "school" doesn't make it good, bad, or even innovative anymore. What matters is the school's ability to educate children. The point of virtual learning is of course *learning*, not virtual technology. Without good curriculum, instruction, training, resources, support, and leadership, virtual schools will flounder. In good virtual schools, the technology is so powerful, well-designed, and intuitive that it becomes an afterthought.

Second, the politics of education also still hold. While virtual schools are not creatures of the Left or Right, they do run into the same roadblocks from special interest groups that other innovations encounter, usually centering on power and money. The roadblocks are especially severe when virtual schools also tie in with other controversial reforms, such as charter schools, contracting out to private management companies, and the interdistrict competition for students generated by open enrollment.

Third, we will always have a need for personal contact, and computers are no replacement for genuine human interaction—or for teachers and tutors. Though there are examples today of computer-based tutoring programs with artificial intelligence and offshore tutoring programs, these are not credible threats to the teaching profession. In the words of Katherine Endacott, CEO of Class.com, "This is another model. It won't replace a classroom, and it won't replace a teacher."

Fourth, virtual schools are not for everybody (nor are they meant to be). According to Tom Scullen, superintendent in Appleton, Wisconsin (which has experimented with virtual schools), "This type of school is not for everyone, but for the kids who need it, this may be their best—or even only—opportunity to succeed."

Finally, this is just the beginning. Over a century we have witnessed steady evolution of distance-learning approaches, structures, and technologies. We don't know what's next, but we can be confident that, as the technology continues its headlong leap to new frontiers and as we understand more about what works (and what doesn't), the education benefits will surely increase with them. Clearly, the use of technology in education will continue to expand and evolve. As one high-school student aptly put it, "we have technology in our blood."

RANDALL GREENWAY is head of school of the Arkansas Virtual School and a former state department of education official, high-school principal, and teacher. **GREGG VANOUREK** is a consultant, writer, and former executive at K12 Inc.

From *Education Next*, Spring 2006. Copyright © 2006 by Hoover Press/Stanford University. Reprinted by permission.

Learner Support Services for Online Students: Scaffolding for Success

STACEY LUDWIG-HARDMAN
Western Governors University, USA

JOANNA C. DUNLAP
University of Colorado at Denver, USA

A critical component of an effective retention program for online students is a learner support services program. While many factors contribute to attrition, at the top of the list are level of interaction and support. To this end, some students in distance learning programs and courses report feelings of isolation, lack of self-direction and management, and eventual decrease in motivation levels. This article describes the types of learner support services strategies that can effectively address these retention challenges. Examples from Western Governors University (WGU) are provided to describe these strategies in action.

Introduction

Distance learning opportunities for students have skyrocketed in popularity. Every year, more universities are starting online programs. Much of this increase is due to the demands of the learner audience who are intrigued by distance education, mostly because they face a number of obstacles that make conventional, brick-and-mortar educational options unviable:

- They live in remote geographic areas
- Conveniently located institutions offer limited program options
- Their work schedules conflict with campus-bound course schedules. This includes people who work shifts, travel frequently on business, work long hours, and/or are in the armed forces
- Personal and family commitments conflict with campus-bound course schedules. This includes having children at home and taking care of aging parents

These obstacles make online learning opportunities attractive—in fact, the obstacles create a built-in audience for online education providers. However, drop out rates associated with distance learning typically range from 20 to 50 percent (Brawer, 1996; Carr, 2000; ERIC, 1984; Kerka, 1995; Parker, 1999). More often than not, distance learning programs report greater attrition rates than traditional on-campus programs. The challenge for online education providers therefore, is not so much how to recruit students, but how to retain them once they have begun. Learner support services are thus a critical component of an effective retention program.

A Challenge for Online Education Providers

While many factors contribute to online student attrition, at the top of the list are level of interaction and support (Moore and Kearsley, 1996). According to Abrami and Bures (1996) some students in distance learning programs and courses report feelings of isolation, lack of self-direction and management, and eventual decreases in motivation levels. These factors are supported by Tinto's (1997) model of institutional departure with its central notion that student persistence is strongly predicted by their degree of academic integration (e.g., performance, academic self esteem, identity as a student, etc.) and social integration (e.g., personal interaction, connection to academic community, etc.).

One of the most consistent problems associated with distance learning environments is a sense of isolation due to lack of interaction (Bennett, Priest and Macpherson, 1999; Harasim, Hiltz, Teles and Turoff, 1995). This sense of isolation is linked with attrition, instructional ineffectiveness, failing academic achievement (Booher and Seiler, 1982), and negative attitudes and overall dissatisfaction with the learning experience (Thompson, 1990). Online learners can easily feel isolated if they do not feel connected to both the greater (university-level) and local (program- and course-level) social context (Abrahamson, 1998; Besser and Donahue, 1996; Brown, 1996; Rahm and Reed, 1998). This can negatively affect retention—students may drop out of a program or course because they do not feel part of a community (DeVries and Wheeler, 1996).

Closely associated with retention is student satisfaction with distance delivered courses. While some studies have reported high satisfaction from learners in online courses (i.e., Hill, 1999; Hill, Rezabek and Murry, 1998; Wayland, Swift and Wilson, 1994), others have indicated that students often experience frustration with distance delivered courses because they do not possess the skills needed to be successful (Ritchie and Newby, 1989; Swift, Wilson and Wayland, 1997). In fact, students' feelings of isolation can be compounded if they are ill equipped to deal with the demands of studying at a distance. Some students do not possess the self-directed skill set, specifically: self-discipline, the ability to work alone, time management, learning independence, the ability to develop a plan for completing work, and so on (Burak, 1993; Dunlap and Grabinger, 2003; Hancock, 1993; Piskurich, 2002). Although often described as a hallmark of adulthood, some people are not self-directed learners (Kerka, 1994). In specifying "successful online learner" guidelines and assessment tools, online education providers list self-direction as a primary quality of successful online learners (e.g., http://www.Colorado.edu/cewww/Fac101/success4.htm, http://ace.coe.wayne.edu/guidelines. html and http://www.ion. Illinois.edu/IONresources/onlineLearning/StudentProfile. html). Compounding the challenge faced by students who feel isolated and disconnected is that self-directed learning skills are developed in a social context (Dunlap and Grabinger, 2003; Kerka, 1999; Long, 1994) through a variety of human-oriented interactions with peers and colleagues, teams, informal social networks, and communities of practice (Kerka, 1994).

Clearly, there is an expectation in distance and online learning programs that learners take on a high level of responsibility and initiative for their own learning (McLoughlin and Marshall, 2000). As Knowles described in his text on self-directed learning (Knowles, 1975, p. 15), "students entering these programs without having learned the skills of self-directed inquiry will experience anxiety, frustration, and often failure ..." To be successful, learners need the skills required for effective online learning, and those skills need to be explicitly taught and supported in the online learning environment. These challenges to the retention of distance learners, interestingly enough, have something in common: they seem to hinge on learners' need for significant support in the distance learning environment through interaction with others (e.g., peers, instructors, and learner support services personnel).

Scaffolding as a Conceptual Framework for Learner Support Services

Tait (2000) describes the central functions of learner support services for students in distance education settings as cognitive, affective, and systemic. Most descriptions of learner support services focus on systemic characteristics—access to the administrative processes and procedures of the educational provider in a timely and accurate manner (e.g., how to register for courses, tracking individual progress on a degree plan, etc.). What is often

ignored, however, is the cognitive function of learner support services, such as guidance, counseling, assessment, coaching, etc. A focus on cognitive outcomes—in particular that learners have various needs, including the need to belong, to interact with each other, and to be a part of a community (Maslow, 1987; Stacey, 1999; Vygotsky, 1978)—leads to creating a learner support services program "where students feel at home, where they feel valued, and which they find manageable" (Tait, 2000, p. 289). Providing this type of support requires more than a technical infrastructure to serve up Web pages on demand—it requires three interrelated elements (Thorpe, 2001):

- **Identity.** The learner has the opportunity to interact with learner support services personnel on a one-to-one basis
- **Individualization.** The interaction that the learner has with learner support services personnel is individualized, based on the specific needs and goals of the learner
- **Interpersonal interaction.** The interaction is mutual and reciprocal, with learning and performance as goals rather than simply information delivery

In a learner support services environment, these elements can be realized through the practice of scaffolding.

The concept, or metaphor, of scaffolding (Wood, Bruner and Ross, 1976) is grounded in the developmental theories of Vygotsky (1978), specifically his concept of assisted learning as described by the "zone of proximal development" (ZPD). The ZPD is:

the difference between the child's developmental level as determined by the independent problem solving and the higher level of potential development as determined through problem solving under adult guidance or in collaboration with more capable peers. (Vygotsky, 1978, p. 86)

Although the concept of ZPD and the scaffolding metaphor were originally used to describe child development, the current view of the ZPD has extended beyond child-adult and novice-expert interaction to include a view that describes the ZPD as "an opportunity for learning with and from others that applies potentially to all participants, and not simply to the less skillful or knowledgeable" (Wells as cited in Anton, 1999). As such, the notions of the ZPD and scaffolding are helpful in considering the support services needs of learners in distance learning settings. Learner support services, if focused on the cognitive features that Tait (2000) describes, can serve to assist performance through the ZPD by promoting a potential for success in a distance learning setting founded on interaction between learners and support services personnel.

Scaffolding involves providing learners with more structure during the early stages of a learning activity and gradually turning responsibility over to them as they internalize and master the skills needed to engage in higher cognitive functioning (Palincsar, 1986; Rosenshine and Meister, 1992). Scaffolding has a number of important characteristics (Greenfield, 1984; McLoughlin and Mitchell, 2000; Wood et al., 1976) to consider when determining the types of learner support services distance students may need:

- Provides structure
- Functions as a tool
- Extends the range of the learner
- Allows the learner to accomplish a task that would otherwise not be possible
- Helps to ensure the learner's success
- Motivates the learner
- Reduces learner frustration
- Is used, when needed, to help the learner, and can be removed when the learner can take on more responsibility

Looking at this list it is clear that the practice of scaffolding is an inherently social process in which the interaction takes place in a collaborative context. The remainder of this article describes how the Western Governors University's learner support services program uses a collaborative context (such as learning communities, advising, and other interactions) to achieve the level of scaffolding needed to address the retention challenges of isolation and lack of needed self-directed learning skills.

Learner Support Services Designed to Support Learners' Self-Direction and Interaction

In order to provide learner support services that help students successfully participate in online learning courses and programs, Western Governors University (WGU) has employed strategies that reflect the collaborative context needed for effective scaffolding. These interactive strategies, which provide the scaffolding needed to enhance students' self-directed learning skills and reduce their feelings of isolation, are summarized in Table 1.

The Recruitment and Admissions Process: Diagnosing Fit Between Learner and Education Provider

Learner support services start with making sure that there is an appropriate fit between the students' learning and professional goals and current capabilities with the offerings and structure of the education provider's online programs. This interaction with potential students not only helps them feel immediately connected with the learning community, but the diagnostic activities help them reflect on their learning goals and strategies, a process important to self-directed learning. Recruitment practices can have a big impact on a student's ability to self-assess whether there is a fit, and for the education provider to do the same. For example, WGU, a unique, competency-based institution, recognizes that learners in their distance delivered degree programs need to possess a high level of

The Recruitment and Admissions Process: Diagnosing Fit Between Learner and Education Provider
<ul><li>Intake interview to discuss learning outcomes expected from courses and programs, and their relationship to personal/professional goals.</li><li>Self-assessment tools to assist the learner in evaluating eligibility and preparedness for courses and programs of interest.</li><li>Diagnostic pre-assessment to identify the learner's strengths and areas for improvement.</li><li>Learning Orientation Questionnaire to determine a learner's readiness for online learning.</li></ul>
Orientation to the Online Learning Experience: To prepare learners for the responsibilities and expectations of participating in an online course or program in a low-stakes, less-threatening environment.
One-on-one Advising: To have a relationship of support with educational provider staff.
Access to a Community of Learners: To have a sense of connection with the education provider and a sense of community with other learners who have similar learning plans.

Table 1. Learner Support Services Strategies for Self-direction and Interaction

self-direction and interest in connecting with other learners if they are to be successful. WGU uses specific tools in the recruitment process—such as an intake interview, self-assessment, diagnostic pre-assessment, and Learning Orientation Questionnaire—to determine a learner's fit with the institution.

Intake Interview

Enrollment counselors and other learner support services personnel must be trained to help learners identify their learning needs by asking them questions that require reflection on their current competencies and their desired goals in order to better identify the knowledge gap and plan for instructional opportunities that will address the gap. All new WGU students are required to complete an intake interview with an enrollment counselor. During the intake interview, an enrollment counselor contacts the student via phone to discuss the program in greater detail, help the student assess fit with the institution, and clarify expectations regarding the personal and professional commitment needed to succeed. The enrollment counselors ask the following types of questions:

- Why is the learner pursuing higher education? Is it for personal enrichment, advancement in the job market, retooling, retraining, or changing careers?
- Is the learner technology literate? Does the learner have the necessary prerequisite skills to successfully use communication tools such as email, threaded discussions, and chat?

- How many hours per week is the learner willing to commit to studies? Does the learner have the time management skills necessary to block out time to study?
- What is the learner's preferred method of learning? Is the learner comfortable with independent study or does the learner require the structure of instructor-facilitated courses?
- What support structures does the learner have at home or in the workplace?
- What challenges or distractions will the learner encounter (family, work, etc.)? Is the learner willing to treat education as a top priority?
- Has the learner taken distance learning courses in the past? If so, what were the learner's experiences?

The intake interview questions are structured to encourage the learner to articulate their individual needs and goals and, with the help of the enrollment counselor, assess whether WGU is a good fit.

Self-Assessment

WGU requires all learners to complete a self-assessment of their competencies gained through prior work and educational experiences. Using a Web-enabled survey, (http://www.wgu.edu/wgu/student/questionnaire.asp), learners are asked to rank their level of competence from zero (no competence) to three (expert competence) against the competency statements or learning objectives for the degree program. The self-assessment also asks the learner to identify short- and long-term goals, strengths, areas for improvement, and preferred methods of communication.

Diagnostic Pre-Assessment

All newly admitted WGU students are required to complete a Web-delivered diagnostic pre-assessment of their competencies in relation to the program requirements. The pre-assessment is used as an advising tool to identify the learner's strengths and areas for improvement.

Learning Orientation Questionnaire

The Learning Orientation Questionnaire (LOQ), developed by The Training Place (http://www.trainingplace.com/), is an online survey that identifies a learner's orientation to learn by looking at three psychological factors that influence learning and performance. These factors consider (1) the learner's emotional investment in learning and performance; (2) strategic self-directedness; and (3) independence or autonomy—all of which are important to effective self-directed learning. These three factors are successful learning attributes and describe how learners generally want or intend to approach learning situationally (The Training Place, 2001).

Learning *orientations* are different from learning *styles* because orientations emphasize the dominant power of emotions and intentions in learning. "Learning orientations …

characterize how individuals differ in the ways they choose to plan, set, perform, and attain goals, intend to commit and expend effort, and subsequently experience learning and achievement" (Martinez, 2000, p. 285). The four learning orientations that the LOQ describes are:

- **Transforming.** WGU learner support services personnel typically recommend independent learning resources for transforming learners because they are highly self-motivated and self-directed and assume responsibility for their learning progress and goals.
- **Performing.** WGU learner support services personnel recommend a mix of independent learning resources and instructor-facilitated courses for performing learners because they typically respond better to short-term goals and semi-structured learning environments.
- **Conforming.** WGU learner support services personnel recommend instructor-facilitated courses to conforming learners because they typically lack the self-motivation and direction to learn independently and prefer structured environments.
- **Resistant.** WGU has not encountered a resistant learner at this time, but would probably counsel a resistant learner out of a distance-delivered program. Resistant learners frequently fail to meet formal learning requirements and expectations.

By providing higher levels of scaffolding through structure and frequent feedback early in the learners' programs, WGU learner support services personnel demonstrate their commitment to help learners move from conforming to performing and from performing to transforming learner orientations. Learner support services personnel assist learners in the development of their self-directed learning skills by encouraging long term goal setting, development of time management skills, self-assessment of learning progress, and greater learning autonomy.

WGU learner support services personnel utilize the outcomes of the intake interview, self-assessment, diagnostic pre-assessment, and Learning Orientation Questionnaire to predict the extent to which a learner will be successful in WGU programs and to develop the learner's personal learning plan. There are times when learner support services personnel recognize that a student is not a good fit for WGU's distance delivered, competency-based programs and those learners may be counseled to consider other educational options. When there is a disconnect between the learner's goals and priorities and the level of commitment required to be successful in a program, a learner is apt to be dissatisfied and may quit the program or discourage others from considering the institution.

Orientation to the Online Learning Experience

Many universities are taking a proactive approach to improving retention, and research bears out the value of a mandatory orientation program (Brawer, 1996; Noel and Levitz, 2000). An orientation program is an education provider's first opportunity to build a community with learners who have actually committed to pursuing their educational goals with the institution.

To be effective, an orientation program needs to provide direction and support for new learners who may be uncomfortable in the distance learning environment. For example, during the early stages of WGU's four week long orientation course, learners are provided with a high level of structure as they become oriented to the community, communication tools, and learning skills needed to work in an online learning environment. As learners begin to show a higher level of comfort with, and interaction in, the environment, the orientation facilitator then encourages learners to take greater responsibility for course content by leading discussions and providing peer feedback. Krauth and Carbajal (1999) further suggest that an orientation should: (a) give students a sense of what it is like to be a distance or online learner; (b) offer tips for being successful in an online learning environment; (c) define technical requirements and prerequisite skills; and (d) describe the steps to access online courses—preferably providing opportunities to practice accessing and navigating through a course. Finding these suggestions to be useful, WGU provides additional information in its orientation courses: (a) suggestions on how learners can create a learning space, develop a study routine, and manage their time assuming a minimum of 10-15 hours per week for their studies; (b) an introduction to research at a distance and how to access the institution's learning resources and e-library; and (c) an introduction to communication tools and skills that will be necessary for students to actively participate in learning communities beyond the orientation course.

WGU's orientation course is an intense introduction to distance learning and WGU's competency-based model of education. By the end of the course, learners are acclimated to the learning community and have practiced applying the self-directed learning skills necessary to be successful in a distance learning environment.

One-On-One Advising

… I just received your note with my degree completion; "Alleluia and Amen" is right! It's finally finished and I need for you to know that without your help and encouragement, it would not have happened! I don't know how to thank you. It was one of the best days of my life and I shall never forget the hours you spent with me on the phone as you poured over [my degree plan] trying to keep me on track. I was overwhelmed trying to figure out the classes I needed. During difficult classes I would say, "I can't do this; I'm not going to make it." But you kept the faith in me. Because my position within the company I work for required a degree, I felt that I was merely complying with that requirement. However, a few days ago I received a 10% pay increase as a result of obtaining my degree … Thank you for everything you've done for me.

Excerpt of a letter from a
distance learner to her advisor

The positive influence advising can have on distance learners' ability to successfully fulfill their educational goals has been well documented (Feasley, 1983; Hezel and Dirr, 1991; Paulet, 1988; Thompson, 1989), and no more eloquently stated than by the learner who wrote the excerpt above. Therefore, a critical learner support service is provision of one-on-one access to advisors (Krauth and Carbajal, 1999). Advisors support learners by helping them identify human and material resources for learning, choose and implement learning strategies, and evaluate learning outcomes. Learners may receive ongoing assistance in such areas as planning academic programs, solving instructional problems, coping with the distance education process, and building skills for career advancement and job hunting. These interactions help students feel connected to the institution while scaffolding self-directness.

WGU's advisors—who are members of the WGU faculty—are called *mentors* and they work one-on-one with students. Mentors provide individualized guidance to learners in dealing with concerns that influence (a) their pursuit of personal and learning goals at a distance, and (b) their ability to be more self-directed in their learning. Mentors scaffold student learning by providing the highest level of structure at the beginning of a learner's program through the development of an individualized, detailed Academic Action Plan. Mentors utilize the items gathered during the admissions process—data from the intake interview, self-assessment, diagnostic pre-assessment, and Learning Orientation Questionnaire—to develop the Academic Action Plan that provides a roadmap for the learner's academic program including information about learning resources and assessment dates. Depending on individual learner's needs, mentors provide various levels of scaffolding by:

- Encouraging learners to articulate their learning goals and plans. In the beginning learners need help developing their learning plan and establishing short-term goals so that they gain the skills necessary to manage their goals and plans later in their programs.

- Helping learners understand their learning orientations, strengths, and areas for improvement early in their programs so that they can use this information to develop their plans, goals, and assessment of their learning progress.

- Advising learners on the exploration and selection of learning opportunities that will meet their needs during the initial development of their learning plans. Later, learners will take greater responsibility for identifying their learning resources.

- Guiding learners as they progress toward established goals and encouraging them to evaluate their own progress.

As the mentoring relationship evolves, learners take greater responsibility for their learning goals and strategies. When less support is required, mentors find that they scaffold learners by offering acknowledgment, positive feedback, and encouragement; being an early warning system for unnoted obstacles or potential problems; providing assistance in clarifying and validating learning plans; and by functioning as a responsive problem-solver/trouble-shooter to assist when academic or administrative issues arise.

Access to a Community of Learners

Learning is a function of the activity, context, and culture in which it occurs—i.e., it is situated (Wenger, 1998). Successful completion of and satisfaction with an academic experience is directly related to students' sense of belonging and connection to the program and courses (Tinto, 1975). Tinto's (1997) model of institutional departure is one of the most widely recognized student retention models which posits that, "other things being equal, the lower the degree of one's social and intellectual integration into the academic and social communities of the college, the greater the likelihood of departure. Conversely, the greater one's integration, the greater the likelihood of persistence" (p. 116). Many of the same motivational effects are evident in contemporary distance education environments, including the same tendency for students to drop out if they lack social interaction with the program (Moore and Kearsley, 1996). Social learning experiences, such as peer teaching, group projects, debates, discussion, and other activities that promote knowledge construction in a social context, allow learners to observe and subsequently emulate other students' models of successful learning. "Successful self-directed learners appear to be highly aware of context in the sense of placing their learning within a social setting in which advice, information, and the skill modeling provided by other learners are crucial conditions for self-directed learning" (Brookfield, 1986, p. 44).

WGU has found that social interaction is a critical component of successful programs and therefore encourages the development of online learning communities. A learning community can be defined as a group of people, connected via technology mediated communication, who actively engage one another in collaborative learner-centered activities to intentionally foster the creation of knowledge, while sharing a number of values and practices, including diversity, mutual appropriation, and progressive discourse. Simply requiring learner interaction in asynchronous environments does not promote a sense of community (Lowell and Persichitte, 2000). WGU has recognized that it cannot force a sense of community through the quantity of interaction, so it strives to support community development by focusing on the nature and quality of interactions.

All of WGU's students have access to a learning community based on the program in which they are enrolled. The learners were introduced to the tools and skills required to actively participate in the community during the orientation course, so most are comfortable with the technology and primarily need support accessing the community itself. Again, WGU mentors provide the greatest scaffolding when new learners are introduced to the community. Mentors invite the learners to join the community and provide detailed instructions on how to access resources, navigate the community, and communicate with other learners via threaded discussions and online chats that are organized by

mentors around specific topic areas. As learners move from the periphery of the community to its center, they become more active and engaged with the culture and hence assume the role of expert or 'old-timer.' This process is referred to as legitimate peripheral participation (Lave and Wenger, 1991) and it is an important step in the development of learning community because the expert learners then scaffold new learners as they get acquainted with the community. Expert learners host their own chats and threaded discussions, and provide feedback to mentors about how to improve the resources and tools in the community.

Connection to a learning community provides the social context needed to help learners feel less isolated. Through authentic sharing between learners and instructors, students have opportunities to interact not only on the content and skills being learned (through collaborative projects, team activities, debates, discussions, role-plays, interviews, etc.), but also on topics such as: (a) different learning and management approaches and strategies to use; (b) resources and references particularly helpful; (c) professional and career goals and opportunities; and (d) personal interests. This type of interaction—which keeps learners actively connected to the learning environment and education provider—can foster learner competencies, such as self-directed learning skills, because it creates a positive psychological climate built upon trusting human relationships (Knowles, 1990).

Conclusion

"The success of distance education, to a greater degree, will depend on the ability of educational institutions to personalize the teaching and learning process" (Saba, 1998, p. 1). Through the use of high-touch, high-interaction learner support services strategies—such as connection to a community of learners and the other scaffolding techniques described in the previous section—online students feel less isolated and are immersed in an environment that supports them as they develop or enhance their self-directed learning skills. These types of learner support services proactively address the challenges of online student retention by acknowledging that: "learning is a very human activity. The more people feel they are being treated as human beings—that their human needs are being taken into account—the more they are likely to learn and learn to learn" (Knowles, 1990, p. 129). Although scaffolding to enhance self-direction and reduce isolation should also occur at the course level (see McLoughlin and Marshall, 2000), individual course instructors may be ill prepared to provide the level of scaffolding needed for individual students or may not attend to scaffolding consistently across learning experiences. Learner support services personnel can provide the consistency and individualized attention learners need to be successful in an online learning environment because they are involved with learners throughout their educational experience with the institution. In this way, regardless of the quality or quantity of scaffolding provided by individual instructors, online learners have specific people to work with that know their particular goals, needs, and strengths. WGU has discovered that learner support services can improve the quality of students' academic experiences, connect them to the university, and help them develop the self-directed learning skills that are necessary to succeed in an online learning environment and thus empower them to achieve their learning goals and change their lives. In this way, learner support services can provide scaffolding for success.

References

Abrahamson, C. E. (1998). Issues in interactive communication in distance education. *College Student Journal, 32*(1), pp. 33–43.

Abrami, P.C., and Bures, E.M. (1996). Computer-supported collaborative learning and distance education. *American Journal of Distance Education, 10*, pp. 37–42.

Anton, M. (1999). The discourse of a learner-centered classroom: Sociocultural perspectives on teacher-learner interaction in the second-language classroom. *The Modern Language Journal 83*, pp. 303–318.

Bennett, S., Priest, A. and Macpherson, C. (1999). Learning about online learning: An approach to staff development for university teachers. *Australian Journal of Educational Technology, 15*(3), pp. 207–221.

Besser, H. and Donahue, S. (1996). Perspectives on … distance independent education: Introduction and overview. *Journal of the American Society for Information Science, 47*(11), pp. 801–804.

Booher, R. K. and Seiler, W. J. (1982). Speech communication anxiety: An impediment to academic achievement in the university classroom. *Journal of Classroom Interaction, 18*(1), pp. 23–27.

Brawer, F. B. (1996). *Retention-attrition in the nineties.* (ERIC Document Reproduction Service No. ED393510). Los Angeles, CA: ERIC Clearinghouse for Community Colleges.

Brookfield, D. (1986). *Understanding and facilitating adult learning.* San Francisco, CA: Jossey-Bass.

Brown, K. M. (1996). The role of internal and external factors in the discontinuation of off-campus students. *Distance Education, 17*(1), pp. 44–71.

Burak, L. (1993). Independent activities teach skills for lifelong learning. *Journal of Health Education, 24*(5), pp. 376–378.

Carr, S. (2000, February 11). As distance education comes of age, the challenge is keeping the students. *The Chronicle of Higher Education*, p. A39.

Cohen, N. H. (1995). *Mentoring adult learners: A guide for educators and trainers.* Malabar, FL: Krieger Publishing Company.

DeVries, J. and Wheeler, C. (1996). The interactivity component of distance learning implemented in an art studio class. *Education Journal.* Retrieved February 10, 2003: http://www2.uiah.fi/~jdevries/intcomp.htm

Dunlap, J. C. and Grabinger, R. S. (2003). Preparing students for lifelong learning: A review of instructional features and teaching methodologies. Manuscript submitted for publication.

ERIC. (1984). *Assessing the student attrition problem.* (ERIC Document Reproduction Service No. ED287522). Los Angeles, CA: ERIC Clearinghouse for Junior Colleges.

Feasley, C. E. (1983). *Serving learners at a distance: A guide to program practice* (ASHE-ERIC Higher Education Research 5). Washington, D.C.: Association for the Study of Higher Education.

Greenfield, P. M. (1984). *A theory of the teacher in the learning activities of everyday life* (pp. 117–138). In B. Rogoff and J. Lave (Eds.), Everyday Cognition: Its Development in Social Context. Cambridge, MA: Harvard University Press.

Hancock, V. (1993). Information literacy for lifelong learning. ERIC Document ED 358 870.

Harasim, L., Hiltz, S. R., Teles, L. and Turoff, M. (1995). *Learning Networks: A Field Guide to Teaching and Learning Online.* Cambridge, MA: The MIT Press.

Hezel, R. T. and Dirr, P. J. (1991). Barriers that lead students to take television-based college courses. *Tech Trends, 36*(3), pp. 33–35.

Hill, J. R. (1999). *Learning about distance education at a distance: Rewards and challenges.* Paper presented at American Educational Research Association. Montreal, Canada.

Hill, J. R., Rezabek, L. R. and Murry, B. (1998). *Web-based instruction: Prospects and challenges.* ERIC document.

Kerka, S. (1994). *Self-directed learning. Myths and realities.* Columbus: ERIC Clearinghouse on Adult, Career, and Vocational Education. (ED 365 818)

Kerka, S. (1995). *Adult learner retention revisited.* Columbus: ERIC Clearinghouse on Adult, Career, and Vocational Education. (ED 166). Retrieved February 20, 2003: http://ericacve.org/docgen.asp?tbl=archive&ID=A002

Kerka, S. (1999). *Self-Directed Learning. Myths and Realities No. 3.* Columbus: ERIC Clearinghouse on Adult, Career, and Vocational Education. Retrieved February 10, 2003: http://ericacve.org/docgen.asp?tbl=mr&ID=94

Knowles, M. S. (1975). *Self-directed learners: A guide for learners and teachers.* San Francisco: Jossey-Bass.

Knowles, M. S. (1990). Fostering competence in self-directed learning. In R. M. Smith (Ed.) *Learning to learn across the life span,* San Francisco: Jossey-Bass, pp. 123–136.

Krauth, B. and Carbajal, J. (1999). *Guide to developing online student services.* Retrieved June 15, 2002: http://www.wiche.edu/telecom/resources/publications/guide/ guide.htm

Lave, J. and Wenger, E. (1991). *Situated learning: Legitimate peripheral participation.* Cambridge: Cambridge University Press.

Long, H. B. (1994). Challenging some myths about self-directed learning. In H. B. Long and Associates (Eds.), *New ideas about self-directed learning,* pp. 1–14. Norman, OK: University of Oklahoma.

Lowell, N. O. and Persichitte, K. A. (2000). A virtual ropes course: Creating online community. *Asynchronous Learning Network Magazine, 4*(1).

Martinez, M. (2000). Successful mentoring, coaching, and guiding relationships from a whole-person approach. In J. A. Woods and J. W. Cortada (Eds.), *The 2001 ASTD Training and Performance Yearbook,* pp. 283–290. Columbus, OH: McGraw-Hill.

Maslow, A. (1987). *Motivation and personality* (3rd ed). New York: Harper & Row.

McLoughlin, C. and Marshall, L. (2000). Scaffolding: A model for learner support in an online teaching environment. Retrieved February 10, 2003: http://cea.curtin.edu.au/tlf/tlf2000/mcloughlin2.html

Moore, M. and Kearsley, G. (1996). *Distance education: A systems view.* Belmont, CA: Wadsworth Publishing Company.

Noel, L. and Levitz, R. (2000). *Are college students satisfied?* Retrieved June 6, 2002: http://www.noellevitz.com/pdfs/Report.pdf

Palincsar, A. S. (1986) The role of dialogue in providing scaffolded instruction. *Educational Psychologist, 21*, pp. 73–98.

Parker, A. (1999). *A study of variables that predict dropout from distance education.* Retrieved September 15, 2001: http://www.outreach.uiuc.edu/ijet/v1n2/parker

Paulet, R. O. (1988). Factors influencing successful counseling in selected distance education programs. *Journal of Research and Development in Education, 21*(3), pp. 60–64.

Piskurich, G. M. (2002). Preparing learners for online learning. Retrieved February 10, 2003: http://www.amanet.org/training_zone/archive/hotzone_jan2002_02.htm

Rahm, D. and Reed, B. J. (1998). Tangled webs in public administration: Organizational issues in distance learning. *Public Administration and Management: An Interactive Journal, 3*(1). Retrieved February 10, 2003: http://www.pamij.com/rahm.html

Ritchie, H. and Newby, T.J. (1989) Classroom lecture discussion vs. live televised instruction: A comparison of effects on student performance, attitude and interaction. *The American Journal of Distance Education, 2*, pp. 36–43.

Rosenshine, B. and Meister, C. (1992). The use of scaffolds for teaching higher-level cognitive strategies. *Educational Leadership, 49*(7), pp. 26–33.

Saba, F. (1998). Enabling the distance learner: A strategy for success. *Distance Education Report.* Retrieved February 10, 2003: http://distance-educator.com/Editorial_1.2.html

Shea, G. F. (1997). *Mentoring.* Menlo Park, CA: Crisp Publications, Inc.

Stacey, E. (1999). Collaborative learning in an online environment. *Journal of Distance Education, 14*(2), pp. 14–33. Retrieved on February 10, 2003: http://cade.icaap.org/vol14.2/stacey.html

Tait, A. (2000). Planning student support for open and distance learning. *Open Learning, 15*(3), pp. 287–299.

The Training Place. (2001). *Learning orientation questionnaire: Measuring online learning ability.* Retrieved on February 21, 2003: http://www.trainingplace.com/

Thompson, G. (1989). The provision of student-support services in distance education: Do we know what they need? In R. Sweet (Ed.), *Post-secondary distance education in Canada: Policies, practices, and priorities.* Athabasca, Alberta: Athabasca University.

Thompson, G. (1990). How can correspondence-based distance education be improved? A survey of attitudes of students who are not well disposed toward correspondence study. *Journal of Distance Education, 5*(1), pp. 53–65.

Thorpe, M. (2001). Rethinking Learner Support: the challenge of collaborative online learning, SCROLLA Symposium on Informing Practice in Networked Learning, Glasgow, Scotland. Retrieved February 10, 2003: http://www.scrolla.ac.uk/papers/s1/thorpe_paper.html

Tinto, V. (1975). Dropout from higher education: A theoretical synthesis of recent research. *Review of Educational Research, 45*(1), pp. 89–125.

Tinto, V. (1997). Classrooms as communities: Exploring the educational character of student persistence. *Journal of Higher Education, 68*, pp. 599–623.

Vygotsky, L. S. (1978). Mind in society: The development of higher psychological processes. Cambridge, MA: Harvard University Press.

Wayland, J. P., Swift, C. O. and Wilson, J. W. (1994). Student attitudes toward distance learning. In B. Engelland and A. J. Bush (Eds.), *Marketing: Advances in theory and thought,* pp. 296–299. Southern Marketing Association, November, New Orleans.

Wenger, E. (1998). *Communities of practice: Learning, meaning, and identity.* Cambridge: Cambridge University Press.

Wood, D. Bruner, J. S. and Ross, G. (1976). The role of tutoring in problem solving. *Journal of Child Psychology and Psychiatry, 17*, pp. 89–100.

Glossary

This glossary of computer terms is included to provide you with a convenient and ready reference as you encounter general computer terms that are unfamiliar or require a review. It is not intended to be comprehensive, but, taken together with the many definitions included in the articles, it should prove to be quite useful.

A

AECT. Association for Educational Communications & Technology. A national association dedicated to the improvement of instruction through the effective use of media and technology.

Alphanumeric. Data that consist of letters of the alphabet, numerals, or other special characters such as punctuation marks.

Analog signals. Audio/video signals currently used in broadcasting where the signal performs transmission tasks by translating continuously variable signals (physical variables such as voltage, pressure, flow) into numerical equivalents, continuously varying and representing a range of frequencies. Current TV and radio signals and phone lines are analog.

Applications software. Software designed to accomplish a specific task (for example, accounting, database management, or word processing).

Archive. Storage of infrequently used data on disks or diskettes.

Artificial intelligence. Hardware or software capable of performing functions that require learning or reasoning (such as a computer that plays chess).

ASCII. American Standard Code for Information Interchange. (The acronym is pronounced "as-key.") An industry standard referring to 128 codes generated by computers for text and control characters. This code permits the computer equipment of different manufacturers to exchange alphanumeric data with one another.

Audiographics. Computer-based technology that allows for the interaction between instructor and students through a simultaneous transmission of voice and data communication and graphic images across local telephone lines.

AUTOEXEC.BAT. An old MS-DOS file that computers read when first turned on. The file provided instructions for running DOS programs.

B

Backup. An extra copy of information that is stored on a disk in case the original data are lost.

Bandwidth. The speed at which data can be transmitted on a communications frequency (measured in Hertz).

Bar code. A code that consists of numerous magnetic lines imprinted on a label that can be read with a scanning device. Often used in labeling retail products.

BASIC. Beginners All-purpose Symbolic Instruction Code. A high-level computer language, considered by many authorities to be the easiest language to learn, and used in one variation or another by almost all microcomputers.

Batch processing. An approach to computer processing where groups of like transactions are accumulated (batched) to be processed at the same time.

Baud rate. The speed of serial data transmission between computers or a computer and a peripheral in bits per second.

Binary. The base-two number system in which all alphanumeric characters are represented by various combinations of 0 and 1. Binary codes may be used to represent any alphanumeric character, such as the letter "A" (100 0001), the number 3 (000 0011), or characters representing certain computer operations such as a "line feed" (000 1010).

Bit. Binary digit. The smallest unit of digital information. Eight bits constitute one byte.

Bit-mapped. Any binary representation in which a bit or set of bits corresponds to an object or condition.

Board. Abbreviation for printed circuit board. Can also refer to any of the peripheral devices or their connectors that plug into the slots inside a microcomputer.

Boot (short for Bootstrap). To start the computer; to load an operating system into the computer's main memory and commence its operation.

Browser. A program that allows a user to view the contents of pages and also to navigate from one page to another.

Buffer. A temporary memory that is capable of storing incoming data for later transmission. Often found on printers to allow the printer to accept information faster than it prints it.

Bug. An error in a program that causes the computer to malfunction. *See also* Debugging.

Bulletin Board System (BBS). An electronic message data base that allows users to log in and leave messages. Messages are generally split into topic groups.

Bus. An electronic highway or communications path linking several devices.

Byte. The sequence of bits that represents any alphanumerical character or a number between 0 and 255. Each byte has 8 bits.

C

CAI. Computer-Assisted Instruction or Computer-Aided Instruction. An educational use of computers that usually entails using computer programs that drill, tutor, simulate, or teach problem-solving skills. *See also* CMI.

Card. Refers to a peripheral card that plugs into one of the internal slots in a microcomputer.

CAT scanner. A diagnostic device used for producing a cross-sectional X ray of a person's internal organs; an acronym for computer axial tomography.

Cathode-ray tube (CRT). *See* Display screen.

CBT. 1. Computer-Based Testing. Refers to the use of computers to present, monitor, or correct examinations. 2. Computer-Based Training. *See also* CAI.

CD-I. Compact Disc-Interactive. A format available to personal computer users that allows access to picture databases and large text; a compact disc standard that includes music compact discs (CD audio), static data (CD-ROM), and graphics.

CD-ROM. Compact Disk Read Only Memory. An auxiliary storage device that contains data that can be read by a computer. Its major advantage is that it can store more information than floppy diskettes.

Central Processing Unit. *See* CPU.

Chip. A small wafer of semiconductor material that forms the base for an integrated circuit, used in a computer.

Clip art. A collection of ready-made graphics.

CMI. Computer-Managed Instruction. An educational use of computers that usually entails the use of computer programs to handle testing, grade-keeping, filing, and other classroom management tasks.

CMICOBOL. COmmon Business Oriented Language. A high-level language, used mostly in business for simple computations of large data amounts.

Coaxial Cable. A thickly insulated metallic cable for carrying large volumes of data or video, consisting of a central conductor surrounded by a concentric tubular conductor. Typically used in networks covering a limited geographic area. Gradually being replaced by fiber optics.

Command prompt. A symbol used to mark the place to type instructions (commands) to DOS.

Compatibility. 1. Software compatibility refers to the ability to run the same software on a variety of computers. 2. Hardware compatibility refers to the ability to directly connect various peripherals to the computer.

Compiler. A program that translates a high-level computer language into machine language for later execution. This would be similar to a human translating an entire document from a foreign language into English for later reading by others.

Compressed Video. System by which a vast amount of information contained in a TV picture and its audio signal is compressed into a fraction of its former bandwidth and sent onto a smaller carrier. Often results in some diminished color, clarity, and motion.

Computer. Any device that can receive, store, and act upon a set of instructions in a predetermined sequence, and one that permits both the instructions and the data upon which the instructions act to be changed.

Computer Bulletin Board Service (CBBS). A computerized data base that users access to post and to retrieve messages.

Computer literacy. Term used to refer to a person's capacity to intelligently use computers.

Computer program. A series of commands, instructions, or statements put together in a way that permits a computer to perform a specific task or a series of tasks.

Computer-Aided Design (CAD). An engineer's use of the computer to design, draft, and analyze a prospective product using computer graphics on a video terminal.

Computer-Aided Instruction. *See* CAI.

Computer-Aided Manufacturing (CAM). An engineer's use of the computer to simulate the required steps of the manufacturing process.

Computer-Assisted Instruction. *See* CAI.

Computer-Based Testing. *See* CBT.

Computer-Based Training. *See* CBT.

CONFIG.SYS. This file, which contains information on how the computer is set up and what it's attached to, is read by the computer every time it boots up.

Configuration. The components that make up a computer (referred to as hardware—a keyboard for text entry, a central processing unit, one or more disk drives, a printer, and a display screen).

Control key. A special function key found on most computer keyboards that allows the user to perform specialized operations.

Copy protected. Refers to a disk that has been altered to prevent it from being copied.

Courseware. Instructional programs and related support materials needed to use computer software.

CPB. Corporation for Public Broadcasting. A nonprofit corporation authorized by the Public Broadcasting Act of 1967 to develop noncommercial radio and TV services in the United States.

CPU. Central Processing Unit. The "brain" of the computer consisting of a large integrated circuit that performs the computations within a computer. CPUs are often designated by a number, such as 6502, 8080, 68000, and so on.

Cracker. A person who seeks to gain unauthorized access to a computer system and is often malicious. *See also* Hacker.

Crash. A malfunction of a computer's software or hardware that prevents the computer from functioning.

Glossary

Crossfooting. The computer's ability to total columns and rows of numeric amounts. The answers are then placed at the end of each row or bottom of each column.

CRT. Cathode-Ray Tube. *See* Display screen.

Cursor. The prompting symbol (usually displayed as a blinking white square or underline on the monitor) that shows where the next character will appear.

Cyberspace. The Internet or the total of all networks.

D

Data. All information, including facts, numbers, letters, and symbols, that can be acted upon or produced by the computer.

Data processing. Also known as electronic data processing (EDP), it is the mathematical or other logical manipulation of symbols or numbers, based on a stored program of instructions.

Database. A collection of related information, such as that found on a mailing list, which can be stored in a computer and retrieved in several ways.

Database management. 1. Refers to a classification of software designed to act like an electronic filing cabinet (which allows the user to store, retrieve, and manipulate files). 2. The practice of using computers to assist in routine filing and information processing chores.

DBS. Direct broadcast satellite.

DDS. Digital Direct Satellite.

Debugging. The process of locating and eliminating defects in a program that cause the computer to malfunction or cease to operate.

Dedicated Line. Communication line leased by a company for its own transmission purposes.

Default format statement. Formatting instructions, built into a software program or the computer's memory, which will be followed unless different instructions are given by the operator.

Demodulation. Process of converting analog signals sent over a telephone line into digital form so that they can be processed by a receiving computer.

Desktop publishing. A layout system that processes text and graphics and produces high-quality pages that are suitable for printing or reproduction.

Directory. A list of related folders (files) that are stored on a hard disk.

Disk, Diskette. A round flat plate with a magnetic coating to store information.

Disk drive. A peripheral device capable of reading and writing information on a disk.

Disk Operating System. *See* DOS.

Display screen. A peripheral that allows for the visual output of information for the computer on a CRT, monitor, or similar device.

Distance education. Distance learning that includes evaluation by distance educators and two-way communication—computer, telephone, mail.

Document. A file that contains information. Documents can be created or changed within a program.

DOS. Disk Operating System. An operating system that allows the computer to run programs.

Dot-matrix. A type of printing in which characters are formed by using a number of closely spaced dots.

Download. To move a file from another computer.

Downtime. Any period of time when the computer is not available or is not working.

Drag. A four-step mouse process that makes it possible to move objects across the desktop.

Dumb terminal. Refers to a terminal that can be used to input information into a computer and to print or display output, but which lacks the capacity to manipulate information transmitted to it from the host computer. *See also* Intelligent terminal.

Dump. Mass copying of memory or a storage device such as a disk to another storage device or a printer so it can be used as a backup or analyzed for errors.

Duplexing. The procedure that allows simultaneous transmission of data between two computers.

DV-I. Digital Video-Interactive. Optical storage media that delivers full-motion, full-screen video, three-dimensional motion graphics, and high-quality audio capabilities.

E

E-lecture: A lecture delivered via electronic mail to individual computers.

Electronic Bulletin Boards. Information services that can be reached via computers connected to telephone line that allow users to place or read messages from other users.

Electronic mail (e-mail). Sending and receiving electronic messages by computer.

Elite type. Any typeface that allows the printing of 12 characters to an inch.

Enter. Adding data into memory via the keyboard.

ERIC. Educational Resources Information Center. An organization sponsored by the Office of Educational Research and Improvement (OERI) that collects and processes printed materials on education that are not available commercially.

Escape key. This function key allows the movement from one program to another program.

Execute. To perform a specific action required by a program.

Exponental notation. Refers to how a computer displays very large or very small numbers by means of the number times 10 raised to some power. For example, 3,000,000 could be printed as 3E + 6 (3 times 10 to the sixth power).

F

Fan fold. A type of paper that can continuously feed into a printer (usually via tractor feed).

FAQ (Frequently Asked Questions). Used to answer the most common questions that could be asked.

Fax. (n.) Short for the word facsimile. A copy of a document transmitted electronically from one machine to another. (v.) To transmit a copy of a document electronically.

Fiber Optics. Newer, high-tech delivery system using attenuated glass (quartz) fiber hardly thicker than a human hair, which conducts light from a laser source. A single glass fiber can carry the equivalent of 100 channels of television or 100,000 telephone calls, with even more capacity possible by encasing many fibers within a cable.

Field. Group of related characters treated as a unit (such as a name); also the location in a record or database where this group of characters is entered.

File. A group of formatted information designed for computer use.

First-generation computers. Developed in the 1950s; used vacuum tubes; faster than earlier mechanical devices, but very slow compared to today's computer.

Fixed disk. *See* Hard disk.

Floppy, Floppy disk. *See* Disk.

Folder. An organized area for storing files. *See also* Subdirectory.

Format. (n.) The physical form in which information appears. (v.) To specify parameters of a form or to write address codes on a blank disk in preparation for using it to store data or programs. *See also* Initialize.

FORTRAN. FORmula TRANslation. A high-level programming language used primarily for numerical and scientific applications.

FTP (File Transfer Protocol). Allows a user to transfer files to and from another computer on the Internet network.

Function keys. Computer keyboard keys that give special commands to the computer (for example, to format, to search text).

G

Gig. Short for gigabyte, it consists of over 1,024 megabytes.

GIGO. Garbage In, Garbage Out. Serves as a reminder that a program is only as good as the information and instructions in the program.

Global. The performance of any function on an entire document without requiring individual commands for each use. For example, a global search-and-replace command will allow the computer to search for a particular word and replace it with a different word throughout the text.

Graphics. 1. Information presented in the form of pictures or images. 2. The display of pictures or images on a computer's display screen.

H

Hacker. A person who is an expert at programming. *See also* Cracker.

Hard copy. A paper copy of the computer's output.

Hard disk. A rigid, magnetically coated metal disk that is usually permanently mounted within a disk drive, although there are also removable disks.

Hard drive. A disk drive that is used to read and write hard disks.

Hardware. Refers to the computer and all its peripheral devices. The physical pieces of the computer.

HDTV. High Definition TV. A television with quality resolution that is higher than current international standards.

Head. Refers to the component of a disk drive or tape system that magnetically reads or writes information to the storage medium.

Hex or Hexadecimal. A numbering system based on 16 (digits 0–9 and letters A–F) rather than on 10. Most computers operate using hex numbers. Each hexadecimal digit corresponds to a sequence of 4 binary digits or bits.

High-level language. An English-like computer language (BASIC, Pascal, FORTRAN, Logo, COBOL) designed to make it relatively convenient for a person to prepare a program for a computer, which in turn translates it into machine language for execution.

Highlight. A selected item; a distinguished word or group of words that are singled out for further action.

Home page. Generally the main page of a Web server.

Hotlink. Shared data between programs in which data changed in one program are automatically changed in the other programs as well.

HTML (Hypertext Markup Language). A hypertext document format; this is used on the World Wide Web.

HyperCard. Brand-name for Apple/Mac product. Simple authoring system for lower level interactive computer-based instruction or information management.

Hypermedia. The connecting of data, texts, video, graphics, and voice in an information system that allows a user to move easily from one element to another.

Hypertext. A collection of documents that contains links or cross-references to other documents.

I

IC. Integrated Circuit. *See* Chip.

Icon. Refers to the use of a graphic symbol to represent something else. When the user clicks on the icon, some action is performed (such as opening a directory).

IHETS. Indiana Higher Education Telecommunication System. A consortium of Indiana higher education operating voice, video, and data networks, through which its members coordinate distance education efforts.

Glossary

Indexing. The ability of a computer to accumulate a list of words or phrases, with corresponding page numbers, in a document, and then to print out or display the list in alphabetical order.

Initialize. 1. To set an initial state or value in preparation for some computation. 2. To prepare a blank disk to receive information by dividing its surface into tracks and sectors. *See also* Format.

Ink jet printer. A class of printer in which the characters are formed by using a number of closely spaced dots that are sprayed onto a page in microscopic droplets of ink.

Input. Information entered into the computer.

Insertion point. Used in word processing, it is the short, blinking (horizontal or vertical) line that indicates where the next typed letter will appear.

Integrated circuit. A tiny complex of electronic components and their connections that is produced in or on a small slice of material. *See* Chip.

Intelligent terminal. A terminal that is capable of doing more than just receiving or transmitting data due to its microprocessor. *See also* Dumb terminal.

Interactive multimedia. Back-and-forth dialogue between user and computer that allows the combining, editing, and orchestrating of sounds, graphics, moving pictures, and text.

Interface. (v.) To connect two pieces of computer hardware together. (n.) The means by which two things communicate. In particular, it refers to the electrical configuration that allows two or more devices to pass information. *See also* Interface card.

Interface card. A board used to connect a microcomputer to peripheral devices.

Internet. A large interconnected set of networks.

I/O. Input/Output. Refers usually to one of the slots or the game port in a microcomputer to which peripheral devices may be connected.

J

Joy stick. An input device, often used to control the movement of objects on the video display screen of a computer for games.

Justification. A method of printing in which additional space is inserted between words or characters to make each line the same length.

K

K. Short for kilobyte (1,024 bytes) and is often used to describe a computer's storage capacity.

Keyboard. The typewriter-like keys that enter input into a computer. Each computer will have basically the same keyboard as a typewriter, with major differences limited to special function keys such as ESCape, RESET, ConTRoL, TABulate, etc.

Kilobyte. *See* K.

L

Language. Used to write programs; they are characters and procedures that the computer is designed to understand.

Laptop. A personal portable computer that can rest comfortably on a user's lap.

Large-Scale Integration (LSI). Refers to a generation of integrated circuits that allowed the equivalent of thousands of vacuum tube switches to be installed on a single chip.

Laser printer. A high-resolution printer that uses a rotating disk to reflect laser beams onto the paper. As the beam touches the paper, electrostatic image areas are formed that attract electrically charged toner. An image is then formed when the toner is fixed onto the paper.

LATA. Local Access and Transport Area. A contiguous geographical region of the United States for telephone exchanges.

LCD. Liquid Crystal Display.

LEC. Local Exchange Carrier. A local telephone company.

Light pen. An input device, shaped much like a mechanical pencil, which, when touched to a display screen, can be used to select or execute certain computer functions.

LISP (LISt Processing). Programming language primarily used in artificial intelligence research.

Local Area Networks (LAN). The linking together of computers, word processors, and other electronic office equipment to form an interoffice network.

Log on. To execute the necessary commands to allow one to use a computer. May involve the use of a password.

Logo. A high-level language specifically designed so that it may be used by both small children and adults. It involves a "turtle"-shaped cursor for much of its operation.

M

M. *See* Megabyte.

Machine language. A fundamental, complex computer language used by the computer itself to perform its functions. This language is quite difficult for the average person to read or write.

Macro. Refers to the use of a simple command to execute a sequence of complex commands while using a computer program. The use of macros can save the user a considerable amount of time and reduce the chance of typing an incorrect key when executing a sequence of commands.

Magnetic Ink Character Recognition (MICR) devices. Computer hardware capable of reading characters imprinted with magnetic ink, such as on checks.

Mainframe. Refers to large computers used primarily in business, industry, government, and higher education that have the capacity to deal with many users simultaneously and to process large amounts of information quickly and in very sophisticated ways. *See also* Time share.

Management Information System (MIS). A systems approach that treats business departments as integrated parts of one total system rather than as separate entities.

MB. *See* Megabyte.

Megabyte. A disk-storage space unit or measurement of memory. It consists of 1,048,576 bytes.

Memory. Chips in the computer that have the capacity to store information. *See also* PROM; RAM; ROM.

Menu. The list of programs available on a given disk to guide the operator through a function.

Menu driven. Refers to software in which the program prompts the user with a list of available options at any given time, thus eliminating the need to memorize commands.

Merge. A command to create one document by combining text that is stored in two different locations (e.g., a form letter can be merged with a mailing list to produce a batch of personalized letters).

Microcomputer. Refers to a generation of small, self-contained, relatively inexpensive computers based on the microprocessor (commonly consists of a display screen, a keyboard, a central processing unit, one or more disk drives, and a printer).

Microprocessor. (The central processing unit [CPU]). It holds all of the essential elements for manipulating data and performing arithmetic operations. A microprocessor is contained on a single silicon chip.

Microsecond. One millionth of a second.

MIDI. Musical Instrument Digital Interface. A protocol that allows for the interchange of musical information between musical instruments, synthesizer, and computers.

Millisecond. One thousandth of a second; abbreviated "ms."

Minicomputer. Refers to a class of computers larger than micros but smaller than mainframe computers, many of which support multiple keyboards and output devices simultaneously.

Minimize. To shrink a window down to a tiny icon to temporarily move it out of the way.

Mnemonics. A computer's system of commands, which are words, letters, or strings that are intended to assist the operator's memory. Abbreviations are used for the command functions they perform (e.g., C for center, U for underline).

Modem. MOdulator/DEModulator. A peripheral device that enables the computer to transmit and receive information over a telephone line.

Monitor. The display screen of a computer.

Motherboard. The main circuit board of a computer.

Mouse. A hand-operated device that is used to move the cursor around on the CRT screen.

Multiplexing. Digital electronics system that allows for the transmission of two or more signals on a single cable, microwave channel or satellite transponder. It doubles the capacity of television transmission and allows for simultaneous feed of independent programs for two audiences.

Multitasking. The ability to run several different programs simultaneously.

N

Nanosecond. One billionth of a second; abbreviated "ns."

National Crime Information Center (NCIC). A computerized information center maintained by the FBI that serves agencies throughout the United States.

Netscape. A popular World Wide Web browser that features integrated support for electronic mail and for reading Usenet news.

Network. A structure capable of linking two or more computers by wire, telephone lines, or radio links.

Newsgroups. A large collection of groups that include government agencies, universities and high schools, businesses, and other areas, all of which can be reached by an information utility.

Nibble. 1. Half a byte. 2. Refers to copy programs that copy small portions of a disk at a time, often used to copy otherwise copy-protected programs.

Nonvolatile memory. Memory that retains data even after power has been shut off. ROM is nonvolatile; RAM is volatile.

Notebook. A small portable microcomputer. *See also* Laptop.

NTU. National Technological University. A consortium of engineering, science, and technical colleges with a satellite delivery system of graduate and professional courses in the sciences.

Numeric keypad. An input device that allows the user to input numbers into a microcomputer with a calculator-like key arrangement.

NUTN. National University Teleconference Network. Network created to provide a means of information sharing and exchange, primarily by satellite-delivered teleconferences, with approximately 260 higher-education institutions as members.

O

Offline. An operation performed by electronic equipment not tied into a centralized information processing system.

Online. An operation performed by electronic equipment controlled by a remote central processing system.

Operating system. A group of programs that act as intermediary between the computer and the applications software; the operating system takes a program's commands and passes them down to the CPU in a language that the CPU understands.

Optical Character Recognition (OCR). A device that can read text and automatically enter it into a computer for editing or storage. Linked to a scanner, this software allows already-printed material to be converted to electronic text without having to type it on a keyboard.

Output. Information sent out of the computer system to some external destination such as the display screen, disk drive, printer, or modem.

P

Parallel. A form of data transmission in which information is passed in streams of eight or more bits at a time in sequence. *See also* Serial.

Pascal. A high-level language, with a larger, more complex vocabulary than BASIC, used for complex applications in business, science, and education.

Password. A code word or group of characters required to access stored material. This provides protection against unauthorized persons accessing documents.

Path. A sentence that tells a computer the exact name and location of a file.

PC. Personal Computer. *See* Microcomputer.

Peripheral. Hardware attachments to a microcomputer, (e.g., printer, modem, monitor, disk drives, or interface card).

Peripheral card. A removable printed-circuit board that plugs into a microcomputer's expansion slot and expands or modifies the computer's capabilities by connecting a peripheral device or performing some subsidiary or peripheral function.

Pica type. Any typeface that allows the printing of 10 characters to an inch.

PILOT. Programmed Inquiry, Learning, or Teaching. A high-level language designed primarily for use by educators, which facilitates the wiring of computer-assisted instruction lessons that include color graphics, sound effects, lesson texts, and answer checking.

Pitch. A measurement that indicates the number of characters in an inch (e.g., pica yields 10 characters to an inch; elite yields 12 characters to an inch).

Pixel. PIXture ELement. Refers to the smallest point of light that can be displayed on a display screen.

Plotter. A printing mechanism capable of drawing lines rapidly and accurately for graphic representation.

Port. An input or output connection to the computer.

Printout. *See* Hard copy.

Program. A list of instructions that allows the computer to perform a function.

PROM. Programmable ROM. A ROM that is programmed after it has been made.

Prompt. A message given on the display screen to indicate the status of a function.

Protocol. A formal set of rules that govern the transmission of information from one piece of equipment to another.

Proxy. A program or computer that performs a service on the user's behalf.

Q

Quit. Exiting or closing a program.

R

RAM. Random Access Memory. The main working memory of any computer. In most microcomputers, anything stored in RAM will be lost when the power is shut off.

Read Only Memory. *See* ROM.

Reboot. Restart the computer.

Retrieve. The transfer of a document from storage to memory.

RF modulator. Radio Frequency Modulator. Refers to a device that converts video signals generated by the computer to signals that can be displayed on a television set.

RISC. Reduced Instruction Set Computer. A processor that is designed for the rapid execution of a sequence of simple instructions rather than on a variety of complex functions.

Robotics. The science of designing and building robots.

ROM. Read Only Memory. A memory device in which information is permanently stored as it is being made. Thus, it may be read but not changed.

RS-232. Industry standard for serial transmission devices. It specifies the gender and pin use of connectors, but not the physical type.

Run. 1. To execute a program. 2. A command to load a program to main memory from a peripheral storage medium, such as a disk, and execute it.

S

Save. To store a program on a disk or somewhere other than a computer's memory.

Scanner. An input device that digitizes an optical image into an electronic image (which is represented as binary data). It can be used to create a computerized version of information or graphics.

Schema. The organization of a relational database in its entirety, including names of all data elements and ways records are linked.

Screen. A CRT or display screen.

Scroll. The ability to view a large body of text by rolling it past the display screen.

Search and replace. Locating a character string in a document and replacing it with a different character string.

Second-generation computers. A computer that was built from transistors; smaller, faster, and with larger storage capacity than the first-generation computers; first computers to use a high-level language.

Serial. A form of data transmission in which information is passed one bit at a time in sequence.

SMPT (Simple Mail Transfer Protocol). These are the rules that define how mail may be sent over the Internet.

Software. The programs used by the computer. Often refers to the programs as stored on a disk.

Sort. To arrange fields, files, and records in a predetermined sequence.

Speech synthesizer. Refers to a peripheral output device that attempts to mimic human speech.

Split screen. A type of dual display that allows some computers to view two or more different video images on the screen at the same time. *See also* Windowing.

Spreadsheet. A program that provides worksheets with rows and columns for calculating and preparing reports.

Stack. A list used to keep track of the sequence of required program routines.

Store. Placing information in memory for later use.

Subdirectory. A directory within a directory that is used to further organize files.

System. An organized collection of hardware, software, and peripheral equipment that works together. *See also* Configuration.

T

TDD (Telecommunications Device for the Deaf). Frequently referred to as Telecommunication Display Device, this terminal device is used widely by hearing-impaired people for text communication over telephone lines.

Telecommunication. Transmission of information between two computers in different locations, usually over telephone lines.

Teleconference. Simultaneous program distributed via AUDIO only. Some call conferencing via satellite on video a "teleconference."

Telephone Bridge. Computerized switching system that allows multisite telephone conferencing.

Telnet. A service that provides a text-based connection to another computer.

Terminal. A piece of equipment used to communicate with a computer, such as a keyboard for input, or video monitor or printer for output.

Third-generation computers. Computers that are built with small-scale integrated circuits. Refers to the present generation of computers based on microchips. Compare to first generation (vacuum tubes) and second generation (transistors).

Time share. Refers to the practice of accessing a larger computer from a remote location and paying for services based on the amount of computer time used. *See* Mainframe.

Toner. Dry ink powder that serves as the "ink" for a laser printer.

Tractor feed. A mechanism used to propel paper through a printer by means of sprockets attached to the printer that engage holes along the paper's edges.

TTY. A teletype terminal that has a limited character set and poor print quality. It is characterized by a noisy mechanical printer.

Turing test. Proposed in 1950, the "Imitation Game" was offered to decide if a computer is intelligent and to answer the question, "Can machines think?" A person asks questions and, on the basis of the answers, must determine if the respondent is another human or a machine. If the answer is provided by a computer and the questioner guesses a human, the computer is deemed to be intelligent.

Typeover. Recording and storing information in a specific location to destroy whatever had been stored there previously.

U

Universal Product Code (UPC). A bar code that appears on virtually all consumer goods; can be read by a scanner or wand device used in point-of-sale systems.

URL (Uniform Resource Locator). This provides a standardized way to represent any location or service that is on the Internet. In HTML documents, it is used to specify the target of a hyperlink.

User friendly. Refers to hardware or software that is relatively easy for a new operator to learn, and which has features to help eliminate operator error.

User group. An association of people who meet to exchange information about computers or computer applications.

Usenet. An Internet group discussion service. It is international in scope and is a large, decentralized information utility.

V

Very Large Scale Integration (VLSI). Describes semiconductor integrated circuits, which are composed of thousands of memory cells or logic elements.

Video conferencing. Allows a video and audio discussion between groups in different locations, using electronic communications.

Video Display Terminal (VDT). A type of terminal that consists of a keyboard and screen. There are two categories—dumb terminals and intelligent (programmable) terminals.

Virtual. Commonly used to describe computer simulations (describes things that appear to be real, but are not really there).

Voice recognition system. A system that allows the user to "train" the computer to understand his or her voice and vocabulary.

Volatile. Refers to memory that is erased whenever the power is removed, such as RAM.

W

WAN. Wide-Area Network. The movement of data between computers in various areas through high-speed links.

Glossary

Web. *See* World Wide Web.

Windowing. The ability of a computer to split a display screen into two or more segments so that several different documents can be viewed and several different functions performed simultaneously.

Word processing. Refers to the use of computers as electronic typewriters capable of entering and retrieving text, storing it on disks, and performing a wide range of editing functions.

World Wide Web. A global document that contains hundreds of thousands of information pages. The pages can be distributed across different Internet machines.

Wraparound. A computer's ability to automatically move words from one line to the next or from one page to the next as a result of margin adjustments, insertions, or deletions.

Write protected. A disk in which the write-enable notch is either missing or has had a write-protect tab placed over it to prevent information from being written to the disk.

Write-enable notch. A notch in a floppy disk that, if uncovered, allows a disk drive to write information to it, and which, if covered, prohibits such writing.

Write-protect tab. A small adhesive sticker used to write-protect a disk by covering the write-enable notch.

Index

Index

Test Your Knowledge Form

We encourage you to photocopy and use this page as a tool to assess how the articles in *Annual Editions* expand on the information in your textbook. By reflecting on the articles you will gain enhanced text information. You can also access this useful form on a product's book support Web site at *http://www.mhcls.com/online/*.

NAME: DATE:

TITLE AND NUMBER OF ARTICLE:

BRIEFLY STATE THE MAIN IDEA OF THIS ARTICLE:

LIST THREE IMPORTANT FACTS THAT THE AUTHOR USES TO SUPPORT THE MAIN IDEA:

WHAT INFORMATION OR IDEAS DISCUSSED IN THIS ARTICLE ARE ALSO DISCUSSED IN YOUR TEXTBOOK OR OTHER READINGS THAT YOU HAVE DONE? LIST THE TEXTBOOK CHAPTERS AND PAGE NUMBERS:

LIST ANY EXAMPLES OF BIAS OR FAULTY REASONING THAT YOU FOUND IN THE ARTICLE:

LIST ANY NEW TERMS/CONCEPTS THAT WERE DISCUSSED IN THE ARTICLE, AND WRITE A SHORT DEFINITION:

We Want Your Advice

ANNUAL EDITIONS revisions depend on two major opinion sources: one is our Advisory Board, listed in the front of this volume, which works with us in scanning the thousands of articles published in the public press each year; the other is you—the person actually using the book. Please help us and the users of the next edition by completing the prepaid article rating form on this page and returning it to us. Thank you for your help!

ANNUAL EDITIONS: Computers in Education, 12/e

ARTICLE RATING FORM

Here is an opportunity for you to have direct input into the next revision of this volume.
We would like you to rate each of the articles listed below, using the following scale:

1. **Excellent: should definitely be retained**
2. **Above average: should probably be retained**
3. **Below average: should probably be deleted**
4. **Poor: should definitely be deleted**

Your ratings will play a vital part in the next revision.
Please mail this prepaid form to us as soon as possible.
Thanks for your help!

RATING	ARTICLE	RATING	ARTICLE
	1. Digital Natives, Digital Immigrants		18. Assessing the Technology Training Needs of Elementary School Teachers
	2. The Myth about Online Course Development		19. An Investment in Tomorrow's University Students: Enhancing the Multimedia Skills of Today's K-12 Teachers
	3. Creating Flexible E-Learning Through the Use of Learning Objects		
	4. Meeting Generation NeXt: Today's Postmodern College Student		20. The Value of Teaching and Learning Technology: Beyond ROI
	5. General Education Issues, Distance Education Practices		21. Boomers and Gen-Xers Millenials: Understanding the New Students
	6. Designing for Learning: The Pursuit of Well-Structured Content		22. Science & Technology: It's A Perfect Match!
	7. Integrating Technology into the Instructional Process: Good Practice Guides the Way		23. Technologies for Teaching Science and Mathematics in K-12 Schools
	8. On the Right Track: Technology for Organizing and Presenting Digital Information		24. SmartTutor: Combining SmartBooks and Peer Tutors for Multi-media On-Line Instruction
	9. A Brief History of Instructional Design		25. Changing Course Management Systems: Lessons Learned
	10. Designing Statistics Instruction for Middle School Students		26. Classroom Assessment in Web-Based Instructional Environment: Instructors' Experience
	11. Changes in Brain Function in Children with Dyslexia after Training		27. MISESS: Web-Based Examination, Evaluation, and Guidance
	12. Implementing PDAs in a College Course: One Professor's Perspective,		28. The Myth about Student Competency
	13. Digital Game-Based Learning		29. Promoting Academic Literacy with Technology: Successful Laptop Programs in K-12 Schools
	14. Podcasting and VODcasting: A White Paper		30. Probing for Plagiarism in the Virtual Classroom
	15. Type II Technology Applications in Teacher Education: Using Instant Messenger to Implement Structured Online Class Discussions		31. The Web's Impact On Student Learning
			32. Software Agents to Assist in Distance Learning Environments
	16. Student Teachers' Perceptions of Instructional Technology: Developing Materials Based on a Constructivist Approach		33. The Virtual Revolution
			34. Learner Support Services for Online Students: Scaffolding for Success
	17. Assessing and Monitoring Student Progress in an E-Learning Personnel Preparation Environment		

ANNUAL EDITIONS

BUSINESS REPLY MAIL
FIRST CLASS MAIL PERMIT NO. 551 DUBUQUE IA

POSTAGE WILL BE PAID BY ADDRESSEE

McGraw-Hill Contemporary Learning Series
2460 KERPER BLVD
DUBUQUE, IA 52001-9902

Ildlndlllndlnnlllblddlullhndldll

ABOUT YOU

Name

Date

Are you a teacher? ❐ A student? ❐
Your school's name

Department

Address

City

State

Zip

School telephone #

YOUR COMMENTS ARE IMPORTANT TO US!

Please fill in the following information:
For which course did you use this book?

Did you use a text with this ANNUAL EDITION? ❐ yes ❐ no
What was the title of the text?

What are your general reactions to the Annual Editions concept?

Have you read any pertinent articles recently that you think should be included in the next edition? Explain.

Are there any articles that you feel should be replaced in the next edition? Why?

Are there any World Wide Web sites that you feel should be included in the next edition? Please annotate.

May we contact you for editorial input? ❐ yes ❐ no
May we quote your comments? ❐ yes ❐ no